Lecture Notes in Artificial Intelligence 1652

Subseries of Lecture Notes in Computer Science
Edited by J. G. Carbonell and J. Siekmann

Lecture Notes in Computer Science

Edited by G. Goos, J. Hartmanis and J. van Leeuwen

Springer

Berlin
Heidelberg
New York
Barcelona
Hong Kong
London
Milan
Paris
Singapore
Tokyo

Matthias Klusch   Onn M. Shehory
Gerhard Weiss (Eds.)

Cooperative Information Agents III

Third International Workshop, CIA'99
Uppsala, Sweden, July 31 – August 2, 1999
Proceedings

Springer

Series Editors

Jaime G. Carbonell, Carnegie Mellon University, Pittsburgh, PA, USA
Jörg Siekmann, University of Saarland, Saarbrücken, Germany

Volume Editors

Matthias Klusch
DFKI German AI Research Center Ltd.
Stuhlsatzenhausweg 3, D-66123 Saarbrücken, Germany
E-mail: klusch@dfki.de

Onn M. Shehory
The Robotics Institute, Carnegie Mellon University
5000 Forbes Ave., Pittsburgh, PA 15213, USA
E-mail: onn@cs.cmu.edu

Gerhard Weiss
Institut für Informatik, Technische Universität München
D-80290 München, Germany
E-mail: weissg@in.tum.de

Cataloging-in-Publication data applied for

Die Deutsche Bibliothek - CIP-Einheitsaufnahme

Cooperative information agents III : third international workshop ; proceedings
/ CIA '99, Uppsala, Sweden, July 31 - August 2, 1999. Matthias Klusch ...
(ed.). - Berlin ; Heidelberg ; New York ; Barcelona ; Hong Kong ; London ;
Milan ; Paris ; Singapore ; Tokyo : Springer, 1999
 (Lecture notes in computer science ; 1652 : Lecture notes in artificial
intelligence)
 ISBN 3-540-66325-8

CR Subject Classification (1998): I.2.11, H.2, H.3, H.4, H.5, I.2

ISBN 3-540-66325-8 Springer-Verlag Berlin Heidelberg New York

© Springer-Verlag Berlin Heidelberg 1999
Printed in Germany

Typesetting: Camera-ready by author
SPIN 10703969   06/3142 – 5 4 3 2 1 0   Printed on acid-free paper

Preface

This volume contains the proceedings of the Third International Workshop on Cooperative Information Agents, held in Uppsala, Sweden, July 31–August 2, 1999.

Modern information environments consist mainly of large, distributed and heterogenous resources which are connected via the Internet, Intranets, or virtual private networks. These environments are open and may dynamically change over time. To cope with such information environments means, in particular, to deal with uncertain, incomplete and vague information. The effective handling of uncertainty is critical in designing, understanding, and evaluating computational systems tasked with making intelligent decisions. It is also crucial to the ultimate success and broad application of information agents on the Internet, as well as in any industrial context. Moreover, any comfortable, reliable human-agent interaction via appropriate types of avatars, and the multi-dimensional representation of the information space available for individual users in the Internet, remains a challenging research topic. The same holds for efficient service mediation by systems of collaborating information agents. In particular, the research area of cooperative adaptive and mobile agents for information management on the Internet is still an uncharted territory in agent technology.

The interdisciplinary CIA workshop series covers the whole thematic range of intelligent and cooperative information agents. Each workshop will focus on a few selected themes of particular relevance and current interest. The CIA-99 workshop were built on the success of CIA-98 ('Learning, Mobility and Electronic Commerce for Information Discovery in the Internet', LNAI Series, Vol. 1435), and CIA-97 ('DAI meets Databases', LNAI Series, Vol. 1202). Main topics of the CIA-99 workshop were mobile information discovery, advances in collaboration, mediation and negotiation, as well as personal assistance and human-agent interaction. This workshop features 10 invited lectures and 16 regular papers selected from 46 submissions.

Acknowledgements. First of all, we gratefully acknowledge the financial support from our Co-Sponsors:

- DEUTSCHE TELEKOM AG, BERKOM GMBH, Berlin (Germany),
- GEORGE MASON UNIVERSITY, Fairfax, VA (USA),
- DAIMLER-CHRYSLER AG, Research & Technology, Berlin (Germany),
- ACTIVE ONLINE SYSTEMS LTD., London (UK), and
- AGENTLINK ESPRIT Network of Excellence for Agent-Based Computing.

The workshop has been organized in cooperation with the special interest group on Distributed Artificial Intelligence (DAI) of the German Computer Science Society and the Computer Science Department of Uppsala University (Sweden).

Moreover, we thank all members of the program committee and all external referees for their very careful work in reviewing and selecting the contributions.

Uppsala, July 1999   Matthias Klusch, Onn Shehory, Gerhard Weiß

Program Committee

Sonia Bergamaschi	(University of Modena, Italy)
Wolfgang Benn	(Technical University of Chemnitz, Germany)
Hans-Dieter Burkhard	(Humboldt University of Berlin, Germany)
Brahim Chaib-draa	(Laval University, Canada)
Yves Demazeau	(Leibniz/IMAG/CNRS, France)
Frank Dignum	(University of Eindhoven, The Netherlands)
Innes Ferguson	(Active Online Systems, London, UK)
Klaus Fischer	(DFKI German AI Research Center Ltd., Germany)
Christian Freksa	(University of Hamburg, Germany)
Erol Gelenbe	(Duke University, USA)
Carl Hewitt	(MIT AI Lab, USA)
Mike Huhns	(University of South Carolina, USA)
Toru Ishida	(University of Kyoto, Japan)
Leonid A. Kalinichenko	(Russian Academia of Sciences, Russia)
Bart Kosko	(University of Southern California, USA)
Sarit Kraus	(University of Maryland, USA)
H.-J. Mueller	(Deutsche Telekom AG, R&D, Darmstadt, Germany)
Joerg P. Mueller	(John Wiley & Sons Corp., London, UK)
San Murugesan	(University of Western Sydney, Australia)
Pablo Noriega	(Institute for AI Research, Spain)
Moira C. Norrie	(ETH Zurich, Switzerland)
Aris Ouksel	(University of Illinois at Chicago, USA)
Mike P. Papazoglou	(Tilburg University, The Netherlands)
Amit Sheth	(University of Georgia, USA)
Carles Sierra	(CSIC AI Research Lab, Catalonia, Spain)
Elizabeth Sonenberg	(University of Melbourne, Australia)
Kurt Sundermeyer	(Daimler-Chrysler AG, R&T, Berlin, Germany)
Katia Sycara	(Carnegie Mellon University, USA)
Peter Thomas	(UWE Bristol, UK)
Robert Tolksdorf	(Technical University of Berlin, Germany)
Jan Treur	(Vrije Universiteit Amsterdam, The Netherlands)
Christian Tschudin	(University of Uppsala, Sweden)
Mike Wooldridge	(QMW College, London, UK)

General Chair

Matthias Klusch (DFKI German AI Research Center Ltd., Germany)

Co-Chairs

Onn Shehory (Carnegie Mellon University, USA)
Gerhard Weiß (Technical University of Munich, Germany)
Larry Kerschberg (George Mason University, USA)

External Reviewers

Ismailcem Arpinar
Paolo Ciaccia
Ariel Felner
Merav Hadad
Catholijn M. Jonker
Ralf Kühnel
Francisco J. Martin
Anandeep Pannu
Terry Payne
Klaus Schild
Leon Sterling
Maksim Tsvetovat

Table of Contents

Information Discovery and Management on the Internet

Information Agents on the Internet – Prototypes, Systems and Applications

Communication and Collaboration

Mobile Information Agents

Rational Information Agents for Electronic Business

Service Mediation and Negotiation

Adaptive, Personal Assistance

Agent Technology from a NASA Perspective

Walt Truszkowski, Harold Hallock
{Walt.Truszkowski, Harold.L.Halloch.1}@gsfc.nasa.gov
NASA Goddard Space Flight Center, Maryland, USA

Remote Agent Team
James Kurien Point-of-Contact
kurien@ptolemy.arc.nasa.gov

Abstract

NASA's drive toward realizing higher levels of autonomy, in both its ground and space systems, is supporting an active and growing interest in agent technology. This paper will address the expanding research in this exciting technology area.

As examples of current work, the Lights-Out Ground Operations System (LOGOS), under prototyping at the Goddard Space Flight Center (GSFC), and the spacecraft-oriented Remote Agent project under development at the Ames Research Center (ARC) and the Jet Propulsion Laboratory (JPL) will be presented.

1. Introduction

This paper presents a discussion of two NASA applications of agent technologies that are being used to support the realization of both ground system and spacecraft autonomy. The LOGOS, which is under prototyping at GSFC, will enable researchers to evaluate the performance and effectiveness of a community of agents operating in a ground system environment. The maturer ARC/JPL Remote Agent project will demonstrate the effectiveness of an agent in partial control of a spacecraft. Each of these domains brings differing resources and constraints that need to be taken into consideration when designing and implementing a participating agent. Working in both the ground system and spacecraft domains is providing NASA with an opportunity for developing a comprehensive agent technology.

2. Background

To establish a context for later discussions, we provide in this section a brief summary and analysis of the responsibilities and functionality of traditional ground and flight systems as viewed from the framework of a total system process, followed by a highlighting of the key drivers when making flight-ground trades. This analysis was done from a near-Earth unmanned scientific satellite system perspective. However, the analysis would mostly carry over to deep space missions.

2.1 Introduction to Ground System Software

Traditionally, the ground system has been almost exclusively responsible for spacecraft planning & scheduling, establishment of communications and (in some cases) processing. The ground has also shouldered the bulk of the calibration burden (both science and engineering) and much of the job of spacecraft Health & Safety (H&S) verification. And when major onboard anomalies/failures arise, ground-based Flight Operations Team (FOT) personnel were charged with determining the underlying cause and developing a long-term solution.

So the traditional ground system has occupied the ironic position of having most of the responsibility for managing the spacecraft and its activities, and yet (with the exception of the planning & scheduling function) relying on the spacecraft to provide nearly all information required for carrying out those responsibilities. Today, in a more conventional workplace setting, this kind of work organization might be analyzed (from a reengineering perspective) to be an artificially fragmented process with unnecessary management layering leading to degraded efficiency and wasteful costs.

From the perspective of reengineering, the standard solution to this type of problem is to re-distribute the processes to empower the local sites, e.g. the spacecraft where most of the information originates, to have more responsibility in the handling of that information. To achieve this type of reengineering there needs to be trades made between ground system functionality and flight system functionality.

A prerequisite to performing these flight-ground trades is to identify all the components of the spacecraft operations process, initially without regards to whether that component is performed onboard or on the ground. The following is a break down of operations into a set of activities. The order of the activities is roughly increasing in time relative to the end-to-end operations process, from defining spacecraft inputs to utilizing spacecraft outputs, although some activities (such as fault detection and correction) are continuous and in parallel with the main line.

1. Planning & scheduling
2. Command loading (including routine table uplink)
3. Science Schedule Execution
4. Science Support Activity Execution
5. Onboard Engineering Support Activities (housekeeping, infrastructure, ground interface, utility support functions, onboard calibration, etc.)
6. Downlinked Data Capture
7. Data and Performance Monitoring
8. Fault Diagnosis
9. Fault Correction
10. Downlinked Data Archiving

11. Engineering Data Analysis/Calibration
12. Science Data Processing/Calibration

Currently, many of the activities listed above are partially automated (for example, planning & scheduling and data and performance monitoring), and may well be fully autonomous (either within the ground or flight systems) in the next 10 years. Some of these functions are already largely performed autonomously onboard. We now give a brief description of each of the operations.

2.1.1 Planning and scheduling

Especially for Low Earth Orbit (LEO) GSFC missions, the ground system planning and scheduling function traditionally has been responsible for generating a detailed and optimized timeline of spacecraft activities. Sometimes (as in the case of Hubble Space Telescope (HST)) this is based on rather complex predictive modeling of the spacecraft's environment and anticipated behavior. The ground system recasts (and augments) the timeline information in an appropriate manner for processing on the spacecraft. The timeline is then executed onboard via a (largely) time driven processor. Often along with the nominal and expected timeline, the ground interleaves in it a large array of alternate branches, to be executed in place of the nominal timeline in the event that certain special conditions or anomalies were encountered. So the resulting product could be a highly coupled, time dependent mass of data which, in the past, occupied a substantial fraction of available onboard storage.

Ironically, the ground system's creation of the timeline data block itself could be almost as highly a time-dependent process as the execution of actual timeline onboard. HST provides a particularly complex example. Long-term scheduling (look-ahead intervals of several months to a year) are used to block-out accepted proposal targets within allowed geometric boundary conditions. The geometry factors are typically dominated by Sun angle considerations, with additional contributions from issues such as moon avoidance, maximizing target orbital visibility, obtaining significant orbital dark time or low sky brightness, and meeting linkages between observations specified by the astronomer.

On the intermediate term (a few weeks to a couple of months), LEO spacecraft targets are ordered and scheduled relative to orbital events such as South Atlantic Anomaly (SAA) entrance/exit and Earth occultation's, and the duration of their associated observations (based on required exposure time computations) were estimated. Concurrently, support functions requiring scheduling, like communications, are interleaved with the science target scheduling.

Lastly, on the short term (a day to a week), final detailed scheduling (both of science targets and support functions) to a precision of seconds is performed using the most accurate available model data (for example, the most recent predicted spacecraft ephemeris), and with the possibility for inclusion of new targets (often referred to as Targets of Opportunity (TOO) not previously considered.

At times the software needed to support the intermediate and short term scheduling processing performed by the ground system has been massive, complex, and potentially very brittle. Further, multiple iterations of the process, frequently involving a lot of manual intervention (at considerable expense), can be required to produce an error-free schedule. Although considerable progress has been made in streamlining this process and reducing its associated costs, the mathematical modeling remains fairly sophisticated and some amount of operational inefficiency is inevitable due to the necessity of relying on approximations during look-ahead modeling.

2.1.2 Command Loading

By contrast to the planning and scheduling function, command loading is quite straightforward. It consists of translating the directives output from planning and scheduling (plus any real-time directives, table loads, etc. generated at and output from the control center) into the language/formats understandable by the flight computer and compatible with the communications medium. As communications protocols and the input interfaces to flight computers become more standardized, this ground system function will become steadily more automated via Commercial Off-the-Shelf (COTS) tools.

2.1.3 Science Schedule Execution

Science schedule execution refers to all onboard activities that directly relate to performing the science mission. They include target acquisition, Science Instrument (SI) configuration, and SI operations on targets (for example, exposure time management)

2.1.4 Science Support Activity Execution

Science support activities are those specifically performed to ensure the success of the science observation, but are not science observations themselves, nor are they routine housekeeping activities pertaining to maintenance of a viable observing platform.. They are highly mission/SI specific activities and may include functions such as Optical Telescope Assembly (OTA) calibration and management and SI direction of spacecraft operation (such as pointing adjustment directives). These activities may be performed in immediate association with ongoing science, or may be performed as background tasks disjoint from a current observation. Although executed onboard, much (if not all) of the supporting calculations may be done on the ground and the results uplinked to the flight computer in the form of tables or commands.

2.1.5 Onboard Engineering Support Activities

Onboard support activities are routine housekeeping functions pertaining to maintenance of a viable observing platform. The exact form of their execution will vary from spacecraft to spacecraft, but general categories are common within a mission type (e.g.., GEO Earth-pointer, LEO celestial-pointer, etc.). Housekeeping functions include angular momentum dumping, data storage & management, attitude & orbit determination and/or prediction, attitude control, and orbit station keeping. These activities may be performed in immediate association with ongoing science, or may be performed as background tasks disjoint from a current observation. .Just as with science support activities, some of the supporting calculations may be done on the ground and the results uplinked to the flight computer in the form of tables or commands.

2.1.6 Downlinked Data Capture

Capture of downlinked telemetry data is rather straightforward and highly standardized. This ground system function will become steadily more automated via COTS (Commercial Off The Shelf) tools.

2.1.7 Data and Performance Monitoring

Monitoring of spacecraft performance and H&S by checking the values of telemetry points and derived parameters is a function that is currently shared between flight and ground systems. While critical H&S monitoring is an onboard responsibility (especially where triggers to safemode entrance are concerned), the ground, in the past, has performed more long term, non-real-time quality checking, such as hardware component trending, accuracy analysis, as well as treatment of more general performance issues (e.g., overall observing efficiency).

2.1.8 Fault Diagnosis

Traditionally prior to launch, the system engineers would identify a whole host of key parameters that need to be monitored onboard, specify tolerances defining in-range vs. out-of-range performance, and identify FSW responses to be taken in real-time and/or FOT responses to be taken in near-real-time. To do this the system engineers have started with a set of failure scenarios in mind, identified the key parameters (and their tolerances/thresholds) that would measure likely symptoms of those failures, figured out how to exclude possible red-herrings (i.e., different physical situations that might masquerade as the failure scenario under consideration), and (in parallel) developed corrective responses to deal with those failures. So the process of transitioning from the symptoms specified by the parameters to the correction action (often a static table entry) that constitutes the diagnosis phase conceptually actually occurs (pre-launch) in the reverse order and the intellectual output of the process is stored onboard.

In the post-launch phase, the system engineers/FOT may encounter an unanticipated problem and must perform a diagnosis function using the telemetry downlinked to the ground. In such cases, operations personnel must rely on their experience (possibly with other spacecraft) and subject matter expertise to solve the problem. When quick solutions are achieved, the process often used is that of pattern recognition (or, more formally, case-based reasoning as will be discussed later), i.e., the recognition of a repetition of clues observed previously when solving a problem in the past. Failing at the pattern recognition level, a more lengthy general analytical phase (the human equivalent of state modeling) typically ensues that is manually intensive and at times very expensive.

2.1.9   Fault Correction

Currently, generating a plan to correct an onboard anomaly, fault, or failure is exclusively a ground responsibility. These plans may be as simple as specification of a mode change or as complex as a major hardware reconfiguration or a FSW code modification. In many cases, canned solutions are stored onboard for execution in response to an onboard trigger or ground command, but creation of the solution itself was done by ground system personnel, either in immediate response to the fault or (at times) many years prior to launch in anticipation of the fault. And even where the solution has been worked out and validated years in advance, conservative operations philosophy has often retained within the ground system power to initiate the solution.

2.1.10   Downlinked Data Archiving

Archiving of downlinked telemetry data (including in some cases distribution of data to users) is rather straightforward and highly standardized. This ground system function will become steadily more automated via COTS tools.

2.1.11   Engineering Data Analysis/Calibration

Traditionally, nearly all spacecraft engineering analysis and calibration functions (with the exception of gyro drift bias calibration and, for the Small Explorer (SMEX) missions, magnetometer calibration) have been performed on the ground. These include attitude sensor alignment and polynomial calibrations, battery depth-of-discharge & state of charge analyses, communications margins evaluations, etc. Often the work in question has been iterative and highly manually intensive.

2.1.12   Science Data Processing/Calibration

Science data processing and calibration have been nearly exclusively a ground system responsibility for two reasons. First, the low computing power of radiation hardened onboard computers, relative to that available in ground systems, has limited the degree to which science data processing can be performed onboard.. Second, the science community generally has insisted that all the science data be brought to the ground. Their position arises from a concern that the data might not be processed as thoroughly onboard as it might on the ground, and that the science data users often process the same data multiple times using different algorithms, calibrations, etc., sometimes years after the data was originally collected.

2.2   Introduction to FSW (Flight Software)

Although highly specialized to serve very precise (and often mission-unique) functions, FSW must simultaneously satisfy a surprisingly broad spectrum of competing needs.

First, it is the FSW that provides the ground system an interface with the flight hardware, both engineering and science. Since these hardware components are constantly being upgraded as their associated technologies continue to advance, the FSW elements that "talk" to the hardware components must regularly be updated as well. Fortunately, as the interface with the ground system (at least here at GSFC) has largely been standardized, the FSW elements that talk to the ground remain largely intact from mission to mission. It is in fact the ability of the FSW to mask changes in flight hardware input/output channels that has provided the ground system a relatively stable environment for the development of standardized COTS products, which in turn has enabled dramatic reductions in ground system development costs.

Second, it is the responsibility of the FSW to respond to events that the ground system cannot deal with, because

1. The spacecraft is out of contact with the ground.
2. The response must be immediate.
3. Critical spacecraft or payload H&S issues are involved.
4. The ground lacks key onboard information for formulating the best response.

Historically, the kinds of functions allocated to FSW for these reasons were ones such as the Attitude Control Subsystem (ACS), safemode processing and transition logic, fault detection and correction, target acquisition logic, etc.

Third, the FSW can be used to streamline (at least in part) those (previously considered ground system) processes where an onboard, autonomous response is cheaper or more efficient. In many of these cases, routine processes may first be performed manually by operations personnel, following which automated ground software is developed to perform the process. After the automated ground process has been fully tested operationally, the software (or algorithms) may then be migrated to the flight system.

Fourth, the process may be performed onboard in order to reduce demand on a limited resource. For example, downlink bandwidth is a valuable, limited quantity on most missions, either because of size/power constraints on spacecraft antennas/transmitters, or because of budget limitations on the size of the ground antenna. In such cases, FSW may be used to compress the output from payload instruments or prune excessive detail from the engineering telemetry stream to accommodate a smaller downlink volume.

As can be seen from even casual consideration of these few examples, the demands placed on FSW are of a widely varying nature. Some require high precision calculation of complex mathematical algorithms. These calculations often must be performed extremely quickly and the absolute time of the calculation must be accurately placed relative to the availability of key input data (i.e., the data latency issue). On the other hand, some FSW functions must process large quantities of data (for example, compression of science instrument output), or must store and manage the data. Other functions must deal with intricate logic trees and orchestrate real-time responses to anomalies detected by self-monitoring functions. And because the FSW is the key line of defense protecting spacecraft H&S, all these functions must be performed flawlessly and continuously, and often (due to onboard processor limitations) must be tightly coupled in several processing loops.

The following is a list of the traditional FSW functions:

1. Attitude Determination and Control
2. Sensor Calibration
3. Orbit Determination/Navigation (traditionally orbit maneuver planning a ground function)
4. Propulsion
5. Executive
6. Command Processing (target scheduling traditionally ground function)
7. Engineering and Science Data Storage
8. Communications
9. Electrical Power Management
10. Thermal Management
11. Science Instrument Commanding
12. Science Instrument Data Processing
13. Data monitoring (traditionally no trending)
14. Fault Detection, Isolation and Recovery (FDIR)
15. Safemode (separate ones for spacecraft and payload instruments)

2.2.1 Attitude Determination and Control, Sensor Calibration, Orbit Determination, Propulsion

Often the first 4 functions reside within a separate Attitude Control System (ACS) processor because of the high Central Processing Unit (CPU) demands of its elaborate mathematical computations. Item 1 includes the control laws responsible for keeping the spacecraft pointing in the desired direction and reorienting the spacecraft to a new direction. Currently, onboard attitude sensor calibration is limited to gyro drift bias calibration (and for some spacecraft a coarse magnetometer calibration).

Orbit determination may be accomplished by measurement (Global Positioning System (GPS) for example), solving the equations of motion, or by use of an orbit propagator. Traditionally, orbit maneuver planning has been the responsibility of the ground, but some experiments will be performed migrating routine stationkeeping maneuver planning onboard Earth Orbiter-1 (EO-1). Regardless whether the orbit maneuver planning is done onboard or on the ground, the onboard propulsion subsystem has responsibility for executing the maneuvers via commands to the spacecraft's thrusters, which also at times may be used for attitude control and momentum management.

2.2.2 Executive, Command Processing, Engineering and Science Data Storage, Communications

The Command & Data Handling (C&DH) processor includes the next 4 functions, and may (depending on the flight system design) include many of the remaining ones. The executive is responsible for coordinating and sequencing all the onboard processing, and separate local executives may be required to control lower level processing within a subsystem. The command processor manages externally supplied stored or real-time commands, as well as internally originated commands to spacecraft sensors, actuators, etc. Again, depending on the design, some command management may be under local control.

The C&DH also have management responsibility for engineering and science data storage (in the past via tape recorders but nowadays usually via solid state storage). Depending on the level of onboard sophistication, much of the bookkeeping job may be shared with the ground, although the trends are towards progressively higher levels of onboard autonomy. Telemetry uplink and downlink are C&DH responsibilities as well, although articulation of moveable actuators (such as high gain antenna gimbals) as well as any supporting mathematical modeling associated with communications (e.g., orbit prediction) are typically the province of the ACS.

2.2.3 Electrical Power Management, Thermal Management SI Commanding, SI Data Processing

Critical H&S functions like spacecraft electrical power and thermal management is usually treated as separate subsystems, although the associated processing may be distributed among several physical processor locations depending on the design of the flight system. This distribution of sub-functionality is particularly varied with regards to science instrument (SI) commanding and data processing given the steadily increasing power of the SIs associated microprocessors. Currently, we are including any onboard processing associated with a spacecraft's Optical telescope Assembly (OTA) within the context of the SI functions.

2.2.4 Data Monitoring, FDIR

The processing associated with the next two functions (data monitoring and FDIR) are even more highly distributed. Typically, the checking of individual data points and the identification of individual errors (with associated flag generation) is done locally, often immediately after the measurement is read out from its sensor. On the other hand, fault recovery is typically centralized so responses to multiple faults can be dealt with in a systematic manner.

2.2.5 Safemode

The last item, safemode, may include several independent sub-functions, depending on the cost and complexity of the spacecraft in question. Typical kinds of safemode algorithms include Sun acquisition modes (to maintain power positive, healthy thermal geometry, and protect sensitive optics), spin-stabilized modes (to maintain attitude stability), and inertial hold mode (to provide minimal perturbation to current spacecraft state). Usually, the processing for one or more of these modes is located in the ACS processor, but there also usually is a fallback mode in a special safemode processor in case the ACS processor itself has gone down. The individual SIs themselves also have separate safemode capabilities, and anomalies causing the C&DH processor to become unavailable are dealt with via a special uplink-downlink card that in the absence of the C&DH processor enables continued (though limited) ground communication with the spacecraft.

2.3 Flight vs. Ground Implementation

Recently expanding levels of onboard autonomy have been enabled by growth in flight data system capacities (CPU, Input/Output (I/O), storage, etc.), as well as the new approaches to and structures for FSW design and development (object-oriented design, expert systems, remote agents, etc.). In particular, operational activities that previously were the private domain of the ground systems (such as planning & scheduling, engineering data analysis and calibration, and science data processing and calibration) now provide exciting opportunities for shifting responsibility from the ground to the flight component.. This would allow taking advantage of the unique strengths inherent in a real-time software system in direct contact with the flight hardware.

The key advantages possessed by the flight component over the ground component are immediacy, currency, and completeness. Only the flight component can instantly access flight hardware measurements, process the information, and respond in real-time. For example, for performance of basic spacecraft functions such as attitude control and thermal/power management, only the FSW has direct access in real-time to critical information needed to define the spacecraft's operational state, as well as the direct access to the spacecraft actuator hardware required to create and maintain the desired state. The FSW is also the only component of the integrated flight/ground operational system with full-time access to all relevant information for applications such as fault detection and Science Instrument (SI) target acquisition.

By contrast, in the past, the advantage of the ground over the flight segment has been the larger, more powerful ground computers that (for example) have enabled the ground system to execute extremely intricate schedule optimization algorithms using highly complex predictive models. However, as the power of the flight computers continues to grow with time, a partial shift of even of these traditional ground monopolies may be justified to take advantage of the real-time information exclusively available onboard. In fact, as this hardware differences between the two platforms environments narrow, the distinction between flight-based vs. ground-based may begin to blur.

In conjunction with ground/space trades, it is an interesting exercise to contemplate what happens to information as it migrates from the spacecraft to the ground system. As Figure 2.1 suggests, in a simplified way, there occur several abstractions that can affect decision-making. The origin of the information is the spacecraft that is the real entity that is the subject of the decision-making process. This information is downloaded to the ground in a raw data format (sequences of zeros and ones) and is stored in a computer memory and converted to what are termed „engineering units". These engineering units form the basis of the information that will be presented to an operator or analyst . The conversion from raw data to engineering units is a mapping, which introduces a level of abstraction. After this conversion the information is still in the computer. The act of presenting it to an operator or analyst , using perhaps some graphical representation, introduces yet another abstraction. The final abstraction process comes when the operator or analyst interprets what he sees with reference to his internal mental model of the spacecraft and its operations.

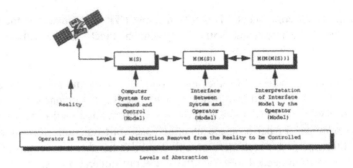

Figure 2.1.   Levels of Abstraction

At each level of abstraction there is the possibility of loosing information, adding information or misinterpreting information. Moving the handling and interpretation of the information closer to the source (the spacecraft) will help alleviate the possibility of errors introduced by the abstraction processes. The introduction of agent technology both on the ground and in space is a step in this direction.

3. LOGOS (Lights-Out Ground Operations System)

This section introduces the concept of agents and related concepts as they are currently understood in the Goddard Space Flight Center (GSFC) context, and discusses the LOGOS (Lights-Out Ground Operations System) which is an environment for demonstrating and evaluating the full spectrum of agent-based capabilities required for comprehensive ground/space systems automation.

3.1   Agents in the Goddard Context

In the literature there are many well-documented attempts to define what an agent is. The intent here is not to add confusion but to construct a definition of agent that is meaningful in the context of currently envisioned NASA/Goddard applications.

Analysis of the role of human operators in current ground system centers has contributed to our understanding of the mandatory and desirable characteristics of agents (or the emergent behaviors of an organization of agents) needed to realize ground system autonomy. A near-term objective of ground system autonomy is to achieve a complete and comprehensive realization of "lights-out" operations. Lights-out operations are just that - operation of a ground control center without the presence or direct intervention of people. Essentially, the agents "replace" in some sense the operators and assume the responsibility for their control center activities. In the current understanding of lights-out operations, human operator intervention is not totally precluded but is supported through operator dialog with an agent or group of agents on an as-needed basis.

The ground system autonomy focus imposes unique requirements on the agents that will be involved in achieving its autonomy. The position we take is that there is a spectrum of agents -- from a minimal agent (reactive) to an intelligent agent (deliberative and social) -- that is needed to support the activities in this domain. In our analysis of ground system autonomy , we have identified the following as typical capabilities that need to be supportable by an agent or a community of agents:

- Ability to initialize a ground system in preparation for a spacecraft contacts.
- Ability to utilize ground system resources to accomplish a goal.
- Ability to maintain operations during a „normal" contact.
- Ability to effectively respond to a fault situation.
- Ability to provide closed-loop support for spacecraft commanding.
- Ability to interact with the outside world in emergency situations.
- Ability to document all ground system operational events.
- Ability to shut down the ground system when not needed in full operational mode.

Analyses of these capabilities have given us a good start at establishing a conceptual understanding of what an agent is and what levels of intelligence it needs to posses. This is addressed in the next subsection.

3.2   Introduction to Agent Concepts

With an understanding of the types of activities that ground control personnel engage in and the prospect of integrating their functionality into the ground software system (via agents), an effort to define the relevant concepts associated with agents was undertaken. Table 3.1 provides a capsule view of the results of that effort. [1]

Table 3.1. Agent Concepts and Definitions/Discussions

Agent Concept	Definition/Discussion
Perception	A software process is said to perceive whenever it obtains data/information from a source in its environment, including itself and communication with other agents. The results of perception are percepts.
Autonomy	A software process is autonomous whenever it acts to achieve a goal according to its own percepts, internal states and knowledge. Inherent is the concept of reasoning.
Competency	A particular capability that an agent possesses
Basic Software Agent	A software process that perceives, is autonomous and has one or more goal-reaching competencies
Attribute	An inherent characteristic or quality that reflects or contributes to, in some way, a capability.

Attribute Understanding	Ability or an agent to modify its mode of communication with others based on an understanding of their communication capabilities.
Adaptable Communication	Ability of an agent to modify its mode of communication with others based on an understanding of their communication capabilities.
Planning	Ability to formulate steps needed to achieve a goal.
Replication	Ability of an agent to clone itself when required to achieve a goal within certain constraints
Temporal Understanding	Ability to understand and reason about time in relation to goal achievement.
Locational Understanding	Ability to understand and reason about self location and the location of others that may be required to support the execution of a goal-achieving plan.
Learning	Ability to increase and/or improve competencies.
Intelligent Agent	An agent is intelligent to the degree that it possesses attribute understanding, adaptable communication planning, replication, temporal understanding, locational understanding a learning capabilities.

Real-world multi-agent systems (like LOGOS to be discussed in 3.3) are designed to effectively employ agents with widely differing levels of intelligence. There is no mandate that all agents in a given agent-based system should have the same level of intelligence. Based on our analysis we feel that in multi-agent systems it is to be expected that the agents would either possess differentiated skills for handling different parts of the application problem or possess the capacity to learn in a nontrivial way (by which it is conceivable that the agent's level of intelligence would be modified).

One important agent-related concept that was adopted for use in the LOGOS relates to the manner in which an agent accomplishes a job. The approach taken essentially amounts to considering an agent as a tool user. The following Figure 3.1 graphically illustrates the idea.

As an example of this concept consider the following. In a control center software system there typically exists an expert system that monitors telemetry from a spacecraft subsystem and reports anomalies to an operator along with suggested corrections if possible. In our approach to agent-based automation of the control center the expert system resource could still be used if the agent knew about it and knew how to interact with it and interpret its results. The monitoring and advise-giving mechanisms would not have to be an integral part of the agent's knowledge base. The agent would have to know how to interpret this information and act on it as would a human operator. In LOGOS there are many examples of this concept in action.

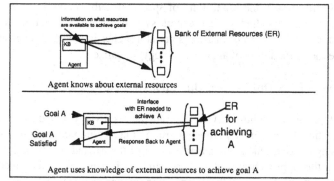

Agent knows about external resources

Agent uses knowledge of external resources to achieve goal A

Figure 3.1 An Agent Using an External Resource to Accomplish a Goal

Before considering the LOGOS concept let us consider, for one more time, the idea of an agent as a surrogate controller. Figure 3.2 illustrates that in a lights-out system environment there are several layers of automation. Agent technology will be required to provide the higher-levels of automation required to compensate for the lack of human presence in the lights-out environment

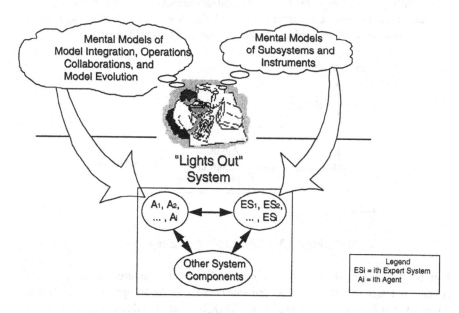

Figure 3.2. View of Operator Integration into a Lights-Out System

As the figure illustrates, the monitoring of spacecraft subsystems is an activity that can and is readily handled by an expert system. However activities such as coordination among a group of operators are at a higher intellectual level which, we feel, require the introduction of agent technology to realize.

3.3 LOGOS (Lights-Out Ground Operations System)

In the development of the initial LOGOS prototype [2] it was decided to distribute the needed operational functionality among a group of agents in a community rather than develop a single monolithic agent capable of all of the needed functionality. Among other things, this approach allows us to research such concepts as the emergence of higher level capabilities from the cooperation of agents with less comprehensive capabilities.

As depicted in Figure 3.3 illustrates the overall operating philosophy for LOGOS is quite straightforward. The agent community of LOGOS attempts to handle any spacecraft anomaly that is not handled by the pass automation process. In the event that it cannot, it establishes an interaction with a remote analyst for help. In doing so it needs to provide to the analyst sufficient contextual information and appropriate representations of what it considers to be the anomaly in order to enable the analyst to successfully address the problem. As the analyst interacts with the community in the solution of the problem the community as whole, as well as individual agents, can learn from the experience. (This particular goal has yet to be achieved.)

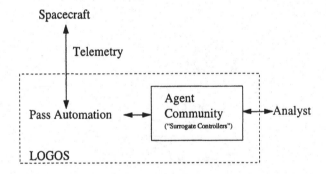

Figure 3.3. The LOGOS Concept

Figure 3.4 illustrates the first version of the LOGOS architecture (currently LOGOS is under redesign to bring about needed enhancements). As the spacecraft sends down telemetry it is formatted and stored in the TPOCC (Transportable Payload Operations Control Center) data server. A GenSAA (Generic Spacecraft Analyst Assistant)/Genie ((Generic Inferential Executor) application, which basically is an expert system, accesses data from this server in its function of executing pass plans and monitoring the health and safety of the spacecraft. Mission Operations Planning and Scheduling System (MOPSS) is the source of pass plan details and is used by

Genie to fabricate a pass script for automating pass activities. Each of these resources is associated with an Interface Agent in the LOGOS agent community. Agents in the community will be addresses shortly

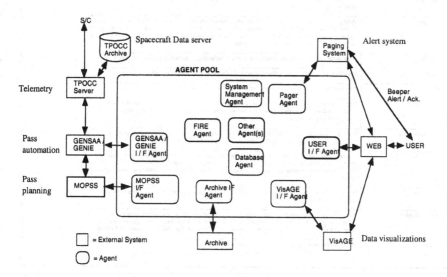

Figure 3.4. Lights-out Ground Operations System (LOGOS) Architecture

The development of LOGOS has been done in the context of object-oriented technology. The implementation of the various agents has been realized in Java. Figure 3.5 give an overview of the agent class hierarchy in LOGOS. Table 3.2 describes the agent class definitions for the LOGOS.

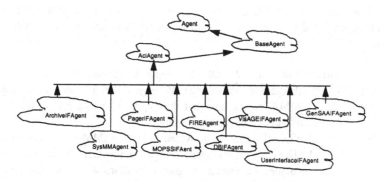

Figure 3.5. Class Hierarchy for LOGOS

Table 3.2. Class Definitions

Agent Class	Description
BaseAgent	BaseAgent defines a default implementation of the Agent interface that all LOGOS agents must support (such as clone, migrate, and runnable)
ActAgent	ActAgent encapsulates the agent-to-agent messaging components used by all agents. For the transport of messages the ActAgent uses a distributed software component framework called Workplace. WorkPlace provides the dynamic peer naming and data distribution services. The actual location of an agent and the transport protocols that are being used for communication are transparent to the agents.
SysMMAgent	Monitors all agents in the system in terms of system resource utilization, event timing and task completion.
MOPSSIFAgent	Monitors satellite pass schedule activity and provides information concerning this schedule.
FIREAgent	Provides procedures for resolving reported mission faults or requests action by a human expert
VisAGEIFAgent	Serves as an interface to Visual Analysis Graphical Environment (VisAGE) which provides data/information visualization functions for spacecraft anomaly analysis and resolution, as well as general monitoring of the LOGOS Agent community as a whole
GenSAAIFAgent	Provides interfaces to GenSAA which is responsible for monitoring and controlling spacecraft behaviors, and to the FIREAgent when an anomaly, not capable of being handled by GenSAA/Genie, is detected.
UserinterfaceIFAgent	Provides security through a user login process, translates messages from human readable form to the internal agent communication language, coordinates the writing of information on external user's displays by other agents, displays administrative or system-level messages, and maintains user-related information (e.g., prefernces, user modeling data, etc.)
DBIFAgent	Provides database management services for the LOGOS databases and is also responsible for the generation of any needed pass or anomaly reports.
ArchiveIFAgent	Responsible for maintaining an interface to an archive of recent and/or historical spacecraft telemetry data. When requested to do so, the Archive Interface Agent will retrieve specified telemetry points, perform any necessary processing on them, and forward them to the VisAGE Interface Agent for presentation to the LOGOS user.
PagerIFAgent	Pages human experts required for needed assistance

There are two agent types that are continuously present in LOGOS. These are the MOPSSAgent and the UserIFAgent. The MOPSSAgent awakens the SyaMMAgent in the event of an impending spacecraft pass, and the UserIFAgent does so if a remote user wishes to communicate with LOGOS. The capabilities supported by these agents are needed by ensure that there is always an interface to the environment outside of LOGOS and that the LOGOS can be readied in a timely fashion to support a mission contact and subsequent operations activities.

As an illustration of LOGOS activity consider the following high-level LOGOS scenario which highlights some of the major capabilities and activities within the system:

- Initialization of LOGOS to support spacecraft contact. The MOPSSIFAgent informs the SysMMAgent that a contact is coming up. The SysMMAgent ensures that the required hardware system elements are up and in good operating condition.
- The GenSAAIFAgent is activated. The SysMMAgent activates the GenSAAIFAgent. This agent brings up the GenSAA/Genie system, which provides for automated pass operations and initial detection of any spacecraft subsystem faults. The Genie script for the contact is activated. This script orchestrates the activities during the pass, including receiving and monitoring telemetry as well as commanding of the spacecraft.

- Once the contact begins, the TPOCC Data Server receives spacecraft telemetry and formats it for use by the GenSAA/Genie system.
- The GenSAAIFAgent monitors the behavior of the GenSAA/Genie system. If a fault is detected that cannot be handled by GenSAA/Genie system then the agent informs the FIREAgent for more extensive fault diagnosis.
- The FIREAgent attempts to diagnose the fault and recommend a solution. If it cannot, it makes the determination that outside help is required. It informs the UserIFAgent to contact the necessary analysts. The PagerIFAgent establishes the contact
- The VisAGEIFAgent is invoked to plan the method of data visualization that will be used to bring the contacted personnel up-to-date on the detected anomaly and to help establish the proper context for their decision making.
- The analysts diagnose the problem and initiate remedial actions through the UserIFAgent.
- The FIREAgent learns from the experience and updates its knowledge base to include information on the remedial actions identified by the analysts for the identified anomaly.
- If the analysts ask for a report on the situation the DBIFAgent will comply and support a report generation function.
- When time comes to end the contact, the SysMMAgent oversees closeout activities which includes data archiving, pass report generation, and shutting down of systems.

The scenario presented above illustrates several important ideas. It illustrates the role of agent as a tool user, it highlights interfaces and interactions with analysts outside the LOGOS on an as-needed basis (one of the hallmarks of lights-out operations), and it illustrates communication and cooperation among agents in the LOGOS community.

Agents within the LOGOS community communicate among themselves via an Agent Communication Language (ACL). This language is highly influenced by the KQML (Knowledge Query and Manipulation Language). In ACL there are currently four basic message types. These are: Request, Reply, Inform and Command. Each ACL message has a unique message id that is used for tracking and record keeping. Each message also includes sender-id, receiver-id, and return-to indicator among other fields. The list of performatives in the ACL includes: Give-Current -Status, Resolve-Anomaly, Query-DB, Insert-DB, Update-DB, Generate-Anomaly-Report, Generate-Pass-Report, Generate-Weekly-Report, Get-Mnemonic-Value, etc. New performatives are added as needs arise. In the new version of LOGOS the ACL will be KQML.

3.4 LOGOS - Next Steps

In addition to updating the agent communication language, new agent architecture will be introduced into the next instantiation of the agent testbed. (the current LOGOS will be used to provide the infrastructure for the new testbed.) The new agent architecture is a component-based architecture. The component approach will allow greater flexibility to the agent designer. A simple agent can be designed by using a minimum number of components that could receive percepts from the environment and react according to those percepts. This type of simple agent would be a reactive agent. A robust agent may be designed using more complex components that allow the agent to reason in a deliberative and/or social fashion, plan, schedule, model the environment, and learn. The following architecture focuses on an agent that is on the highly robust side of the scale; it contains components for modeling, reasoning, and planning. These components give the agent a higher degree of intelligence when interacting with its environment. Figure 3.5 details the agent architecture, showing the components needed to allow an agent to act with a high degree of intelligence.

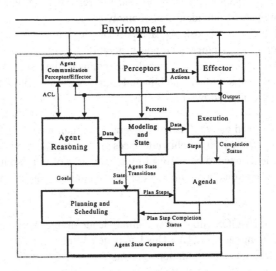

Figure 3.5. New Agent Architecture

Percepts received through sensors, communication with external software/systems, and other environmental entities are received through a Perceptor component. These percepts are passed from the perceptor to the Modeling and State component where a model's state is updated as needed. (Note, the modeling component maintains models of the environment, other agents in the community, and the agent itself.) A special perceptor is used to send and receive messages with other agents, this is the Agent Communication Perceptor/Effector. Incoming Agent Communication Language

(ACL) messages are formatted and passed to the Agent Reasoning component. The Agent Reasoning component reasons with received ACL messages, knowledge that it contains, and information that is acquired from the Modeling and State component to formulate goals for the agent when necessary. Goals are then acquired by the Planning component along with state and state transition information. The Planning component formulates a plan for the agent to achieve the desired goals. When a plan has been developed, the Agenda keeps track of the execution of the plan's steps. Steps are marked when they are ready for execution and the completion status of each step is also tracked by the Agenda. The Execution component manages the execution of steps and determines the success or failure of each step's execution. Output produced during a step execution can be passed to an Effector or the Reasoning component. The Modeling and State component will record state changes. When a plan is finished execution, a completion status is passed to the Planning component for evaluation of the plan for future use. If the Agent Reasoning component is dealing with data from the environment it may decide to either set a goal (for more deliberative planning) or react quickly in an emergency situation. The Agent Reasoner can also carry on a dialog with another agent in the community through the Agent Communication Perceptor/Effector.

What is a component? A component is a software module that performs a defined task. Components when combined with other software components can constitute a more robust piece of software that is easily maintained and upgraded. Each component in the architecture can communicate information to/from all other components as needed through a publish and subscribe communication mechanism, message passing, or a request for immediate data. Components may be implemented with a degree of intelligence through the addition of reasoning and learning functions in each component. Thus, a component needs to implement certain interfaces and contain certain properties. Components must implement functionality to publish information, subscribe to information, and be able to accept queries for information from other components or objects. Components need to keep a status of their state, and need to know what types of information they contain and need from external components and objects to function.

The LOGOS experience has to-date had been a successful and rewarding one. Because of its initial success longer-range missions like the Nanosat mission, a constellation of small satellites which will make multiple remote and in-situ measurements in space, has plans to evaluate the role that agent technology can play in support of autonomous ground and space operations.

4. Remote Agent

We now turn from ground-based autonomy to autonomy onboard a spacecraft. This section describes a flight experiment that will demonstrate the Remote Agent approach to spacecraft commanding and control. In this approach, the Remote Agent software may be considered to be an autonomous „remote agent" of the spacecraft operators in the sense that the operators rely on the agent to achieve particular goals. The operators do not know the exact conditions on the spacecraft, so they do not tell the agent exactly what to do at each instant of time. They do, however, tell the agent exactly which goals to achieve in a period of time as well as how and when to report in.

The Remote Agent (RA) is formed by the integration of three separate technologies: an on-board planner-scheduler, a robust multi-threaded executive, and a model-based fault diagnosis and recovery system. This Remote Agent approach is being designed into the New Millennium Program's Deep Space One (DS1) mission as an experiment. The New Millennium Program is designed to validate high-payoff, cutting-edge technologies to enable those technologies to become more broadly available for use on other NASA programs. The experiment is slated to be exercised in May of 1999.

4.1 Remote Agent Design Approach and Architecture

The New Millennium Autonomy Architecture rapid Prototype (NewMaap) effort [3] identified the key contributing technologies: on-board planning and replanning, multi-threaded smart executive, and model-based failure diagnosis and repair. In NewMaap, we learned how to take advantages of the strengths and weaknesses of these three technologies and merge them into a powerful system. After successful completion of the prototype, the RA was selected as one of the NMP technologies for DS1. It will be uplinked to the spacecraft as a software modification and demonstrated as an experiment.

Figure 4.1 shows the communications architecture for the Remote Agent. Note that all interactions with the hardware are the responsibility of the real-time software. The RA is layered on top of that software, but also gathers information from all levels to support fault diagnosis.

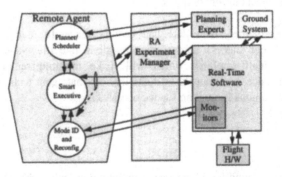

Figure 4.1. Remote Agent Communication Architecture

Several spacecraft commanding styles are possible. Goal-oriented commanding is the intended operating mode for most of a RA mission; provision has been made for updating the goals in flight. In a typical planning cycle, the executive is executing a plan and gets to an activity that can be interpreted as "time to plan the next segment." The executive calls the planner with the current and projected spacecraft state including the health of all devices. The planner/scheduler generates a new plan using priorities, heuristics, and domain models including system constraints. The planner sends this plan to an executive that creates an agenda of plan items and executes the agenda. Plan execution robustness is added by making use of the Model-based Mode Identification and Reconfiguration (MIR) system. The MIR system includes monitors, mode identification for nominal and failure conditions, communication of state to the executive and proposals of reconfiguration actions to take in the event of failures. Each of the components of the Remote Agent will be described in more detail, but first the Remote Agent experiment for the Deep Space One mission will be described in more detail.

4.2 The Deep Space One Remote Agent Experiment

The Remote Agent eXperiment (RAX) for Deep Space One is a demonstration of RA capabilities. Since an alternate method of control is used for most of the mission, RAX is focused on demonstrating specific autonomy capabilities rather than controlling all aspects of spacecraft behavior. The Remote Agent controls the following spacecraft hardware and software: the camera for use in autonomous navigation, the Solar Electric Propulsion (SEP) subsystem for trajectory adjustment, the attitude control system for turns and attitude hold, the navigation system for determining how the actual trajectory is deviating from the reference trajectory and what SEP thrusting profile is needed to stay on the reference trajectory, and the Power Amplification and Switching Module (PASM) for use in demonstrating fault protection capabilities.

Four failure modes are covered by RAX. These are:
  F1. Power bus status switch failure
  F2. Camera power stuck on
  F3. Hardware device not communicating over bus to flight computer
  F4. Thruster stuck closed

4.3 Mission Scenario

The Remote Agent experiment is executed in two phases, a 12 hour Phase One followed a couple of weeks later by a several day Phase Two.

In Phase One, we start slowly by first demonstrating the executive operating in the manner of a low-level sequencer by accepting commands to turn devices on and off. Next, a „scripted" mode is demonstrated with execution of plans uplinked from the ground. The main demonstration here will be commanding the spacecraft to go to and stay in a known, safe, standby mode and then take a series of optical navigation (OpNav) images. In addition, Failure mode F1 will be demonstrated by injecting power bus switch status readings indicating that a power bus is unexpectedly off. The fault diagnostic system will examine this information along with other information that indicates that devices on the bus are still communicating normally with the flight computer and conclude that the failure is in the switch status sensor and not in the bus itself. No action will result

In Phase Two, we initiate on-board planning. Based on the spacecraft initial state and the uplinked goals, the planner will generate a multi-day plan including imaging for optical navigation, thrusting to stay on the reference trajectory, and simulated injection of faults to test out failures F2, F3, and F4. First the camera power stuck on failure (F2) is injected. When the executive is unable to turn off the camera when the plan so dictates, the executive realizes that the current plan should be aborted and replanning is indicated. This might be necessary, for example, because the initial plan's assumptions on power consumption are incorrect with the camera on when it should be off. The plan is declared failed, the spacecraft is sent to a standby mode while the planner is requested to replan based on the new information that the camera power switch is stuck on. When the new plan is received by the executive, execution resumes including navigation and SEP thrusting. Near the end of the three-day plan, the planner is called to generate the plan for the next three days. This plan includes navigation and SEP thrusting as before. It also includes two simulated faults. First, a failure of a hardware device to communicate is injected (F3); the proper recovery is to reset the device without interrupting the plan. Next, injecting an attitude control error monitor above threshold simulates a thruster stuck closed failure (F4). The correct response is to switch control modes so that the failure is mitigated.

4.4 RA Capabilities Demonstrated with DS1 RAX

The above scenario has been designed to demonstrate that the DS1 Remote Agent meets the following autonomy technology goals:

- Allow low-level command access to hardware.
- Achieve goal oriented commanding.
- Generate plans based on goals and current spacecraft state expectations.
- Determine the Health State of hardware modules.
- Demonstrate model-based failure detection, isolation, and recovery.
- Coordinate hardware states and software modes.
- Replan after failure given a new context.

4.5 RA Components

The major components of the Remote Agent are discussed as follows.

4.5.1 Planner/Scheduler

The highest level commanding interface to the Remote Agent is provided the Planner/Scheduler (PS). Given the Spacecraft State and a set of goals, PS generates a set of synchronized high-level activities that, once executed, will achieve the goals. PS maintains a database of goals for the mission, and the mission profile that spans a very long time horizon, potentially the duration of the entire mission. Ground controllers can add, modify, or delete goals from the mission profile by issuing a command to Remote Agent.

Over the duration of a mission PS is invoked by the executive to return a synchronized network of activities, the plan, for each short-term scheduling horizon into which the mission is partitioned. Typically each short-term horizon covers several days. When PS receives a request from EXEC, it identifies the next scheduling horizon and retrieves the goals relevant to that horizon from the mission profile. It merges in the expected initial Spacecraft State provided by EXEC and generates a fully populated plan. PS then sends that plan to EXEC for execution. A new plan will be requested in two situations, both of which are handled identically by PS:

- Nominal operations: in this case EXEC reaches the activity Planner_Plan_Next_Horizon toward the end of the current plan horizon. EXEC will issue a request for a new plan. This request will define the new initial state as the expected final state of the current plan. This will allow transition from the old to new plan without any interruption of execution.

- Fault response: if MIR detects an anomaly that will impact the executability of current or future tasks in the plan, the EXEC will request a new plan to resume normal operations after having put the spacecraft in a safe standby mode. In this case the initial state describes the standby state for each subsystem modeled in the plan and health information describing possibly degraded modes for failed subsystems.

PS consists of a heuristic search engine, the Incremental Refinement Scheduler (IRS) that operates in the space of incomplete or partial plan [6]. Since the plans explicitly represent time in a numeric (or metric) fashion, the planner makes use of a temporal database. As with most causal planners, PS begins with an incomplete plan and attempts to expand it into a complete plan by posting additional constraints in the database. These constraints originate from the goals and from constraint templates stored in a model of the spacecraft. The temporal database and the facilities for defining and accessing model information during search are provided by the HSTS system. For more details on PS and the HSTS system see [4] and [5]. Figure 4.2 illustrates the PS architecture.

Each subsystem in the model is represented in the PS database. Each subsystem has a set of dynamic state variables whose value is tracked over time. PS uses tokens to represent both actions and states that occur over finite time intervals. A token is associated with a value of a state variable occurring over a finite time interval. Each value has one or more associated compatibility's, i.e., and sets of constraints between tokens. An example of the atomic temporal constraints that belong to compatibility can be expressed in English as „While the spacecraft is taking asteroid pictures requested by navigation, no ion thrusting is allowed".

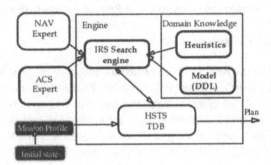

Figure 4.2. Planner/Scheduler Architecture

Table 4.2 describes three plans that PS would generate during a 6-day period that includes replanning due to spacecraft failure. The first CPU time column reports the actual run time of PS on a PowerPC/VxWorks flight hardware testbed. The next column reports the estimated time to generate the same plans using only 25% of DS1's slower RAD6000 processor.

Scenario	Tokens	Constraints	CPU time on PPC testbed (mm:ss)	Est. CPU time on RAD6000 (hh:mm:ss)
1st horizon	105	141	7:13	4:48:00
Replan in 1st horizon	69	66	4:01	2:40:00
2nd horizon	126	192	13:49	9:12:00

Table 4.2 PS Metrics for Performance

4.5.2 Executive

The Smart Executive (EXEC) is a reactive plan execution system with responsibilities for coordinating execution-time activity. EXEC's functions include plan execution, task expansion, hardware reconfiguration, runtime resource management, plan monitoring, and event management. The executive invokes the planner and MIR to help it perform these functions. The executive also controls the lower-level software by setting its modes, supplying parameters and by responding to monitored events.

The top-level operational cycle, including the planning loop, is described as follows. EXEC requests a plan by formulating a plan request describing the current execution context. It later executes and monitors the generated plan. EXEC executes a plan by decomposing high-level activities in the plan into primitive activities, which it then executes by sending out commands, usually to the real-time flight software (FSW). EXEC determines whether its commanded activities succeeded based either on direct feedback from the recipient of the command or on inferences drawn by the Mode Identification (MI) component of MIR. When some method to achieve a task fails, EXEC attempts to accomplish the task using an alternate method in that task's definition or by invoking the Mode Reconfiguration (MR) component of MIR. If MR finds steps to repair the failing activity without interfering with other concurrent activities, EXEC performs those steps and continues on with the original definition of the activity. If the EXEC is unable to execute or repair the current plan, it aborts the plan, cleans up all executing activities, and puts the controlled system into a standby mode. If continued autonomous operation is allowed, EXEC requests a new plan from PS while maintaining standby mode. EXEC resumes execution of the new plan when it is received.

In the Periodic Planning Cycle as shown in Figure 4.3, our approach separates an extensive, deliberative planning phase from the reactive execution phase, executing infrequently generated plans that extended over time periods. Plans normally include the task of planning for the next horizon—i.e., the planner sets aside a good time for its own (next) computation. The planner extends the plan to address the goals of the next planning horizon and returns the result to the executive. The executive then merges the extended plan with the end of the currently running plan. This enables Remote Agent to engage in activities, which span multiple planning horizons (such as a 3-month long ion engine burn), without interrupting them.

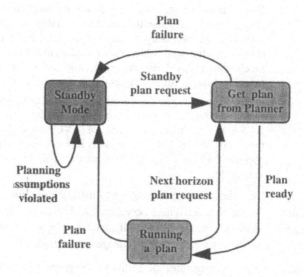

Figure 4.3 Executive Periodic Planning Cycle

We now summarize how the EXEC capabilities described above are demonstrated within the RAX scenarios.

First, EXEC demonstrates the multi-level commanding, allowing ground operators to specify low-level commands to the hardware as part of a sequence, to generate plans from ground, or to request and execute plans generated on-board the spacecraft. Low-level commanding and ground-based planning are demonstrated in Phase One of the RAX experiment. In this phase a plan is up-linked from the ground which contains both high-level activities (like turning to a target) and low-level activities (using the EXEC-ACTIVITY tokens turn PASM on and off).

Second, EXEC demonstrates plan request generation and execution. As part of executing a plan phase two, EXEC demonstrates a number of important capabilities involved in token decomposition.

- EXEC demonstrates context sensitive behavior in the management of the ion propulsion system. Before executing a thrust command, EXEC requires that IPS be in standby mode. If it is already in standby mode, EXEC proceeds to the thrusting, otherwise it will put IPS into the standby mode before proceeding.

- EXEC demonstrates time-driven token durations. For example, it terminates a thrust segment based on a timeout, rather than external confirmation.

- EXEC demonstrates event-driven token duration's, in which picture taking tokens are not allowed to terminate until confirmation the picture has finished

- EXEC demonstrates goal-oriented achievement (don't achieve things that are already true). Because the planner is unable to determine how many thrust segments are necessary to achieve the total desired thrust, it inserts thrust tokens into the plan, which may not need to be executed. EXEC tracks how much thrust has been achieved, and only executes thrust tokens (and associated turns) for so long as thrust is actually necessary..

- EXEC demonstrates the coordination of activity details across subsystems that are below the level of visibility of the planner. There is a constraint that ACS is in that thrust-vector-control (TVC) mode shortly after IPS has started thrusting. When EXEC commands IPS into thrusting mode, it also sends the command to ACS to enter TVC mode based on its own lower-level domain knowledge.

Third, EXEC demonstrates the ability to maintain required properties in the face of failures. In the thruster failure scenario, EXEC learns from a MIR state update that the current thruster mode is faulty. It invokes MIR with a recovery request and then executes MIRs recommendation to change to a degraded thruster control mode.

Fourth, EXEC demonstrates the ability to recognize plan failure, abort the plan, enter standby mode, and request and execute a replan. This occurs in the MICAS (Microelectronics Integrated Camera And Spectrometer) failure scenario, in which EXEC learns from MIR that MICAS is stuck on and cannot be turned off. EXEC requests a recovery from MIR so that it can turn MICAS off, but since there is no way to fix this problem MIR informs EXEC that it has no recovery. Since the plan requires MICAS to be off, EXEC aborts the plan, terminating a thrusting segment if necessary. It then enters a degraded standby mode, in which it leaves MICAS on despite the usual desire to turn off all unnecessary devices in standby mode, and requests a plan for the planner. In its plan request, EXEC informs the planner that MICAS is stuck on. Later, in executing the new plan, ground finds a way to fix MICAS and informs MIR of this fact. When EXEC learns from MIR that MICAS can now be shut off, this new information does not cause EXEC to abandon the plan, since the planner did not require MICAS to be broken. However, the next time EXEC asks for a plan, it informs the planner about the restored health of MICAS, so that the planner can now plan to switch MICAS off when desired. More details about EXEC can be found in References [6, 7.. and 8].

4.5.3   Diagnosis and Repair

We refer to the Diagnosis and Repair engine of the Remote Agent as MIR, for Mode Identification and Reconfiguration, which emphasizes the model-based diagnosis and control flavor of the system. MIR eavesdrops on commands that are sent to the on-board hardware managers by the EXEC. As each command is executed, MIR receives observations from spacecraft sensors. MIR combines these commands and observations with declarative models of the spacecraft's components to determine the current state of the system and report it to the Exec. A very simple example is shown

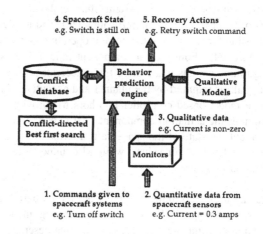

Figure 4.4 Information Flow in MIR

schematically in Figure 4.4. In the nominal case, MIR merely confirms that the commands had the expected effect on Spacecraft State. In case of failure, MIR diagnoses the failure and the current state of the spacecraft and provides a recovery recommendation. A single set of models and algorithms are exploited for command confirmation, diagnosis and recovery.

The RAX mission scenario demonstrates the following MIR capabilities: state identification throughout the experiment, diagnosis of sensor failure, diagnosis and recovery recommendations for device failures, and overriding of a MIR diagnosis via a ground command. RAX is fully responsible for responding to real failures within scope should they occur during the experiment. However, since we cannot depend on failures occurring during the experiment, injecting false sensor readings consistent with the failures will simulate failures F1-F4. RAX will be expected to take the appropriate corrective actions, though in reality none are necessary.

F1 illustrates MIR's ability to disambiguate between a sensor failure and failure of the device being sensed. MIR combines power distribution models with the sensed nominal current draw and communication status of devices to conclude that the power switch must be on and that a switch sensor failure, though unlikely, has occurred. Failures F2-F4 are diagnosed in a similar fashion and include the possibility of recovery. In F4, given only an attitude error and models of the spacecraft dynamics, MIR infers that one of a particular pair of thruster valves is stuck closed. MIR is then able to recommend that no matter which one of the two valves is stuck, switching ACS control modes will mitigate the problem.

The MIR component of the RA architecture, embodied in a system called Livingstone, consists of two parts: Mode Identification (MI) and Mode Reconfiguration (MR). MI is responsible for identifying the current operating or failure mode of each component in the spacecraft. Following a component failure, MR is responsible for suggesting reconfiguration actions that restore the spacecraft to a configuration that achieves all current goals as required by the planner and executive. Livingstone can be viewed as a discrete model-based controller in whom MI provides the sensing component and MR provides the actuation component. MI's mode inference allows the executive to reason about the state of the spacecraft in terms of component modes, rather than in terms of low level sensor values, while MR supports the run-time generation of novel reconfiguration actions.

Livingstone uses algorithms adapted from model-based diagnosis [9, 10] to provide the above functions. The key idea underlying model-based diagnosis is that a combination of component modes is a possible description of the current state of the spacecraft only if the models associated with these modes are consistent with the observed sensor values. Following de Kleer and Williams [10], MI uses a conflict directed best-first search to find the most likely combination of component modes consistent with the observations. Analogously, MR uses the same search to find the least-cost combination of commands that achieve the desired goals in the next state. Furthermore, both MI and MR use the same system model to perform their function. The combination of a single search algorithm with a single model, and the process of exercising these through multiple uses, contributes significantly to the robustness of the complete system. Note that this methodology is independent of the actual set of available sensors and commands. Furthermore, it does not require that all aspects of the spacecraft state are directly observable, providing an elegant solution to the problem of limited observability.

The use of model-based diagnosis algorithms immediately provides Livingstone with a number of additional features. First, the search algorithms are sound and complete, providing a guarantee of coverage with respect to the models used. Second, the model building methodology is modular, which simplifies model construction and maintenance, and supports reuse.. Third, the algorithms extend smoothly to handling multiple faults and recoveries that involve multiple commands. Fourth, while the algorithms do not require explicit fault models for each component, they can easily exploit available fault models to find likely failures and possible recoveries.

An important Livingstone feature is that the behavior of each component state or mode is captured using abstract, or qualitative, models [11, 12]. These models describe qualities of the spacecraft's structure or behavior without the detail needed for precise numerical prediction, making abstract models much easier to acquire and verify than quantitative engineering models. Examples of qualities captured are the power, data and hydraulic connectivity of spacecraft components and the directions in which each thruster provides torque. While such models cannot quantify how the spacecraft would perform with a failed thruster for example, they can be used to infer which thrusters are failed given only the signs of the errors in spacecraft orientation. Such inferences are robust since small changes in the underlying parameters do not affect the abstract behavior of the spacecraft. In addition, abstract models can be reduced to a set of clauses in propositional logic. This form allows behavior prediction to take place via unit propagation, a restricted and very efficient inference procedure.

All told, the MIR model for the DS1 spacecraft represents fifty-seven components of twelve different types, their behavior, and their interconnections. It is important to note that the MIR models are not required to be explicit or complete with respect to the actual physical components. Often models do not explicitly represent the cause for a given behavior in terms of a component's physical structure. For example, there are numerous causes for a stuck switch: the driver has failed, excessive current has welded it shut, and so on. If the observable behavior and recovery for all causes of a stuck switch are the same, MIR need not closely model the physical structure responsible for these fine distinctions. By modeling only to the level of detail required to make relevant distinctions in diagnosis (distinctions that prescribe different recoveries or different operation of the system) we can describe a system with qualitative "common-sense" models which are compact and quite easily written.

Models are always incomplete in that they have an explicit unknown failure mode. Any component behavior, which is inconsistent with all known nominal and failure modes, is consistent with the unknown failure mode. In this way, MIR can infer that a component has failed, though the failure was not foreseen or was simply left unmodeled because no recovery is possible. Additional technical details about Livingstone can be found in [13]

5. Future Directions - Some Speculations

Extrapolating from the LOGOS and Remote Agent examples, its safe to say that the future of agent technology work in NASA is exceptionally bright. A major accomplishment will be the integrating of ground-based and space-based autonomous systems into a single autonomous system with a ground and a space component. This integration could support some interesting and valuable investigations and demonstrations. For example, the migration of an autonomous process from the ground to space could be viewed as an agent moving from one community to another. This would be an interesting way to achieve adaptable autonomy.

In closing we cite three scenarios that are in NASA's future:

- A Principal Investigator (PI) talking, in a natural language, to an onboard agent serving as a PI-surrogate which is responsible for the management of the PIs scientific instrument and the planning and scheduling of detailed approaches for realizing the science agenda established by the PI.
- The spacecraft itself, considered as an agent, initiating and maintaining a dialog with an automated ground system and/or a human for either status reporting or anomaly handling.
- A constellation of autonomous spacecraft deciding among themselves how best to achieve some scientific goal.

6. Acknowledgments

At Goddard the authors wish to thank James Rash, Tom Grubb, Troy Ames, Carl Hostetter, Chris Rouff, Jeff Hosler, Matt Brandt, Dave Kocur, Kevin Stewart, Jay Karlin, Victoria Yoon, Chariya Peterson, and Dave Zock (who are or have been members of the Goddard Agent Group) for their major contributions. For more information on LOGOS the interested reader is invited to browse the GSFC agent web page at http://agents.gsfc.nasa.gov for access to current papers and working documents.

At ARC and JPL the authors wish to thank Douglas E. Bernard[1], Gregory A. Dorais[3], Chuck Fry[3], Edward B. Gamble Jr.[1], Bob Kanefsky[3], James Kurien[3], William Millar[3], Nicola Muscettola[2], P. Pandurang Nayak[4], Barney Pell[4], Kanna Rajan[3], Nicolas Rouquette[1], Benjamin Smith[1], Brian C. Williams[5] ([1] Jet Propulsion Laboratory, [2] Recom Technologies @ Ames, [3] Caelum Research @ Ames, [4] RIACS @ Ames

The material on the Remote Agent was based on a paper presented at IEEE Aerospace98 Conference

7. References

[1] Goddard Agent Group Working Paper, "Intelligent Agent-based Systems in the NASA/GSFC Context", http://agents.gsfc.nasa.gov/products.html

[2] Goddard Agent Group Working Paper, "LOGOS Requirements and Design Document", http://agents.gsfc.nasa.gov/products.html

[3] B. Pell, D. E. Bernard, S. A. Chien, E. Gat, N. Muscettola, P. Nayak, M. D. Wagner, and B. C. Williams, „A Remote Agent Prototype for Spacecraft Autonomy," SPIE Proceedings Volume 2810, Denver, CO, 1996.

[4] N. Muscettola, „HSTS: Integrating planning and scheduling," in Fox, M., and Zweben, M., eds, *Intelligent Scheduling*, Morgan Kaufman,

[5] N. Muscettola, B. Smith, S. Chien, C. Fry, G. Rabideau, K. Rajan, D. Yan, „Onboard Planning for Autonomous Spacecraft," in Proceedings of the fourth International Symposium on Artificial Intelligence, Robotics and Automation for Space (i-SAIRAS 97), July 1997.

[6] Barney Pell, Ed Gamble, Erann Gat, Ron Keesing, Jim Kurien, Bill Millar, P. Pandurang Nayak, Christian Plaunt, and Brian Williams, „A hybrid procedural/deductive executive for autonomous spacecraft," In P. Pandurang Nayak and B. C. Williams, editors, Procs. of the AAAI Fall Symposium on Model-Directed Autonomous Systems, AAAI Press, 1997.

[7] Barney Pell, Erann Gat, Ron Keesing, Nicola Muscettola, and Ben Smith, „Robust Periodic Planning and Execution for Autonomous Spacecraft," In Procs. of IJCAI-97, 1997.

[8] Erann Gat and Barney Pell, „Abstract Resource Management in an Unconstrained Plan Execution System," in Proc. of IEEE Aeronautics (AERO-98), Aspend, CO, IEEE Press, 1998 (To appear).

[9] J. de Kleer and B. C. Williams, „Diagnosing Multiple Faults," Artificial Intelligence, Vol 32, Number 1, 1987.

[10] J. de Kleer and B. C. Williams, „Diagnosis With Behavioral Modes," Proceedings of IJCAI-89, 1989.

[11] D. S. Weld and J. de Kleer, *Readings in Qualitative Reasoning About Physical Systems*, Morgan Kaufmann Publishers, Inc., San Mateo, California, 1990.

[12] J. de Kleer and B. C. Williams, *Artificial Intelligence*, Volume 51, Elsevier, 1991.

[13] B. C. Williams and P. Nayak, „A Model-based Approach to Reactive Self-Configuring Systems," Proceedings of AAAI-96, 1996.

Digital City Kyoto:
Towards a Social Information Infrastructure

Toru Ishida*, Jun-ichi Akahani**, Kaoru Hiramatsu**,
Katherine Isbister**, Stefan Lisowski***,
Hideyuki Nakanishi*, Masayuki Okamoto*
Yasuhiko Miyazaki****, Ken Tsutsuguchi****

* Department of Social Informatics, Kyoto University
** NTT Communication Science Laboratories
***Omron Software
****NTT Cyber Communication Laboratories

Abstract. This paper proposes the concept of digital cities as a social information infrastructure for urban life (including shopping, business, transportation, education, welfare and so on). We propose the *three layer architecture* for digital cities: a) the *information layer* integrates both WWW archives and real-time sensory information related to the city, b) the *interface layer* provides 2D and 3D views of the city, and c) the *interaction layer* assists social interaction among people who are living/visiting in/at the city. We started a three year project to develop a digital city for Kyoto, the old capital and cultural center of Japan, based on the newest technologies including GIS, 3D, animation, agents and mobile computing. This paper introduces the system architecture and the current status of Digital City Kyoto.

1. Introduction

As the number of Internet users is continuing to increase, various community networks are being tested [1]. The Internet is used not only for research and businesses but for everyday urban life. While the Internet makes research and businesses global, life is inherently local. The concept of digital cities is thus proposed to build an arena in which people in regional communities can interact and share knowledge, experience, and mutual interests.

Various digital cities have been created around the world. In the US, America Online (AOL) has developed a series of digital cities [2]. Each AOL digital city collects tourist and shopping information of the corresponding city. The success of AOL digital cities shows that people need regional information services for their everyday life. Since the word "digital city" is a registered trademark of AOL, though there are numerous activities on regional community networking in the US, we cannot find any other activity named "digital city" in the US.

In Europe, on the other hand, the European Digital Cities Conference has been held annually from 1994 to discuss a wide variety of topics including "the role of cities, towns, and regions in the deployment of advanced telematics solutions within the development of the Information Society." As an example of the experiments performed, Digital City Amsterdam was started four years ago. This city was built as a platform for various community networking systems and thus particularly focuses on social interaction among digital citizens. We were able to see how social interaction increased in the digital city. Though Digital City Amsterdam succeeded to introduce the city metaphor in the regional information services, since there is no direct mapping between digital and physical Amsterdam, the ratio of Amsterdam based digital citizens decreased from 45% in 1994 to 22% in 1998 [3]. This fact highlights the design issue of how much reality we should put into digital cities. If we make digital cities without strong connections to the corresponding physical cities, the connection may gradually disappear.

Recent activities on digital cities typically include 3D technologies. We can find several VRML-based trials such as those for Helsinki [4], Berlin, and Washington D.C. The Virtual Los Angeles [5] is designed to allow community members to directly participate in the urban planning process, and is a good example of a high quality 3D virtual city. The question is, however, what level of 3D reality is technologically and psychologically appropriate for implementing digital cities. Another question is who should/can develop and maintain the 3D digital cities. Moreover, as the 3D models become more accurate, more computational power and communication bandwidth are required to view digital cities at home. Though there exist various technical and organizational problems on implementing and using 3D in the Internet, we think the 3D technology will take an important role in establishing connections between digital and physical cities.

In October 1998, we started a project to develop a digital city as a social information infrastructure for Kyoto. Digital City Kyoto makes available different city metaphors: a 2D map and a 3D virtual space, which are easy to understand for non-technical people. WEB information is collected and linked to the 2D/3D city. Real-time sensory data from the physical city is also mapped to the digital city. People can get information related to the physical city such as traffic, weather, parking, shopping, and sightseeing. Digital City Kyoto also encourages social interaction among residents and tourists. This paper describes the basic concepts of digital city design in Section 2, and reports the current status of Digital City Kyoto in Sections 3 to 5. Since digital cities create regional information spaces in the Internet, we will discuss cross-cultural communication for bridging digital cities in Section 6.

2. Design Concepts for Digital Cities

The first design policy for Digital City Kyoto is to make it *real* by establishing a strong connection to physical Kyoto. Our digital city is not an imaginary city existing only in cyberspace. Instead, our digital city complements the corresponding physical city, and provides an information center for everyday life for actual urban communities. We think "digital" and "physical" make things "real." For example, in computerized organizations, such as universities and advanced companies, we cannot figure out their activities without looking into networks (E-mail, WEB and so on). As in those organizations, digital activities will become an essential part of urban life in the near future. The second design policy is to make the digital city *live* by dynamically integrating WEB archives and real-time sensory information created in the city. We will not produce contents nor select them. We will provide a tool for viewing and reorganizing vivid regional information created by people in the city.

We propose the system architecture of digital cities as follows. Figure 1 shows the three layer model for designing digital cities. The first layer is called the *information layer* where WWW archives and realtime sensory data are integrated and reorganized using the city metaphor. The geographical database is used for the integration of those types of information. The second layer is called the *interface layer* where 2D maps and 3D virtual spaces provide an intuitive view of digital cities. The animation of moving objects such as avatars, cars, busses, trains, and helicopters demonstrate dynamic activities in the cities. If the animation reflects real activities of the corresponding physical city, each moving object can become a media for social interaction: you may want to click the object to communicate with it. The third layer is called the *interaction layer* where residents and tourists interact with each other. Community computing experiments [6,7] especially agent/multiagent technologies are applied to encourage interactions in digital cities.

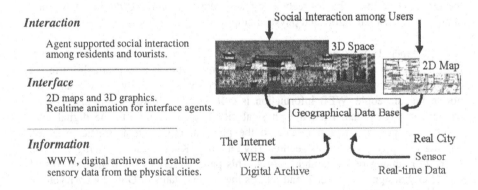

Interaction

Agent supported social interaction among residents and tourists.

Interface

2D maps and 3D graphics.
Realtime animation for interface agents.

Information

WWW, digital archives and realtime sensory data from the physical cities.

Social Interaction among Users

3D Space

2D Map

Geographical Data Base

The Internet
WEB
Digital Archive

Real City
Sensor
Real-time Data

Figure 1: The Three Layers Model for Digital Cities

3. Human Interface in Digital City Kyoto

To explain Digital City Kyoto, we start with the second layer, the *interface layer*. The human interface of current WEB sites is mainly by text: users search information by keywords and software robots retrieve information. This search-and-retrieve metaphor works well, especially if the needed information is distributed worldwide. The AOL digital cities inherit the same metaphor for their interface design. As the Internet is used for everyday life, however, we believe that the geographical interface will become more important in digital cities.

In Digital City Amsterdam, 2D maps represent an abstract city consisting of more than thirty squares with cultural, recreational, technological, civic, and political themes. Though the city does not directly correspond to the physically existing city, Digital City Amsterdam introduced geographical metaphors and spatial constraints, and succeeded to introducing neighboring feelings in digital citizens. If we want to integrate WEB information and real-time sensory data, however, we need more direct mapping between physical and digital cities. In Digital City Kyoto, we thus adopted GIS (geographical information system) as the core of the system architecture. Figure 2 shows maps for Kyoto with two different scales (left: 1/100,000, right: 1/1000). These maps are commercially available at reasonable prices. One interesting technology we are planning to apply is to omit irrelevant details and to produce a simplified map that is intuitively easy to understand.

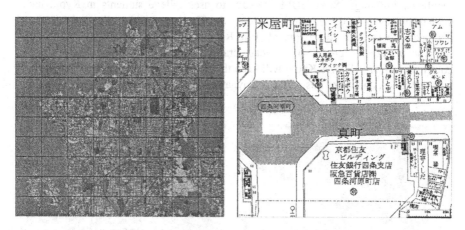

Figure 2: 2D Maps for Digital City Kyoto (Provided by Zenrin Corp.)

The 3D graphic technology becomes a key component of the interface when used in parallel with the 2D maps. The 3D aspect to a digital city allows non-residents to get a good feel for what the city looks like, and to plan physical visits. Residents of the city can use the 3D interface to pinpoint places or stores they would like to visit, and to test walking routes.

VRML (Virtual Reality Modeling Language) is the most well known 3D WEB technology and has been used in various digital city projects. Though VRML has been available for years, it is surprising that 3D technologies on the WEB have not yet become common. Some problems with VRML are its slowness and difficulty in modeling complex objects. Without significant effort, it is difficult to create a realistic VRML space that doesn't look like a plastic model. Though there are various approaches for building 3D experiences, we started with 3DML [8] for our initial prototype. People are comfortable moving through 3D spaces with game interfaces such as those currently offered by Doom or Quake, and now offered by the 3DML WEB plug-in. We decided to use photos mapped onto 3D blocks and 2D planes, rather than precise 3D modeling. This approach does not solve all the problems, but significantly diminishes some of them. Since 3DML coding is far more intuitive than VRML, the costs of developing the 3D space is dramatically reduced. Several days of VRML programming can be equivalent to several hours of 3DML coding. We are able to achieve sufficient graphic realism and detail, while at the same time an average PC can perform the 3D walk through. Some problems exist when downloading gif or jpeg compressed photos: as with any site on the WEB using many graphics, it takes some time when using telephone line connections.

Figure 3 shows the 3DML implementation of Shijo Shopping Street (Kyoto's most popular shopping street) and the hundreds of years old Nijo Castle in Kyoto. 3DML is not well suited to reproducing gardens and grounds, but has no problem with modern rectilinear buildings. Since 3DML is easy to use, college students in Kyoto have started to join us in cooperatively building the 3D Kyoto. This follows the "bazaar approach" to software development (Eric Raymond, The Cathedral and the Bazaar http://www.tuxedo.org/~esr/writings/cathedral-bazaar/). We hope that have contributors from all over Kyoto will keep the project from being a small handful of stagnant areas, and make this a vast and dynamic city.

Figure 3: 3D Interfaces for Digital City Kyoto (By Stefan Lisowski)

As described above, we are developing a human interface to Digital City Kyoto that combines 2D maps with several 3DML spots. At the same time, we started discussing various problems with the shopping street community: since we are using photos, information in the photos becomes old; the advertisements in the photos quickly become out-of-date; and some photos include registered trademarks. It is important for engineers, researchers and shop owners to start thinking of these issues. One solution we're working to implement, is a WEB and ftp interface to allow individual shopkeepers to update the advertisement photos on their 3D buildings by themselves.

3D Kyoto impacts different research areas such as architecture and disaster protection. In the area of architecture, researchers are eager to have a digital environment for simulating interactions between humans and environments. Since 3D Kyoto can be run on PCs connected to the Internet, network simulations with a large number of participants become feasible. In the area of disaster protection, the researchers normally must investigate a lot of photos (for example, 12,000 photos for one destroyed city). One group in Kyoto University has been trying to post all those photos on the WEB, but 3D technology may provide a better solution. Though it is impossible to make a precise 3D model for destroyed cities, the photo-based 3D approach can overcome this problem, see Figure 4 which consists only of 3D cubes and 2D planes, plus gif files with transparency.

Figure 4 : 3D City after the Earthquake (By Stefan Lisowski)

4. Information Sharing in Digital City Kyoto

The digital city integrates WEB and sensory data. As shown in Figure 1, GIS is the core of the system. The geographical database connects 2D/3D interfaces to WEB/sensory information. From the viewpoint of system architecture, it is also important not to directly connect the interface and information layers. Introducing the geographic database allows us to test various interface/information technologies independently.

After digital cities become popular, people will register their pages to their digital city, but until then, we need some technology to automatically determine the XY coordinates of each WEB page. The automatic address conversion thus becomes a key technology for providing fresh information from the Internet. While the ratio of the Internet users in Kyoto is less than 10%, the number of pages is increasing rapidly. We thus started extracting addresses from the WEB pages and converted them into XY coordinates using the geographic database. The WEB pages, which we could assign XY coordinates, should include precise addresses, famous and unique landmarks, or precise route information. In Kyoto, however, since the city is 1,200 years old, there are various ways to express the same address, and this makes the process very complicated. We have gathered over 600,000 pages that we acquired at a Yahoo regional link and have started developing a learning agent to extract rules for selecting valuable WEB pages and determining XY coordinates from the information contained in the WEB pages. So far, we selected 4,000 candidate pages and determined the precise XY coordinates for 2,000 of them.

Figure 5(a) shows the results of locating those pages on the 2D map. We can see how WEB pages are distributed in the city. The interesting fact is that most of them are located in the center of the city: the main shopping area of Kyoto. Various new data retrieval methods are now under development. Figure 5(b) shows the result of retrieving WEB pages for bus stops in Kyoto. The result clearly shows where those bus stops are located. It appears that the side effect of geographical WEB retrieving is to display the spatial distribution of the retrieved objects in the city.

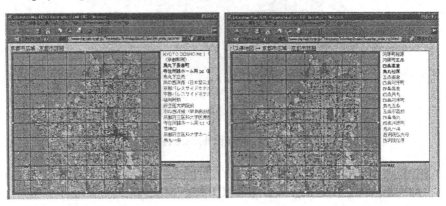

    (a) WEB Sites in Kyoto   (b) Bus Stops in Kyoto
Figure 5: Locating WEB Pages on the 2D Map

As the real-time sensory information, we are considering bus schedules, traffic status, weather condition, and live video from the fire department. In Kyoto City, for example, more than three hundred sensors have already been installed and they are gathering the traffic data of more than six hundred city buses. Each bus sends its location and route data in every few minutes. Such dynamic information makes our digital city live. During the first trial we are using real-time bus data and display them on the digital city. Since we can simulate the ideal bus schedule, the differences between real and ideal clearly indicate to users the traffic status. In future, we expect to get information from various private companies such as the availability of parking lots, restaurant tables, and so on. WEB retrieval under the constraint of sensory data is definitely an interesting research issue. We can also use real-time information to make a plan for daily shopping.

Other obvious real-time data is the location of the users, both tourists and residents, in the actual city. Several technologies such as GPS (Global Positioning System) are becoming available to locate each user's position. Real-time city information is more important for people who are doing something in the physical city than for those who are sitting in front of desktop computers. For example, people would like to know when the next bus is coming, where the nearest vacant parking lot is, whether they can reserve a table at the restaurant, and what is on sale at the department store just in front of them.

However, mobile users face limitations in operating their devices. Furthermore, their circumstances and context to get information dynamically change while moving [9]. We are now implementing a prototype application providing live information to mobile users. This application supports them in getting to their destinations within the city by public transportation, mainly by bus. Since in Kyoto, just as most big cities, buses hardly keep to their schedule because of heavy traffic jams, real-time bus information is sometimes more important than the timetable.

5. Social Interaction in Digital City Kyoto

Social interaction is an important goal in digital cities. Even if we build a beautiful 3D space, if there is no one living in the city, the city cannot be very attractive. Similarly, even if we have a virtual town where people often visit to chat, if there is no connection to the corresponding physical city, this town cannot be an information infrastructure for the city.

We plan to use both experimental and traditional digital community building tools to encourage social interaction in Digital City Kyoto. Traditional tools will include newsgroups, email lists, and bulletin boards. We have set up a newsgroup server, and we plan to use this server to encourage both local and tourist conversations about topics that are relevant to real life in Kyoto. Visitor newsgroups might include topics such as stories about travel experiences in Kyoto, best things to bring on one's trip, best restaurants for different kinds of cuisine, and so forth. Local newsgroups might include requests for more specialized sorts of resource help, such as the best place to find and buy a special item, or places for people with a particular hobby to meet. Newsgroups and email lists are very approachable and comfortable technologies for newcomers to the internet, and we hope that providing these simple-to-use resources will encourage visitors and locals to establish thriving community exchanges on the Digital City Kyoto site, that help them in their real life activities in Kyoto.

We are also interested in developing new ways to encourage community to form, using cutting-edge technologies, and ways to support social interaction among residents and visitors. One way we hope to encourage cross-cultural interaction in the Digital City, is by implementing a digital bus tour for foreign visitors to the site. The tour will be a point of entry for foreigners to the digital city, as well as to Kyoto itself. We hope the tour will increase visitor interest in and use of the digital city, and will lead to a richer community around Kyoto Digital City. By providing local information and stories, we hope the tour guide will encourage dialogue and relationships among those participating, both during and after the tour, and will encourage visitors to reach out to and communicate with the local users of the Kyoto Digital City. We also hope that the tour will increase interest in Kyoto's history and lore among friends and family of those who participate, because the stories that the agent tells will be chosen partly based on how easy and attractive they are for retelling to others.

The tour will be implemented within the WEB environment, using I-Chat and Microsoft's Peedy Agent (see Figure 6). The tour guide agent will lead chatting visitors through sections of Kyoto simulated using 3DML. The agent can easily bring up web pages to supplement stories.

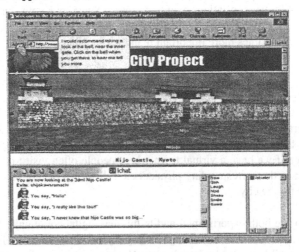

Figure 6: Digital Bus Tour with Agent Guide (By Katherine Isbister)

To prepare for creating the tour guide agent, we participated in several guide-led tours of Kyoto. We noticed that tour guides often told stories, supplementing the rich visual environment of Kyoto with explanations of what Japanese people, both past and present, did in each place. While visitors looked at the buildings, and took things in visually, the guide would create a narrative context for the site, providing visitors with stories they could share with their fellow tour members, as well as with people back home. Tour guides were very sensitive to peoples' interest-level in timing their storytelling, and allowed people time to talk to each other about what they saw and heard. We would like to recreate this sort of rich social and educational experience with our digital bus tour.

We are currently compiling a database of stories related to the sites that will be part of the Kyoto Digital City, and categorizing the stories to allow customization of the tour guide's storytelling. We will use this database to create the agent-led tour of the 3DML interface to the Kyoto digital city. The agent's tour narrative will be triggered by the group's approach to each of the sites on the tour. We plan to vary the agent's narrative to adapt to each visitor group's interest level. Current ideas for tracking visitor interest include noting the amount of conversation among visitors within the chat environment, searching for positive conversation key words while at the site, as well as directly asking visitors in prototype tours to rate stories and to indicate if they would like more information and/or stories about a site. We plan to develop and incorporate direct feedback mechanisms into the final interface to the guide agent, as well. We are also interested in extending the tour guide's abilities to make a story-tool that local web-site hosts (such as shop owners or temple leaders) could use to provide stories for tours.

Developing the agent's story-timing mechanisms and user-interest tracking techniques will contribute to the research on the construction of social interface agents, with implications for using such agents in other types of environments. We hope that developing the tour itself will contribute to our larger, social interaction goals for Kyoto Digital City, by helping to build a self-sustaining community within the city, and encouraging foreign visitors to learn more about Kyoto.

Another trial for social interaction in digital cities uses avatars in the 3D space to bridge residents and visitors. Figure 7 shows the animation of avatars walking in cities with a background image. The technology allows a number of avatars to walk around the city in real-time. By making a link between avatars and people walking in the corresponding physical city, we can realize communication between digital tourists and physical residents.

Figure 7: People Walking with Real Images (By Ken Tsutsuguchi)

As the walking motion can be generated by the user's machine via a WEB browser plug-in, only the walking position/velocity and direction needs to be downloaded. Thus, large number of 3D human walking animation can be created rapidly in real-time. Aside from the avatar, adding a virtual population makes it possible to activate the digital city. This technology is based on the animation system called WWWalk [10], which simulates human walking along an arbitrary 3D walking path.

6. Cross-Cultural Communication in Digital Cities

Digital cities enable us to overcome the geographical limitations of communication. We can meet people who have different cultural backgrounds in digital environments. Since digital cities create regional information spaces in the Internet, cross-cultural communication becomes an essential issue. Then, how we can support cross-cultural communication in digital cities? To support worldwide business, standardization of data formats such as CALS in electronic commerce has been extensively studied. However, for human communities, standardization can not be a solution. In this section, we discuss a digital environment that can mediate cross-cultural differences.

We have developed an embodied character that acts in a three-dimensional meeting space called FreeWalk [12]. It is sometimes difficult to begin talking if users have different cultural backgrounds. The helper character provides common topics to break the ice. We loaded safe and unsafe topics into the conversation database of the character. Figure 8 shows a three-dimensional meeting space where the character is posing a question to users.

Figure 8: FreeWalk with a Helper Character (by Hideyuki Nakanishi)

Suppose a group of people with different cultural backgrounds is planning to work collaboratively. It is important to know each other beforehand to make the remote collaboration run smoothly. We have developed a system that uses a large electronic screen called Silhouettel to help the socialization process [13]. Figure 9 shows how this system works in a media room. When the two screens are connected by high speed network, the system overlays video images of two separated groups on a large screen, and shows personal information, such as name, cultural information (e.g. nationality, language), and information about the collaboration (e.g. period, skill) in both languages. The user can change the information displayed by touching the menu on the screen. By integrating the system into the digital city framework, we think that groups of people in different digital cities can collaborate with each other.

Figure 9: Silhouettel (by Masayuki Okamoto)

We are conducting a social psychological experiment to test the effectiveness of those systems using an international dedicated line between Kyoto University and Stanford University to see how this system contributes to communication among different cultures.

7. Conclusion

The Digital City Project is a three-year initiative sponsored by NTT. Established in October of 1998, the project consists primarily of researchers from NTT and Kyoto University, but also includes a wide variety of people from other organizations. Contributors include several different universities in Kyoto and leading computer companies. Researchers and designers from overseas have also joined the project.

Besides technological problems, we have encountered numerous non-technical research issues such as security, privacy, and intellectual property rights. To gain a better understanding of the big picture of digital cities, we are planning to have an International Symposium and Workshop on Digital Cities in Kyoto, in September 1999. Through designing Digital City Kyoto, and collaborating with worldwide activities on digital cities, we hope to develop an avenue towards the social information infrastructure for urban life in the 21st century. All activities of Digital City Kyoto can be found at http://www.digitalcity.gr.jp/.

Acknowledgement

We wish to thank Drs. Tohkura, Shimohara and Kuwabara of NTT Communication Science Laboratories, and Prof. Nass of Stanford University for their help on the digital city project. We also thank Zenrin Corp. and Hitachi Co. Ltd. for their contribution to this project.

References

1. A. J. Kim, "Community Building on the Web: Secret Strategies for Successful Online Communities," Addison-Wesley (forthcoming).
2. http://www.digitalcity.com/
3. P. van den Besselaar and D. Beckers, "Demographics and Sociographics of the Digital City," *Community Computing and Support Systems*, Lecture Notes in Computer Science 1519, Springer-Verlag, pp. 109-125, 1998. http://www.dds.nl/
4. http://www.hel.fi/infocities/
5. W. Jepson and S. Friedman, "The Virtual World Data Server & The Virtual Los Angeles Project," http://www.aud.ucla.edu/~bill/ACM97.html.
6. T. Ishida Ed., *Community Computing: Collaboration over Global Information Networks*, John Wiley and Sons, 1998.
7. T. Ishida Ed., *Community Computing and Support Systems*, Lecture Notes in Computer Science 1519, Springer-Verlag, 1998.
8. http://www.flatland.com/
9. Y. Miyazaki, K. Fujimoto, K. Sugiyama, "Agent Model on Information Kiosk Systems Supporting Mobile Users," Intelligent Agents in Cyberspace, *1999 AAAI Spring Symposium*, AAAI Press, 1999.
10. K. Tsutsuguchi, Y. Suenaga, Y. Watanabe and K. Shimohara, "Human Walking Animation System in Three-dimensional Modeled Scene," *Trans. IPS Japan*, Vol. 38(4), pp.787-796, 1997.
11. K. Isbister, *Reading Personality in Onscreen Interactive Characters: An Examination of Social Psychological Principles of Consistency, Personality Match, and Situational Attribution Applied to Interaction with Characters*, Doctoral dissertation, Stanford University, 1998.
12. H. Nakanishi, C. Yoshida, T. Nishimura and T. Ishida, "FreeWalk: Supporting Casual Meetings in a Network," *CSCW-96*, 308-314, 1996.
13. M. Okamoto, H. Nakanishi, T. Nishimura and T. Ishida, "Silhouettell: Awareness Support for Real-World Encounter," *Community Computing and Support Systems*, Lecture Notes in Computer Science 1519, Springer-Verlag, pp. 316-329, 1998.

Autonomous Search for Information in an Unknown Environment*

Erol Gelenbe

School of Computer Science
University of Central Florida
Orlando, FL 32816
erol@cs.ucf.edu

Abstract. The search for information in a complex information space –
such as the Web or large digital libraries, or in an unkown robotics environment – requires the design of efficient and intelligent strategies for (1)
determining regions of interest, (2) detecting and classifying information
of interest, and (3) searching the space by autonomous agents. This paper discusses strategies for directing autonomous search based on spatio-
temporal distributions. We discuss a model for search assuming that the
environment is static, and where the information that agents have is updated as they pursue their discovery of the environment. Autonomous
search algorithms are designed and compared using simulations.

1 Introduction

The purpose of this research is to consider general methodologies for autonomous
navigation in virtual spaces, in which an agent searches with the help of "sensors". Sensors are algorithms which allow the agent to examine its current location in virtual space, and determine whether it contains information which
it wants. Motion of the agent in virtual space refers to motion between web or
digital library servers.

Autonomous search in a multidimensional environment has been traditionally studied in different virtual spaces such as robotics or animal psychology. It
raises two main questions: (1) what is an adequate representation of the world,
and (2) what should be the location of the robots or agents at any given time.
Given an initial location, the agent must find a path in an environment, possibly
through obstacles whose spatial locations are known or are being discovered.
This continuous path cannot in general be predetermined because information
about the path and the obstacles is often only incrementally available over time.
The autonomous agent has to sense the contents of the "terrain" where it currently resides as well as of its immediate neighbourhood, and it must make
decisions about the *"next step"* as it collects information. In [3] comparisons are
made between robotic navigation and three great sailors of the past: Magellan,

* This research was supported by the U.S. Army Research Office, Grant No. DAAH04-
96-1-0448.

Columbus, and Ulysses. Magellan knows where are all the obstacles are located, and has to come up with a map of the world by navigating around the obstacles. Columbus does not know anything, and has to discover all the environment and the obstacles and, like Magellan, Columbus must create a map. Ulysses has a complete global map, but the environment changes often due to the will of the gods against Ulysses' travels; in his case we could consider that the map is composed of static and dynamic areas. In another study [18] *Clustering by discovery* is discussed. Landmarks are present in the environment considered; they can be detected by the sensors of the agent during the exploration. We define a logical road *(LR)* to be a straight line between two landmarks. The physical road *(PR)* considers the real shapes of the obstacles. During motion, the symbolic mobile "builds" a map with the landmarks already defined. There are two kinds of maps: topological maps describe the pattern of landmarks and their connections with the logical road, while metric maps give the location of each landmark in a Cartesian space. The knowledge of these two maps permits the partioning of space into clusters which depend on the scale and the environment. Clustering by discovery is then the technique for identifying clusters in a map being learned by exploration. The clustering problem consists in finding the optimized partition of a given set of points called landmarks in clusters. They change during the motion of the agent in the environment. Other studies of robotic or of animal search are listed in the bibliography. Learning models that are capable of forming a cognitive map to be used in search and navigation are discussed in [16] using either discrete elements of topographic information, or continuously available and updated information gathered during the search process. An important general issue is the coordination of multiple agents. A recent approach developed for collaboration and non-interference between agents is based on *Social Potential Fields* [23] where a global controller defines (possibly distinct) pair-wise potential laws for ordered pairs of components (i.e. agents, obstacles and objectives) of the system. The volume edited by Meyer, Roitblat and Wilson [22] presents many ideas from animal cooperation and social interaction in the design of robotic search systems.

2   A model of the environment and of agent motion

The information units we use in our research are *Scenes*; they are typically multicriteria representations of the virtual area in which the agent is searching. Each scene is "tiled" with a set of *Blocks* or locations (x, y). The Blocks' size relates to the granularity of the information we are dealing with. A block may be as small as a page of data, or it may be a whole digital library, or a complete web server. In mathematical terms, a Scene is a finite closed subset R of Cartesian space which is augmented by the probability of finding information at each block (x, y).

In a distributed-control framework, each agent determines its movement by observing the local environment, and applying some computed *control law* designed so that the system as a whole will achieve the goals of search and detection.

Our investigation will use prior information from the Scene, and local information sensed by an individual agent, to decide in an on-line manner the next move it should make. The criterion being optimized can be the rate at which potential information locations are being visited. This study uses three representations of the virtual space which we call scenes:

- Scene-1 is the currently available objective information; it is a map which associates with each point $(x, y) \in R$ an *a priori* probability $q(x, y)$ of the presence of information, as well as the physical possibility (or difficulty) of moving to that point. The physical ease or difficulty of moving from point (x, y) to neighboring point (u, v) is represented by a rate $\gamma(x, y, u, v)$ – this rate will be low (or even zero) when this movement is laborious or impossible due to obstacles or other impediments, while it can be relatively high when the terrain presents no difficulties. An example is given in Figure 1.
- Scene-2 is the knowledge one has of reality, i.e. of the presence and absence of information. It is thus the "test-bed" that one would use for any proposed strategy.
- Scene-3 is the map used for decision making. It contains the most recent values of the motion rates or directional virtual space strengths $\mu(x, y, u, v)$ which are the decision variables used by the agent.

In the approach considered in this paper, the agent must decide where to move from its current location (x, y) at time t to some neighboring point. It does so by calculating the rate of motion $\mu(x, y, u, v)$ from (x, y) to a neighboring point (u, v). We will denote by $N(x, y)$ the set of neighbouring points of (x, y) of which typically there will be eight.

2.1 A simple greedy algorithm

The above discussion now leads to a simple algorithm for agent motion, assuming that the environment is static, except for the effect the agent itself has on this information due to its discovery that information exists or does not exist after visiting a given point (x, y). The algorithm uses the *a priori* probability $q(x, y)$ that there is information at point (x, y). This probability is only modified by the visits that the agent makes. Indeed, when (x, y) is visited, either the information is found and removed, setting $q(x, y) \leftarrow 0$, or information is not found, leading to the same result.

The simplest algorithm we may consider is one in which the agent always moves in the direction where the probability of finding information is greatest. This simple *"greedy" algorithm* can be expressed as:

$$\mu(x, y, u, v) = \mu_m, \quad if \quad q(u, v) = \max\{q(a, b) : (a, b) \in N(x, y)\}, \quad (1)$$
$$= 0, \quad otherwise, \quad (2)$$

where μ_m is some maximum speed at which the agent can move. Note that in the case of equal values of the largest $q(u, v)$ for the immediate neighbours of (x, y), the direction of motion would be chosen at random among those neighbours for which the probability is greatest. This algorithm is fast, and can be quite effective (as the resulting simulations described next section show), and it will not trap the agent in local maxima simply because $q(x, y)$ is reduced to zero after point (x, y) is visited. Random motion when all neighbouring probabilities are equal will eventually move the agent away from a local maximum, though the escape from that area may be relatively slow and disorganized. However it does take only a local view of the search, and does not incorporate a more long range view.

The performance of the Greedy Algorithm on the hypothetical search space of Figure 1 is shown in Figure 2, and compared with a random search. In these experiments we assume that the "difficulty" of motion is the same at all points and in each direction. The measure of performance is the percentage of information actually found. The experiment is run as follows. The probabilistic data of Figure 1 is used by the Greedy Algorithm, and the various tests reported on Figure 2 are run on *instances* or realizations of the presence of information obtained by drawing at random the presence of information in each location using the spatial distribution of Figure 1. We clearly see that the greedy algorithm provides a significant improvement in the rate of finding information both with respect to a random search and with respect to a systematic sweeping search through all the servers or locations.

An obvious search strategy is a Systematic Sweep, and it is very reasonable to ask how any algorithm might perform as compared to that simple (and widely used) approach. The answer of course is simple too: this strategy which does not take into account available information about the search space will perform on the average as well as (or as poorly as) a random search in which no location is visited twice. In fact, for any given instance of a probabilistic or "actual" distribution of information, the Systematic Sweep policy's performance, in terms of number of information found on the average (or exactly) per unit time can be obtained by inspection from the available data, as long as the point where the search originates is known. In further work we will also consider variants of the Systematic Sweep which combine a more refined optimization technique.

3 Motion with long term objectives in a static environment

If the agent takes a strictly local decision based on its perception of its immediate neighborhood, it should move so that its overall motion reflects the local perception of the distribution of information. However, if the agent can make use of global information, its motion should match its perception of its coverage of the whole virtual space. This can be done if the direction and speed of motion is selected so that the long run probability $p(x, y)$ of the location of the agent, matches the relative probability $Q(x, y)$ of finding information at each point (x, y) in the virtual space. We denote by (x_0, y_0) the starting point for the search; typically it will be on the boundary of R.

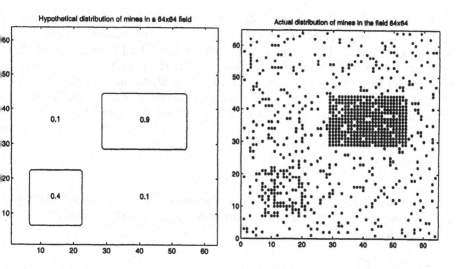

Fig. 1. Probabilistic (left) and actual (right) distribution of information in a 64x64 virtual space

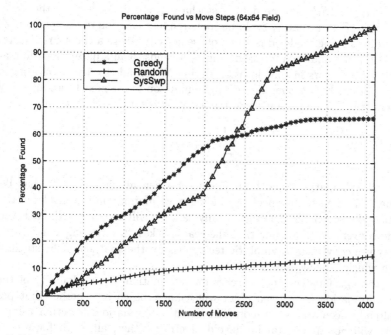

Fig. 2. Random versus Greedy and Sweep Algorithms for the virtual space of Figure 1

We will now formally construct $\{Z_t, \ t \geq 0\}$ the random process representing agent location. Let $\{Z_t^i, \ t \geq 0, \ i = 0, 1, 2, ...\}$ be a sequence of random processes which take values in R, the region of interest. Each of the $\{Z_t^i\}$ is assumed to be a continuous time, discrete state-space Markov chain with transition rates $\mu^i(x, y, u, v)$ from state (x, y) to state (u, v), where $\mu^i(x, y, u, v) = 0$ if $(u, v) \notin N(x, y)$ so that agent motion is being constrained to take place between adjacent points in R. These processes $\{Z_t^i\}$ are constructed recursively as follows:

- $Z_0^1 = (x_0, y_0)$,
- Let $T_i = inf\{t : t > 0, \ Z_t^i \neq Z_0^i\}$;
- then $Z_0^{i+1} = Z_{T_i}^i$, $i = 1, 2, ...$

Furthermore, let $\{S_i, \ i = 0, 1, 2, ...\}$ be a sequence of positive random variables representing the time spent by the agent to investigate, with its sensors, each successive location it visits. Then:

- $Z_t = Z_t^1$ for $0 \leq t \leq T_1$,
- $Z_t = Z_{T_1}^1$ for $T_1 \leq t \leq T_1 + S_1$,
- $Z_{t+\sum_{i=1}^{j-1}(T_i+S_i)} = Z_t^j$ for $0 \leq t \leq T_j, j = 2, ...$,
- $Z_t = Z_{T_j}^j$ for $\sum_{i=1}^{j-1}(T_i + S_i) + T_j \leq t < \sum_{i=1}^{j}(T_i + S_i)$.

In general, the $\{S_i\}$ may be doubly stochastic, and dependent on the past of the process $\{Z_t\}$, in that S_i could be some random function of the location $Z_{T_i}^i$. Thus what is being modeled is a two phase activity where a agent first starts in location (x_0, y_0) and then moves during T_1 seconds to an adjacent location, and then uses its sensors in that location during S_1 seconds to detect information, after which it takes another T_2 seconds to move on to the next location, etc. We will denote by d_i the instant when the agent enters its $i - th$ location:

$$d_i = \sum_{j=1}^{i-1}(T_j + S_j) + T_i. \tag{3}$$

When all information have been found, or when all the region R has been searched, or when the chances for finding new information is considered to be minimal, the search should stop. In any case we will have $i \leq |R|$. However it will be convenient to assume that the search takes "a very long time" so that we may use convenient asymptotic techniques for the analysis of the stochastic system which is being considered.

As the agent moves and searches for information, the probability of there being information at a given point will change, based on whether that point has already been visited or not. The agent's information detection using its sensors will not in general be devoid of errors either, although for the sake of simplicity the present paper assumes that the agent is capable of perfect detection. Thus, once a point (x, y) has ben visited once, additional visits are superfluous from information detection viewpoint (although they may be needed in terms of the agent's motion plan. Thus after a move to (x, y), both $q(x, y)$

and *all* the $Q(u,v), (u,v) \in X \times Y$ need to be updated, $Q(x,y)$, which is a normalized version of $q(x,y)$ is given by:

$$Q(x,y) = \frac{q(x,y)}{\sum_{all\ (u,v)} q(u,v)}. \tag{4}$$

In this section we will design and evaluate a Simplified Infinite Horizon Optimization (SIHO) Algorithm that attempts to optimize the rate of finding information into the "infinite horizon" at each step. The SIHO Algorithm computes the transition rates $\{\mu^i(x,y,u,v)\}$ at each $i-th$ step so that the long run probability, after the $i-th$ step, that the agent visits a point in R matches closely the probability of finding information at that point.

Recall the structure of the process $\{Z_t,\ t \geq 0\}$. A continuous time Markov chain with rates $\{\mu^i(x,y,u,v),\ (u,v) \in N(x,y)\}$ determines the motion of the agent between time d_{i-1} ($d_0 = 0$) and time $d_i + T_i$; then the agent stays at point (x_i,y_i) to search for information during a time S_i, and then motion starts again, etc. In the following, we will be dealing with quantities subsequent to the $i-th$ step of motion, and therefore they should all be indexed by i. However, for the sake of notational simplicity, we will drop that index.

Since we will be working with the stationary probability distribution $p(x,y)$ of the agent's location, we need to make sure that the underlying stochastic process representing the motion of the agent is ergodic. This is achieved by associating positive (but sometimes very small) rates of motion at each point (x,y) for the stochastic process which represents agent motion in R. Consider a cost function which determines how well the long run probability $p(x,y)$ that point (x,y) is visited during the search actually fits the known *a priori* probability that there is information at that point:

$$C = \frac{1}{2} \sum_{all\ (x,y)} [p(x,y) - Q(x,y)]^2, \tag{5}$$

Note that $p(x,y)$ can be calculated from the previously defined quantities:

$$p(x,y) \sum_{all\ (u,v) \in N(x,y)} \mu(x,y,u,v) = \sum_{all\ (u,v) \in N(x,y)} \mu(u,v,x,y) p(u,v), \tag{6}$$

with

$$\sum_{all\ (x,y)\ in\ the\ plane} p(x,y) = 1, \tag{7}$$

under the assumption that the agent travels for a very long time around the search space. We may write (6) in matrix notation:

$$p = \mu p, \tag{8}$$

where p is the vector of stationary probabilities $p(x,y)$ and μ is the rate matrix $[\mu(x,y,u,v)]$.

The motion to the neighboring points $N(x, y)$ of the point (x, y) by choosing the direction which yields the highest rate of motion. These rates are updated using the gradient rule to obtain values of μ which yield minima of C:

$$\mu^{new}(x, y, u, v) = \mu^{old}(x, y, u, v) - \eta \frac{\partial C}{\partial \mu(x, y, u, v)}\Big|_{old} \tag{9}$$

where $\eta > 0$, and the algorithmic challenge is to carry out this computation at low cost, or to approximate it by a faster algorithm. Note that at each gradient descent step we need to compute the new value of p using the new value of μ, which is a costly $O(n^3)$ computation, though it can be accelerated because the matrix μ is sparse. Note that this approach includes in the decision, both the *expected long term behavior* of the search (via the probabilites $p(x, y)$), and the currently available information about the probability of finding information at each point (via $Q(x, y)$). The gradient descent (9) is repeated till the point of diminishing returns is attained:

$$|\mu^{new}(x, y, u, v) - \mu^{old}(x, y, u, v)| \leq \epsilon, \tag{10}$$

for a stopping criterion $\epsilon > 0$. The resulting values $\mu(x, y, u, v)$ will then used in the following manner. The agent will move to a point $(U, V) \in N(x, y)$ such that:

$$\mu(x, y, U, V) = max_{(u,v) \in N(x,y)}\{\mu(x, y, u, v)\}. \tag{11}$$

Again, if there are several (U, V) satisfying the above relationship, then one of those should be selected at random.

When a agent visits some location (x, y) it is presumed to sense whether information is there or not. In which case it will update the probability distribution in the following manner:

$$q^{after-visit}(x, y) \Leftarrow \text{``}small - value\text{''} (e.g.\ 0.01), \tag{12}$$

since we wish to avoid unnecessary repeated visits of the agent to the same point; after a visit, either information is detected and the work there is done, or information is not detected so that the agent need not visit the point again. The result of detection also needs to be stored in Scene-2 which is the information one has obtained about reality. Note that after $q(x, y)$ is modified, we have

$$q'(u, v) = q(u, v),\ if\ (u, v) \neq (x, y),$$
$$q'(u, v) = q^{after-visit}(u, v),\ if\ (u, v) = (x, y).$$

Note also that <u>all</u> the $Q(u, v)$ need to be updated using (4) to the new value:

$$Q'(u, v) = \frac{q'(u, v)}{\sum_{all\ (a,b)} q(a, b)}. \tag{13}$$

Let us now turn to the computation of the gradient in (9). Of course, the computationally significant portion will be to compute the partial derivatives, and we will be making use of the cost function (5) and also of the equation for the steady-state probabilities $p(x, y)$ (6). The computationally costly portion of the algorithm is precisely (6), (13), and (14) which must be used repeatedly at each gradient descent step, and which includes the solution of linear systems of size $|X||Y| \times |X||Y|$, i.e. the size of the whole plane of motion. Fortunately this computation can be accelerated because the matrices are very sparse, since motion of the agent is only possible in adjacent directions. Note that:

$$\frac{\partial C}{\partial \mu(x, y, u, v)} = \sum_{all\ (a,b)} [p(a, b) - Q(a, b)] \frac{\partial p(a, b)}{\partial \mu(x, y, u, v)}. \tag{14}$$

We use the two system equations (6) and (7), which in matrix notation can be written as

$$[0, 0, ...0, 1] = [p_1, p_2, ..., p_n, 0] \begin{bmatrix} \mu_{11} & \mu_{12} & \cdots & \mu_{1n} & 1 \\ \mu_{21} & \mu_{22} & \cdots & \mu_{2n} & 1 \\ \cdot & \cdot & \cdots & \cdot & \cdot \\ \mu_{n1} & \mu_{n2} & \cdots & \mu_{nn} & 1 \\ * & * & \cdots & * & * \end{bmatrix} \tag{15}$$

where

$$\mu_{ij} = \mu(u, v; x, y), p_i = p(u, v) \text{ and } p_j = p(x, y)$$

with

$$i = u + vw, j = x + yw \text{ and } n = wh.$$

Here w and h denote the width and height of the information virtual space. Because each point in the plane is taken to have only 8 (and 5 or 3 at boundaries) ajacent neigbours, we have

$$\mu_{ij} = \mu(u, v; x, y) = 0, \text{if } (u, v) \notin N(x, y).$$

As we noted before the rate transition matrix is sparse. Let us denote the matrix which appears on the right-hand-side of (15) as $\mathbf{M}$. Note that the bottom row of $\mathbf{M}$ can be arbitary However to make $\mathbf{M}$ invertible, the unassigned values $*$ should be properly set. Since:

$$\mu_{ii} = - \sum_{j=1, j \neq i}^{n} \mu_{ij},$$

and by consequence the determinant of the sub-matrix

$$\mu = \begin{bmatrix} \mu_{11} & \mu_{12} & \cdots & \mu_{1n} \\ \mu_{21} & \mu_{22} & \cdots & \mu_{2n} \\ \cdot & \cdot & \cdots & \cdot \\ \mu_{n1} & \mu_{n2} & \cdots & \mu_{nn} \end{bmatrix}$$

is zero: $|\mu| = 0$. Neverthless $\mathbf{M}$ has an inverse provided the $*$ are properly chosen.

Taking the derivative of (15) with respect to μ_{ij} we obtain:

$$0 = [p'_1, p'_2, ..., p'_n, 0]_{ij} \mathbf{M} + [0, ..., -p_i, ... \ p_i, ..., 0]$$

$$\qquad\qquad\qquad\qquad \uparrow \qquad \uparrow \qquad\qquad (16)$$

$$\qquad\qquad\qquad\qquad i \qquad\ j$$

where $[p'_1, p'_2, ..., p'_n, 0]_{ij}$ denotes the derivative of $[p_1, p_2, ..., p_n, 0]$ with respect to μ_{ij}. If $[X]_{(kl)}$ denotes the (kl) element of matrix X, then

$$\frac{\partial p_\nu}{\partial \mu_{ij}} = p_i([\mathbf{M}^{-1}]_{(i\nu)} - [\mathbf{M}^{-1}]_{(j\nu)}). \qquad (17)$$

For implementation purposes in relation to the virtual space coordinates, we revert to the notation $(a, b) \rightarrow \nu$, $(u, v) \rightarrow i$ and $(x, y) \rightarrow j$ so that:

$$\frac{\partial p(a, b)}{\partial \mu(u, v; x, y)} = p(u, v)([\mathbf{M}^{-1}]_{(u,v;a,b)} - [\mathbf{M}^{-1}]_{(x,y;a,b)}). \qquad (18)$$

Using (18) in (14) we obtain

$$\frac{\partial C}{\partial \mu(u, v; x, y)} = \sum_{all(a,b)} p(u, v) \left[p(a, b) - Q(a, b) \right] \left\{ [\mathbf{M}^{-1}]_{(u,v;a,b)} - [\mathbf{M}^{-1}]_{(x,y;a,b)} \right\}.$$

$$(19)$$

We can now summarize the gradient based SIHO algorithm for computing the direction in which the agent moves from a given point (x, y):

1. From all the current *old* values of $\mu(a, b, c, d)$, calculate $p(x, y)$ using (6).
2. Calculate the derivative of the cost C with respect to the desired $\mu(x, y, u, v)$ for all $(u, v) \in N(x, y)$ using (19).
3. Use the gradient descent (9) to deterinformation the new values of all the $\mu(x, y, u, v)$, for $(u, v) \in N(x, y)$.
4. Move in the direction (x, y) to (U, V) according to (11).

3.1 Experimental evaluation of the SIHO Algorithm

The SIHO algorithm performs well in taking advantage of the global information available about the search space. This is illustrated with some simulation results. We show an example of a probabilistically defined search space in Figure 3, which includes an "actual" virtual space obtained by a random generation of information locations from this probabilistic data. Throughout the simulations discussed here it is assumed that once the autonomous agent reaches a location in the search space it will correctly detect or correctly reject the presence of information (zero false alarm rate). On the Figure 3 we show simulation runs for SIHO, the Greedy Algorithm, and of the Random search. We clearly see that the rate of attaining information locations, in particular in the initial portion of the search (i.e. before each of the algorithms reaches the point of "diminishing returns"), is far greater with the SIHO algorithm than with the alternatives.

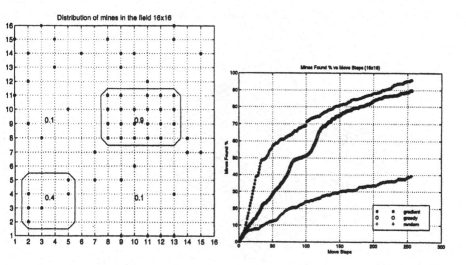

Fig. 3. "Actual" 16x16 virtual space (left) and SIHO, Greedy, Random algorithm performance (right)

SIHO will be more time consuming in computation time; however this may be a viable price to pay for the performance improvement.

It is interesting to visualize search paths in Cartesian space which are followed by the SIHO algorithm. On Figure 4 we show the *a priori* probabilistic virtual space information of a 32 by 32 sized search space. The path followed by a agent or agent under the control of a single run of the SIHO algorithm is shown in Figure 5, where we clearly see that the SIHO algorithm does not pursue a myopic greedy approach but that the moving agent or agent actually covers the areas where the probability of finding information is largest.

This paper contributes to the design of search strategies with probabilistic *a priori* information. However there remains much more work to do than what has been currently achieved. Issues that we are currently pursuing include the use of actual search space sensory data rather than probabilistic data to direct the search, the use of learning techniques from on-line sensory data to gather information about the virtual space so as to direct the search, questions of false alarm rates and detection errors which will impact the search strategy, neural network approximations for computing the potential virtual space which controls agent motion, and the use of information gradients from sensors (e.g. chemical sensors) to direct the search.

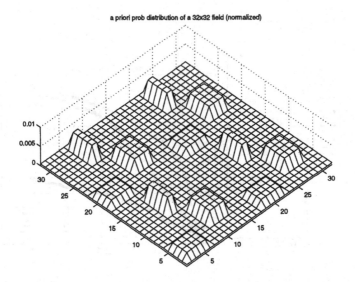

a priori prob distribution of a 32x32 field (normalized)

Fig. 4. A 32 by 32 Probabilistic Test Field Representation

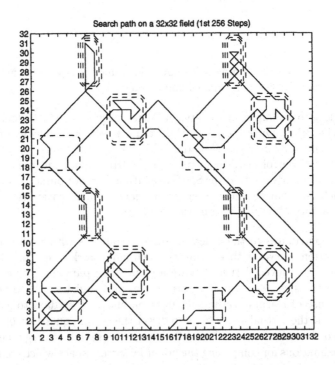

Search path on a 32x32 field (1st 256 Steps)

Fig. 5. SIHO Search Path on 32 by 32 Probabilistic Test Field

References

1. A.C. Kamil, F. Lindstrom, J. Peters "The detection of cryptic prey by blue jays (Cyanocitta cristata): I. The effects of travel time", *Animal Behaviour* Vol. 33 (4) pp. 1068-1079, 1985.
2. J. McNamara, A. Houston "A simple model of information use in the exploitation of patchily distributed food", Animal Behaviour Vol. 33 (2), pp. 553-560, 1985.
3. C. Jorgensen, W. Hamel and C. Weisbin. "Autonomous robot navigation", *BYTE*, Vol. 11, pp. 223-235, Jan. 1986.
4. N. Rao "Algorithmic framework for learned robot navigation in unknown terrains" *Computer* pp. 37-43, 1989.
5. P. Pf. Spelt , E. Lyness and G. deSaussure. "Developpment and training of a learning expert system in an autonomous mobile robot via simulation", *Simulation*, pp. 223-228, 1989.
6. C.R. Weisbin, G. deSaussure, J.R. Einstein and F.G. Pin. "Autonomous mobile robot navigation and learning", *Computer* pp. 29-35, 1989.
7. E. Gelenbe, "Random neural networks with negative and positive signals and product form solution", *Neural Computation*, Vol. 1, No. 4, pp 502-511, 1989.
8. E. Gelenbe, "Stability of the random neural network model", *Neural Computation*, Vol. 2, No. 2, pp. 239-247, 1990.
9. Z. Shiller and Y.R. Gwo. "Dynamic motion planning of autonomous vehicles", *IEEE Transaction On Robotics and Automation*, Vol. 7, no. 2, pp. 241-249, 1991.
10. G. Beni and J. Wang. "Theoretical problems for the realization of Distributed Robotic Systems", *Proc. IEEE Int. Conf. on Robotics and Automation*, pp. 1914-1920, 1991.
11. M.J. Mataric, "Distributed approaches to behavior control", *Proc. SPIE, Vol. 1828, Sensor Fusion V*, pp. 373-382, 1992.
12. Y. Shoham and M. Tennenholtz "On the synthesis of useful social laws for artificial robot societies", *Proc. 10th National Conf. on Artificial Intelligence*, pp. 276-281, 1992.
13. S. Gross and J.L. Deneubourg, "Harvesting by a group of robots", *Proc. 1st European Conf. on Artificial Life*, pp. 195-204, 1992.
14. G. Lucarini, M. Varoli, R. Cerutti, and G. Sandini, "Cellular Robotics: simulation and hardware implementation" *Proc. IEEE Int. Conf. on Robotics and Automation*, pp. 846-852, 1993.
15. T. Ueyama and T. Fukuda. "Self-organization of Cellular Robots using random walk with simple rules", *Proc. IEEE Int. Conf. on Robotics and Automation*, pp. 595-600, 1993.
16. N. Schmajuk, H.T. Blair "Place learning and the dynamics of spatial navigation: A neural network approach," *Adaptive Behavior* Vol. 1, No. 3, pp. 353-385, 1993.
17. N. Schmajuk, A.D. Thieme, H.T. Blair "Maps, routes, and the Hippocampus: A neural network approach", *Hippocampus*, Vol. 3, No.3, pp. 387-400, 1993.
18. D. Maio, and S. Rizzi. "Map learning and clustering in autonomous systems", *IEEE Transaction On Pattern Analysis And Machine Intelligence*, Vol. 15, no. 12, pp. 1286-1297, 1993.
19. E. Hou and D. Zheng "Mobile robot path planning based on hierarchical hexagonal decomlocation and artificial potential virtual spaces", *Journal of Robotic Systems*, pp. 605-614, 1994.
20. L.E. Parker "Designing control laws for cooperative robot teams", *Proc. IEEE Int. Conf. on Robotics and Automation*, pp. 582-587, 1994.

21. E. Rimon and J.F. Canny "Construction of C-space roadmaps from local sensory data: what should the sensors look for?", *Proc. IEEE Int. Conf. on Robotics and Automation*, pp. 117–123, 1994.
22. J.A. Meyer, H.L. Roitblat and S.W. Wilson (eds.) " From Animals to Animats 2: Proceedings of the Second International Conference on Simulation of Adaptive Behavior (Complex adaptive systems)" pp. 432-510. MIT Press, Cambridge, MA, 523 p., 1992.
23. J. Reif and H. Wang, "Social potential virtual spaces: A distributed behavioral control for autonomous robots", *Proc. Workshop on the Algorithmic Foundations of Robotics*, pp. 331–345, 1994.
24. S. Benhamou "Spatial memory and searching efficiency," *Animal Behaviour* Vol. 47 (6), pp. 1423-1433, 1994.
25. E. Gelenbe, Z.-H. Mao, Y.-D. Li "Function approximation with spiked random networks", *IEEE Trans. on Neural Networks*, Vol. 10, No. 1, pp. 3–9, 1999.

Resource Management in Agent-Based Distributed Environments

Alexander Brodsky[1], Larry Kerschberg[1], and Samuel Varas[2]

[1] Center for Information Systems Integration and Evolution
Department of Information and Software Engineering
George Mason University
Fairfax, VA 22030-4444
{brodsky, kersch}@gmu.edu
[2] Industrial Engineering Department
University of Chile Republica 701
svara@dii.uchile.cl

Abstract. This paper presents an agent-based architecture for optimally managing resources in distributed environments. The agent-based approach allows for maximal autonomy in agent negotiation and decision-making. A three-layer agency-based architecture is proposed, consisting of the user, agency and application domain layers. Agencies correspond to enterprise functional units, and agents are associated with agencies. A formal model of resources and constraints is presented, and it is shown that, under certain assumptions, optimal resource decompositions and allocations can be achieved. A distributed protocol is developed for agencies and agents to negotiate and exchange resources autonomously, while still satisfying both local and global constraints.

1 Introduction

Agent-based architectures are becoming increasingly important, particularly in the areas of electronic commerce, cooperative information integration, logistics, and other supply-chain types of applications. Many aspects of agent-based architectures have been studied, including agent coordination, communication, negotiation and cooperative problem-solving.

Although considerable work has been done in agent-based negotiation, the problem of optimal management of distributed resources under local and global constraints remains open. In this paper we are concerned with distributed resource management in the presence of both communication and site (agency) failures. More specifically, the contributions of this paper are as follows. First, we present an agency-based architecture to support the functional workflow of an enterprise. Next we introduce the concept of enterprise resources and resource distribution and show that they are related to constraints. We then adapt our previous constraint results [3, 13], to reduce the problem of optimal resource distribution to the problem of optimal constraint management. Third, based on the reduction, we adapt the generic distributed protocol framework of [3] to the agency-based architecture. The suggested protocol guarantees the following desirable properties, in the presence of agency and network failures:

- *consistency*, i.e., the current overall state of resources in all agencies satisfy the enterprise constraints,
- *safety*, i.e., the distribution of resource among local sites (agencies) is such that constraint satisfaction at all agencies guarantees satisfaction of all enterprise constraints,
- *optimality* of resource constraints distribution in terms of some required criterion, e.g., the minimal probability of not violating local resource constraints at the agencies, and
- *last-resort resource update refusal*, i.e., a resource update at a local agency is only refused if there is not enough overall resource slack in the maximally connected subnetwork of agencies. In particular, if all agencies are connected, then an update is refused only if the resource update violates the enterprise resource constraints.

1.1 Motivation: Crisis Management Scenario

To motivate the problem of distributed resource management, we consider the following scenario. Emergency service providers (e.g., fire fighters, medical personnel, military etc.) and disaster relief agencies such as the Red Cross, must be prepared to respond efficiently to crises such as floods, fires and earthquakes. In order to perform Crisis Management, these agencies must find, coordinate, allocate, deploy and distribute various resources (such as food, clothing, equipment, emergency personnel, transportation) to the victims of a crisis. These resources are typically geographically distributed among many warehouses, suppliers, military units, local fire departments, bus terminals, etc.

These agencies operate autonomously, so that we have a loosely-connected federation of agencies that are called upon to coordinate their resources and services during the crisis. Each location may maintain a *local database* that stores and monitors information about available resources and their quantities within a particular agency. Our *distributed database*, therefore, is a loosely-connected collection of local databases, which are related because of a global constraint on resources.

The global constraint on resources may originate, for example, from a number of pre-defined crisis management scenarios that require that certain amounts of resources be delivered to any potential disaster area within bounded time using available transportation. For example, a Hurricane Relief Mission to Florida may require that the following resources be delivered there in 24 hours: 1) sufficient canned food to feed 30,000 people for 4 days, 2) a supply of tents to support a tent city of 20,000 people, 3) medicines and vaccines to inoculate the tent city residents against cholera, 4) computers and communications equipment to support the coordination, command and control functions of the mission, 5) 10 medical units with medical personnel and portable facilities to care for victims, and 6) military and civilian personnel to staff the mission.

For this scenario, the global resource constraint would reflect that, for each resource type above, the overall amount of this resource available at all locations reachable within 24 hours (with the available transportation), be greater than or equal to the amount required in the scenario. Note that some resources are composed of other resources, which also should be reflected by the global constraint. For example, each of the required 10 medical units (resource 1) is composed of 2 physicians (resource 2), 5 paramedics (resources 3) and must have 2 tents (resource 4), 2000 vaccination packages (resource 5), 500 first aid packages (resource 6), etc. In turn, each vaccination package may be composed of certain quantities of other items and so on.

When an agency database in the distributed enterprise is being updated, for example when a certain amount of materiel is taken from a warehouse (not necessarily for crisis support), the update can only be allowed if it satisfies the global integrity constraint, which depends, in general, on the global database instance, not just on the updated local instance. Therefore, verification of the global constraint would require a distributed transaction involving possibly hundreds of loosely-connected distributed sites, which could be an extremely expensive and time-consuming operation, especially when protocols such as two-phase commit are used to guarantee the standard properties of transaction atomicity, consistency, isolation and durability (e.g., [6]). Moreover, such a distributed transaction would often not be possible in the presence of agency and network failures, whereas the robustness feature, i.e., the ability to operate in the presence of (partial) failures, is crucial for applications such as Crisis Management. In short, local verification of the global constraint can significantly reduce distributed processing costs and increase system robustness in the presence of failures. We will show in this paper, that there are mechanisms by which we can provide agencies with reasonable autonomy while preserving both local and global resource constraints.

This paper is organized as follows. Next section proposes an agent-based architecture, and its functionality. Section 3 presents a model to represent resources and resource constraints. Section 4 reviews the results of [3, 13] relevant to the distributed protocol for resource management of agencies, which is presented in Section 5. Finally, Section 6 concludes and briefly outlines future research directions.

We now present an agency-based architecture to enable the optimal allocation, distribution and management of resources.

2 Agency-Based Architecture for Resource Management

The example of the crisis management scenario indicates that a request may impact multiple agencies, each of which is specialized to perform certain activities, allocate its resources, and provide services in support of the scenario. In addition, an agency will coordinate with other agencies to provide end-to-end services for user requests. In many cases, an agency will not have all the necessary resources, and will have to negotiate for resources with other agencies and possibly with external sites.

We assume that our enterprise is geographically distributed, so we wish to give each site as much *autonomy* as possible over its resources, and as much responsibility as possible in its decision-making regarding its resource and service allocations. This is especially important when agencies must react quickly to user requests.

Our model assumes that the agencies have local resources and services that they control, can negotiate for resources and services related to their application domain, and must compete for shared resources and services provided by other agencies within the enterprise. For example, in a request involving food, clothing and medical supplies, the Transportation Agency would be called upon to coordinate and allocate resources to ensure that supplies arrive at their destination in a timely fashion. These resources could be taken from the enterprise transportation services, as well as from commercial and military transportation services. The assets allocated to each agency take the form of supplies, resources and services which have certain constraints placed upon them, such as a maximum and minimum inventory levels, utilization constraints, as well as distribution constraints. Ideally, each agency should manage its own assets, make decisions in a timely fashion, and commit resources and services to user requests, subject to both local and global constraints.

2.1 The Agency Model

Figure 1 depicts a three-layer architecture, similar to the Knowledge Rover architecture [8, 7] consisting of a User Layer, an Agency Layer, and an Application Domain Layer.

At the User Layer requesting users access the system through a service-oriented view. The service-oriented view then submits user requests to the Coordination Agent, who is aware of the current state of the system including all applicable constraints. The Coordination Agent then routes the user request to an Executive Agent residing at the Agency Layer. The Executive Agent decomposes the request into a collection of activities and workflows to be handled by the agencies residing at the Agency Layer.

Each agency is organized according to its functional role within the enterprise. For example, the Clothing Agency would handle all requests regarding the allocation of resources involving clothes. The Clothing Agency has a collection of clothing agents who are specialists in different lines of clothing, for example heavy-duty boots, shirts, pants, etc. In addition, each agency deals with its respective application domain - in this case the Clothing Domain - residing at the Application Domain Layer.

Within the Clothing Domain, for example, would be local assets stored at enterprise warehouses, as well as external assets available through pre-established contracts, or through a negotiation process with suppliers to contract for specific quantities, prices, and delivery schedules. Each application domain has associated with it one or more Field Agents whose job is to monitor the activities of the domain suppliers, and to report back to its agency any significant events and

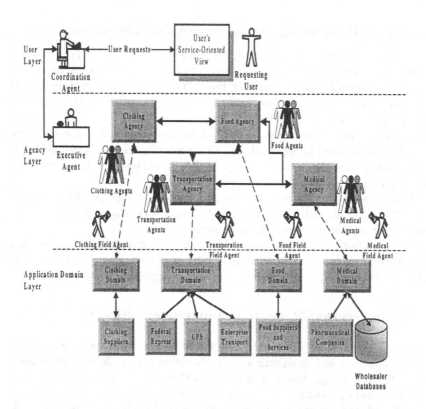

Fig. 1. Three-Layer Agency-based Enterprise Architecture

2.3 Agency Decision-Making and Negotiation Mechanisms

The general strategy for agent decision-making is the following: 1) an agency attempts to allocate locally-controlled resources and services so as to satisfy one or more user requests while satisfying the collection of local constraints, 2) if local constraints do not allow the agency to commit its resources, then it enters into negotiations with other agencies to request a redistribution of resources in such a manor that all agency local constraints are satisfied, and therefore the global constraints are also satisfied, and 3) if resources are not available within the enterprise, then they would be negotiated with suppliers affiliated with the enterprise in a real-time fashion.

The next section introduces a formal framework for the specification of resources and services, and presents a protocol framework that allows agencies to negotiate for, and share resources and services.

The key aspect of this approach is that we allow maximum *autonomy* and *responsibility* over local assets, while providing a resource sharing protocol that guarantees optimal allocation of resources among agencies the enterprise.

3 Agency-Based Resource Management Model

Enterprise resources are allocated to the various agencies that are responsible for their management and distribution. This allocation can be done in an optimal fashion, both at design time as well as at run-time; this is discussed in detail in Varas' doctoral dissertation [13]. Once the allocation to the agencies has been accomplished, the enterprise begins operations by fulfilling user requests that are coordinated by the agencies.

We now present our model for resource characterization that will be used in this paper.

3.1 The Resource Allocation Model

Let $r_1, r_2, \ldots, r_k$ be quantities of basic resources (e.g, commodities, human resources, transportation, etc.) managed by the enterprise. These basic resources may be allocated to agencies, and some of them may be shared among agencies. Enterprise constraints include limitations on the basic resources, e.g., a particular location must maintain certain minimal amounts of resources for emergency; or cannot store more than a certain maximal amount of a basic resource.

In addition to basic resources and their amounts, the enterprise can define derived resources, formulated in terms of basic ones. For example, while an amount of blankets in each warehouse can be basic resource, the overall amount could be a derived one. Or, the cost to purchase a set of all items in a warehouse is a derived resource, which is expressed as a linear combination of basic or derived resources. Of course, an amount of a derived resource can always be expressed in terms of basic resources. Constraints on basic and derived resources in the enterprise constitute the *enterprise constraints* or boundaries. More formally, an *enterprise resource state* is defined as follows:

Definition 1 *An* enterprise resource state *is a tuple* (Var, P, E, Val, C), *where:*

- Var *is a set* $\{r_1, \ldots, r_k, r_{k+1}, \ldots, r_n\}$ *of resource variables,* $\{r_1, \ldots, r_k\}$ *for basic resources and* $\{r_{k+1}, \ldots, r_n\}$ *for derived resources.*
- P *is a partition of basic resource variables among m agencies:*

$$\{r_1, \ldots, r_{i_1}\}, \ldots, \{r_{i_{j-1}+1}, \ldots, r_{i_j}\}, \ldots, \{r_{i_{m-1}+1}, \ldots, r_k\}$$

where basic resource variables $\{r_{i_{j-1}+1}, \ldots, r_{i_j}\}$ *are managed by agency j*
- E *is a set (conjunction) of equations*

$$r_{k+1} = a_{1,1} * r_1 + \quad \ldots + a_{1,k} * r_k$$
$$r_{k+2} = a_{2,1} * r_1 + \quad \ldots + a_{2,k} * r_k$$
$$\vdots$$
$$r_n = \quad a_{n-k,1} * r_1 + \ldots + a_{n-k,k} * r_k$$

which express the derived resource variables in terms of the basic resource variables.
- Val *is an instantiation* $r_1 = v_1, \ldots, r_k = v_k$ *of values into basic resource variables, and*
- C *is a set of range constraints on (basic and derived) resource variables of the form*

$$l_1 \leq r_1 \leq u_1, \ldots, l_n \leq r_n \leq u_n$$

where $l_1, \ldots, l_n$ *are real non-negative constants, and* $r_1, \ldots, r_n$ *are either real non-negative constants or* ∞[1]

Each equation in E can be given an interpretation, for example, one equation may denote a constraint on the total number of blankets that the enterprise may stock, while another may denote an upper bound on the total transportation costs that may be incurred by the enterprise.

For agencies to perform their tasks, they manipulate basic resource values assigned to them, e.g., certain quantities are being used or sent, certain quantities are received, etc. However, when these updates are performed, the enterprise must adhere to the overall constraints C, whose satisfaction depends not only on specific resource values at agency j being updated, but also on the values at other agencies. As local resources are depleted and as local constraints are potentially violated, agencies will negotiate with their neighbors for needed resources, thereby preserving both local and global constraints.

The derived resource equations and the lower and upper bounds for all resources define the global enterprise constraints, which can be expressed as a set

---

[1] To be strict, with ∞, $\leq$ should be replaced with $<$.

of inequalities (constraints) as follows:

$$
\begin{aligned}
r_1 &\leq u_1 \\
r_2 &\leq u_2 \\
&\vdots \\
r_k &\leq u_k \\
a_{1,1} * r_1 + a_{1,2} * r_2 \ldots + a_{1,k} * r_k &\leq u_{k+1} \\
a_{2,1} * r_1 + a_{2,2} * r_2 \ldots + a_{2,k} * r_k &\leq u_{k+2} \\
&\vdots \\
a_{n-k,1} * r_1 + a_{n-k,2} * r_2 \ldots + a_{n-k,k} * r_k &\leq u_n \\
-r_1 &\leq -l_1 \\
-r_2 &\leq -l_2 \\
&\vdots \\
-r_k &\leq -l_k \\
-a_{1,1} * r_1 - a_{1,2} * r_2 \ldots - a_{1,k} * r_k &\leq -l_{k+1} \\
-a_{2,1} * r_1 - a_{2,2} * r_2 \ldots - a_{2,k} * r_k &\leq -l_{k+2} \\
&\vdots \\
-a_{n-k,1} * r_1 - a_{n-k,2} * r_2 \ldots - a_{n-k,k} * r_k &\leq -l_n
\end{aligned}
$$

In the following sections we will simply assume that the enterprise constraints consists of a set of linear inequalities over real variables, which express basic resource quantities.

An important task of the enterprise is to manage the constraints locally, which is discussed in the next section. Succeeding sections formalize the problem in more detail and provide a distributed protocol for the exchange of resources among agencies.

4 Review of Constraint Decompositions

In this section we define the central notion of *safe decompositions*, and formulate our problem as one of finding the best feasible safe decomposition of a global constraint. The problem formulation in this section, except for the notion of *resources*, is applicable to all types of constraints.

Our work on constraint decompositions in [3, 13], which is being reviewed here, was motivated by the works [2, 1, 12, 11] which deal with local verification of numeric constraints, and the works [9, 10, 5], which consider applications of parametric linear constraint queries and their connection to Fourier's elimination method [4]. While the setting in [9, 10, 5] is very different from the one in [3, 13], they used similar techniques for parametric characterization of constraints (in our case satisfying safety). However, the work on parametric queries assumes that the number of parameters (i.e., coefficients) is bounded, whereas the main technical difficulty in [3, 13] is that *safe* decompositions do not have a bound on the number of parameters.

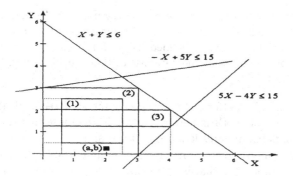

Fig. 2. Safe decompositions of Ω

4.1 Optimal Safe Decompositions

Safe Decompositions.

Definition 2 *A constraint C in variables $\vec{x}$ is a Boolean function from the domain of $\vec{x}$, to the Boolean set, i.e., C: $Domain(\vec{x}) \rightarrow \{True, False\}$*

By a slight abuse of notation $\vec{x}$ will denote either a vector or a set of variables.

Definition 3 *A variable partition $\mathbb{P}$ of the set of variables $\vec{x}$ is defined as $\mathbb{P} = (\vec{y}_1, \ldots, \vec{y}_M)$, such that $\vec{y}_1 \cup \vec{y}_2 \cup \ldots \cup \vec{y}_M = \vec{x}$, and $\vec{y}_i \cap \vec{y}_j = \emptyset$ for all i, j $(1 \leq i, j \leq M, i \neq j)$.*

Definition 4 *Let Ω be a constraint, and $\mathbb{P} = (\vec{y}_1, \ldots, \vec{y}_M)$ be a partition of variables. We say that $\mathbb{C} = (C_1, \ldots, C_M)$ is a decomposition of Ω, if in every constraint C_i all free variables are from $\vec{y}_i$. Sometimes we will use $\mathbb{C}$ to indicate the conjunction $C_1 \wedge .. \wedge C_M$. We say that a decomposition $\mathbb{C} = (C_1, \ldots, C_M)$ is safe if $C_1 \wedge .. \wedge C_M \models \Omega$, i.e., $C_1, \ldots, C_M$ is subsumed by Ω.*

Definition 5 *Let $\vec{x}^0 = (\vec{y}_1^0, \ldots, \vec{y}_M^0)$ be a database instance. We say that $\vec{x}^0$ satisfies a decomposition $\mathbb{C} = (C_1, \ldots, C_M)$ if $\vec{y}_i^0$ satisfies C_i for all $1 \leq i \leq M$.*

Example 1. Consider the following set Ω of linear constraints: $X + Y \leq 6, -X + 5Y \leq 15, 5X + 4Y \leq 15$, and both variables X and Y are non-negative. A graphic representation of Ω is given in Figure 2. For the partition $\mathbb{P} = (\{X\}, \{Y\})$ (i.e., two sites with a single variable each), consider three safe decompositions $\mathbb{C}_1, \mathbb{C}_2, and \mathbb{C}_3$ as follows:

$$\mathbb{C}_1 = (C_{11}, C_{12})$$
$$= (\{0.5 \leq X \leq 2.5\}, \{0.5 \leq Y \leq 2.5\})$$
$$\mathbb{C}_2 = (C_{21}, C_{22}), and$$
$$= (\{0.0 \leq X \leq 3.0\}, \{0.0 \leq Y \leq 3.0\}), and$$
$$\mathbb{C}_3 = (C_{31}, C_{32})$$
$$= (\{0.0 \leq X \leq 4.0\}, \{1.25 \leq Y \leq 2.0\}).$$

$\mathbb{C}_1$ is a safe decomposition of Ω because every point (X,Y) that satisfies C_{11} and C_{12} will also satisfy Ω. Geometrically, this means that the space (1) defined by $\mathbb{C}_1$ is contained in the space defined by Ω. Similarly, $\mathbb{C}_2$ and $\mathbb{C}_3$ are safe decompositions of Ω. Note that the database instance (a, b) satisfies $\mathbb{C}_2$, but not $\mathbb{C}_1$ and $\mathbb{C}_3$.

Note that rectangle (1) (for $\mathbb{C}_1$) is strictly contained in rectangle (2) (for $\mathbb{C}_2$). Hence, the decomposition $\mathbb{C}_2$ is better than $\mathbb{C}_1$ in the sense that, in $\mathbb{C}_2$ we will have to perform global updates less frequently than in $\mathbb{C}_1$, i.e., less overhead.

Since safe decompositions are not unique, an important question is how to choose a safe decomposition that is optimal according to some meaningful criterion. In our example, the rectangle with the maximal area may be a good choice. In fact, if update points (X,Y) are uniformly distributed over the given space (defined by Ω), then the larger area (volume in the general case) corresponds to greater probability that an update will satisfy local constraints, and thus no global processing will be necessary. We defer the discussion on optimality criteria to Section 4.1.

Decomposition of Constraints over Agencies. We suggest the following general framework for selecting optimal feasible decompositions:

$$maximize\ f(s)$$
$$s.t.\ s \in \mathbb{S} \tag{1}$$

where $\mathbb{S}$ is the set of all feasible decompositions, and $f : \mathbb{S} \to \mathbb{R}$ (real numbers) is the objective function discussed in the next subsection.

Definition 6 *Let Ω be a constraint, $\mathbb{C} = (C_1, \ldots, C_M)$ be a decomposition of Ω, $\theta = \{k+1, \ldots, M\}$ be a subset of sites $\{1, \ldots, M\}$, and $\vec{x}^0 = (\vec{y}_1^0, \ldots, \vec{y}_M^0)$ be a database instance. We consider the following properties of $\mathbb{C}$:*

1. *Safety. $\mathbb{C}$ has this property if it is a safe decomposition of Ω.*
2. *Local Consistency. $\mathbb{C}$ has this property w.r.t. $\vec{x}^0 = (\vec{y}_1^0, \ldots, \vec{y}_M^0)$ if every local instance $\vec{y}_i^0$ satisfies its local constraint C_i $(1 \leq i \leq M)$. Clearly, local consistency and safety imply global consistency.*
3. *Partial Constraint Preservation. $\mathbb{C} = (C_1, \ldots, C_M)$ has this property w.r.t. local constraints $C_1', \ldots, C_M'$ outside $\theta = \{k+1, \ldots, M\}$ if $C_i = C_i'$ for all $1 \leq i \leq M$, i.e., local constraints outside θ are fixed to $(C_1', \ldots, C_k')$, respectively.*
4. *Resource Partition B_θ. The resource partition property is given only for families of constraints in which the resource characterization, defined in Section 4.2, is possible (e.g., linear constraints considered in this paper). Namely, the global constraint Ω is associated with the global resource bound $\vec{b}$, each local constraint C_i in the decomposition is associated with a resource $\vec{r}_i$, and each subset of sites θ is associated with the cumulative resource $\vec{r}_\theta$.*

A partition of the global resource bound between θ and $\bar{\theta}$ (i.e., all sites except θ) is a pair $(\vec{B}_\theta, \vec{B}_{\bar{\theta}})$, such that $\vec{B}_\theta + \vec{B}_{\bar{\theta}} = \vec{b}$, which is identified by $\boldsymbol{B}_\theta$. We say that a decomposition $\mathbb{C}$ has a resource bound partition property w.r.t. a partition $\vec{B}_\theta$, if the cumulative resource $\vec{r}_\theta$ is bounded by $\vec{B}_\theta$, and $\vec{r}_{\bar{\theta}}$ is bounded by $\vec{B}_{\bar{\theta}}$. [2]

Given a set Pr of properties that contains safety and possibly other properties above, the set $\mathbb{S}_{Pr}$ of feasible (safe) decompositions w.r.t. Pr is the set of all decompositions of Ω that satisfy the properties in Pr.

Before we discuss how the decomposition problems can be solved effectively, we consider possible candidates for function f.

Optimization Criteria. There are many feasible (minimally-constrained) safe decompositions in $\mathbb{S}$, and we would like to formulate a criterion to select the best among them. This criterion should represent the problem characteristics, and the decomposition goals. Possible criteria include:

- Maximize the probability that an update will not violate the existing local constraints (decomposition).
- Minimize overall expected cost of computations during an update.
- Maximize the expected number of updates before the first update that violates local constraints.
- Maximize the expected length of time before an update violates local constraints.

Many other optimization criteria are possible. However, any reasonable criteria should be monotonic, as defined below.

Definition 7 Let f be a function from the set of safe decompositions of Ω to $\mathbb{R}$. We say that f is monotonic if for every two decompositions $\mathbb{C}_1, \mathbb{C}_2$ of Ω, $\mathbb{C}_1 \models \mathbb{C}_2$ implies $f(\mathbb{C}_1) \leq f(\mathbb{C}_2)$.

Intuitively, being monotonic for an optimization criterion means that enlarging the space defined by a decomposition can only make it better.

Note, that if f is monotonic, then $f(\mathbb{C}_1) = f(\mathbb{C}_2)$ for any two equivalent decompositions $\mathbb{C}_1$ and $\mathbb{C}_2$.

As we will see in Section 4.2, it is often necessary to consider a subspace of all safe decompositions (without loosing an optimal decomposition).

Definition 8 Let $\mathbb{S}$ be a set of safe decompositions of Ω.[3] A subset $\mathbb{S}'$ of $\mathbb{S}$ will be called a monotonic cover of $\mathbb{S}$ if for every decomposition $\mathbb{C}$ in $\mathbb{S}$ there exists a decomposition $\mathbb{C}'$ in $\mathbb{S}'$, such that $\mathbb{C}'$ subsumes $\mathbb{C}$ (i.e., $\mathbb{C} \models \mathbb{C}'$).

---

[2] Note that the notion of resource bound partition is more flexible than constraint preservation, and allows one to perform concurrent constraint decompositions.

[3] Not necessarily the set of all safe decompositions of Ω.

The following proposition states that optimal decompositions are not missed when the search space is restricted to a monotonic cover and the optimization function is monotonic.

Proposition 1 *Let* $\mathbb{S}$ *be a (sub) set of all safe decompositions of* Ω, $\mathbb{S}'$ *be a monotonic cover of* $\mathbb{S}$, *and* f *be a monotonic function from* $\mathbb{S}$ *to* $\mathbb{R}$. *Then, the following two optimization problems yield the same maximum.*

1. *Problem 1. max* $f(s)$, *s.t.* $s \in \mathbb{S}$.
2. *Problem 2. max* $f(s)$, *s.t.* $s \in \mathbb{S}'$.

4.2   Split Decompositions and Resource Distributions

This section addresses the general partition case. Let $\mathbb{P} = (\vec{y}_1, \vec{y}_2, \dots, \vec{y}_M)$ be a partition of $\vec{x}$, where $\vec{y}_i$ is the subset of variables at site i, $(\mid \vec{y}_i \mid = n_i)$, and $\vec{x}$ is the vector of all variables in our problem.

Split Decompositions. The first problem in the general case is that, for a safe decomposition, a constraint C_i at site i may be characterized by an unbounded set of atomic linear constraints; thus the size of a parametric description (using coefficients of those constraints) is unbounded. To overcome this problem, we reduce the search space to the set of what we call *compact split* decompositions, for which we prove that: (1) there does exist a parametric description of bounded size and (2) the optimum of the objective function among all safe decompositions *can always be found* in the subspace of split decompositions.

Definition 9 *Let* $\Omega = A\vec{x} \leq \vec{b}$ *be a constraint on* $\vec{x}$, *and* $\mathbb{P} = (\vec{y}_1, \dots, \vec{y}_M)$ *be a variable partition of* $\vec{x}$. *A split of* Ω, *denoted by* $D(\vec{r}_1, \dots, \vec{r}_M)$, *is a tuple* $(A_1\vec{y}_1 \leq \vec{r}_1, \dots, A_M\vec{y}_M \leq \vec{r}_M)$ *of constraints, where* A_i, $1 \leq i \leq M$, *is the matrix composed of the columns of* A *that are associated with* $\vec{y}_i$. *We say that a split* $D(\vec{r}_1, \dots, \vec{r}_M)$ *is safe if it is a safe decomposition of* Ω. *For a subset* θ *of sites, say* $\{k+1, \dots, M\}$, *a (partial)* θ-split *of* Ω, *denoted by* $D(\vec{r}_{k+1}, \dots, \vec{r}_M)$, *is a tuple* $(A_{k+1}\vec{y}_{k+1} \leq \vec{r}_{k+1}, \dots, A_M\vec{y}_M \leq \vec{r}_M)$ *of constraints.*

Note that the vectors $\vec{r}_i$ above have the same dimension as the vector $\vec{b}$, which equals to the number of constraints in Ω. Recall that, by Proposition ??, $D(\vec{r}_1, \dots, \vec{r}_M)$ is satisfiable if and only if for all i, $1 \leq i \leq M$, $A_i\vec{y}_i \leq \vec{r}_i$ is satisfiable.

For our classification we introduce the notion of *tight form* for a system $A\vec{x} \leq \vec{b}$,[4] which states, intuitively, that the values of $\vec{b}$ are tight. This is formalized as follows.

---

[4] $A\vec{x} \leq \vec{b}$ in this definition denotes any system of linear constraints, not just the global constraint.

Definition 10 *We say that a constraint $A\vec{x} \le \vec{b}$ is tight, if there does not exist $\vec{b}'$, such that $\vec{b}' \le \vec{b}$, $\vec{b}' \ne \vec{b}$, and $A\vec{x} \le \vec{b}$ is equivalent to $A\vec{x} \le \vec{b}'$. We say that a split $D(\vec{r}_1, \dots, \vec{r}_M)$ is tight if every satisfiable constraint $A_i\vec{y}_i \le \vec{r}_i$ in it $(1 \le i \le M)$ is tight.*

Claim. For any satisfiable system $A\vec{x} \le \vec{b}$ (respectively split) there exists an equivalent system (respectively split) that is tight. Furthermore, every tight constraint $A\vec{x} \le \vec{b}$ is satisfiable.

Definition 11 *We say that a split $D(\vec{r}_1, \dots, \vec{r}_M)$ of Ω is compact if*

$$\sum_{i=1}^{M} \vec{r}_i \le \vec{b}$$

The next theorem shows that the maximum of a monotonic function in the space of safe decompositions can always be found in the subspace of compact splits.

Theorem 1 *Let $\Omega = A\vec{x} \le \vec{b}$ be a satisfiable global constraint, f be a monotonic function from the set of all safe decompositions of Ω to $\mathbb{R}$, $\mathbb{P} = (\vec{y}_1, \dots, \vec{y}_M)$ be a variable partition of $\vec{x}$, and $\vec{x}^0 = (\vec{y}_1^0, \dots, \vec{y}_M^0)$ be an instance of $\vec{x}$. Let $\mathbb{S}$ and $\mathbb{SS}$ be the sets of all safe decompositions and all compact splits of Ω, respectively, and let $\mathbb{S}_{\vec{x}^0}$ and $\mathbb{SS}_{\vec{x}^0}$ be the sets $\mathbb{S}$ and $\mathbb{SS}$ restricted to decompositions that satisfy $\vec{x}^0$. Then,*

1. $max\, f(s)$ s.t. $s \in \mathbb{S} = max\, f(s)$ s.t. $s \in \mathbb{SS}$
2. $max\, f(s)$ s.t. $s \in \mathbb{S}_{\vec{x}^0} = max\, f(s)$ s.t. $s \in \mathbb{SS}_{\vec{x}^0}$

Following Theorem 1, from now on we only consider compact splits. Vectors $(\vec{r}_1, \dots, \vec{r}_M)$ can be viewed as resources assigned to agencies, because they represent how much of vector $\vec{b}$ is distributed to each agency. The following subsection presents a parametric resource characterization of splits and a parametric formulation of the optimization problem in terms of resources.

Constraint Resource Characterization. This subsection characterizes (compact) splits in terms of *resources*, which allows (in the next subsection) to reduce *compact split* (safe decompositions) to *resource distributions*. In turn, *resource distributions* can significantly simplify the management of a distributed protocol, because of their small size as compared with the size of a (safe) decomposition. Also, as explained in the next subsection, *resource distributions* support concurrent constraint (re-)decompositions.

More specifically, we formulate the properties of *compactness*, *local consistency (lc)*, *partial constraint preservation (pcp)*, and *resource bound partition (rp)* for splits in terms of resources. Then, the optimization problem is formulated in terms of such a characterization. First, we introduce the concept of *resources* of (compact) splits.

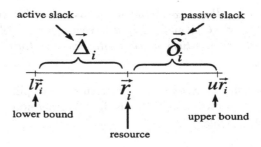

Fig. 3. Resource Representation at site i

Definition 12 (Resource Parameters) *Let* $\Omega = A\vec{x} \leq \vec{b}$ *be a satisfiable global constraint,* $D(\vec{r}_1, \ldots, \vec{r}_M)$ *be a tight compact split of* Ω, $\vec{x}^0 = (\vec{y}_1^0, \ldots, \vec{y}_M^0)$ *be an instance of* x, *and* θ *be a subset* $\{k+1, \ldots, M\}$ *of sites* $\{1, \ldots, M\}$. *Then, we say that:*

1. $\vec{b}$ *is the* global upper bound *of resources in* Ω.
2. $\vec{r}_i$ *is the* resource *assigned to site* i, $1 \leq i \leq M$.
3. $\vec{r} = \sum_{i=1}^{M} \vec{r}_i$ *is the* global resource.
4. $\vec{\delta} = \vec{b} - \vec{r}$ *is the* global passive slack *of* Ω *w.r.t.* $D(\vec{r}_1, \ldots, \vec{r}_M)$.
5. $(\vec{\delta}_1, \ldots, \vec{\delta}_M)$ *such that* $\vec{\delta}_i \geq 0$, $1 \leq i \leq M$ *and* $\sum_{i=1}^{M} \vec{\delta}_i = \vec{\delta}$, *is a partition of* $\vec{\delta}$. *Each* $\vec{\delta}_i$, $1 \leq i \leq M$, *is called the* passive slack *at site* i.
6. $\vec{ur}_i = \vec{r}_i + \vec{\delta}_i$ *is the* upper resource bound *at site* i, $(1 \leq i \leq M)$.
7. *Given an instance* $\vec{y}_i^0$ *at site* i, $\vec{lr}_i = A_i \vec{y}_i^0$, $1 \leq i \leq M$, *is the* lower resource bound *at site* i *w.r.t.* $\vec{y}_i^0$.
8. *Given an instance* $\vec{y}_i^0$ *at site* i, $\vec{\Delta}_i = \vec{r}_i - \vec{lr}_i$, $1 \leq i \leq M$, *is the* active slack *at site* i *w.r.t.* $\vec{y}_i^0$.

Finally, we define the cumulative parameters for θ, *namely cumulative resources, resource upper and lower bounds, and passive and active slacks by* $\vec{r}_\theta = \sum_{i \in \theta} \vec{r}_i$, $\vec{ur}_\theta = \sum_{i \in \theta} \vec{ur}_i$, $\vec{lr}_\theta = \sum_{i \in \theta} \vec{lr}_i$, $\vec{\delta}_\theta = \sum_{i \in \theta} \vec{\delta}_i$, *and* $\vec{\Delta}_\theta = \sum_{i \in \theta} \vec{\Delta}_i$, *respectively.*

The above resource parameters are shown in Figure 3. In this figure, each resource $\vec{r}_i$ is bounded between its lower and upper bound ($\vec{lr}_i$ and $\vec{ur}_i$), the difference between upper bound ($\vec{ur}_i$) and the resource is the passive slack $\vec{\delta}_i$, and the difference between the resource ($\vec{r}_i$) and its lower bound ($\vec{lr}_i$) is the active slack ($\vec{\Delta}_i$).

The following proposition characterizes the split properties of *compactness*, *local consistency (lc)*, *partial constraint preservation (pcp)*, and *resource bound partition (rp)* in terms of the resource parameters.

Proposition 2 (Parametric Feasible Properties) *Let* $\Omega = A\vec{x} \leq \vec{b}$ *be a global satisfiable constraint,* $\mathbb{P} = (\vec{y}_1, \ldots, \vec{y}_M)$ *be a variable partition of* $\vec{x}$, $\vec{x}^0 =$

$(\vec{y}_1^0, \ldots, \vec{y}_M^0)$ be an instance of $\vec{x}$, θ be a subset of sites, say $\theta = \{k+1, \ldots, M\}$, $\bar{\theta}$ be the set $\{1, \ldots, k\}$, and $D(\vec{r}_1^0, \ldots, \vec{r}_k^0)$ be a (partial) $\bar{\theta}$-split that satisfies $(\vec{y}_1^0, \ldots, \vec{y}_k^0)$. Then, for any split $D(\vec{r}_1, \ldots, \vec{r}_M)$

1. $D(\vec{r}_1, \ldots, \vec{r}_M)$ is compact iff the global resource $\vec{r}$ is bounded by the global upper bound $\vec{b}$, i.e., $\vec{r} \leq \vec{b}$. We denote this condition by $\Phi_{compact}(\vec{r}_1, \ldots, \vec{r}_M)$.
2. $D(\vec{r}_1, \ldots, \vec{r}_M)$ satisfies local consistency w.r.t. $\vec{x}^0$ iff the resource $\vec{r}_i$ assigned to site i is bounded from below by its lower bound $\vec{lr}_i$, i.e., for every site i, $1 \leq i \leq M$, $\vec{lr}_i \leq \vec{r}_i$. We denote this condition by $\Phi_{lc}(\vec{r}_1, \ldots, \vec{r}_M)$.
3. $D(\vec{r}_1, \ldots, \vec{r}_M)$ satisfies partial constraint preservation w.r.t. $\bar{\theta}$-split $D(\vec{r}_1^0, \ldots, \vec{r}_k^0)$ iff the resources at each site outside θ are fixed, i.e., $r_1 = r_1^0, \ldots, r_k = r_k^0$. We denote this condition by $\Phi_{pcp}(\vec{r}_1, \ldots, \vec{r}_M)$.

We will also denote by $\Phi_{rp, \vec{B}_\theta}(\vec{r}_1, \ldots, \vec{r}_M)$ the condition stating that $D(\vec{r}_1, \ldots, \vec{r}_M)$ satisfies resource partition w.r.t. a resource bound partition $\vec{B}_\theta$.

Theorem 2 (Resource Optimization) Let $\Omega = A\vec{x} \leq \vec{b}$ be a satisfiable global constraint, f be a monotonic function from the set of all safe decompositions to $\mathbb{R}$, $\mathbb{P} = (\vec{y}_1, \ldots, \vec{y}_M)$ a variable partition of $\vec{x}$, $\vec{x}^0 = (\vec{y}_1^0, \ldots, \vec{y}_M^0)$ be an instance of $\vec{x}$, and Pr be the subset of properties $\{compactness, lc, pcp, rp\}$ that must contain compactness or resource bound partition. Then, solving the optimization problem

$$max\ f(s)$$
$$s.t.\ s \in \mathbb{SS}_{Pr}$$

is equivalent to solving the parametric problem [5]

$$max\ f(D(\vec{r}_1, \ldots, \vec{r}_M))$$
$$s.t.\ \Phi_{Pr}(\vec{r}_1, \ldots, \vec{r}_M)$$

Resource Distributions and Concurrent Splits. The resource characterization of the previous subsection assumes that information from all sites is used. However, in order to support distributed and autonomous protocols we would like to make constraint decompositions and re-decompositions involving only a (small) subset of sites, say $\theta = \{(k+1), \ldots, M\}$ of sites $\{1, \ldots, M\}$. To do that a formulation of the decomposition problem can only involve or affect information that is stored in sites θ. We capture this idea using the notion of (full or partial) *resource distribution* as follows.

Definition 13 Let $\Omega = A\vec{x} \leq \vec{b}$ be a global constraint, $D(\vec{r}_1, \ldots, \vec{r}_M)$ be a compact split of Ω, $(\vec{\delta}_1, \ldots, \vec{\delta}_M)$ be a partition of the global passive slack $\vec{\delta}$, $\vec{x}^0 = (\vec{y}_1^0, \ldots, \vec{y}_M^0)$ be a database instance, θ is a subset, say $\{k+1, \ldots, M\}$, of sites. A resource distribution is a tuple (of triples) $((\vec{lr}_1, \vec{r}_1, \vec{ur}_1), \ldots, (\vec{lr}_M, \vec{r}_M, \vec{ur}_M))$ [6];

---

[5] we will sometimes write $f(D(\vec{r}_1, \ldots, \vec{r}_M))$ as $f(\vec{r}_1, \ldots, \vec{r}_M)$.

[6] Note $(\vec{lr}_i, \vec{r}_i, \vec{ur}_i)$'s are defined in Definition 12.

a θ-resource distribution is $((\vec{lr}_{k+1}, \vec{r}_{k+1}, \vec{ur}_{k+1}), \ldots, (\vec{lr}_M, \vec{r}_M, \vec{ur}_M))$. We say that the resource distribution is permissible if

$$\sum_{i=1}^{M} \vec{ur}_i = \vec{b} \text{ and } \vec{lr}_i \leq \vec{r}_i \leq \vec{ur}_i, \text{ for every } 1 \leq i \leq M$$

Given a resource bound partition $\vec{B}_\theta$, we say that the θ-resource distribution $((\vec{lr}_{k+1}, \vec{r}_{k+1}, \vec{ur}_{k+1}), \ldots, (\vec{lr}_M, \vec{r}_M, \vec{ur}_M))$ is permissible w.r.t. $\vec{B}_\theta$ if

$$\sum_{i \in \theta} \vec{ur}_i = \vec{B}_\theta \text{ and } \vec{lr}_i \leq \vec{r}_i \leq \vec{ur}_i, \text{ for every } i \in \theta$$

Note that if θ is the set of all sites, the resource distribution permissibility is equivalent to θ resource distribution permissibility.

The key advantage of a resource distribution is its small size of $O(nc)$ as compared with the size $O(nc * nv)$ of a constraint decomposition, where nc and nv are the number of constraints and variables, respectively, in the global constraint. In fact, nv may be as large as the size of a database, for example when the global constraint reflects that the summation of some quantity, one per relational tuple, is bounded by a constant.

The following proposition motivates the notion of permissible distribution and provides a local criterion for a subset θ of sites to decide whether a feasible resource distribution exists, after database instances have been updated (i.e., lower bounds).

Proposition 3 (θ-Resource Distribution Feasibility) *Let θ be a subset, say $\{k+1, \ldots, M\}$, of sites $\{1, \ldots, M\}$, and $\bar{\theta}$ be its complement, $\vec{B}_\theta$ be a resource bound partition. Then,*

1. *Given a database instance $(\vec{y}_{k+1}^0, \ldots, \vec{y}_M^0)$ at sites θ (and thus lower bounds $(\vec{lr}_{k+1}, \ldots, \vec{lr}_M))$, the following are equivalent:*
   (a) *There exists a compact split of Ω satisfying resource partition $\vec{B}_\theta$ and local consistency w.r.t. to an instance $(\vec{y}_{k+1}^0, \ldots, \vec{y}_M^0)$ at θ.*
   (b) *There exists a θ-permissible resource distribution w.r.t. $\vec{B}_\theta$ (with the above lower bounds).*
   (c) $\vec{lr}_\theta = \sum_{i \in \theta} \vec{lr}_i \leq \vec{B}_\theta$
2. *The combination of θ-permissible resource distribution w.r.t. $\vec{B}_\theta$ and $\bar{\theta}$-permissible resource distribution w.r.t. $\vec{B}_{\bar{\theta}}$ constitutes a permissible resource distribution.*

The optimization functions f are defined in terms of the information of all sites (i.e., $D(\vec{r}_1, \ldots, \vec{r}_M)$), whereas we need to work with the information only on a subset θ of sites. To do that, we define the notion of θ-localizer as follows.

Definition 14 *Let Ω be a constraint over $\vec{x}$, and $\mathbb{S}$ be the set of all splits of Ω, $f : \mathbb{S} \to \mathbb{R}$ be a function. Let $\theta = \{k+1, \ldots, M\}$ be a subset of sites*

$\{1, \ldots, M\}$, $\bar{\theta}$ *its complement,* $\mathbb{S}_\theta$ *be the set of all θ-splits. Then, function f_θ :* $\mathbb{S}_\theta \to \mathbb{R}$ *is called θ-localizer of f if for any $\vec{r}_1^0, \ldots, \vec{r}_k^0$, and for every two splits* $D(\vec{r}_1^0, \ldots, \vec{r}_k^0, \vec{r}_{k+1}, \ldots, \vec{r}_M)$ *and* $D(\vec{r}_1^0, \ldots, \vec{r}_k^0, \vec{r}_{k+1}', \ldots, \vec{r}_M')$ *in* $\mathbb{S}$,

$$f(\vec{r}_1^0, \ldots, \vec{r}_k^0, \vec{r}_{k+1}, \ldots, \vec{r}_M) \geq f(\vec{r}_1^0, \ldots, \vec{r}_k^0, \vec{r}_{k+1}', \ldots, \vec{r}_M') \Leftrightarrow$$
$$f_\theta(\vec{r}_{k+1}, \ldots, \vec{r}_M) \geq f_\theta(\vec{r}_{k+1}', \ldots, \vec{r}_M')$$

(i.e., f_θ preserves monotonicity for any resource instantiation outside of θ).

We are now ready to formulate a theorem to be used for concurrent (re-)decompositions of the global constraints.

Theorem 3 *Let $\Omega = A\vec{x} \leq \vec{b}$ be a global constraints, θ be a subset, say $\{k + 1, \ldots, M\}$, of sites $\{1, \ldots, M\}$ and $\bar{\theta}$ be its complement, $\mathbb{S}$ be the set of all compact splits of Ω, $f : \mathbb{S} \to \mathbb{R}$ be a monotonic function and f_θ be its θ-localizer, $\vec{B}_\theta$ be a resource bound partition, and $D(\vec{r}_1^0, \ldots, \vec{r}_k^0)$ be a (partial) $\bar{\theta}$-split for sites outside θ. Let Pr be a subset of properties that contains rp and $\Phi_{\theta-Pr}$ be the condition (1) $\vec{r}_\theta \leq \vec{B}_\theta$ for the case that Pr contains just rp, and the conditions (2) $\vec{r}_\theta \leq \vec{B}_\theta, l\vec{r}_i \leq \vec{r}_i$ for every $i \in \theta$, for the case of Pr that contains both rp and lc. Then,*

1. *For Pr being the set of properties $\{rp, pcp\}$ or $\{rp, pcp, lc\}$, let $(\vec{r}_{k+1}', \ldots, \vec{r}_M')$ be a solution to the problem*

$$max f_\theta(\vec{r}_{k+1}, \ldots, \vec{r}_M)$$
$$s.t. \Phi_{\theta-Pr}$$

   Then, $(\vec{r}_1^0, \ldots, \vec{r}_k^0, \vec{r}_{k+1}', \ldots, \vec{r}_M')$ is a solution to the problem

$$max f(\vec{r}_1, \ldots, \vec{r}_M)$$
$$s.t. \Phi_{Pr}$$

2. *For Pr being the set of properties $\{rp\}$ or $\{rp, lc\}$, let $(\vec{r}_{k+1}', \ldots, \vec{r}_M')$ be a solution to the problem*

$$max f_\theta(\vec{r}_{k+1}, \ldots, \vec{r}_M)$$
$$s.t. \Phi_{\theta-Pr}$$

   and $(\vec{r}_1', \ldots, \vec{r}_k')$ be a solution to the problem

$$max f_{\bar{\theta}}(\vec{r}_{k+1}, \ldots, \vec{r}_M)$$
$$s.t. \Phi_{\bar{\theta}-Pr}$$

   Then, $(\vec{r}_1', \ldots, \vec{r}_k', \vec{r}_{k+1}', \ldots, \vec{r}_M')$ is a solution to the problem

$$max f(\vec{r}_1, \ldots, \vec{r}_M)$$
$$s.t. \Phi_{Pr}$$

Proof. The proof follows from the fact that f has a θ-localizer, and from Propositions 2 and 3.

5 Distributed Agency Resource Protocol

In this section we propose a protocol to manage linear arithmetic constraints over a distributed system and which possesses the desirable protocol properties. In fact, the protocol manages resource distributions as a mechanism to manage updates and constraint decompositions (as is described in Subsection 4.2).

First, we explain a distributed transaction primitive called RESOURCE_TRANSFER that we use in the protocol. RESOURCE_TRANSFER($i,j,\vec{rc}$) works on a pair of sites (agencies), and transfers the *resource-contribution* $\vec{rc}$ from the *giving* agency i to the *receiving* agency j. The effect of the transfer is that the resource upper bound $\vec{ur}_i$ at agency i will be decreased by $\vec{rc}$, after which $\vec{ur}_j$ at agency j will be increased by $\vec{rc}$. Also, we assume that with every change in a resource upper bound $\vec{ur}_i$ the corresponding resource $\vec{r}_i$ is updated correspondingly simply by making $\vec{ur}_i$ tight. It is assumed that standard distributed transaction techniques are used to ensure that (1) under no circumstances (possibly involving failures) resource-contribution is added to $\vec{ur}_j$ of the receiving agency before it has been reduced from $\vec{ur}_i$ of the giving agency, and (2) the standard ACID properties (i.e., atomicity, consistency, isolation, and durability) of distributed transactions. It is important to note that distributed transaction protocols to ensure these properties (e.g., two-phase commit) are less expensive for transactions involving two agencies only, as is done in our RESOURCE_TRANSFER. We can now provide the basic assumptions for our protocol as follows:

Distributed Protocol Assumptions.

1. For the purpose of constraint management, we assume that the global enterprise is abstracted by real values for the vector of variables $\vec{x} = (\vec{y}_1, \dots, \vec{y}_M)$, where $(\vec{y}_1, \dots, \vec{y}_M)$ is a partition of $\vec{x}$. However, any actual database model, e.g., relational or object-oriented, can be used, in which values for $\vec{x}$ are either explicitly stored or expressed as views (e.g., aggregations).

2. The global constraint is of the form $\Omega = A\vec{x} \leq \vec{b}$, i.e., Ω is a system of linear constraints. Local constraints are assumed to be compact splits of Ω.

3. The global database is composed of M distributed agencies, where at each agency i, $1 \leq i \leq M$, values for variables $\vec{y}_i$ are stored. Since $(\vec{y}_1, \dots, \vec{y}_M)$ is a partition of $\vec{x}$, i.e., there is no variable replication [7] i.e., $\vec{y}_i \cap \vec{y}_j = \emptyset$, for every $i \neq j$. Furthermore, each agency i, $1 \leq i \leq M$, has a local transaction manager that guarantees the standard ACID properties (i.e., atomicity, consistency, isolation, and durability), as well as mechanisms for back-up and recovery from failure. We thus assume that every response to an EVENT in a protocol is run as a local transaction. We also assume that

---

[7] If there is replication, e.g., a variable x appears at two agencies, then, technically, it can be reduced to a partition by replacing x with x_1 and x_2 and adding the constraint $x_1 = x_2$ to Ω. However, as we further comment in the discussion subsection at the end of this section, this is not a good solution, and other approaches to extend our results with replication techniques would be a better choice.

all agencies are assigned a unique ID from a domain with total ordering, say, ID's are integers 1 through M.

4. Local update $\vec{y}_k^0$ at agency k means that the current values for $\vec{y_k}$ are to be replaced with the new values $\vec{y}_k^0$, i.e., updates are formulated in absolute terms. Thus, if a new update $\vec{y_k}^0$ arrives while the previous update $\vec{y_k}'$ is pending, it is interpreted as replacing the previous update request (i.e., canceling it) with the new one. Note that update requests formulated in relative terms (e.g., add/subtract certain values to/from the current values of $\vec{y_k}$), can always be translated to absolute terms, and so this assumption is not a limitation. We use it to simplify the formulation of the protocol.

5. Failure and communication model: both agencies and communication links may fail, but persistent storage does not fail, i.e., after a agency recovers from a failure, the database instance is as before the failure. We assume that the agency failures stop agency execution without performing any incorrect actions. We also assume that the underlying communication system at each agency indicates which other agencies are *connected* and *operational*, through the flag CONNECTED(i, j), which is implemented at the communication layer.[8] It is further assumed that the uncertainty time (i.e., between the time the agency j becomes disconnected or not operational, and the time when CONNECTED(i, j) turns FALSE) is bounded by a constant. Also, when a message is sent, say from i to j, then within bounded time either this message is acknowledged at i, or the CONNECTED(i, j) turns FALSE. In the following, when we say that "agency j is *operational* and *connected* to agency i" we will mean that the CONNECTED(i, j) flag at agency i is TRUE and remains so until the relevant task (e.g., sending a message and receiving an acknowledgment) is completed.

We can now formulate the protocol.

The DAR Protocol.

1. Every agency k maintains, in addition to its local instance $\vec{y}_i^0$ and the global constraint Ω, the triple $(\vec{lr}_k, \vec{r}_k, \vec{ur}_k)$, where $((\vec{lr}_1, \vec{r}_1, \vec{ur}_1), \ldots, (\vec{lr}_M, \vec{r}_M, \vec{ur}_M))$ is a permissible resource distribution (thus the local constraint $A_k \vec{y}_k \leq \vec{r}_k$ is also implicitly given). Safe (re-)decompositions are performed by updating the permissible resource distribution.

2. In addition, every agency k has a *mechanism* to dynamically collect information about the *resource distribution* for all agencies. While the triple $(\vec{lr}_k, \vec{r}_k, \vec{ur}_k)$ for i is always accurate, the triples for the other agencies may not be. The collection mechanism can be implemented by periodically passing around the *resource distribution* information, with a time-stamp of the latest known update attached to each triple. Also, the *resource distribution*

---

[8] Whether this is done by trying to send packets and not receiving an acknowledgment within a TIMOUT period, or by whatever additional mechanism is orthogonal to our protocols of this section.

information will be passed with every message being sent among distributed agencies. We assume that the collection mechanism is implemented so that it ensures that the information on the *resource distribution* triples for all connected agencies is at most T seconds old, where T is a constant time bound, for those agencies that are connected to k for at least that period of time (i.e., T seconds).

3. For each maximal connected subset θ^* of agencies, an EXECUTIVE AGENT will be selected, which will be responsible for periodic optimal resource redistribution, as described below. If more than one EXECUTIVE AGENT is in $\theta*$, the agency with the minimum ID will be assigned the responsibility for resource redistribution.[9], i.e., each EXECUTIVE AGENT in θ^* decides that it is responsible for resource redistribution in θ^* if it has the minimal ID (which are assumed to be known at agency k).

4. Every agency remembers the PENDING_UPDATE (i.e., an update that was requested but still neither performed nor refused) as well the as PENDING_RESOURCE, that reflects requests for resource contributions as explained below.

5. The distributed protocol at each agency k reacts in response to the events below as follows:

EVENT 1: update-request $\vec{y}_k^0$
Agency k assigns $\vec{y}_k^0$ to PENDING_UPDATE.

EVENT 2: status change
This event is triggered when PENDING_UPDATE, RESOURCE_DISTRIBUTION, PENDING_RESOURCE, or CONNECTED condition (that reflects operational agencies connected k) are changed at agency k. If a resource contribution is received from agency i (via the RESOURCE_TRANSFER transaction) in response to k requests for update resource contribution, then PENDIND_RESOURCE is reduced by the quantity requested from i. Also, if PENDING_UPDATE is not empty, agency k reevaluates it as follows:

(a) If $\vec{y}_k^0$ satisfies the local constraint (i.e., by Proposition 3, $A_k y_k \leq \vec{ur}_k$), agency k performs the update and empties PENDING_UPDATE.

(b) Otherwise, agency k checks if for the *maximal* set θ^* of agencies that are *operational* and *connected* to k, $\vec{lr}_{\theta^*}' \not\leq \vec{ur}_{\theta^*}$. By Proposition 3, this means that there does not exist a compact split of Ω satisfying resource partition $\vec{ur}_\theta$ and local consistency w.r.t. database instances in θ^*. In this case, PENDING_UPDATE is refused and the structure for PENDING_UPDATE is emptied (to indicate that there is no pending update).

(c) Otherwise, find a minimal subset θ of θ^* such that $\vec{lr}_\theta' \leq \vec{ur}_\theta$, where $\vec{lr}_\theta'$ is the cumulative lower bound in θ that reflects PENDING_UPDATE. By Proposition 3, this condition means that there exists a compact split of Ω satisfying resource partition $\vec{ur}_\theta$ and local consistency w.r.t. database instances in θ, including PENDING_UPDATE. The cumulative resource contribution vector $\vec{rc}$ to be requested from agencies

---

[9] Recall that ID's are assumed to be integers, i.e., they have total order.

in θ will be computed as follows: for every component $\vec{rc}_j$ of $\vec{rc}$

$$\vec{rc}_j = max\{0, (A_k y_k^0 - \vec{ur}_k - \vec{pr}_k)_j\}$$

where $\vec{pr}_k$ is the current PENDING_RESOURCE at k. Intuitively, $\vec{rc}$ above is the minimal (non-negative) resource contribution vector that is necessary, in addition to already PENDING_RESOURCE, for agency k to make PENDING_UPDATE.

(d) Agency k partitions $\vec{rc}$ among agencies in θ so that taking the corresponding parts from each part will preserve a permissible resource distribution in θ. Then agency k sends a request to each agency in θ asking for the corresponding contribution. Finally, $\vec{rc}$ is added to PENDING_RESOURCE.

EVENT 3: request for update resource contribution $\vec{rc}$
This event is triggered when such a request is received from another agency, say i that needs additional resource to make an update. First, the maximum contribution vector $max\_\vec{rc}$ is computed as the (component-wise) maximum contribution that can be taken out of $\vec{ur}_k$ so that (1) the current instance will still satisfy the local constraint and (2) PENDING_UP-DATE, if not empty, will satisfy the local constraint after PENDING_RE-SOURCE is received. Then, the actual resource contribution $\vec{rc}'$ is computed as the (component-wise) minimum of the requested $\vec{rc}$ and $max\_\vec{rc}$. Finally, RESOURCE_TRANSFER($\vec{rc}',k,i$) is initiated.

EVENT 4: request for redistribution resource contribution
This request can only be sent from a an EXECUTIVE AGENT that took the responsibility of resource redistribution. If the ID of the requesting agency is not smaller than k, then nothing is done (since then the requesting agency should not be responsible for resource redistribution). Otherwise, k initiates RESOURCE_TRANSFER($max\_\vec{rc}$, k, i), where $max\_\vec{rc}$ is as defined in EVENT 3. Intuitively, agency k gives away as much resource as possible, leaving only what is necessary to keep local consistency for the current local database instance as well as for PENDING_UPDATE when PENDING_RESOURCE will arrive.

EVENT 5: initiation of resource redistribution
This is a composite event, which only occurs at the EXECUTIVE AGENT responsibly for resource distribution. This event is triggered periodically when certain criteria are met. For example, a resource redistribution can be initiated every time that (1) the optimal probability to satisfy local constraint is higher by at least $\alpha\%$ than the current probability (based on the current resource distribution) and (2) the previous re-decomposition was performed at least time t ago. The action here is a *request for redistribution resource contribution* sent to all operational agencies that are connected to k.

EVENT 6: optimal re-decomposition
This is a composite event, which only occurs at the EXECUTIVE AGENT responsible for redecomposition. This event is triggered at time t after

the initiation of the resource redistribution, where t is computed so that for connected agencies it will suffice to transfer their resources to the responsible EXECUTIVE AGENT. The action here is as follows:

(a) For the maximal set θ^* of operational agencies connected to k, agency k finds the optimal θ^* compact split, w.r.t. resource partition $\vec{ur}_{\theta^*}$ and satisfying local consistency w.r.t. both the current database instance and PENDING_UPDATEs in θ^*. (This can be done using the formulation of Theorem 3, when the lower bound for each agency i in θ^* in the theorem is taken as the current resource $\vec{r}_i$ in the resource distribution.) The optimal compact split gives the (tight) resource $\vec{r}_i$ for each agency i in θ^*.

(b) Agency k initiates RESOURCE_TRANSFER($\vec{rc}$, k, i) for each agency i in θ^*, where $\vec{rc}$ is the resource contribution that will update $\vec{ur}_i$ to the optimal resource $\vec{r}_i$ computed above. [10]

End of Distributed Agency Resource Protocol.

The DAR protocol is designed to satisfy the desirable properties of global and local *Consistency*, decomposition *Safety*, snap-shot *Optimality*, and *Last-resort update refusal* (the CSOL-properties) as stated in the following proposition:

Proposition 4 *The suggested Distributed Protocol, that operates under the Distributed Protocol Assumptions satisfies the following* **CSOL** *properties:*

Consistency: At all times, the database instance $\vec{x} = (\vec{y}_1, \ldots, \vec{y}_M)$ satisfies the global constraint Ω; every local instance $\vec{y}_i$ at every site i must satisfy the local constraint C_i.

Safety: At all times, the constraint decomposition is safe.

Optimality: When triggered to do so, the EXECUTIVE AGENT responsible for resource redistribution, redistributes resources in the maximal set θ^* of operational and connected agencies, in the optimal way, i.e., so that the resulting resource distribution will correspond to the optimal θ^* compact split, w.r.t. resource partition $\vec{ur}_{\theta^*}$ and satisfying local consistency w.r.t. both the current database instance and PENDING_UPDATEs in θ^*. This is under the assumption that the EXECUTIVE AGENT responsible for resource redistribution has the correct information about the resource distribution in θ^* at the time of the re-decomposition.

Last-Resort Update Refusal: Let $\vec{y}_i^0$ be a new update for site i, and let θ^* be a maximal set of *operational* and *connected* agencies that contains the agency i (i.e., no resources outside θ^* are available). Last-Resort Update Refusal means that an agency k refuses an update $\vec{y}_i^0$ only if, based on the information of the resource distribution available at agency k, there does not exist a safe (compact split) decomposition of Ω that satisfies resource partition $\vec{ur}_{\theta^*}$ (i.e., the cumulative resource upper bound in θ^*) and preserves

---

[10] Note that since the optimal resources are tight (see Section 4.2) RE-SOURCE-DISTRIBUTOR effectively leaves the entire passive slack in θ^* to itself.

local consistency w.r.t. the database instance in θ^* that would be created by the update.

Global and local consistency are the standard properties that we would like to preserve. *Safety* allows one to check only *local consistency* to guarantee *global consistency*. *Optimality* is restricted to the information known to the responsible EXECUTIVE AGENT at the time of resource redistribution. Clearly, this information may not be updated, and, furthermore, may also change after the redistribution decision has been made. We expect that there will be a trade-off in each specific protocol between how often a coordinator will update its knowledge regarding the current resource distribution and the cost of maintaining such knowledge. Finally, *Last-resort update refusal* says, intuitively, that the protocol refuses updates (and re-decompositions), only when there is no choice under the circumstances, i.e., no agency outside of θ^* can be reached (that is, θ^* is a maximal set) and, based just on the information at agencies in θ^*, we cannot guarantee satisfaction of global and local consistency.

Discussion on Distributed Protocol Features. The Distributed Protocol uses a number of tunable parameters and criteria, whose selection will affect various system trade-offs. One such parameters is how often should the enterprise perform an optimal redistribution of the enterprise constraints resources (i.e., EVENT 5, initiation of resource redistribution), so that the "right" trade-off is achieved between the optimality of a decomposition and the cost of redecomposition.

Another important trade-off is how accurate should the estimate on the current resource distribution be, versus how much overhead the protocol can tolerate for achieving this accuracy. This trade-off will influence how often the information about the resource distribution is circulated. One extreme case is that any change affecting a resource distribution would be run as a global distributed transaction (with ACID properties), and then the knowledge regarding the resource distribution could be made completely accurate at all times. However, the cost of doing so may eliminate most of the benefits of autonomous processing, and thus seems to be excessive. The other extreme is that the optimal redistribution is never done, but rather resources will be passed based on the needs of updates. It is possible that this extreme may be the best solution for some cases. In our Distributed Protocol we suggested an intermediate solution, in which it was assumed that the accuracy is maintained up to a certain time T and subject to a certain minimal deviation from the optimal decompositions. However, which specific parameters and criteria should be used here for various application scenarios remains to be studied carefully.

Another important issue still left open is that of replication, since we assumed that variables are partitioned among distributed agencies. As we commented earlier, the replication case can technically be reduced to a partition, by replacing every basic resource variable x that appears in more than one agency with separate variables $x_1, x_2, \ldots$ for each agency, and adding the equality constraint among these variables to the global constraint. However, this solution is not good, because safe decompositions in this case would force each copy of x to have a specific value. That would cause the problem that, effectively, updates at individual agencies (without simultaneously involving other agencies) would not be possible. A better solution seems to be integrating data replication techniques into our decomposition technique. Clearly, the question of how such integration of constraint decomposition and data replication techniques can be done would require more study and is outside the scope of this paper.

An interesting related problem arises when the global constraint Ω is not fully dimensional, i.e., it implies an equation. For example, to simplify the idea, Ω may imply $x_1 = x_2$. This case has exactly the same problem as the one introduced by replication; it seems that a good solution for this situation would be to treat it as replication, for example, to use one variable, say x_1 as the prime copy that would appear in Ω, while the other variable x_2 will be treated as a replicated copy using data replication techniques.

6 Conclusions

This paper has presented a novel and scalable agent-based approach to the management of shared enterprise resources which are subject to both local and global constraints. A three-layer agency-based model allows a family of agents to be specialized and organized into agencies, each of which plays a functional role within the organization.

A formal resource model is presented, together with the concept of resource constraints. It is shown that this model admits to optimal resource decompositions at both design-time and at run-time, under the assumption of linear constraints. This allows shared resources to be allocated to agencies in an optimal manner. Moreover, the agencies may operate autonomously so long as they satisfy local resource constraints, and may cooperate with their neighboring agencies to obtain needed resources, subject to global resource constraints.

We have presented the DAR protocol, which allows agencies to communicate, negotiate for, and exchange resources, while ensuring that all applicable constraints are satisfied. The beauty of this approach, however, is that we preserve the notion of agent autonomy, which is very important in multiagent systems. The protocol also ensures that agency databases are updated in a consistent manner, thereby preserving local and global database states.

Future work will involve extending the constraint and resource formalisms to handle other than linear constraints. We also wish to investigate different types of agency organizations, as well as more general resource distribution protocols.

Finally, we feel that for cooperative information agents to succeed in providing information and other services to organizations, they must interface with real enterprise databases, and our research suggests that this is indeed possible. Our results show that the resource management, negotiation, and exchange protocol provides an optimal and scalable solution to a very important open problem.

Acknowledgements

This research was sponsored in part by the Defense Advanced Research Project Agency (DARPA) within the Advanced Logistics Program under contract number N00600-96-D-3202, and by the National Science Foundation (NSF) grants IIS-9734242 and IRI-9409770.

References

1. D. Barbará and H. Garcia-Molina. The Demarcation Protocol: A technique for maintaining constraints in distributed database systems. *VLDB Journal*, 2(3).
2. D. Barbará and H. Garcia-Molina. The demarcation protocol: A technique for maintaining arithmetic constraints in distributed database systems. In *Proc. 3rd International Conference on Extending Data Base Technology, EDBT92*, pages 373–388. Springer-Verlag, 1992.
3. A. Brodsky, L. Kerscberg, and S. Varas. On optimal constraint management in distributed databases. Technical report, George Mason University, 1998.
4. J.B.J. Fourier. *Reported in: Analyse de travaux de l'Academie Royale des Sciences, pendant l'annee 1824, Partie Mathematique, Historyde l'Academie Royale de Sciences de l'Institue de France 7 (1827) xlvii-lv. (Partial English translation in: D.A. Kohler, Translation of a Report by Fourier on his work on Linear Inequalities. Opsearch 10 (1973) 38-42.).* 1824.
5. T. Huynh, L. Joskowicz, C. Lassez, and J.L. Lassez. Practical tools for reasoning about linear constraints. *Fundamenta Informaticae, Special issue on Logic and Artificial Intelligence*, 15(4):357–379, 1991.
6. S. Jajodia and L. Kerschberg. *Advanced Transaction Models and Architectures*. Norwall, MA, Kluwer Academic Publishers, first edition, 1997.
7. L. Kerschberg. Knowledge rovers: Cooperative intelligent agent support for enterprise information architectures. In Kandzia and Klusch, editors, *Cooperative Information Agents*, volume 1202 of *Lecture Notes in Computer Science*, pages 79–100, Berlin, 1997. Springer-Verlag.
8. L. Kerschberg. The role of intelligent agents in advanced information systems. In Small, Douglas, Johnson, King, and Martin, editors, *Advances in Databases*, volume 1271 of *Lecture Notes in Computer Science*, pages 1–22. Springer-Verlag, 1997.
9. J-L. Lassez. Querying constraints. In *Proc. 9th ACM SIGACT-SIGMOD-SIGART Symp. on Principles of Database Systems*, 1990.
10. Jean-Louis Lassez and Michael Maher. On Fourier's algorithm for linear arithmetic constraints. *Journal of Automated Reasoning*, 9:373–379, 1992.
11. S. Mazumdar and Z. Yuan. Localizing global constraints: A geometric approach. In *In Proceedings of the 9th International Conference on Computing and Information. ICCI'98*, 1998.
12. N. Soparkar and A. Silberschatz. Data-value partitioning and virtual messages. In ACM, editor, *Proc. 9th ACM SIGACT-SIGMOD-SIGART Simposium on Principles of Database Systems*, Nashville, Tennessee, 1990.
13. S. Varas. *On Optimal Constraint Decomposition, Monitoring, and Management in Distributed Environments*. PhD thesis, George Mason University, 1998.

A Multi-agent Architecture for an Intelligent Website in Insurance

Catholijn M. Jonker[1], Remco A. Lam[1,2], and Jan Treur[1]

[1] Vrije Universiteit Amsterdam, Department of Artificial Intelligence
De Boelelaan 1081a, 1081 HV Amsterdam, The Netherlands
URL:http://www.cs.vu.nl/~{jonker,treur}. Email: {jonker,treur}@cs.vu.nl

[2] Ordina Utopics BV, Leusden, The Netherlands

Abstract. In this paper a multi-agent architecture for intelligent Websites is presented and applied in insurance. The architecture has been designed and implemented using the compositional development method for multi-agent systems DESIRE. The agents within this architecture are based on a generic broker agent model. It is shown how it can be exploited to design an intelligent Website for insurance, developed in co-operation with the software company Ordina Utopics and an insurance company.

1 Introduction

An analysis of most current business Websites from the perspectives of marketing and customer relations suggests that Websites should become more active and personalised, just as in the nonvirtual case where contacts are based on human servants. Intelligent agents provide the possibility to reflect at least a number of aspects of the nonvirtual situation in a simulated form, and, in addition, enables to use new opportunities for one-to-one marketing, integrated in the Website. The generic agent-based architecture for intelligent Websites presented in this paper offers these possibilities. It is shown how the architecture has been applied in a project on intelligent Websites in co-operation with an insurance company. The test bed chosen for this project was information and documents that need to be exchanged between insurance agents and the insurance company main office. The goal of the intelligent Website is to provide insurance agents with an accurate account of all available documents and information regarding a specific topic. The supporting software agents are able to provide a match (either strict or soft) between demand and available information. They also support pro-active information provision, based on profiles of the insurance agents that are dynamically constructed.

In Section 2 the insurance application domain is introduced. In Section 3 the global design of an intelligent Website is presented; the different types of agents participating in the Website are distinguished. In Section 4 the generic broker agent architecture is described and applied to obtain the internal structure of the agents involved in the Website. In Section 5 the application of the architecture to insurance is discussed in more detail and illustrated by some example behaviour patterns.

2 Application Domain: Insurance

One of the largest insurance companies in the Netherlands works solely on the basis of (human) insurance agents. To better support these agents a Website was created with information about products offered by the firm, forms to support administrative actions and other related information. The site's aim is to support the insurance agent with their work. To do this a simple setup has been chosen. The Website is structured around four main sections: Store, Desk, Newsstand and Office.

The *store* is the place to go if you want more information about the insurance products offered. The various insurance policies can be found under this heading. Also, request forms for more information, brochures and personalized proposals can be found in this section. From the store a couple of useful programs can be downloaded as well: spreadsheets, an anti-virus toolkit and an insurance dictionary.

When the insurance agent is stuck with a problem, he or she can turn to the *desk* section with questions. Apart from a Frequently Asked Questions page also a form for specific questions the agent might have, is available. In this Website section the editorials can be found that address in depth a certain problem an insurance agent might have. Finally, an address book is available, in which the various departments and teams operating within the company can be found.

At the *newsstand* the visitors of the site can find the latest information. Newsletters can be found. A calendar can be checked for upcoming events and various links to other interesting sites are offered here. Whenever new interesting sites are added, the visitor can be notified of this be email, if he or she wants this. Also an assorted amount of articles is available.

At the *office*, the sale of insurance products is supported. Here resources to improve the insurance agent's job can be found, like telemarketing scripts, newsletter articles, advertisements that only need further filling out and sales letters. Also, the agent can find its personal production figures for the firm's products.

All this makes the Website a collection of variable information sources. Images, programs, documents, addresses, phonebooks and personal data make it span almost all possible information types. Apart from it having so many different types of information, new information is being added daily. Keeping uptodate with the latest relevant information, can take time with so many different types of information and daily updates. To help the insurance agent managing this the supporting multi agent system was developed to keep the agent uptodate on the latest interesting information.

The aim is that the multi agent system integrated in the Website improves the use of the resources such a Website offers. From the visitors point of view, more interesting information can be found, even things the visitor did not think of before. The agent, with its intimate knowledge of who the user is and what he wants can shorten the time needed for visiting the website. Application forms can be offered, already (partially) filled out by the agent. The maintainers can use information collected through the multi agent system to develop a more direct form of marketing. Without much research the appropriate visitor can be contacted about new products or offers that are interesting to him or her. Visitor information can be used to find out what a visitor is interested in and so a personalised product offer could be offered.

3   A Multi-agent Architecture for Intelligent Websites

In this section a global multi-agent architecture, that can be used as a basis for an intelligent Website, is introduced. First, in Section 3.1 the top level process composition of the multi-agent system is presented. In Section 3.2 for each of the two types of agents in the multi-agent architecture, basic (external) agent characteristics and behaviours are identified and requirements are expressed. After this global view, in Section 4 the internal structure of the agents is discussed. Although the architecture is generic, for reasons of presentation some of its aspects will be illustrated in the context of the insurance application.

3.1   The Overall Architecture

The domain has been identified as a multi-agent domain. Therefore, it makes sense to start with the agents as the highest process abstraction level within the system. Four classes of agents are distinguished at the level of the multi-agent system: *customers* (human agents), *Personal Assistant agents* (software agents), *Website Agents* (software agents), *employees* (human agents); see Fig. 1. The shaded area at the right hand side shows the agents related to the Website; the shaded area at the left hand side shows the two agents at one of the customer sites. In this figure, for shortness only two Website Agents, one employee, one Personal Assistant agent and one customer (user of the Personal Assistant) are depicted. In the application to insurance, the Website Agents are one-to-one related to the departments within the (insurance) company responsible for distinguished parts of the Website.

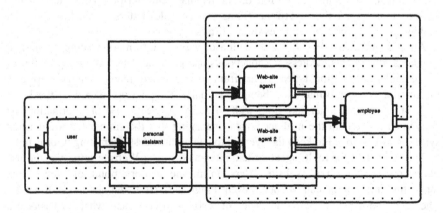

Fig. 1. The overall multi-agent architecture

Note that the Personal Assistant is involved as a mediating agent in all communication between its own user and all Website Agents. From the user it can receive information about his or her interests and profile, and it can provide him or her with information assumed interesting. Moreover, it can receive information from any of the Website Agents, and it can ask them for specific information. The Website Agents communicate not only with all Personal Assistants, but also with each other and with employees. The customer only communicates with his or her own Personal Assistant. This agent serves as an interface agent for the customer. If a customer visits the Website for the first time this Personal Assistant agent is instantiated and offered to the customer (during all visits).

3.2 The Software Agents

In this section the agents are considered from outside only. Which structures are inside remains hidden; the internal structure will be presented in Section 4. The following external agent concepts to define interaction characteristics are used:
- *interaction with the world* (observation, action performance)
- *communication with other agents*

For the Website agents the interaction characteristics are:
Observation
- its own part of the Website
- presence and behaviour of customers visiting the Website

Performing actions
- making modifications in the Website
- showing Web-pages to a customer and PA

Communication with other agents
- from PA: requests for information, customer profile information, customer privacy constraints
- from other WA: info on scopes, customer info

For the Personal Assistants the interaction characteristics are:
Observation
- notice changes and offers at the Website
- look at the Website for items within the customer's needs

Communication with other agents
- from WA: info on available information, offers
- from Customer: customer needs and preferences, privacy constraints
- to WA: customer needs, profile information
- to Customer: info on available information

4   The Internal Design of the Software Agents

The agents in the application have been designed on the basis of a generic model of a broker agent. The process of brokering involves a number of activities. For example, responding to customer requests for objects (the word *object* will be used to indicate either a product or an information object such as a text or a form) with certain properties, maintaining information on customers, building customer profiles on the basis of such customer information, maintaining information on products, maintaining provider profiles, matching customer requests and product information (in a strict or soft manner), searching for information on the WWW, and responding to new offers of products by informing customers for whom these offers fit their profile. In this section a generic broker agent architecture is presented that supports such activities. This generic model has been used as a basis for both the Website Agents and the Personal Assistant agents introduced in Section 3.

4.1   A Generic Broker Agent Architecture

For the design of the generic broker agent the following main aspects are considered: process composition, knowledge composition, and relations between knowledge and process composition. A compositional generic agent model (introduced in [2]), supporting the weak agency notion (cf. [11]) is used. At the highest abstraction level within an agent, a number of processes can be distinguished that support interaction with the other agents. First, a process that manages communication with other agents, modelled by the component agent interaction management in Fig. 2.

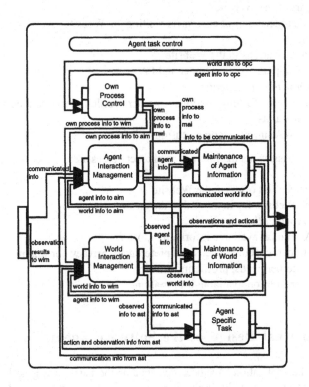

Fig. 2. Composition at the highest level within the broker agent

This component analyses incoming information and determines which other processes within the agent need the communicated information. Moreover, outgoing communication is prepared. Next, the agent needs to maintain information on the other agents with which it co-operates: maintenance of agent information. The component maintenance of world information is included to store the world information (e.g., information on attributes of objects). The process own process control defines different characteristics of the agent and determines foci for behaviour. The component world interaction management is included to model interaction with the world (with the World Wide Web world, in the example application): initiating observations and receiving observation results.

The agent processes discussed above are generic agent processes. Many agents perform these processes. In addition, often agent-specific processes are needed: to perform tasks specific to one agent, for example directly related to a specific domain of application. The broker agent may have to determine proposals for other agents. In this process, information on available objects (communicated by information providing agents and kept in the component maintenance of world information), and about the scopes of interests of agents (kept in the component maintenance of agent information), is combined to determine which agents might be interested in which objects. Fig. 2 depicts how the broker agent is composed of its components.

Part of the exchange of information within the generic broker agent model can be described as follows. The broker agent needs input about scopes of interests put forward by agents and information about attributes of available objects that are communicated by information providing agents. It produces output for other agents about proposed objects and the attributes of these objects. Moreover, it produces output for information providers about interests. For more details; see [5].

4.2 Internal Design of a Website Agent and Personal Assistant

The broker agent architecture provides an appropriate means to establish the internal design of the two types of agents involved. In this section four of the components of a Website Agent are briefly discussed. For a Website Agent, the internal storage and updating of information on the world and on other agents (the beliefs of the agent) is performed by the two components maintenance of world information and maintenance of agent information. Profile information on customers is obtained from Personal Assistants, and maintained with the customer's permission. Also identified behaviour instances of the Personal Assistants can give input to the profile. Maintenance of world information includes: info on available information. Maintenance of agent information includes: info on customer profiles, customer privacy constraints, other WA's scopes. Within the agent specific task component matching techniques are employed to relate demands and offers.

For the Personal Assistant, as for the Website Agent, the internal storage and updating of information on the world and on other agents is performed by the two components maintenance of world information and maintenance of agent information. Maintenance of world information includes information on available information. Maintenance of agent information includes: customer needs and profile, customer privacy constraints, WAs scopes

5 The Multi-agent System's Behaviour

The multi-agent system's behaviour will be explained for two cases: behaviour initiated by an information request of a user (user initiated), and behaviour initiated by update or addition of information to the Website (Website initiated). In both cases, after initiation a reactivity chain is trigered. In the first case the main reactivity chain follows the path user-PA-WA-PA-user; the first half of this path deals with the queries, and the second half (back) with answers on these queries. In the second case the main reactivity chain follows the path WA-PA-user-PA-WA; here the first half deals with volunteerly offered information (one-to-one marketing), and the second half (back) with feedback on usefulness of the offered information (in order to update profile information).

5.1 Information Used in the System

This system is a prototype, as such it does not work with the actual information on the Website. Instead a sample of the information objects on the Website was taken and a description of each of these was made.

Fig. 3. User interface for asking questions and stating user interest

In deliberation with people from the insurance company the following attributes were selected to describe the information:
- **Title:** The title of the information object.
- **Author:** The department or person that created the information object.
- **Subject:** Subject of the information object.

- **First Relation:** The first related subject.
- **Second Relation:** The second related subject.
- **Date:** Date of creation/availability.
- **Language:** What language the information is in.
- **Persistency:** An indication of how soon the information will be outdated.
- **Kind:** The form which the information object takes (mailform, text, audio, etc.).
- **Type:** The type of of information the information object contains (FAQ, newsletter, personal information, etc.).
- **URL:** The hyperlink to where the actual information object can be found

5.2   Behaviour Initiated by a User

When a user asks a question, several things happen simultaneously in the Personal Assistant agent. The question is analysed to find similarities to previous questions and if these exist, new interests are created. Also, the agent tries to respond to the information request by finding information available within the PA itself and by contacting the appropriate Website Agents. To keep things clear, first it is described how an answer to a question is found. Next, the process of updating the user profile is discussed.

Handling a question. First the behaviour as it appears to the user is described after which a more detailed description is given of what happens within the multi agent system itself.

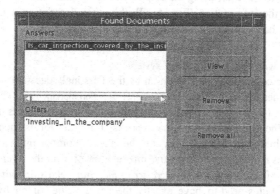

Fig. 4. Display for the answers to questions and offers made by a PA

The user interaction
A user wants information about car insurance. So the user communicates this question to the personal assistant using the interface (Fig. 3). The user selects the subject 'car insurance' in the scrollable list under the heading 'Subjects' and presses the button 'Question'. The Personal Assistant will start to acquire useful information on behalf of its user.

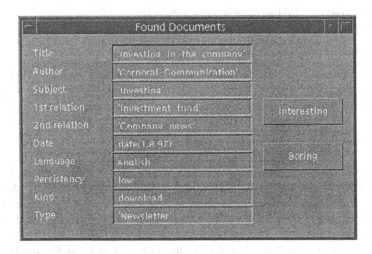

Fig. 5. Details of the information found

First it looks into all the information it has already gathered and then it will contact appropriate Website Agents for more information. All the gathered information is then communicated to the user, using the display in Fig. 4. Each title is clickable to get a description of the information (Fig. 5). Within this description a user can indicate whether or not he or she evaluates the information as interesting.

The processes within the multi-agent system
When the user communicates a question to the Personal Assistant agent, this agent analyses this question in the component agent interaction management. The question itself is then related to the task specific component determine proposals in the Personal Assistant. In the component determine proposals this question is then matched to the information objects in the memory of the agent (component maintenance of world information). It is matched against all the information objects the agent has knowledge of. Two types of matching are covered: *strict matching* and *soft matching*. For strict matching, attributes need to have exactly the same value, or an overlapping value range. For soft matching, it can be specified when values of attributes are considered close (but not necessarily equal) to each other. This closeness relation may be based on various techniques. In the current prototype the closeness relation for the subject attribute is taken as a point of departure, abstracting from the manner in which it is determined (it is assumed to be specified in any manner). One of the matching rules is:

```
if        query(Q:QUERY_ID, scope(subject, S:SUBJECT))
  and     object_scope(O:OBJECT_ID, scope(related_subject, S:SUBJECT))
  then    possible_answer_to_query(O:OBJECT_ID, Q:QUERY_ID);
```

Subject is being matched with the related subject. If this rule succeeds, the object is selected as a possible answer. For this possible answer to become a definite answer, the object must not differ on another attribute; see the following rule:

```
if            query(Q:QUERY_ID, scope(A:ATTRIBUTE, V1:VALUE))
and           object_scope(O:OBJECT_ID,scope(A:ATTRIBUTE, V2:VALUE))
and           not A:ATTRIBUTE = subject
and           not V1:VALUE = V2:VALUE
then          rejected_answer_for_query(O:OBJECT_ID, Q:QUERY_ID);
```

Then with the following rule the final answer to the question is derived:

```
if            possible_answer_to_query(O:OBJECT_ID, Q:QUERY_ID)
and           not rejected_answer_for_query(O:OBJECT_ID, Q:QUERY_ID)
then          selected_answer_to_query(O:OBJECT_ID, Q:QUERY_ID);
```

Simultaneously, in the same component, the Website Agents the Personal Assistant is aware of are considered for further information. This is done in three steps. First, the Personal Assistant agent looks for a Website Agent that is known to provide information about the same subject (part of the Personal Assistant's agent model for the Website Agent, expressed in webagent_subject(W:WA, S:SUBJECT) within component maintenance of agent information) as the subject to which the question refers:

```
if            query(Q:QUERY_ID, scope(subject, S:SUBJECT))
and           webagent_subject(W:WA, S:SUBJECT)
then          main_wa_for_answer(W:WA, Q:QUERY_ID)
and           found_wa_for_query(Q:QUERY_ID);
```

This rule will not succeed however when the question does not contain a subject term or when no appropriate Website Agent subjects are known. Then the Personal Assistant agent can fall back to a second method of finding an appropriate Website Agent, by considering another part of its agent models of Website Agents:

```
if            query(Q:QUERY_ID, S:SCOPE)
and           can_provide_scope(W:WA, S:SCOPE)
then          secondary_wa_for_answer(W:WA, Q:QUERY_ID)
and           found_wa_for_query(Q:QUERY_ID);
```

Finally as a fail-safe, each personal assistant has a default Website Agent it can contact when it does not know whom to turn to. This default WA is stored in the component own process control and is for this purpose also available in the component determine proposals. The final selection of the WA to contact is done by the following three rules:

```
if            main_wa_for_answer(W:WA, Q:QUERY_ID)
then          selected_wa_for_answer(W:WA, Q:QUERY_ID);

if            secondary_wa_for_answer(W:WA, Q:QUERY_ID)
then          selected_wa_for_answer(W:WA, Q:QUERY_ID);

if            not found_wa_for_query(Q:QUERY_ID)
and           default_wa(W:WA)
then          selected_W:WA_for_answer(W:WA, Q:QUERY_ID);
```

Now the selected_wa_for_answer terms and the selected_object_for_query terms are transferred to the component agent interaction management where communication is initiated to the selected Website Agent(s).

A Website Agent receives the question and handles it in the same way the Personal Assistant handled it. The component determine proposals tries to find a match with the known information objects. The matches it comes up with are then communicated back to the Personal Assistant. By the component agent interaction management of the PA the received answer is then passed on to its user.

```
if        communicated_by(query_answer(Q:QUERY_ID, object_scope(O:OBJECT_ID,
          S:SCOPE)), pos, W:WA)
then      to_be_communicated_to(query_answer(Q:QUERY_ID, object_scope(O:OBJECT_ID,
          S:SCOPE)), pos, user);
```

However, the information about the object is also stored by the personal assistant, so that in the future it can supply this information by itself.

Update of user profile. In this prototype focus lay on the agent interaction and document selection. Profile management had a lower priority. Therefor the used mechanisms for profile management are very simple, without extensive research behind them. As stated earlier, the PA compares questions with each other. When similarities are found in enough questions, these similarities are then added as new user interests to the system. This is done in the (composed) component interest creator.

A question is first compared to all other questions. A simple method has been chosen to create these candidates, whenever three different questions match on one or more attribute values, these attribute-value pairs are combined to a candidate interest specification:

```
if        asked(query(Q1:QUERY_ID, scope(A:ATTRIBUTE, V:VALUE)))
and       asked(query(Q2:QUERY_ID, scope(A:ATTRIBUTE, V:VALUE)))
and       asked(query(Q3:QUERY_ID, scope(A:ATTRIBUTE, V:VALUE)))
and       not Q1:QUERY_ID = Q2:QUERY_ID
and       not Q1:QUERY_ID = Q3:QUERY_ID
and       not Q2:QUERY_ID = Q3:QUERY_ID
then      candidate_for_interest(candidate_id(Q1:QUERY_ID, Q2:QUERY_ID,
          Q3:QUERY_ID), scope(A:ATTRIBUTE, V:VALUE));
```

Extra constraints could be added to the creation of these candidates. For example, the questions must be asked within a certain (temporal) distance of each other. The three query id's are combined to create a temporary candidate id. The created candidate is then compared to the already existing interests.

```
if        candidate_for_interest(C:CANDIDATE_ID, scope(A:ATTRIBUTE, V1:VALUE))
and       belief(interest(I:INTEREST_ID, scope(A:ATTRIBUTE, V2:VALUE))
and       not V1:VALUE = V2:VALUE
then      different(C:CANDIDATE_ID, I:INTEREST_ID);
```

Because this component is reasoning about changes in interests, it is at a meta-level compared to the component maintenance of agent information, in which the interests are maintained. So reasoning about interests is done by encapsulating them with the term belief, as was done in the above rule.

```
if      new_interest_id(I:INTEREST_ID)
and     approved_candidate(C:CANDIDATE_ID, S:SCOPE)
then    to_be_created(interest(I:INTEREST_ID, S:SCOPE));
```

If a candidate is not a duplicate of an already existing interest it can be added to the user interests. First a unique interest identifier is created and then the new interest is created in the component maintain agent information by way of an information link.

5.3 Behaviour Initiated by the Website

For a second type of behaviour, iniatied by the Website, also first the behaviour to directly serve the user interaction is discussed, and next the behaviour of to update the user profile is described in more detail.

Offering the user new information. First the behavior as it appears to the user is described after which a more detailed description is given of what happens within the multi agent system itself.

The user interaction
Every once in a while the Personal Assistant will notify its user on its own initiative of interesting information it has found. This is done in the same display where answers to information requests are displayed (see Fig. 4). But now on the bottom half of the screen. Again, the user can click on a title to get more information about the proposal (Fig. 5). As with the responses to an information request, the user can choose to accept the proposed information or to reject it.

The processes within the multi-agent system
When new information becomes available at the Website, the Website Agent starts to look for possible interested parties. Just as the Personal Assistant has built a profile of its user, the Website Agent has built a profile of the Personal Assistants it has been in contact with. In the component determine proposals of the Website Agent this information is matched to the Personal Assistants interests it has collected over time:

```
if      new_object_scope(O:OBJECT_ID, S:SCOPE)
and     interest(P:PA, I:INTEREST_ID, S:SCOPE)
then    partly_matched_new_object(O:OBJECT_ID, P:PA, I:INTEREST_ID);
```

For each scope in the new object a comparison is done against the interests. When they match, the object is partly selected: that specific scope is matched to the interest. However, on another scope, the interest and the new object may differ. Only if none of these differences exist will the object be selected. The offer is then made in the component agent interaction management.

The Personal Assistant receives this offer and compares it to its own user interests, which are specific to the user. This is done in the Personal Assistant's determine proposals, the same way as it is done in the Website Agent:

```
if          offered_object_scope(O:OBJECT_ID, S:SCOPE)
  and       interest(I:INTEREST_ID, S:SCOPE)
  then      partly_matched_offer(O:OBJECT_ID, I:INTEREST_ID);
```

Again, when no conflicting scopes can be found between the interest and the offered object it is selected with the following rule:

```
if          partly_matched_offer(O:OBJECT_ID, I:INTEREST_ID)
  and       not rejected_offer(O:OBJECT_ID, I:INTEREST_ID)
  then      accepted_offer(O:OBJECT_ID, I:INTEREST_ID);
```

The selected offer is then communicated to the user, who can reply to the offer.

Update of user profile. After the user has told the Personal Assistant whether it found the offer interesting or not, a profile update process is initiated: the reply is used to update the user interests, if necessary, by removing those interests repeatingly receiving negative feedback.

This feedback is used in the component interest remover to select interests for removal. As for the creation of new interests, a simple mechanism is used to select interests for removal. A kind of circular list is kept of the last three responses to offers based on an interest. This list only has three objects and when all three objects show a negative response, that interest is marked for removal:

```
if          last3_suggestions_response(last_id1, rejected, I:INTEREST_ID)
  and       last3_suggestions_response(last_id2, rejected, I:INTEREST_ID)
  and       last3_suggestions_response(last_id3, rejected, I:INTEREST_ID)
  then      to_be_confirmed(remove(I:INTEREST_ID))
```

An interest so marked for removal is not automatically removed. For this, the user has to give its approval. When the user disapproves of the removal, the three last responses to that interest are then reset so that again three rejections in a row must be received before the agent considers the interest for removal again. But when the user approves the removal is seen through.

```
if          removal_response(I:INTEREST_ID, confirmed)
  and       believe(interest(I:INTEREST_ID, S:SCOPE))
  then      to_be_removed(interest(I:INTEREST_ID, S:SCOPE));
```

As with the interest creator, this component reasons about changes in interests and is therefore at a meta-level compared to the component maintenance of agent information. The interest is then removed by an information link, similar to how interests are created.

6 Discussion

In this paper a multi-agent architecture for intelligent Websites is presented, based on information broker agents, and its application to an intelligent Website for insurance is described. A Website, supported by this architecture has a more personal look and feel than the usual Websites. Within the architecture, also negotiation facilities (e.g., as in [11]) can be incorporated. Applications of broker agents (addressed in, e.g., [3], [4], [7], [8], [9], [10]), often are not implemented in a principled manner: without an explicit design at a conceptual level, and without support maintenance. The generic broker agent architecture used here was designed and implemented in a principled manner, using the compositional development method for multi-agent systems DESIRE [1]. Due to its compositional structure it supports reuse and maintenance; a flexible, easily adaptable architecture results. Moreover, within the broker agent model facilities can be integrated that provide automated support of the agent's own maintenance [5]. In [6] a compositional verification method for multi-agent systems has been introduced. Using this approach, the multi-agent architecture introduced here can be verified: the required properties on the system, the agents, and their internal components can be expressed using a temporal language, and logical relationships between these properties can be proven. For the particular application in insurance the generic broker agent model has been instantiated with domain ontologies and domain knowledge. In the prototype some of these instantiations have been done in an ad hoc manner, without the intention to propose these instantiations as a generic approach for more domains. Actually, current research addresses more principled manners to use dynamic taxonomies in profile creation and techniques from inductive logic programming to induce profiles from examples.

Acknowledgements

Pascal van Eck (Vrije Universiteit) supported other experiments with some variants of the broker agent model. The authors are also grateful for discussions with employees of Ordina Utopics (in particular, Richard Schut) and an (anonymous) insurance company.

References

1. Brazier, F.M.T., Dunin-Keplicz, B., Jennings, N.R., Treur, J., Formal specification of Multi-Agent Systems: a real-world case. In: V. Lesser (ed.), Proceedings of the First International Conference on Multi-Agent Systems, ICMAS'95, MIT Press, Cambridge, MA, 1995, pp. 25-32. Extended version in: International Journal of Cooperative Information Systems, M. Huhns, M. Singh, (eds.), special issue on Formal Methods in Cooperative Information Systems: Multi-Agent Systems, vol. 6, 1997, pp. 67-94.

2. Brazier, F.M.T., Jonker, C.M., Treur, J., Compositional Design and Reuse of a Generic Agent Model. In: Applied AI Journal. In press, 1999.

3. Chavez, A., Maes, P., Kasbah: An Agent Marketplace for Buying and Selling goods. In: Proceedings of the First International Conference on the Practical Application of Intelligent Agents and Multi-Agent Technology, PAAM'96, The Practical Application Company Ltd, Blackpool, 1996, pp. 75-90.

4. Chavez, A., Dreilinger, D., Gutman, R., Maes, P., A Real-Life Experiment in Creating an Agent Market Place. In: Proceedings of the Second International Conference on the Practical Application of Intelligent Agents and Multi-Agent Technology, PAAM'97, The Practical Application Company Ltd, Blackpool, 1997, pp. 159-178.

5. Jonker, C.M., Treur, J., Compositional Design and Maintenance of Broker Agents. Technical Report, Vrije Universiteit Amsterdam, Department of Artificial Intelligence, 1998.

6. Jonker, C.M., Treur, J., Compositional Verification of Multi-Agent Systems: a Formal Analysis of Pro-activeness and Reactiveness. In: W.P. de Roever, H. Langmaack, A. Pnueli (eds.), Proceedings of the International Workshop on Compositionality, COMPOS'97, Lecture Notes in Computer Science, vol. 1536, Springer Verlag, 1998, pp. 31.

7. Kuokka, D., Harada, L., On Using KQML for Matchmaking. In: V. Lesser (ed.), Proceedings of the First International Conference on Multi-Agent Systems, ICMAS'95, MIT Press, Cambridge, MA, 1995, pp. 239-245.

8. Martin, D., Moran, D., Oohama, H., Cheyer, A., Information Brokering in an Agent Architecture. In: Proceedings of the Second International Conference on the Practical Application of Intelligent Agents and Multi-Agent Technology, PAAM'97, The Practical Application Company Ltd, Blackpool, 1997, pp. 467-486.

9. Sandholm, T., Lesser, V., Issues in Automated Negotiation and Electronic Commerce: Extending the Contract Network. In: V. Lesser (ed.), Proceedings of the First International Conference on Multi-Agent Systems, ICMAS'95, MIT Press, Cambridge, MA, 1995, pp. 328-335.

10. Tsvetovatyy, M., Gini, M., Toward a Virtual Marketplace: Architectures and Strategies. In: Proceedings of the First International Conference on the Practical Application of Intelligent Agents and Multi-Agent Technology, PAAM'96, The Practical Application Company Ltd, Blackpool, 1996, pp. 597-613.

11. Wooldridge, M., Jennings, N.R., Agent Theories, Architectures, and Languages: a survey. In: [12], pp. 1-39.

12. Wooldridge, M., Jennings, N.R. (eds.), Intelligent Agents, Proc. of the First International Workshop on Agent Theories, Architectures and Languages, ATAL'94, Lecture Notes in AI, vol. 890, Springer Verlag, 1995.

Formation of Cooperative Behavior among Information Agents in Web Repository Change Monitoring Service

Santi Saeyor Mitsuru Ishizuka

Dept. of Information and Communication Engineering,
Faculty of Engineering,
University of Tokyo,
7-3-1 Hongo, Bunkyo-ku, Tokyo 113-8656, JAPAN
{santi,ishizuka}@miv.t.u-tokyo.ac.jp

Abstract. The Web repositories are exposed in form of a huge amount of heterogeneous information sources. The information is overwhelming the users. Besides the target information itself, the changes upon the previously released information are significant and worth being notified to those who perceived the out of date information as soon as possible. The changes made in Web repositories occur at unpredictable rates. Unfortunately, stock type information source has no means to inform its prospective users about the changes. While the stock type information source occupies a large percentage of sources on the Web, it is necessary to have a system that monitors changes on the Web, and provides comprehensive presentation to the prospective users. In this paper, we proposes a mechanism that provides change monitoring and presentation service for a large group of users by coalition among service agents. The service agents keep improving the overall utilization factor by several schemes based on the decision made by game analysis. We apply a cost model to the service mechanism in order to study the cooperative behavior of the service agents. The reduction of cost is designed to comply with the level of cooperation among service agents. This paper presents a paradigm for the service and the formation of cooperative behavior of the agents in the community.

1 Introduction

Browsing through the sites for new updates is not only time consuming task but also vain in case that there is no change made on the sites once visited. This puts a significant load to the users besides exploring brand new information. We need some representatives to do such burdensome and tedious jobs for us.

This paper presents the evolution of mechanism that detects and evaluates changes on the Web, provides it in comprehensive form, and push the information to prospective users. The mechanism is evolved on multi-user basis. This paper proposes the coalition among service agents in order to maintain the performance both in the benefit of users and resource usage of the system. With this system, the ubiquitous stock type information sources on the Web have no need to provide any effort to convey their updates to the users.

We incorporate shared resource management in our system in order to enable the framework a larger scale of service. The service agents attempt to increase the utilization factor of the overall system by several schemes. Each scheme tries to increase identical services in the monitoring service. These identical or virtually identical requests give a significant impact on the utilization of our service. As long as we can implement the service with reasonable resource allocation, more users can have access to the service. A useful tool for decision making we use here is the game theory. We use the basics of game theory in several decision making situations during matchmaking process in resource management issue.

2   Distributed change monitoring

The architecture of a unit of change monitoring service is shown in Fig.1. The service is provided openly on the Web. Each user accesses the service via the Internet using any browser with Java Virtual Machine. Requests can be made directly to the *Service Agent* which is the front end of the service. The functions

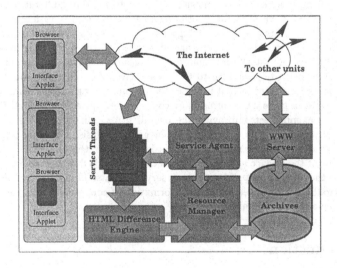

Fig. 1. *Each unit of monitoring service agent.*

of main modules can be listed as follows:

– **Resource Manager:** All resources for the service are handled by this module. The results from the HTML Difference Engine will be kept in the archives by Resource Manager.

- **Service Threads**: Each Web page monitoring request will be handled by a service thread. The thread keep monitoring and comparing revisions of the Web page.
- **Service Agent**: This is the heart of the service that interacts with users and other modules in order to retrieve and compare Web pages.
- **HTML Difference Engine**: The service threads implement the Difference Engine in order to compare the content of updated pages and see whether there are significant changes in them. At the same time, it will summarize the updated information into another HTML document by an innovative algorithm described in [1].
- **WWW server**: The page archives contain the old and new version of Web pages together with summary pages. When the users are notified by the Service Agent, they can view the summary pages with their browsers via the WWW server.

The system is composed of a number of service agents distributed on the Internet as shown in Fig. 2. Each Service Agent announces the local service to the Matchmaking Agent in order that the identical or virtually identical requests can be relayed to the previously allocated services. The requests are served at

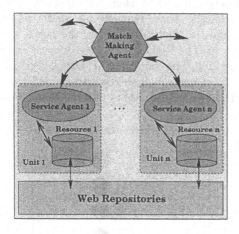

Fig. 2. *A number of service agents announce services to the Matchmaking Agent.*

arbitrary sites as shared services. Fig. 3. shows the life cycle of each service. The cycle begins when a user connects to a front end Service Agent. The requests made by the users are dispatched to appropriate Service Agents distributed in the network. The assigned pages will be monitored and compared to the old revisions by the service threads every period T. The changes will be assigned scores. The score for each kind of change is determined by its significance. This policy is used in order to prevent notification of trivial changes. The agent evaluates

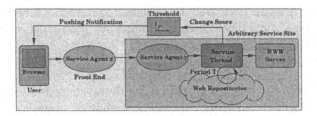

Fig. 3. *Life cycle of each change monitoring service.*

the significance of changes in a document by summing up all scores. The more significant, the more score we assign to the change. If the total score exceeds a specific threshold, the changes are considered significant and will be notified to the users. The services terminate when service termination commands are issued by the users.

3 Resource management

When serving a large number of users, we expect to have some identical or virtually identical requests. These requests can share the same resource. The more identical or virtually identical requests, the better utilization factor we can get from the service. The Resource Manager in each unit deals dynamically with the request matching. The conditions of virtually identical requests change dynamically upon the changes in Web repositories and the parameters of the requests made by the users. In the case of pushing changes and difference infor-

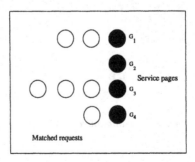

Fig. 4. *Groups of requests with the identical or virtually identical requests.*

mation, we push the information to prospective users. This implies that each user has different degree of interest and attitude against the detected changes. Fig. 4. shows that among different service pages, there are some identical requests. We can express the utilization of resource as following equations.

$$N = \sum_{i=1}^{M} G_i \qquad (1)$$

$$M = P_{diff} N \qquad (2)$$

$$\psi = \frac{N - M}{M} = \frac{1 - P_{diff}}{P_{diff}} \qquad (3)$$

where:
N = number of all request
M = number of different kinds of requests
G_i = number of matched requests for i^{th} group
P_{diff} = Probability of having different kinds of requests
ψ = Utilization factor

We can see obviously that if we share resource among users, we are likely to get more profit than serving each user separately. The utilization factor, finally, depends on the P_{diff} which ranges from $\frac{1}{N}$ to 1. The range tells us that our utilization factor ranges from 0 to $N - 1$.

The amount of identical or virtually identical requests can vary dynamically. This is the case when some requests among currently identical requests are satisfied by the changed conditions but some are not. For examples, we decide to push changes information to the user if we found that the change score is higher than specific threshold points. Suppose we have 2 users who specified the score thresholds for an identical page at 1500 and 1000 points. Both requests are considered identical if the change score is 2000 points. However, if the change score falls between 1000 and 1500 points, the requests are no longer identical. The Resource Manager analyzes the characteristic of changes on Web pages. A

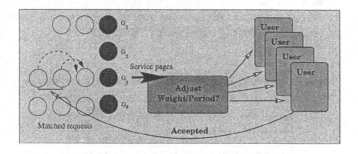

Fig. 5. *Increasing request hit rate by asking users to modify appropriate parameters.*

parameter to check is the notification threshold. In some cases, some users specified high thresholds with high frequency of monitoring. If the Resource Manager found that the change rates of those pages are relatively slow, it may ask the users to adjust threshold weight of notification or monitoring frequency. Adjusting these parameters has probability to increase more matched requests as shown in Fig. 5.

Meanwhile, the Resource Manager detects hot requests shared by a large number of users. The hot requests trend to be interesting pages. The Resource Manager may recommend these requests to the users recorded in the Matchmaking Agent as shown in Fig. 6. If some users accept the recommendation, the

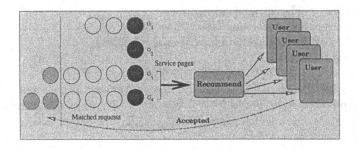

Fig. 6. *Increasing identical or virtually identical requests by recommending hot requests to the users.*

utility factor of the service trends to be increased according to the increasing matched requests. However, the Resource Manager has to make decision based on facts and experience in the past whether it should ask the users to adjust some parameters or recommend some hot requests to the users. The Resource Manager makes a decision by investigating the probability of improvement from the payoff matrix of the game. We consider how to make decision based on our service games from the following expected payoff matrix.

Table 1. Expected payoff matrix for the games of the service.

			User	
			No Adj.	Adjust
		No Adj.	$< p_0, q_0 >$	$< p_1, q_1 >$
Service Agent		Adjust	$< p_2, q_2 >$	$< p_3, q_3 >$

The Payoff $< x_1, x_2 >$ indicates that the Service Agent has an expected payoff of x_1 (where an improvement is worth 1, and no improvement is worth 0 for the Service Agent) and the user has an expected payoff of x_2. In the case of our service $x_1 + x_2$ must be 1.

We define the utility as:
$$utility(ServiceAgent, 1) \longleftarrow improvement$$
$$utility(ServiceAgent, 0) \longleftarrow \neg improvement$$
$$utility(User, 1) \longleftarrow improvement$$
$$utility(User, 0) \longleftarrow \neg improvement$$

Improvement occurs when:

$improvement \longleftarrow ServiceAgent(D) \wedge User(D) \wedge improve\_if\_follow(D)$

$improvement \longleftarrow ServiceAgent(Adj.) \wedge User(NoAdj.) \wedge improve\_if\_sa\_un$

$improvement \longleftarrow ServiceAgent(NoAdj.) \wedge User(Adj.) \wedge improve\_if\_sn\_ua$

Right here, the $improve\_if\_follow(D)$ is the p_0 or p_3 depends on the instruction of the Service Agent, the $improve\_if\_sa\_un$ is the p_2 and the $improve\_if\_sn\_ua$ is the p_1. Suppose that the Service Agent is to choose a strategy with $p_a = P_{ServiceAgent}(Adjust)$ and the user is to choose a strategy with $p_u = P_{User}(Adjust)$. In this setup, the probability of having improvement $P(improve)$ is defined by

$$P(improve) = p_a p_u p_3 + (1 - p_a)(1 - p_u)p_0 + (1 - p_a)p_u p_1 + p_a(1 - p_u)p_2 \quad (4)$$

In a randomized equilibrium from the Service Agent view, the payoff for $Adjust$ and $NoAdjustment$ must be equal. The payoff for asking for adjustment is the above formula with $p_a = 1$, the payoff for asking no adjustment is the formula with $p_a = 0$. These are equal, so we have

$$(1 - p_u)p_0 + p_u p_1 = p_u p_3 + (1 - p_u)p_2 \quad (5)$$

Similarly for the user

$$(1 - p_a)p_0 + p_a p_2 = p_a p_3 + (1 - p_a)p_1 \quad (6)$$

Solve for p_u and p_a we derive

$$p_u = \frac{p_2 - p_0}{p_1 + p_2 - p_0 - p_3} \quad (7)$$

and

$$p_a = \frac{p_1 - p_0}{p_1 + p_2 - p_0 - p_3} \quad (8)$$

Substitute in equation (4), we derive

$$P(improve) = \frac{p_1 p_2 - p_0 p_3}{p_1 + p_2 - p_0 - p_3} \quad (9)$$

The service agent checks whether the $P(improve)$ is above 0.5 which means the system has probability to improve the service more than 0.5, if it asks the user for adjustment. In our service, the probability p_3 can be derived by a function that evaluates how significant a request for adjustment is. The probability p_2 comes from the experience in the past which is, in other words, how much the user refuses the suggestion. The probability p_1 comes from the improvement made when the user adjusts the service profile without suggestion from the

Service Agent. Finally, the probability p_0 comes from the self-improvement rate occurred as the conditions of changes in Web repositories vary in time domain. We can see obviously that the variables used in the game analysis above can be evaluated at ease from the statistic of the service. The Service Agent can make decision to deal or not to deal with the user by calculating the P(improve) based on transactions in the past. Moreover, each decision trends to be more exact as the experience of the Service Agent increases.

4 Matchmaking among service agents

Besides the self-organization in each service unit, the distributed service units work in coordination with the Matchmaking Agent as shown previously in Fig. 2. The coalition among Service Agents is made possible by the Matchmaking Agent. The agent has 3 main functions as follows:

1. **Request matching**: The agent tries to match nearly identical requests and dispatches them to appropriate Service Agent in the community.
2. **Issuing suggestions to users and Service Agents**: The agent has opportunity to evaluate the resource sharing efficiency because it holds the service profiles of the Service Agents in the community. It tries to adjust the load balancing and utilization factor of the overall system. The utilization factor can be improved if the agent can find new users who request nearly identical requests to the existing ones. The Matchmaking Agent also implements the same game analysis policy described in previous section to issue suggestions to the users.
3. **Providing information of services on demand**: Service Agents in the community may query the service profiles from the Matchmaking Agent. There are necessary when a Service Agent deals with the users according to the access behavior of others.

The Matchmaking Agent cooperates with the Service Agents in the community by interpretation of incoming request objects as follows:

4.1 Request Object

The request object is a common template for requests posted to the Matchmaking Agent. A request object consists of requested function, input, output, owner, and time stamp. The functions currently implemented are listed as follows:

- **Declaration of service profiles**: In order to made the existing requests available to other service units, the Service Agent declares its service profiles to the Matchmaking Agent.
- **Load request**: When the Resource Manager considers that the load in the unit is still low compared to the available resources, it may give charity to the community by issuing a load request to the Matchmaking Agent. The constraint of the request object indicates the acceptable number of

Request Object:

Function:	*Request_function*
Input:	*Description, Constraint* *Input_obj*
Output:	*Description, Constraint* *Output_obj*
Owner:	*Service_Agent*
Time:	*Issued_time*

Fig. 7. *The template of a request object.*

requests. The agent assigns requests to the service unit if available. The Matchmaking Agent returns the request object that the output was assigned a set of requests back to the service unit.

- **Load distribution request**: In some cases such as a service unit becomes overloaded or needs to be temporarily closed, the service unit has to distribute its services to others. It issues one or more request objects to the Matchmaking Agent in order to distribute the requests to available service units.

- **Effectively identical requests matching**: When a user request a service, the Service Agent in charged consults with the Resource Manager in the unit about an effectively identical request. In the case of no effectively identical request available, the Service Agent sends this request object to be served by the Matchmaking agent. In the worst case, there is no effectively identical request in the community, the Matchmaking Agent relays the request to an appropriate service unit. This can be both the service unit that issued a load request or the site which the Matchmaking Agent considers that the load is still low. However, the elected service unit has right to refuse the request base upon constraint on the location. If the request is not accepted by any service site, the in charged Service Agent takes the request into its own service unit.

4.2 Matching process

The Matchmaking Agent performs the request matching of incoming request objects. The agent investigates the function of each request and processes the input and output of the request according to the function. The request objects come to the agent in asynchronous fashion. In order to match the requests efficiently, the request objects should be interpreted at different priorities from the highest to the lowest: declaration of service profiles, load request, load distribution request, and request matching respectively.

The Declaration of service profiles should be rendered as fast as possible in order to provide the updated information about available requests. The load request should be rendered before load distribution request in order to register the demands. When the load distribution request or the supplies come to the Match-making Agent, they can be distributed immediately. This comes from the fact that load distribution request has probability to be denied by any limited service units if load request is not available. The lowest priority is the request matching because this operation requires more processing effort and needs information of request with higher priorities.

When effectively identical requests are found, the users who request will be redirected to the service units where the requests are available.

4.3 Decision making in matching process

A cost model is applied to the service mechanism to investigate cooperative behavior of service agents in the community. The invited users under the invitation of preference adjustment requests and the new users gather together to get assigned to appropriate service groups. This implies that they desire to play in an assignment game in order to improve profits. Right in this process, the requests will be clustered into groups of prospectively identical requests. These groups are applied to a cost model for finding acceptable matches. The cost for a service is defined on the concept that the more effectively identical requests, the lower the cost of each service in the identical group. We define C_i, the cost per service for each user in the ith group based on F which is the full cost per user, as follows:

$$C_i = F(1 - k\frac{e^{\frac{g_i}{N}} - 1}{e - 1}) \quad where \ 0 \leq k \leq 1 \tag{10}$$

The cost reduction increases exponentially according to the number of identical requests in the group. This create a persuasion for the users to join a large group even the request for that group is not exactly matched what they want since this can reduce their costs. Another effect of the cost model is that the service costs in the community become lower remarkably as the number of identical requests increases. As a result, the competitiveness of the community becomes higher in case that we consider the service in multiple communities. The above is the evaluation of the value of services on the service provider side. The evaluation of services on the user side can be derived from the evaluation of distance between existing services and the service in need. We define the appreciation value of the jth user against the service of the ith group by u_{ij}. Then, the difference value for the service of group i^{th} viewed by the user j^{th} is $a_{ij} = u_{ij} - C_i$. If we have a set of service groups $G = \{g_1, g_2, ...g_n\}$, and a set of users $H = \{h_1, h_2, ..., h_m\}$, then we can find the maximum profit combination by finding the maximum value of $\sum a_{ij}$ among the combination space of G and H.

5 Related work

From the standpoint of tracking and viewing changes on the Web, the works that are most similar to ours are that of Douglis, et al. [2],[3]. They used the

AT&T Internet Difference Engine to compare revisions of Web pages of some enterprises from time to time. We attempt to improve the service for a larger scale of users. We manage the shared resources among users in order to enable induced push mode of changes and differences. Besides, our difference engine implements the *Longest Common Tag Sequence (LOCTAGS)* algorithm [1], which is capable of comparing context exactly where the revisions should be compared. The results from the HTML Difference Engine are comprehensive change presentation pages which precisely display down to the cell level of structured text. In addition to a target page, we assume that the child pages are likely to have relevant information. Therefore, the service agent can be requested to watch the target down to its child pages. If needed, the agent can also be requested to watch deep down to the grandchild pages. However, the grandchild level is limited to the pages in the same domain of each child page.

The Do-I-Care agent [6] applies social discovery and filtering to inform the users when changes are detected. Moreover, it takes advantage of training the agent by groups of users where some interesting information may be offered to the user via the effort of others. We agree with the idea but we need a simpler way for evaluation of changes. The scoring method we use is straightforward and can be carried out quickly while providing a way for the users to adjust the threshold values upon their experiences [1]. In our system, the social filtering effect occurs when the Resource Manager cooperates with the Service Agent and the Matchmaking Agent in order to find hot requests to recommend to the users.

6 Summary

In this paper, we presented the mechanism of Web repositories change monitoring service that notifies the users about changes in Web repositories and creates comprehensive summary pages of the changes. The improvement of overall utilization factor is derived from the resource management within each service unit and the cooperation among service units. The Matchmaking Agent is the key of coalition. The coalition among service units brings about a broader scope for request matching. Moreover, the Matchmaking Agent has potential to balance the services among service units. At the same time, the mechanism of load transfer based on coalition among the service units strengthen the robustness of the service.

Decision making process of both Matchmaking Agent and Service Agent in each service unit relies on the game analysis. The expected payoff values based on experience in the past have direct impacts to the decision. The users that are engaged to the service assignment game are grouped to appropriate service group based on cost model. The cost model promotes the degree of cooperation by compromising the user needs based upon the maximum profits. As a result, this increases the identical requests dramatically compared to matching only by similarity of incoming requests.

References

1. Santi Saeyor and Mitsuru Ishizuka: WebBeholder: A Revolution in Tracking and Viewing Changes on The Web by Agent Community, in *proceedings of WebNet98, 3rd World Conference on WWW and Internet*, Orlando, Florida, USA, Nov. 1998.
2. Fred Douglis, Thomas Ball, Yih-Farn Chen and Eleftherios Koutsofios: The AT&T Internet Difference Engine: Tracking and viewing changes on the web *World Wide Web* Volume 1 Issue 1, 1998. pp. 27-44
3. Fred Douglis: Experiences with the AT&T Internet Difference Engine 22nd International Conference for the Resource Management & Performance Evaluation of Enterprise Computing System (CMG96), December, 1996.
4. F. Douglis, T. Ball, Y. Chen, E. Koutsofios. Webguide: Querying and Navigating Changes in Web Repositories. In *Proceedings of the Fifth International World Wide Web Conference*, Paris, France, May 1996. pp. 1335-1344.
5. Jeffrey M. Bradshaw: Software Agents AAAI Press/The MIT Press, 1997.
6. Brian Starr, Mark S. Ackerman, Michael Pazzani: Do-I-Care: A Collaborative Web Agent *Proceeding of ACM CHI'96*, April, 1996.
7. Imma Curiel: Cooperative Game Theory and Applications, Kluwer Academic Pubishers, 1997
8. Theo Driessen: Cooperative Games, Solution and Applications, Kluwer Academic Publishers, 1988
9. Aglet-Workbench - Programming Mobile Agents in Java, IBM Tokyo Research Lab.,URL=http://www.trl.ibm.co.jp/aglets/
10. Kazuhiro Minami and Toshihiro Suzuki: JMT (Java-Based Moderator Templates) for Multi-Agent Planning *OOPSLA'97 Workshop*, 1997.

GETESS — Searching the Web Exploiting German Texts[‡]

Steffen Staab[1], Christian Braun[2], Ilvio Bruder[3], Antje Düsterhöft[4], Andreas Heuer[4],
Meike Klettke[4], Günter Neumann[2], Bernd Prager[3], Jan Pretzel[3], Hans-Peter Schnurr[1],
Rudi Studer[1], Hans Uszkoreit[2], and Burkhard Wrenger[3]

[1] AIFB, Univ. Karlsruhe, D-76128 Karlsruhe, Germany
[2] DFKI, Stuhlsatzenhausweg 3, D-66123 Saarbrücken, Germany
[3] GECKO mbH, Koch-Gotha-Str. 1, D-18055 Rostock, Germany
[4] Universität Rostock, Fachbereich Informatik, D-18051 Rostock, Germany
http://www.getess.de

Abstract. We present an intelligent information agent that uses semantic methods and natural language processing capabilites in order to gather tourist information from the WWW and present it to the human user in an intuitive, user-friendly way. Thereby, the information agent is designed such that as background knowledge and linguistic coverage increase, its benefits improve, while it guarantees state-of-the-art information and database retrieval capabilities as its bottom line.

1 Introduction

Due to the vast amounts of information in the WWW, its users have more and more difficulties finding the information they are looking for among the many heterogeneous information resources. Hence, intelligent information agents that support the gathering and exploitation of web site contents are in the primary focus of a number of research communities these days. Currently, syntactic methods of information retrieval prevail in realistic scenarios (cf., e.g., [3]), such as in general search engines like AltaVista, but the limits inherent in these approaches often make finding the proper information a nuisance. On the other end of methodologies, semantic methods could provide just the right level for finding information, but they rely on explicitly annotated sources (cf., e.g., [7]) or on complete and correct natural language understanding systems, both of which cannot be expected in the near future.

Therefore our information assistant, GETESS[1], uses the semantics of documents in the WWW — as far as it is provided explicitly or as it can be inferred by an incomplete natural language understanding system, but relies on syntactic retrieval methods, once the methods at the semantic level fail to fulfill their task. In particular, we consider an information finding approach that, *(i)*, has semantic knowledge for supporting the retrieval task, *(ii)*, partially, but robustly, understands natural language, *(iii)*, allows for advanced ways of interaction that appear natural to the human user, *(iv)*, integrates

---

[‡] Corresponding author: S. Staab, e-mail: staab@aifb.uni-karlsruhe.de,
tel.: +49-721-6087363, fax: +49-721-693717
[1] GErman Text Exploitation and Search System

knowledge from unstructured and semi-structured documents with knowledge from relational database systems, and, *(v)*, reasons about this knowledge in order to support the user dialogue and the retrieval of implicit knowledge.

In our project, we decided to aim at an information agent that provides information finding and filtering methods for a restricted domain, *viz.* for prospective tourists that may travel in a certain region and are looking for all kinds of information, such as housing, leisure activities, seesights, etc. The information about all this cannot be found within a narrowly restricted format — neither in a single database nor in a single web site. Rather, the information agent must gather information that is stored in an open and dynamic environment on many different web servers, often in unstructured text, and even in some databases, such as a booking database of a hotel chain. In order to improve on common information retrieval systems, at least part of what is stated in the (HTML) texts must be made available semantically. However, since automatic text understanding is still far from perfect, we pursue a *fail-soft* approach that is based on extracting knowledge from text with a robust parser, but also integrates and falls back onto common information retrieval mechanisms when the more elaborate understanding component fails.

In the following, we first give an example of how GETESS may assist an user in finding tourist information on the web that will be used for the purpose of illustration throughout the rest of this paper. Then, we draft the architecture of GETESS with its overall sharing of the work load. From this outline we will then motivate and describe some key issues of the major subsystems of GETESS.

2 Example Scenario

The GETESS intelligent assistant knows about a multitude of sites offering tourist information on the web. This first contact may be established by different means, such as by manual registration of sites through the information provider or by automatic classification methods that simply have to determine whether a web site offers tourist information. Our current testbed consists of a few hundred text documents which include different types of information that might be of interest to a prospective tourist. Examples are information about the regional administration or about activities in particular places. A typical example scenario that illustrates the range of services we want to offer to an information seeker is given in the following.

First, we have documents like (1a) and (1b) that contain the italicized propositions.

(1) a. *... The island Usedom belongs to Mecklenburg-Vorpommern....*
    b. *... The Usedom music festival is a touristic highlight every summer. ...*

Then, a tourist who is planning to travel the region might look for places and activities and she may pose queries like (2a) to (2c).

(2) a. *cultural events, Mecklenburg-Vorpommern*
    b. *Which cultural events take place in Mecklenburg-Vorpommern?*
    c. *I am searching for cultural events in Mecklenburg-Vorpommern.*

These example queries may differ in their types, but ultimately they are geared toward the same goal, *viz.* the retrieval of cultural events in Mecklenburg-Vorpommern, such as the one in Usedom. The GETESS intelligent assistant must understand this information request, integrate informations from different documents (e.g., it must integrate the propositions from (1a) and (1b) in order to retrieve the Usedom music festival as a correct answer) and present a list of references to the information seeker. The first three of this long list may be given in (3a) to (3c), together with some hints, (4), that may help the user to narrow down the choices she is looking for.

(3) a. *Rostock, Concert series of the Hochschule[2] für Musik und Theater, http://...*
  b. *Usedom music festival, http://...*
  c. *Ralswiek, Störtebecker theater festival, http://...*

(4) You might want to reduce your hit rate by refining your search to MUSIC EVENT, THEATER EVENT, SHOW EVENT, or EDUCATIONAL EVENT.

Then, the dialogue may continue with query (5):

(5) *What type of music is played on Usedom?*

Resulting in answer (6) by GETESS:

(6) The Usedom music festival features classical music.

And the user may proceed with

(7) *Show me folklore music events.*

This may result in

(8) There are no folklore music events known in Mecklenburg-Vorpommern. You might want to check out related categories like
  a. *Folklore dance event: Ribnitz-Damgarten International Folklore dance festival, http://...*

This result here may happily suffice the information seekers request and serve as an ongoing illustration in the further course of this paper.

3 Architecture

The front end of the GETESS agent (cf. a depiction of its main modules in Figure 1) provides a user interface that is embedded in a *dialogue system* controlling the history of interactions (cf. Section 4). Single interactions are handed to the query processor that selects the corresponding analysis methods, *viz.* the natural language processing module (NLP system; also cf. Section 6) or the information retrieval and database query mechanisms (cf. Section 5). While the latter ones can be directly used as input to the *search system*, the natural language processing module first translates the natural language query into a corresponding database query, before it sends this formal query to the search system.

In order to process queries and search for results, three kinds of resources are provided by the back end of the GETESS assistant. First, archived information is available in several content databases (the abstract DB, the index DB and the DB repository), the function of which is explained below. Second, the lexicon and the ontology provide

---

[2] College for music and theatre.

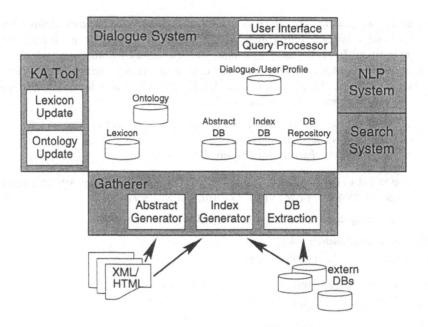

Fig. 1. The architecture of GETESS

metaknowledge about the queries, *viz.* about the grammatical status of words and their conceptual denotations. Third, a database incorporating dialogue sequences and user profiles, gives control over dialogue interactions.

While dialogue sequences and user profiles are acquired during the course of interactions and the metaknowledge is provided by the human modeller with the help of knowledge acquisition tools (*KA Tools*), the content databases must be filled automatically, since the contents of typical web sites change almost on a daily basis. For this task the *gatherer* searches regularly through relevant XML/HTML-pages and databases of specified sites in order to generate corresponding entries in the abstract database, the index database and the database repository.

The content in the abstract database is derived from a robust, though incomplete natural language understanding module that parses documents and extracts semantic information building a so called "*abstract*" for each document. These abstracts are sets of facts, *i.e.* tupels, like hostsEvent(Usedom, music-festival-1), that could be extracted from natural language text, like "The Usedom music festival ..." in example (1b). The index generator builds access information for full text search with information retrieval methods, while the DB repository offers relevant views onto extern databases.

Subsequently, we will first introduce the front end, the dialogue system. The key issues here are concerned with *facilitating* user interaction at different levels of expertise (Section 4). At the back end of the system, the tools for gathering, database management and information retrieval provide the technical platform for efficiently updating and communicating with the agent's information repositories (Section 5). The natural language processing component in GETESS is employed by the dialogue system as well as by the back end in order to understand natural language queries and extract information from natural language texts, respectively, and, thus, *enhance* the quality of the web search (Section 6). Finally, we outline the function of the ontology that constitutes the "glue" of the system at the semantic level (Section 7).

4 Dialogue System

The dialogue system constitutes the interface of the GETESS intelligent assistant. In order to facilitate the user's task of finding the information he is looking for, users should be able to communicate conveniently at their level of expertise. This means the agent should allow for intuitive interaction by natural language queries as well as for formal queries that may be the preferred mode of interaction by a human expert user. Indepent of the concrete mode of interaction, the GETESS assistant should react quickly and accurately while using the capabilities of the different modal actions.

In particular, GETESS provides four types of interaction, *viz.* natural language, graphical interface, keyword search and formal database query. Since the methods for natural language processing as well as for keyword search and formal database queries form major components, their description has been delegated to subsequent sections (6 as well as 5, respectively).

Thus, this chapter serves the following three goals: First, it is described how reasoning about user interactions may support the user's goal in quickly finding the appropriate information. Second, it is sketched how single interactions are treated as elements of a complex dialogue. Hence, the user does not have to start from scratch every time he inititiates a new query, but can instead refer to his previous queries, e.g. by requests like "Show me folklore music events." (7) that implicitly relates to *folklore music events in Mecklenburg-Vorpommern* — the location need not be restated explicitly. Finally, we give a glimpse on the use of the graphical interface.

The Knowledge Base of the Dialogue System. Knowledge is crucial for all modes of interaction, because we want the system to give appropriate responses to the user when problems arise. For instance, when a query results in an abundance of hits, the system must reason about why this problem might have occured and how it might be solved. Knowledge that allows for this type of reasoning is encoded in the *knowledge base of the dialogue system* (KBD).

The KBD includes all the definitions available in the ontology (cf. Section 7). These definitions help with explaining to the user why a query might have been too unspecific or with giving him hints how he might try to rephrase the query such that he gets the information he is looking for. For example, if the user seeks for information on the local offers of "cultural events", the hit rate for a database query may be reduced by the choice of one of the refined search terms "music events", "theater events", "show events" and "educational events" (cf. (4)). Vice versa, a too specific choice like "folk music event" might result in no hits, but the hint towards more general search terms might bring up similar events such as "folklore dance event" in (8a) that may be of interest. Further help is also provided through important terminological links such as synonyms, homonyms, antonyms and terms that may be parts of other terms, e.g. the show of a magician may be part of a circus show and, hence, the circus show might be a viable entertainment alternative to a magician's show.

In addition to the definitions of the ontology, the KBD features definitions and rules about dialogue concepts. At the moment, this part is tuned to map different interactions onto common requests to the database.[3] For example, the user input "Which cultural events take place in Mecklenburg-Vorpommern" (2b), which may also be supplemented by restrictions from the graphical interface, has the same meaning, i.e. it constitutes the same speech act, as "I am searching for cultural events in Mecklenburg-Vorpommern" (2c). Therefore, both inputs must be mapped onto the same query to the database.

Both types of knowledge provide user support that reduces the number of inquiries the user has to pose to the system and, hence, accelerates the dialogue compared to common keyword retrieval interactions.

Complex Dialogues. As indicated by examples (3) and (4), information finding rarely produces an instantaneous hit — after the user has formulated just a single query. This is true for syntactic methods and it will improve only to a limited amount with semantic methods either. However, when a user's sequence of interactions is perceived as being executed in order to achieve a goal, such as illustrated by the user's requests in Section 2, then this task of finding the proper information can be substantially facilitated. For this purpose, we provide a query processor that analyses not only the single interactions, but also views them as being embedded into a more global structure.

The methodology we use is based on work done by Ahrenberg et al. [1], who structure the dialog hierarchically into segments that are opened by a request and closed by the appropriate answer. Our assumption here is that users typically have a request for a certain piece of information and give related information in order to succeed. For example, they give a *topic*[4], which here boils down to a type restriction, like "cultural event", and spatial information about where these events should occur. The task of the dialogue system lies in zooming in or out on relevant information according to the interaction initiated by the user. For example, two user interactions[5] like, *(i)*, "Which cultural events take place in Mecklenburg-Vorpommern?" (2b), and, *(ii)*, "Show me folklore music events" (7) return a large set of documents first (with feedback such as in (4)), but a much smaller set of data after the second interaction has narrowed down the focus.

Hence, we here identify *dialogue segments*, *interactions* and *topics* as the major parameters (though not the only ones) that the dialogue system keeps track of. By this way the user's single interactions may all convey towards the common information finding goal and, thus, facilitate the human-computer interaction.

The Graphical Interface. Besides of the natural language query capabilities and the possibility of directly composing a formal query, the GETESS system features a graphical interface. This interface constitutes an intermediate level of access to the system

---

[3] In the linguistic literature this mapping is defined by the way natural language propositions, requests or questions can be considered as so called *speech acts* [2].

[4] The "topic" in a dialogue corresponds to what the dialogue is about. Usually, it is given only implicitly in natural language statements. In our setting it may also be given explicitly, *e.g.* through the graphical interface.

[5] Each interaction corresponds loosely to a speech act as introduced above, but might also be an act in the graphical user interface. Examples are *update* (users provide information to the system), *question, answer, assertion* or *directive*.

between the most professional (and fastest) one, *viz.* the formal query, and the most intuitive one (that requires a somewhat more elaborate interaction), *viz.* the natural language access. The graphical interface does not require from the user to learn the syntax of a particular query language or the concepts that are available in the ontology, but expects some basic understanding of formal systems from the user. This interface visualizes the ontology in a manner suited for selecting appropriate classes and attributes and, thus, allows the assembly of a formal query through simple mouse clicks. For this purpose, the ontology is visualized by a technology based on hyperbolic geometry [14, 9]: classes in the center of the visualization are represented with a big circle, surrounding classes are represented with a smaller circle. This technique allows fast navigation to distant classes and a clear illustration of each class and its neighboring concepts.

5 Gathering, Database Management and Information Retrieval

In this section, we outline the back end of GETESS that gathers data from the web and stores it in a way that allows for efficient retrieval mechanisms as far as keyword search and formal queries are concerned.

The back end of GETESS employs a typical gatherer-broker structure, *viz.* a Harvest search service [4] with a database interface. Though we use the tools provided by another project, SWING [13], the setting of GETESS puts additional demands on the gatherer-broker system: *(i)*, the GETESS search engine has to work with facts contained in the abstracts, *(ii)*, ontology knowledge must be integrated into the process of analysing internet information as well as answering user queries, *(iii)*, internet information can be of different types (*e.g.*, HTML, XML texts), and, *(iv)*, data collections such as information stored in databases must also be accessible via the GETESS search engine. These different requirements must be met both during the main process of gathering data and during the querying process (broker).

The gatherer process. Periodically, internet information is analysed via internet agents in order to build a search index for the GETESS search engine. Information (*e.g.* HTML-texts, Postscript-files, ...) is checked to find keywords. Additionally, the GETESS gatherer initiates the abstract generation on these information (cf. Sections 6, 7). The two kinds of index data ('simple' keywords and abstracts) are stored in databases.

The broker process. As indicated above, the dialogue system maps the user's queries (with the help of the natural language processing module and the definition in the ontology) onto formal or keyword queries in IRQL, the Information Retrieval Query Language [12], which is based on SQL99. The IRQL language combines different kinds of queries — both database and information retrieval queries — thus providing access to the index data. The query result set may be ranked with a function the shape of which will have to be determined by future experiments. The ranked result set is then presented to the user via the dialogue system.

The integration of different types of information (full text, abstracts, relational database facts) during gathering and querying has put forth and still requires demand for research, however at the same time it raises new possibilities of posing queries, because:

1. Conventional search engines support an efficient search for keywords or combinations of keywords over a whole document. This is still possible, but the GETESS

abstracts also provide relational information for the documents. Exploiting this type of information, we can realise attributed queries. That means users have the possibility to search for terms in special attributes, such as for instances of a particular concept.

2. Searching for particular integer values, for instance prices or distances is nearly impossible with a conventional information retrieval approach. The GETESS assistant will allow the comparison of integer and real values, *e.g.* to search for all prices that fall below a threshold. In addition, one may also determine minimum, maximum and average values as well as sort and group results by particular values.

3. Database functionality brings up answers from the abstract databases that are composed of different abstracts. That means, for answering a query of an user we may refer and exploit facts derived from different websites. Thereby, it is not even necessary that these websites are connected by links, but all the algebraic operations given through database functionality can be employed in order to deduce information. For instance, a music festival may be announced on one web site (1a), the corresponding reviews are found in another one. Database technology allows for retrieving all the events that take place in a particular location like Usedom and that also received a good note in the corresponding reviews.

This functionality is implemented in an object relational database system. It will be employed in a distributed database solution, which provides for data storage at different local servers. Having made available different languages for accessing this repository of information, we are now researching a common language level, the IRQL described above, for accessing structured information (abstracts) and unstructured information (for instance HTML or XML) with the same interface. This language will then reduce the burden on the dialogue system, because the dialogue system will not have to distinguish between formal and keyword search anymore. Thus, IRQL will enhance the overall robustness of the system.

6 Natural Language Processing

The GETESS intelligent assistant uses the natural language processing (NLP) component in order to, *(i)*, linguistically analyse user queries specified in the dialogue system, *(ii)*, to generate the linguistic basis for the extraction of facts from NL-documents, and, *(iii)*, generate natural language responses from facts in the abstract database.

The design of the NLP component is based on two major design criteria: First, the GETESS system requests a high degree of robustness and efficiency in order that the agent may be applied in a real-world setting. The reason is that we must be able to process arbitrary sequences of strings efficiently, because "broken" documents appear on real web sites, and that the number of documents that must be processed is too large in order to allow for response times of several minutes per sentence. Second, we employ the same shallow NL core components and linguistic data managing tools for processing texts and extracting information as well as for analysing a user's query. Thus, we can reduce the amount of redundancies as far as possible and keep the system in a consistent state with regard to its language capabilities. For instance, when the internal linguistic representation of an NL query and the abstracts use the same data sources, and if we also use the same knowledge sources for NL-based generation, inconsistencies as a result of unshared data can be reduced.

For the purpose of a short presentation here, we abstract from two major components of the natural language processing component in GETESS. We do not elaborate on the natural language generation part that also includes features for summarizing facts from the abstract database. Moreover, we are well aware that our project serves an international tourist community and, therefore we will have to add multi-lingual access as well as multi-lingual presentations of the query results. However, at the current state of the project, we focus on parts of Germany as the touristic goal that we want to provide information about and, hence, focus on the analysis of German documents only.

Shallow text processing. The shallow text processor (STP) of GETESS is based on and an extension of SMES, an IE-core system developed at DFKI (see [16, 17]). One of the major advantages of STP is that it makes a clean separation between domain independent and dependent knowledge sources. Its core components include: *(i)*, a text scanner, which recognizes, *e.g.*, number, date, time and word expressions, as well as text structure, like sentence markers and paragraphs; *(ii)*, a very fast component for morphological processing which performs inflectional analyses including processing of compounds and robust lexical access (*e.g.* analysing "events" as the plural of "event"); *(iii)*, a chunk parser based on a cascade of weighted finite state transducers. The chunk parser performs recognition of phrases (specific phrases like complex date expressions and proper names, and general phrases, like nominal phrases and verb groups), collection of phrases into sentences, and determination of the grammatical functions (like the deep cases, which determine the direction in which a particular relation holds; *e.g.* in example (1a) Mecklenburg-Vorpommern encloses Usedom and not vice versa).

STP has large linguistic knowledge sources (e.g., 120.000 general stem entries, more than 20.000 verb–frame entries). The system is fast, and can process 400 words in about one second running all components. In order for adapting STP for the GETESS assistant, we have evaluated STP's coverage on a corpus provided by our industrial partner. Though evaluation is blind, because the current knowledge sources have not been specified using any part of this corpus, we could analyse over 90% of all word forms and found that a majority of the remaining forms can be covered by domain specific lexica.

Extraction of facts. Finally, a word on the extraction of facts — and thus the generation of abstracts: The STP generates a linguistic analysis, *i.e.* it determines syntactic relations between words, *e.g.* between a verb and its subject. How these linguistic cues are exploited in order to go from natural language to a formal description is explained in the following section that elaborates on the semantic level of GETESS.

7 Ontology

As already mentioned, the scope of syntactic methods for gathering, using and querying of information is very limited and often unsatisfactory. A semantic reference model, an ontology, which structures the content and describes relationships between parts of the content helps to overcome these limitations. With the ontology in GETESS, we aim at two major purposes: First, it offers inference facilities that are exploited by the other modules, as, *e.g.*, described in Section 4, the dialogue module may ask for the types a particular instance belongs to in order to present alternative query options to the user. Second, the ontology acts as a mediator between the different modules. This latter role is explained here in more detail, since it illustrates how ontological design influences the working of the GETESS agent and, in particular, the extraction of facts from natural language texts.

The text processing (cf. Section 6) of natural language documents and queries delivers syntactic relations between words and phrases. Whether and how this syntactic relation can be translated into a meaningful semantic relation, depends on how the tourism domain is conceptualized in the ontology. For example (cf. Fig. 2), the natural language processing system finds syntactic relations between the words "music festival" and "Usedom" in the phrase "Usedom music festival". The word "Usedom" refers to Usedom which is known as an instance of the class Island in the database. "music festival" refers to a — so far — unknown instance, music-festival-1 of the class MusicFestival. The database refers to the ontology for the description of the classes Island and MusicFestival. Querying the ontology for semantic relations between Island and MusicFestival results in hostsEvent, which is inherited from the class Region to the class Island. Then, a corresponding entry between Usedom and music-festival-1 is added to the abstract, *i.e.* the set of extracted facts, of the currently processed document in the abstract database.

This example shows that the design of the ontology determines, *(i)*, the facts that may be extracted from texts, *(ii)*, the database schema that must be used to store these facts and, thus, *(iii)*, what information is made available at the semantic level. Hence, the ontology might con-

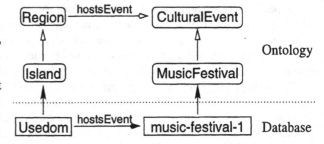

Fig. 2. Interaction of Ontology with NLP system and Database Organization

stitute an engineering bottleneck. However, we try to overcome this problem by a dual approach. On the one hand, we try to ease the burden on the knowledge engineer by a graphical, easy-to-use, knowledge engineering interface in the line of Protege-II [8]. On the other hand, we relieve the decision of which concepts to model by using the linguistic and statistical analyses of the text processing component. These analyses do not only indicate frequent, though yet unmodelled, concepts, but they also help to narrow down the choice of where new concepts should be placed in the ontology. Thus, the composition as well as the adaptation of the ontology is facilitated.

8 Related Work

The GETESS project builds on and extends a lot of earlier work in various domains. In the natural language community, research like [10] fostered the use of natural language application to databases, though these applications never reached the high precision and generality required in order to access typical databases, e.g. for accounting. Here, our approach seems better suited, since some of the deficits of natural language understanding techniques are counterbalanced by information retrieval facilities and an accompanying graphical interface.

Only few researchers, e.g. Hahn et al. [11], have elaborated on the interaction between natural language understanding and the corresponding use of ontologies. We think this to be an important point since underlying ontologies cannot only be used as submodules of text understanding systems, but can also be employed for a more direct access to the knowledge base and for providing an intermediate layer between text representation and extern databases.

As far as queries of conceptual structures are concerned, we agree with McGuiness & Patel [15] that usability issues play a vital role in determining whether a semantic layer can be made available to the user and, hence, we elaborated on this topic early on [9]. We, thereby, keep in mind that regular users may find lengthy natural language questions too troublesome to deal with and, therefore, prefer an interface that allows fast access, but which is still more comfortable than any formal query language.

Projects that compare directly to GETESS are, *e.g.*, Paradime [16][6], MULINEX [6] and MIETTA [5]. However, none of these projects combines information extraction with similarly rich interactions at the semantic layer. Hence, to the best of our knowledge we are the only one integrating unstructured, semi-structured and highly-structured data with a variety of easy-to-use facilities for human-computer interaction.

9 Conclusion

In the project GETESS (GErman Text Exploitation and Search System) we decided to build an intelligent information finder that relies on current techniques for information retrieval and database querying as its bottom line. The support for finding informations is *enhanced* through an additional semantic layer that is based on ontological engineering and on a partial text understanding component.

In order to *facilitate* web search, intuitive communication with the GETESS agent is considered a crucial point. Here, analyses of complex dialogues allow for refining, rephrasing or refocusing succeeding queries, and thus eliminate the burden of starting from scratch with every single user interaction. Thereby, several modes of interaction are possible, besides keyword search and SQL-queries one can mix natural language queries with clicking in the graphical query interface.

Having built the single modules for our system, the next task is bringing these components together. Given the design methodology of achieving entry level features first and then working towards "the high ceiling" (*viz.* complete text understanding and representation), we expect benefits on the parts of economic and research interests early in the project. The system is general enough in order to be applied to many realistic scenarios, e.g. as an intelligent interface to a company's intranet, even though it is still far from offering a general solution for the most general information finding problems in the WWW. Further research will have to address many of the remaining open issues, such as an evaluation of the overall system, a general methodology for mapping ontological models to database schemata or semi-automatic modeling of ontologies from example texts.

---

[6] Actually, GETESS uses the same linguistic core machinery as Paradime.

Acknowledgements

The research presented in this paper has been partially funded by the German Bundesministerium für Bildung, Wissenschaft, Forschung und Technologie (BMBF) under grant number 01IN802 (project "GETESS´´).

References

1. L. Ahrenberg, N. Dahlbäck, A. Jönnson, and A. Thure. Customizing interaction for natural language interfaces. *Computer and Information Science*, 1(1), 1996.
2. J.L. Austin. *How to Do Things with Words*. Oxford University Press, 1962.
3. J.P. Ballerini, M. Büchel, D. Knaus, B. Mateev, M. Mittendorf, P. Schäuble, P. Sheridan, and M. Wechsler. SPIDER retrieval system at TREC 5. In *Proc. of TREC-5*, 1996. http://www-nlpir.nist.gov/pubs.
4. C.M. Bowman, P.B. Danzig, R.D. Hardy, U. Manber, and M.F. Schwartz. The harvest information discovery and access systems. *Networks and ISDN Systems*, 1995. http://ftp.cs.colorado.edu/pub/cs/techreports/schwartz/Harvest.Conf.ps.Z.
5. P. Buitelaar, K. Netter, and F. Xu. Integrating different strategies for cross-language information retrieval in the MIETTA project. In D. Hiemstra, F. de Jong, and K. Netter, editors, *Language Technology in Multimedia Information Retrieval. Proc. of the 14th Twente Workshop on Language Technology*, TWLT 14, pages 9–17. Universiteit Twente, Enschede, 1998.
6. J. Capstick, A.K. Diagne, G. Erbach, H. Uszkoreit, F. Cagno, G. Gadaleta, J.A. Hernandez, R. Korte, A. Leisenberg, M. Leisenberg, and O. Christ. MULINEX: Multilingual web search and navigation. In *Proc. of Natural Language Processing and Industrial Applicatons*, 1998.
7. S. Decker, M. Erdmann, D. Fensel, and R. Studer. Ontobroker: Ontology based access to distributed and semi-structured information. In R. Meersman et al, editor, *Database Semantics, Semantic Issues in Multimedia Systems*, pages 351–369. Kluwer, Boston, MA, 1999.
8. H. Eriksson, Y. Shahar, S. W. Tu, A. R. Puerta, and Mark A. Musen. Task modeling with reusable problem-solving methods. *Artificial Intelligence*, 79(2):293–326, 1995.
9. D. Fensel, S. Decker, M. Erdmann, and R. Studer. Ontobroker: The very high idea. In *Proceedings of the 11th International Flairs Conference*, 1998.
10. B. Grosz, D. Appelt, P. Martin, and F. Pereira. Team: An experiment in the design of transportable natural-language interfaces. *Artificial Intelligence*, 32(2):173–243, 1987.
11. U. Hahn, M. Romacker, and S. Schulz. How knowledge drives understanding: Matching medical ontologies with the needs of medical language processing. *AI in Medicine*, 15(1):25–51, 1999.
12. Andreas Heuer and Denny Priebe. IRQL — Yet another language for querying semistructured data? Preprint CS–01–99, Universität Rostock, Fachbereich Informatik, 1999.
13. A. Heyer, H. Meyer, A. Düsterhöft, and U. Langer. SWING: Der Anfrage- und Suchdienst des Regionalen Informationssystems MV-Info. In *Tagungsband IuK-Tage Mecklenburg-Vorpommern. Schwerin, 27./28. Juni 1997*, 1997.
14. J. Lamping and R. Rao. The hyperbolic browser: A focus + context technique for visualizing large hierarchies. *Journal of Visual Languages & Computing*, 7, 1996.
15. D. McGuinness and P. Patel-Schneider. Usability issues in knowledge representation systems. In *Proc. of AAAI-98*, pages 608–614, 1998.
16. G. Neumann, R. Backofen, J. Baur, M. Becker, and C. Braun. An information extraction core system for real world german text processing. In *5th International Conference of Applied Natural Language Processing*, pages 208–215, Washington, USA, March 1997.
17. G. Neumann and G. Mazzini. Domain-adaptive information extraction. Technical report, DFKI, Saarbrücken, November 1998.

An Agent-Based System for Intelligent Collaborative Filtering

Colm O' Riordan[1] and Humphrey Sorensen[2]

[1] I.T. Centre, National University of Ireland, Galway
[2] Computer Science Dept., University College Cork, Ireland.

Abstract. This paper describes a multi-agent approach to collaborative filtering. The system combines traditional content filtering (using a semantic network representation and a spreading activation search for comparison) and social filtering (achieved via agent communication which is effectively triggered by user feedback). Collaborative relationships form between the agents as agents learn to trust or distrust other agents. The system aids users in overcoming the problem of information overload by presenting, on a daily basis, a 'personalised newspaper' comprising articles relevant to the user.

1   Introduction

In recent years, with the increasing popularity of the Internet, more and more online information has become available to users. This increase in information has created a scenario where users have difficulty in sifting through the information to find the items of interest to them.

This paper describes a system that has been developed to help users cope with the vast quantities of available on-line information. The system has undergone extensive empirical analysis using available test document collections. To date, this system has helped users overcome the problem of information overload.

The system developed combines a *content* filtering algorithm with a *collaborative* filtering technique. The content filtering module utilises a semantic network representation to represent information. The collaborative approach attempts to simulate "word of mouth" techniques prevalent in human communication. Thus, for example, people working within the same domain, or people with similar interests, may have information filtered based not solely on the content but also on other readers' recommendations.

We adopt the agent paradigm in our system as the task of personalised information filtering seems to require the same properties associated with agents—intelligence and autonomy. The content filtering is effected by a set of filtering agents. The collaboration between users with shared interests is modeled and implemented using a set of collaborating agents.

The overall result provided to the user by the system is a personalised, virtual newspaper comprising articles selected from an underlying information source. The selected articles should satisfy different interests a user may have.

2 Background

2.1 Information Retrieval and Information Filtering

Information retrieval (IR) is a well established field in information science, which addresses the problems associated with retrieval of documents from a collection in response to user queries. Information filtering (IF) is a more recent specialisation within information science, having come to the fore due to increasing volumes of online transient data. Similarities and dissimilarities between IR and IF have been well debated [1] and a relatively coherent viewpoint has emerged. The primary dissimilarities relate to the nature of the data set and the nature of the user need.

The chief components of an IR/IF system are *representation* (ranging from using indexes, vector representation or matrices, to the more recent models—neural networks, connectionist networks and semantic networks), *comparison* (to estimate relevance of documents for a given query), and *feedback* (often incorporated to improve the performance. This usually involves the user stating his/her satisfaction or dissatisfaction with returned documents. On receiving this feedback, the query (or profile) is usually modified to attain better results and the comparison process begins again.)

The main metrics used to test the accuracy of the retrieval/ filtering algorithm are *precision* and *recall*. These are defined as:

$$\text{Precision} = \frac{\text{Number of relevant items retrieved}}{\text{Number of items retrieved}}$$

$$\text{Recall} = \frac{\text{Number of relevant items retrieved}}{\text{Number of relevant items in database}}$$

Typically, the precision decreases as recall increases and vice-versa.

2.2 Collaborative Filtering

Different criteria may be used to filter documents/articles—the filtering and retrieval techniques mentioned thus far all use the content of the documents as the basis for the filtering. Malone [8] describes three categories of filtering techniques—cognitive, social and economic. Cognitive filtering is based solely on the content of the articles. Social filtering techniques are based on the relationships between people and on their subjective judgments. Economic filtering bases filtering on the cost of producing and reading articles. For example, a USENET News filtering system may filter out articles that have been cross-posted to many groups.

Collaborative filtering is a form of social filtering—it is based on the subjective evaluations of other readers. Approaches employing collaborative filtering use human judgments, which do not suffer from the problems which automatic techniques have with natural language, such as synonymy, polysemy and homonymy. Other language constructs, at a pragmatic level, like sarcasm, humour and irony may also be recognised.

Sample collaborative systems include the Tapestry system [4] which was developed to aid users in the management of incoming news articles or mails, and GroupLens[1] which is a "distributed system for gathering, disseminating, and using ratings from some users to predict other user's interests in articles" [10].

In the Tapestry system, in order to receive recommendations, users must know in advance the names of authors who have previously recommended the articles, i.e., the "social filtering is still left to the user". [12]. In Grouplens, the scoring method used is based upon the heuristic that people who agreed in the past are likely to agree again in the future. The main difficulties with GroupLens are the limited number of newsgroups catered for, and that for the system to be effective a a large number of recommendations should be made, thereby requiring an inordinate amount of time on behalf of the users.

Other common examples of social or collaborative filtering include *recommender systems*. In these systems, users rate different interests, such as videos (e.g *Bellcore's video recommendation* [7]) and musicians (e.g. Firefly[2], previously known as Ringo [12]). Films or musicians are then recommended to the user based on comparisons with other users' rankings.

Social or collaborative filtering addresses issues ignored by simple cognitive systems, which have been predominant to date. The large quantities of on-line information can clearly be rendered more manageable via word-of-mouth recommendations among cooperating consumers.

However, existing systems either promote collaboration within a limited domain or require explicit user intervention. For a collaborative filtering system to be most beneficial it should i) filter articles with high precision and recall, ii) promote cooperation with other users over a reasonably large domain and iii) be unobtrusive in its operation.

---

[1] http://www.cs.umn.edu/Research/GroupLens/
[2] Available at http://www.firefly.com/

2.3 Agents

The term *agent* has become one of the more pervasive buzzwords over the past few years. The number of products and companies using, or claiming to use, 'agent' technology has steadily increased; this trend seems set to continue with some predicting an even more widespread application of agent-technology—"in 10 years time most new IT development will be affected, and many consumer products will contain embedded agent-based software" [5].

The existence of many various definitions and interpretations that abound, is due mainly to the fact that numerous classes of agent exist, each with their own set of properties. The concept of an agent was first introduced by Hewitt, in his *Actor Model* [6]. Today, numerous strands of agent research exist, each applying different methodologies to different types of problems. Hence, the difficulty in defining the term *agent*. Nwana [9] uses different means of classifying agents—mobility, reactiveness, possession of certain basic properties and, finally, classification by the role they fulfill.

Our system adopts the agent paradigm. Filter agents filter information streams on behalf of the users (using a content filtering algorithm). Editor agents select articles offered by the filter agent. These agents participate in collaboration in an attempt to improve the performance (precision and recall) of the filtering.

3 System Architecture

3.1 Motivations

The goals of this system were:

1. To achieve accurate filtering on behalf of the user.
2. To allow effective feedback to cater for changing information needs and to attempt to improve filtering accuracy.
3. To attempt to improve on traditional content filtering systems by using collaborative filtering.
4. To implement this collaborative filtering to provide an effective, easy-to-use system that operates over a varying range of domains.
5. To create a virtual personalised newspaper for each user with article selection based on both content and collaborative filtering.

3.2 Architecture Overview

The system allows both content and collaborative filtering of information. The collaborative filtering operates in a transparent manner—the user is not aware when agents are collaborating on his/her behalf. We will discuss the content filtering module and collaborative filtering modules as separate sections (although the performance of the content filter determines the frequency of collaborative activity). A diagrammatic representation of the system architecture is given in Figure 1.

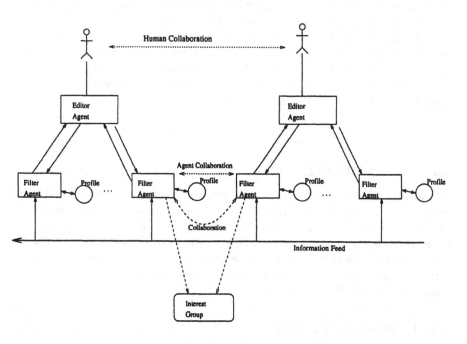

Fig. 1. System Architecture

Each user may have many filtering agents, each with a profile dedicated to a distinct information need (created by the user by providing key-words, phrases or a body of text representing his/her information need). The filtering agents, operating on the user's behalf, use this initial profile to create a network representation which is then used to filter incoming articles. The articles are then ranked in order of relevancy.

Associated with each user in the system is an editor agent whose primary function is to provide a 'personalised newspaper' to the user every morning by selecting the most relevant articles as determined by its filtering agents.

On reading an article, the user is asked to provide feedback (either positive or negative). Positive feedback causes an increase in the editor's confidence in that particular agent. It also leads to a modification of the network representation of the user's information need. This modification is incorporated in an attempt to increase the precision of the filtering by representing more accurately the user's information need. Negative feedback, on the other hand, causes a decrease in the editor's trust.

These changes to the editor agent's trust level has the effect that, if the trust is decreased, then that the agent's articles are less likely to be included in the future editions of the newspaper, thereby increasing the probability that the newspaper will contain relevant articles. On the other hand, the more positive feedback an agent receives, the higher its confidence level and hence the greater the chances that agent's filtered articles will be presented to the user. A user may also offer direct explicit feedback to any agent operating on his/her behalf. This involves offering text (words, phrases, sentences, relevant paragraphs) to change the filter's profile. This may be desired by the user for two different reasons—the filter agent is not filtering accurately enough or the user's specific information need in a given domain has changed considerably.

3.3   Content Filtering

The system adopts a semantic network representation (consisting of weighted nodes and weighted edges) of the user's information need. An effort is made to pay more attention to phrases than terms due to their higher resolving power. Comparison is achieved via a spreading activation search mechanism. Feedback is implemented via re-weighting of nodes and edges with the possible incorporation of new nodes and edges. The content filtering module (representation, comparison and feedback) is described in [14], [11].

3.4   Collaborative Filtering

In a multi-user environment, users with common interests (e.g., a group of researchers studying the same field) may wish to allow collaborative filtering with people filtering in the same domain. A user may register one of his/her agents with a 'collaborative group'; this indicates the user's desire to allow one of his/her agents to engage in collaborative filtering (through learning from other registered agents and by offering to teach other registered agents).

If the editor's trust level in a particular filtering agent falls below a certain threshold, the agent will attempt to improve its performance. This may result in one of two actions: if it is a personal filter (i.e., not registered to a collaborative group), then the user is prompted to provide more information representing his/her information need; if it is registered to a collaborative group, an effort is made by the agent to learn from other agents filtering in the same domain.

The agent communication is effected via the Contract Net Protocol (CNP) [13]—the agent wishing to learn from other agents 'offers' a contract to other agents registered with the same group; those agents who believe they can help in achieving higher precision filtering (i.e. those with a higher trust level) 'bid' for the contract by sending their trust-level to the contractor. The contractor then offers the 'contract' to one or more of these agents based both on their respective confidence measures and on their past dealings; these agents in turn become obliged to teach the filter agent by modifying the contractor's profile. (This involves addition of terms and phrases to the network representation and re-weighting of existing terms/phrases). This process may be repeated again in the future if the precision of the filter does not improve. The agent remembers past dealings with other agents that did not improve filtering. Over time, the offering of bids will become more restrictive, i.e., an agent will not offer contracts as readily to some other agents whose previous collaboration did not improve filtering precision.

3.5 Typical Scenario

This section enumerates the different steps involved in using the system. These steps include actions performed by the user and events within the system, some of which are transparent to the user (denoted below by the use of italics).

1. A user joins the system by registering. *On joining the system, an editor agent is created for that user.*
2. The user creates a set of profiles representing distinct information needs. *This causes a set of filter agents (one for each information need) to be created (with an initial system-defined confidence).*
3. A user may register any of these agents with the existing 'collaborative groups' or may create his/her own collaborative groups.
4. *The initial profiles are transformed into network representations.*
5. *Each evening, incoming news articles are compared to the profiles by the filter agents, who rank all articles and then pass rankings to the editor agent.*
6. *The editor agent uses the assigned relevancy and its trust in the filter agent to decide which articles to include or exclude in the virtual newspaper.*
7. The user may offer feedback on any of the articles presented.
8. *Following feedback, the agent's trust in the filter agents is decreased or increased. Associated profiles are modified.*
9. *If an agent's confidence falls below a threshold, collaboration takes place and the agent's profile and confidence are modified before the next iteration of filtering.*
10. *Over time, the agents learn to collaborate more readily with certain agents rather than others. These decisions are based on previous dealings and subsequent feedback.*
11. The user may at any time offer direct feedback to any agent which causes a change in that agent's profile.

3.6 Agent Collaboration

This section deals with architecture of the different classes of agents operating in the system and the communication mechanisms used. The agents in our system may be classified as deliberative agents, each possessing a logical model of the environment within which it exists. Each also possesses a set of tasks and goals and an ever-changing knowledge which is used by the agents to satisfy its goals.

Filter Agents: The goal of each of the filter agents is to effectively filter a particular domain on the user's behalf. The agent can gauge its success in this regard by changes that occur to its confidence level. This confidence level is, in turn, based on user feedback which can be taken as a measure of the filter's effectiveness. Figure 2 depicts the features of a filter agent.

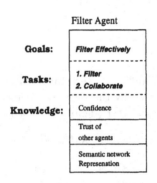

Fig. 2. Filter Agent

The tasks of each filter agent are as follows:

To filter incoming articles: using graph representations of the incoming articles.
To respond to requests for collaboration if possible:
If another agent, A, requests aid/collaboration, the filter agent, F, is obliged to offer help if the following conditions hold at that time: the agents involved are filtering the same domain, the confidence of F is above the threshold and the confidence of F is greater than that of A.

The knowledge possessed by each of the filter agents is as follows:

Confidence level: based on feedback.
Trust level in other agents registered in its domain or interest group:
based on measures of difference in agent performance, following agent collaboration.
A semantic network representation: The user's information need is represented using a semantic network.

This filter agent learns (modifies its knowledge) in order to attain a more accurate model of its changing environment. The knowledge is modified by communication with the editor agent (via user-feedback) and communication with other filter agent.

Editor Agents The tasks assigned to each user's editor (depicted in Figure 3) are:

To present on a daily basis a 'newspaper' of articles to the user:
These articles are chosen from highly-ranked articles filtered by the filter agents. The articles are presented to the user via the user interface which allows the user to offer feedback as appropriate. The editor selects the N (user defined) articles with the highest pr (probable relevancy) rating. This rating is defined for an article A by:

$$pr(A) = \sum_{i=1}^{n} (\ rating(A, i) \times confidence(i)\ )$$

where n is the number of filters filtering on behalf of the editor agent. The summation is used to ensure that articles deemed relevant by more than one filter agent may have a greater probability of being included in the final 'newspaper'.

To communicate feedback from the user to the filter agents operating on behalf of that editor:
Feedback offered by the user via the user interface is relayed to the filter agents by the editor agent. This feedback alters the individual filter agents as described earlier.

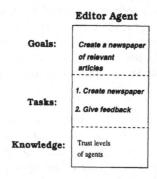

Fig. 3. Editor Agent

The knowledge possessed by each editor comprises the trust levels of each of its filter agents. This knowledge is continually updated as a result of feedback from the user.

Contract Net Protocol Different classes of agent interaction occur in our system. Interaction and communication between editor and filter agents adheres to a master-slave paradigm. The filter agents communicate their filtering results to the editor agent, the editor agent selects the appropriate articles for inclusion and the editor passes any feedback to the individual filter agents.

Communication between individual filter agents, active in the same domain, is effected using the contract net protocol (CNP). This protocol contains three phases—announcement, bidding, awarding. The contract network protocol amongst agents is explained more formally in [3].

Formation of Collaborative Relationships If after awarding a contract, an agent's confidence does not increase, i.e., user-feedback has not improved, the agent will not collaborate as readily with the successful bidder. Checks are made to see if any improvement has occurred after n iterations of feedback (n is at present hard-coded into the system). Each agent maintains a trust level in other agents registered in the group. Over time, after collaborations, these trust levels will vary, leading to either stronger or weaker relationships in the other agents filtering in the domain.

4 Results

4.1 Filtering Engine

We tested the effectiveness of the filtering engine by running the engines on commonly used document test collections and plotting precision against recall. The collections comprise a large set of documents, a set of queries (information needs) and a set of human relevance judgments. The documents and queries vary in size. In simulating user feedback we selected articles for feedback by offering the highest ranked documents that were also deemed relevant according to the provided relevancy judgments.

We describe the results obtained in tests using the MEDLINE document collection. The results presented in this section have been obtained from trials involving the MEDLINE collection (1033 articles, 30 queries/topics). The vast majority of results compare favourably with other systems that have been tested against MEDLINE articles. We compare our results with the results achieved by the LSI system over this collection (taken from [2]). The following 9-point graph (Figure 5) shows the comparison of the two systems (the values for the LSI performance using 90 dimensions.)

Dumais' trials also included the calculation of the mean precision achieved with LSI for a range of values for the number of dimensions (See Table 1).

We also calculated the mean precision for our system with different levels of feedback—5 iterations, 10 iterations and full feedback. (See Table 2). LSI and other retrieval systems view the document set as a whole and derive statistics

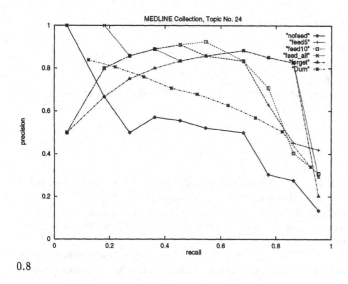

0.8

Fig. 4. Comparison with LSI(90 domains) over MEDLINE

Precision	Number Of Domains
0.414173	10
0.724983	50
0.717937	100
0.633250	300
0.589000	500
0.544683	800
0.531173	1033

Table 1. Mean Precision values for LSI over MEDLINE

based on the the whole collection. Our system, on the other hand, filters articles one at a time with no attention paid to the document set as a whole.

5 Conclusion

This paper describes a multi-agent approach to information filtering. Individual content-filter agents are described. Precision-recall graphs are included to illustrate the performance. Collaborative filtering is modeled as a set of co-operating communicating agents. These 'share knowledge' by modifying other profile representations to attempt attain higher precision content filtering. The agents, over time, develop collaborative relationships which model real-world collaborative relationships between users with similar interests.

Mean Precision	Number of Iterations of Feedback
0.419906	5
0.525376	10
0.661820	full feedback
0.552563	full feedback with forgetting

Table 2. Mean Precision values for our system with different levels of feedback

References

1. N. Belkin and B. Croft. Information filtering and information retrieval: Two sides of the same coin? *Communications of the ACM*, 35(2), December 1992.

2. S. Deerwester, S.Dumais, T. Landauer, G. Furnas, and R. Harshman. Indexing by latent semantic analysis. *Journal of the American Society for Information Science*, 41(6):391–407, 1990.

3. M. Fisher and M. Wooldridge. On the formal specification and verification of multi-agent systems. *International Journal of Cooperative Information Systems*, 6(1):37–65, 1997.

4. D. Goldberg, D. Nichols, B.M. Oki, and Douglas Terry. Using collaborative filtering to weave an information tapestry. *Communications of the ACM*, 35(12):61 – 70, December 1992.

5. C. Guilfoyle. Vendors of agent technology. *UNICOM Seminar on Intelligent Agents and their Business Applications*, pages 135–142, 1995.

6. C. Hewitt. Viewing control structures as patterns of passing messages. *Artificial Intelligence*, 8(3):323–364, 1977.

7. W. Hill, L. Stead, M. Rosenstein, and G. Furnas. Recommending and evaluating choices in a virtual community of use. *Computer-Human Interfaces (CHI '95)*, 1994.

8. Malone, Grant, Turbak, Brobst, and Cohen. Intelligent information sharing systems. *Communications of the ACM*, 30(5):390–402, 1987.

9. H. S. Nwana. Software agents : An overview. *Knowledge Engineering Review*, 11(3):1–40, 1996.

10. P. Resnick, N.Iacovou, M. Suchak, P. Bergstrom, and J. Reidl. Grouplens : An open architecture for collaborative filtering of netnews. *Proceedings of ACM 1994 Conference on CSCW*, pages 175 – 186, 1994.

11. Colm O' Riordan. *Multi-Agent Collaborative Filtering*. Msc. thesis, University College Cork, 1997.

12. U. Shardanand and P. Maes. Social information filtering: Algorithms for automating "word of mouth". *Computer-Human Interfaces (CHI '95)*, 1995.

13. R. Smith. The contract net protocol: High-level communication and control in a distributed problem solver. *IEEE Transactions on Computers*, 12(29):1104, 1113, 1980.

14. H. Sorensen, A. O'Riordan, and C. O'Riordan. Personal profiling with the informer filtering agent. *Journal Of Universal Computer Science*, 3(8), 1996.

Inter-Agent Communication in Cooperative Information Agent-Based Systems

Hassan Gomaa

Department of Information and Software Engineering, George Mason University
Fairfax, VA 22030-4444, USA
hgomaa@isse.gmu.edu

Abstract. This paper describes several different approaches for information agents to communicate and cooperate with each other in agent-based systems. The paper describes different communication patterns for inter-agent cooperation. In particular, three patterns of inter-agent communication are described in more detail, brokered communication, subscription/notification communication, and negotiated communication. In each case, the pattern is described and examples of its use are given. The cooperative inter-agent interactions are described in the Unified Modeling Language (UML) notation. Agent-based systems can be designed using these different patterns of inter-agent communication. Examples are given from electronic commerce, real-time monitoring, and travel reservation systems.

1. Introduction

This paper describes several different approaches for information agents to communicate and cooperate with each other in agent-based systems. The agent-based system consists of distributed objects, which can be clients, agents, or servers. The paper describes different communication patterns for inter-agent cooperation and gives examples of their use in cooperative information agent-based systems. The cooperative agent interactions are described in the Unified Modeling Language (UML) notation.

Section 2 presents an overview of cooperation among agents. Section 3 describes the different ways in which distributed information agents can communicate with each other. Section 4 presents an overview of the Unified Modeling Language. Section 5 describes brokered communication between distributed agents. Section 6 gives an example of inter-agent cooperation in an Agent-Based Electronic Commerce System. Section 7 then describes inter-agent communication using a subscription and notification pattern. Finally, Section 8 describes inter-agent negotiation using a negotiation pattern.

2. Cooperative Information Agent-Based Systems

An agent-based system is a highly distributed system, in which agents are active concurrent objects that act on behalf of users. Agents are intermediaries between clients, which are typically user interface objects, and servers, which are typically entity objects that store persistent information. Usually, several agents participate in the problem solving activity, communicating with each other. This leads to a more distributed and scaleable environment. More information on multi-agent systems is given in [6, 11, 14, 15, 16]. Several researchers have addressed interaction protocols in multi-agent systems [5, 12, 13, 20, 22, 23]. This paper describes inter-agent communication patterns that may be used in the design of agent-based systems. An *inter-agent cooperation pattern* describes a sequence of message interactions between cooperating agents, which can be reused in different cooperative information agent-based systems. In this paper, the patterns are described in the UML notation and examples are given of their use.

Agents may communicate with each other in many different ways, either directly or indirectly. Client agents act on behalf of their clients while server agents provide agent services for the client agents.

3. Message Communication in Cooperative Agent-Based Systems

An important goal of a software architecture for a distributed cooperative information agent-based system is to provide a concurrent message-based design that is highly configurable. The concept is that the software architecture can be mapped to many different system configurations, is reusable, and can evolve as new requirements are introduced [8, 9]. In this architecture all objects are concurrent and distributed. Objects are clients, agents or servers. All communication between them is by means of messages.

A designer of a distributed agent-based system, where distributed objects potentially reside on different nodes, needs to consider a wide variety of alternatives for message communication [7]. In this paper, three styles of communication are explored in more detail for inter-agent communication, brokered communication, subscription/notification communication, and negotiated communication:

a) *Brokered communication.* An object broker mediates interactions between clients and servers. It frees the client from having to maintain information about where a particular service is provided and how to obtain the service.

b) *Subscription/notification communication.* With this form of group communication, clients subscribe to events they wish to be notified of. When an event of interest arises, a message is sent to all clients on the subscription list notifying them of the event.

c) *Negotiated communication.* In a negotiated communication, agents will make proposals to each other, and respond with offers that may be accepted, rejected, or counter offered.

4. Overview of the Unified Modeling Language

Object-oriented concepts are considered important in software reuse and evolution because they address fundamental issues of adaptation and evolution. Object-oriented methods are based on the concepts of information hiding, classes, and inheritance. Information hiding can lead to more self-contained and hence modifiable and maintainable systems. Inheritance provides an approach for adapting a class in a systematic way. With the proliferation of notations and methods for the object-oriented analysis and design of software systems, the Unified Modeling Language

(UML) [2, 21] is an attempt to provide a standardized notation for describing object-oriented models.

In **use case modeling**, the functional requirements of the system are defined in terms of use cases and actors [2]. **Structural modeling** provides a static view of the information aspects of the system [2]. Classes are defined in terms of their attributes, as well as their relationship with other classes. **Behavioral modeling** provides a dynamic view of the system. The use cases are refined to show the interaction among the objects participating in each use case [10]. Object collaboration diagrams are developed to show how objects collaborate with each other to execute the use case.

For analyzing inter-agent communication, the behavioral view is the most informative. In this paper, all agent interactions are depicted on UML object collaboration diagrams (e.g., Fig. 1), which show the objects (client, agent, or server) participating in a use case and the sequence of message interactions among them.

5. Brokered Communication between Distributed Agents

In a distributed object environment, clients and servers are designed as distributed objects. An Object Broker [18] is an intermediary in interactions between client agents and server agents, and also in interactions between server agents and server entity objects. It frees client agents from having to maintain information about where a particular service is provided and how to obtain that service. It also provides *location transparency*, so that if the server agent is moved to a different location, only the object broker need be notified.

Server agents register the services they provide and the location of these services with an Object Broker. Instead of a client agent having to know the location of services provided by server agents, it queries the Object Broker for services provided. A client agent sends a message identifying the service required, for example to withdraw cash (service) from a given bank (server name). The Object Broker receives the client request, determines the location of the agent (e.g., the node the agent resides on), and forwards the message to the agent at the specific location. Alternatively, it returns a service handle to the client agent, as shown in Fig. 1, which can then request the service at the server. The latter approach, which is referred to as the *Handle-driven Design* approach, is as follows:

1. Client Agent sends a request to the Object Broker.
2. The Object Broker looks up the location of the server agent and returns a service handle to the client.
3. The Client Agent uses the service handle to request the service from the appropriate Server Agent.
4. The Server Agent services the request and sends the response directly to the Client Agent. This approach is more efficient if the Client and Server Agents are likely to have a dialog that results in the exchange of several messages.

The above mode of communication, in which the Client Agent knows the service it requires but not its location is referred to as "white page" object brokering. Another type of brokering is through "yellow page" object brokering, where the Client Agent knows the service type it requires but not which specific Server Agent. This interaction is shown in Fig. 2. The Client Agent sends a query request to the Object Broker requesting all server agents of a given type, e.g., software travel agents. The Object Broker responds with a list of all server agents that match the client agent's request. The Client Agent, after consultation with the user, selects a specific Server Agent. The Client Agent then communicates with the Server Agent using the service handle returned to it by the broker.

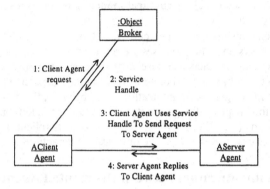

Fig. 1. Inter-Agent Communication Using Object Broker (White Pages)

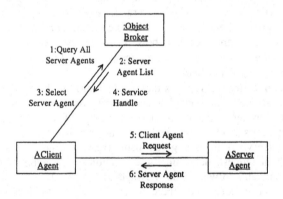

Fig. 2. Inter-Agent Communication Using Object Broker (Yellow Pages)

6. Inter-agent Cooperation in Agent-Based Electronic Commerce

6.1 Agent Support for Electronic Commerce Problem

In the electronic commerce problem [3], there are customers and suppliers. Each customer has a contract with a supplier for purchases from that supplier as well as one or more bank accounts through which payments to suppliers can be made. Each supplier provides a catalog of items, accepts customer orders, and maintains accounts with each customer for receiving payment.

A customer is able to browse through several world wide web-based catalogs [1] provided by the suppliers, and make selections of items that need to be purchased. The customer needs to specify a contract, which will be used for charging the purchase. The customer's order needs to be checked against the available contracts to determine if the contract is valid. Each contract has operations funds committed to it. It needs to be determined that there are sufficient funds available for the customer order. Assuming that contract and funds are in place, a delivery order is created and sent to the catalog supplier. The supplier confirms the order and enters a planned shipping date. As time passes, the shipping order is monitored and both supplier and customer are notified if there is a shipping delay. When the order is shipped, the customer is notified. The customer acknowledges when the shipment is received and the delivery order is updated. After receipt of shipment, authorization for payment of the invoice is now made. The invoice is checked against the contract, available funds, and the delivery order status, after which the invoice is sent to accounts payable, which authorizes payment of electronic funds to the customer's bank.

An approach to addressing the electronic commerce problem using software agents is outlined in this section and described in more detail in Section 6.2. In this example, there are client agents and server agents, where each agent defines the business rules for some aspect of the electronic commerce domain. In this application, the client agents are user agents that act on behalf of users and assist users to perform their jobs. To achieve this, they interact with server agents. The server agents receive requests from client agents. To satisfy a client agent request, a server agent typically interacts with server objects and with other agents.

In the Electronic Commerce problem, there are two types of user agent, the Customer Agent and the Supplier Agent. There is one instance of the Customer Agent for each customer and one Supplier Agent for each supplier. There are three server agents, with many instances of each. The server agents are:

- Requisition Agent, one instance for each requisition.
- Delivery Order Agent, one instance for each delivery order.
- Invoice Agent, one instance for each invoice.

To maintain low coupling between clients, agents, and servers, an object broker is used to maintain the location of the specific services. Servers and agents register their services and locations with the object broker. When a service is required, the location of the service is determined by sending a message to the object broker, as shown in Figs. 1 and 2.

6.3 Object Collaborations in Agent-Based Electronic Commerce System

There are two actors (user types) and six use cases in this application. The two actors are the customer and the supplier. The actor initiates three use cases, Browse Catalog, Place Requisition, and Confirm Delivery. The supplier initiates three use cases, Process Delivery Order, Confirm Shipment, and Send Invoice. These are the main use cases in the application; there are other use cases for querying the servers and monitoring progress, which have been omitted for brevity.

For each use case, an object collaboration diagram is developed. The object collaboration diagrams are then merged to create the software architecture for the Agent-Based Electronic Commerce System, as depicted in Fig. 3. It consists of an object collaboration diagram in which message sequences corresponding to the key use cases are depicted. The cooperating agents and servers are depicted on the diagram. User interface objects, which provide GUI interfaces to the customer and server actors have been omitted to avoid clutter on the diagram.

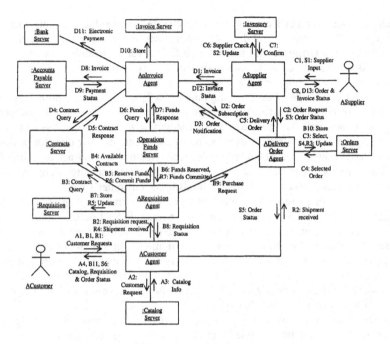

Fig. 3. Object Collaboration in Agent-Based Electronic Commerce System

The first use case, Browse Catalog, is based around the customer making catalog selections, assisted by the Customer Agent. The steps in this use case are:

A1: The Customer Agent is instantiated to assist the customer. Based on the customer's request, the Customer Agent selects one or more catalogs for the customer to browse.

A2: Customer Agent requests information from Catalog Server.

A3: The Catalog Server sends Catalog Information to the Customer Agent.

A4: The Customer Agent displays the catalog to the user.

In the Place Requisition use case, the customer makes a catalog selection, the Customer Agent instantiates a Requisition Agent and sends it a requisition. In this use case, the Requisition Agent communicates with the Contracts Server and Operations Funds Server, as well as with the Delivery Order Agent and the Customer Agent. It instantiates a Delivery Order agent and sends the purchase request to it. The steps in this use case are:

B1: Customer selects items from catalog and requests creation of a requisition.

B2: The Customer Agent instantiates the Requisition Agent, passing to it the customer's requisition request.

B3: The Requisition Agent sends a Contract Query to the Contracts Server.

B4: The Contracts Server returns the contracts available between the customer and the supplier.

B5: The Requisition Agent send a Reserve Funds request to the Operations Funds Server, to hold the funds from a given contract for this requisition.

B6: The Operations Funds Server confirms that the funds have been reserved.

B7: The Requisition Agent approves the requisition and sends it to be stored at the Requisition Server.

B8: The Requisition Agent sends the Requisition Status to the Customer Agent.

B9: The Requisition Agent instantiates a Delivery Order Agent and sends the purchase request to it.

B10: The Delivery Order Agent creates a new delivery order and stores it with the Delivery Server.

B11: The Customer Agent displays the Requisition Status to the User.

In the next use case, Process Delivery Order, the Supplier Agent queries the Delivery Order Agent for a new delivery order; the agent selects a delivery order is retrieved notification to a Supplier agent. The Supplier agent displays the order to the supplier (via the user interface). The Supplier enters the shipping information, including the shipping date. The customer eventually acknowledges receipt of the goods and the delivery order is updated to reflect the receipt date. The steps in the use case are as follows:

C1: Supplier requests a new delivery order.

C2: The Supplier Agent sends the request to the Delivery Order Agent

C3, C4: The Delivery Order Agent selects a deliver order.

C5: The Delivery Order Agent sends the Delivery Order to the Supplier Agent.

C6, C7: The Supplier Agent checks that the items are available in inventory.

C8: The Supplier Agent displays the Delivery Order and inventory information to the supplier.

In the Confirm Shipment use case, the supplier prepares the shipment manually and then confirms the shipment:

S1: Supplier inputs the shipping information.

S2: Supplier Agent updates the inventory stored at the inventory server.

S3: The Supplier Agent sends the Order status to the Delivery Order Agent.

S4: The Delivery Order Agent updates the Delivery Order Server.

S5: The Delivery Order Agent sends the Order status to the Customer Agent.

S6: The Customer Agent displays the Order status to the user.

In the Confirm Delivery use case, when the shipment arrives at the customer, the customer confirms the delivery:

R1: The Customer acknowledges the receipt of shipment.

R2: The Customer Agent sends a Shipment Received message to the Delivery Order Agent.

R3: The Delivery Order Agent updates the Delivery Order at the server.

R4: The Customer Agent sends a Shipment Received message to the Requisition Agent.

R5: The Requisition Agent updates the status of the requisition stored at the Requisition Server.

R6, R7: The Requisition Agent commits the funds for this requisition with the Operations Funds Server.

In the Send Invoice use case, the Supplier agent instantiates an Invoice Agent to follow through on the invoice. Usually this is done when the items have been shipped. The Invoice Agent subscribes to the Delivery Order agent to be notified when the goods have been received. When the receipt event occurs, the Invoice Agent sends the invoice to the Accounts Payable Server. The steps in the use case are as follows:

D1: The Supplier Agent sends the invoice information to the Invoice Agent.
D2: The Invoice Agent subscribes to the Delivery Order agent.
D3: The Delivery Order Agent notifies the Invoice Agent that the goods have been received.
D4: The Invoice Agent sends a Contract Query to the Contracts Server.
D5: The Contracts Server confirms the contract.
D6: The Invoice Agent sends a Funds Query to the Operations Funds Server.
D7: The Operations Funds Server confirms that the funds are available and committed.
D8: The Invoice Agent sends the invoice to the Accounts Payable Server.
D9: The Accounts Payable Server sends the Payment Status to the Invoice Agent.
D10: The Invoice Agent stores the invoice at the Invoice Server.
D11: The Invoice Agent sends the electronic payment to the Customer's Bank Server.
D12: The Invoice Agent sends the Invoice Status to the Supplier Agent.
D13: The Invoice Agent displays the Invoice Status to the Supplier.

7. Inter-agent Communication by Subscription and Notification

This section describes how information agents can cooperate using a subscription and notification pattern. An example is given of a Real-Time agent that monitors some external entity for specific external events. The Real-Time Agent maintains a subscription list of client agents who wish to be notified of these events. The agent may observe several events and must determine which of these is significant. When a significant event occurs to the external entity, the Real-Time agent updates an event archive and notifies client agents, via an Event Distributor object, who have subscribed to receive events of this type.

The Subscription and Notification inter-agent communication pattern is depicted on the object collaboration diagram (Fig. 4), which shows three use cases, a simple query use case, an event subscription use case and an event notification use case. In the query use case that does not involve a subscription, a client makes a request to the Client Agent, which queries the Event Archive Server and sends the response to the Client. The event subscription use case consists of the following collaboration:

S1: Client Agent receives a subscription request from a user.
S2: The Client Agent sends a subscription message to the Subscription Server.
S3: The Subscription Server confirms the subscription.
S4: The Client Agent informs the user.

Now consider the event notification use case:
E1: An event arrives at the Real-Time Monitoring Agent.

E2: The Real-Time Monitoring Agent determines that this is a significant event and sends an update message to the Event Archive Server.

E3: The Real-Time Monitoring Agent sends an Event Notification message to the Event Distributor object.

E4, E5: The Event Distributor queries the Subscription Server to get the list of event subscribers (i.e., client agents that have subscribed to receive events of this type).

E6: The Event Distributor sends a multicast message to all client agents that have subscribed for this event.

E7: The Client Agent sends the relevant date to the client.

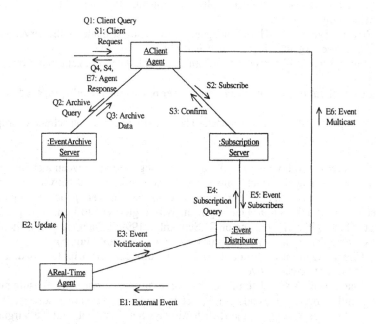

Fig. 4. Inter-Agent Communication using Subscription and Notification

8. Negotiation among Information Agents

In multi-agent systems, it is necessary to have a negotiation pattern to allow agents to cooperatively make decisions [4, 19,]. In the negotiation paradigm, a client agent acts on behalf of the user and locates an appropriate server agent, e.g., a software travel agent, via the object broker's yellow pages (Fig. 2). The client agent then makes a proposal to the server agent. The server agent attempts to satisfy the client's proposal, which may involve communication with other server agents. Having determined the available options, the server agent then offers the client agent one or more options that come closest to matching the original client agent proposal. The client agent may then request one of the options, propose further options, or reject the offer. If the server agent can satisfy the client agent request, it accepts the request; otherwise it rejects the request.

In order to provide the agent services described in the previous paragraph, an inter-agent negotiation pattern is required, as described next. For cooperating information agents that wish to negotiate with each other, the following communication services are provided:

The Client Agent, who acts on behalf of the client, may:

a) Propose service. The client agent proposes a service to the server agent. This proposed service is **negotiable,** meaning that the client agent is willing to consider counter offers.

b) Request service. The client agent requests a service from the server agent. This requested service is **non-negotiable,** meaning that the client agent is not willing to consider counter offers.

c) Reject server offer. The client agent rejects an offer made by the server agent.

The Server Agent, who acts on behalf of the server, may:

a) Offer a service. In response to client proposal, a server agent may offer a counter-proposal.

b) Reject client request/proposal. The server rejects the client's proposed or requested service.

c) Accept client request/proposal. The server accepts the client's proposed or requested service.

Consider the following example involving negotiation between a client agent and a software travel agent, which follows a scenario similar to that between a human client and a human travel agent. For example, consider a travel agency example, where a user wishes to take an airplane trip from Washington DC to London departing on 14 September 1999 and returning on 21 September 1999, for a price of less than $700. A use case depicting the negotiation procedure is given next (Fig. 5):

1. Client Agent uses Propose Service to propose the trip to London with the constraints given above.

2. The Travel Agent determines that three airlines service the Washington DC to London route. It sends a Request to the three respective servers, the United Airlines Server Agent, the British Airways Server Agent, and the Virgin Atlantic Server Agent for flights on those dates. It receives responses from all three with the times and prices of the flights.

3. The Travel Agent sends an Offer Service message to the client agent consisting of the available flights at the proposed price. If only more expensive flights are available, the Travel Agent offers the cheapest it can find. In this case, it determines that the two best offers for the proposed dates are from UA for $750 and BA for $775. There is no flight below $700, so it offers the two available flights that come closest to the proposed price. It sends the Offer Service message to the Client Agent.

4. Client Agent displays the choice to the user, who selects the UA offer. The Client Agent may either Request Service (one of the choices offered by the server agent) or Reject the server offer if the user does not like any of the options and propose a service on a different date. In this case, the Server Requests the UA flight.

5. The Travel Agent makes a reservation request to the UA Server Agent.

6. Assuming the seat is still available, the UA Server confirms the reservation.
7. The Travel Agent responds to the client agent's Request Service with an Accept Request message. If the flight is no longer available, the Travel Agent would send a Reject Request message.

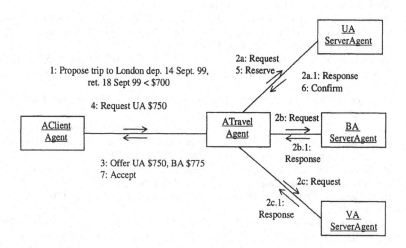

Fig. 5. Example of Information Agent Negotiation

9. Conclusions

This paper has described several different approaches for information agents to communicate and cooperate with each other in agent-based systems. The paper has described different communication patterns for inter-agent cooperation. In particular, three patterns of inter-agent communication have been described in more detail, brokered communication, subscription/notification communication, and negotiated communication. In each case, the pattern was described and examples of its use were given. The cooperative inter-agent interactions were described in the Unified Modeling Language (UML) notation. Agent-based systems can be designed using these different patterns of inter-agent communication.

10. Acknowledgements

The authors gratefully acknowledge several valuable discussions with J. Cunningham, L. Kerschberg, and A. Motro. This research was supported in part by DARPA and American Management Systems, Inc. Thanks are also due to the anonymous reviewers for their comments on an earlier draft of this paper.

11. References

1. T. Berners-Lee, R. Cailliau, A. Loutonen, H. F. Nielsen, and A. Secret, "The World-Wide Web," Communications of the ACM, vol. 37, pp. 76-82, 1994.

2. G. Booch, J. Rumbaugh, I. Jacobson, "The Unified Modeling Language User Guide", Addison Wesley, Reading MA, 1999.

3. N. S. Borenstein, "Perils and pitfalls of practical cybercommerce," CACM, vol. 39, pp. 36-44, 1996.

4. R. Davis and R. Smith, "Negotiation as a Metaphor for Distributed Problem Solving," Artificial Intelligence, vol. 20, pp. 63-109, 1983.

5. R. Fritzen, T. Finin, D. McKay, and R. McEntire, "KQML - A Language and Protocol for Knowledge and Information Exchange," International Distributed Artificial Intelligence Workshop, Seattle, WA, 1994.

6. Genesereth and S. P. Ketchpel, "Software Agents," CACM, vol. 37, pp. 48-53, 1994.

7. H. Gomaa, *Software Design Methods for Concurrent and Real-Time Systems*, Addison Wesley, 1993.

8. H. Gomaa, "Reusable Software Requirements and Architectures for Families of Systems", *Journal of Systems and Software*, April 1995.

9. H. Gomaa, L. Kerschberg, et. al., "A Knowledge-Based Software Engineering Environment for Reusable Software Requirements and Architectures," *Journal of Automated Software Engineering*, Vol. 3, Nos. 3/4, August 1996.

10. H. Gomaa, "Use Cases for Distributed Real-Time Software Architectures", Journal of Parallel and Distributed Computing Practices, Vol. 1, No. 2, 1998.

11. R. V. Guha and D. B. Lenat, "Enabling Agents to Work Together," CACM, vol. 37, pp. 126-142, 1994.

12. A. Haddadi, "Cooperation and Coordination in Agent Systems", Springer-Verlag, 1996.

13. N. R. Jennings, "Coordination Techniques for Distributed Artificial Intelligence," in *Foundations of Distributed Artificial Intelligence*, M. P. Georgeff and N. R. Jennings, Eds.: Wiley InterScience, 1996.

14. Kerschberg, L., "Knowledge Rovers: Cooperative Intelligent Agent Support for Enterprise Information Architectures." Cooperative Information Agents, P. Kandzia and M. Klusch, eds., Springer-Verlag, Berlin, 79-100, 1997.

15. Kerschberg, L., "The Role of Intelligent Agents in Advanced Information Systems." Advanced in Databases, C. Small, P. Douglas, R. Johnson, P. King, and N. Martin, eds., Springer-Verlag, London, 1-22, 1997.

16. M. Klusch, "Utilitarian Coalition Formation Between Information Agents," In Cooperative Knowledge Processing, S. Kirn and G. O'Hare, Eds. London: Springer-Verlag, 1996.

17. P. Maes, "Designing Autonomous Agents: Theory and Practice from Biology to Engineering and Back," In Special Issues of Robotics and Autonomous Systems. Cambridge, MA, London, England: The MIT Press, 1990, pp. 194.

18. Mowbray T. and W. Ruh, "Insider CORBA – Distributed Object Standards and Applications", Addison Wesley, Reading MA, 1997.

19. J. Pitt, M. Anderton, and R.J. Cunningham, "Normalized Interactions between Autonomous Agents: A Case Study in Inter-Organizational Project Management", Computer Supported Cooperative Work: The Journal of Collaborative Computing 5:201-222, Kluwer 1996.

20. J. S. Rosenschein and G. Zlotkin, *Rules of Encounter: Designing Conventions for Automated Negotiation among Computers*. Cambridge, MA,: MIT Press, 1994.

21. J. Rumbaugh, I. Jacobson, G. Booch, "The Unified Modeling Language Reference Manual", Addison Wesley, Reading MA, 1999.

22. M. Wooldridge, "Issues in Agent-Based Software Engineering," in *Cooperative Information Agents*, vol. 1202, *Lecture Notes in Artificial Intelligence*, P. Kandzia and M. Klusch, Eds. Kiel, Germany: Springer-Verlag, 1997, pp. 1-18.

23. M. Wooldridge and N. R. Jennings, "Intelligent Agents: Theory and Practice," *The Knowledge Engineering Review*, vol. 10, pp. 115 - 152, 1995

Intention Reconciliation in the Context of Teamwork: An Initial Empirical Investigation*

David G. Sullivan[1], Alyssa Glass[1], Barbara J. Grosz[1], and Sarit Kraus[2]

[1] Harvard University, Cambridge, MA 02138, USA
{sullivan,glass,grosz}@eecs.harvard.edu
[2] Bar Ilan University, Ramat Gan 52900, Israel
and Institute for Advanced Computer Studies,
University of Maryland, College Park, MD 20712, USA
sarit@cs.biu.ac.il

Abstract. With growing opportunities for individually motivated agents to work collaboratively to satisfy shared goals, it becomes increasingly important to design agents that can make intelligent decisions in the context of commitments to group activities. In particular, agents need to be able to reconcile their intentions to do team-related actions with other, conflicting intentions. We present the SPIRE experimental system that allows the process of intention reconciliation in team contexts to be simulated and studied. SPIRE enables us to examine the influence of team norms and environmental factors on team members faced with conflicting intentions, as well as the effectiveness of different intention-reconciliation strategies. We discuss results from pilot experiments that confirm the reasonableness of our model of the problem and illustrate some of the issues involved, and we lay the groundwork for future experiments that will allow us to derive principles for designers of collaboration-capable agents.

1 Introduction

As a result of the ubiquity of computer networks and the phenomenal growth of the Internet, computer systems increasingly are becoming elements of complex, distributed communities in which both people and systems act. Many applications have been proposed that require members of such communities to work collaboratively to satisfy a shared goal (Decker and Li 1998; Sen et al. 1997; Sycara and Zeng 1996). In such situations, agents need to form teams to carry out actions, making commitments to their team's activity and to their individual actions in service of that activity. As rational agents, team members must be able to make individually rational decisions about their commitments and plans. However, they must also be responsible to the team and, dually, able to count on one another. Thus, decision making in the context of teamwork is complex and presents a number of new challenges to the developers of intelligent agents.

This paper focuses specifically on the decision making that self-interested, collaborative agents must perform when their commitment to a group activity conflicts with opportunities to commit to different actions or plans. We describe the initial results of an empirical investigation into the process of intention reconciliation that agents must perform in such situations. The experimental framework we have developed allows us to explore both the effect of team norms and policies on an agent's decisions about

---
* This research has been supported by National Science Foundation grants IRI-95-25915, IRI-96-18848, and CDA-94-01024. Michael Epstein participated in the development of the SPIRE system. We thank Luke Hunsberger, Martha Pollack, and the reviewer for helpful comments on previous drafts.

conflicting intentions and the effectiveness of various intention-reconciliation strategies that agents can adopt in the face of team norms. Our longer-term goal is to derive principles that system designers can use in constructing computer-based agents that participate in teams. While we recognize that no single approach can adequately meet the needs of every designer in every type of environment, we hope to provide insight into the types of factors that affect individual and team behavior and outcomes, and thus assist developers working in a variety of domains.

2 Intention Reconciliation in the Context of Teamwork

Research on collaboration in multi-agent systems, including our work on SharedPlans (Grosz and Kraus 1996, 1999) and that of others (Levesque et al. 1990; Kinny et al. 1994; Tambe 1997), has established that commitment to the joint activity is a defining characteristic of collaboration. Although theories differ in the ways they encode this commitment, they agree on its centrality. At the same time, research on rationality and resource-bounded reasoning (Doyle 1991; Horty and Pollack 1998; inter alia) has established the need for agents to dynamically adapt their plans to accomodate new opportunities and changes in the environment. However, efforts in this area have mainly focused on plan management and evolution in the context of individual plans. Our work brings these two threads of research together; it addresses the need for collaborative agents to manage plans and intentions in multi-agent contexts, reasoning jointly about commitments to individual plans and commitments to group activities.

2.1 The Problem

Our investigation focuses on the problem of intention reconciliation that arises because rational agents cannot adopt conflicting intentions (Bratman 1987; Grosz and Kraus 1996; inter alia). If an agent has adopted an intention to do some action β and is given the opportunity to do another action γ that would in some way preclude its being able to do β, then the agent must decide between doing β and doing γ: it must *reconcile* intentions, deciding whether to maintain its intention to do β or to drop that intention and instead adopt an intention to do γ.

In particular, we are concerned with intention reconciliation in the context of teamwork, i.e., situations in which at least one of the conflicting intentions is related to an agent's commitment to a team plan. Although "defaulting" on a team-related commitment for the sake of another opportunity may at times appear beneficial from a purely individualistic perspective, agents may need to be concerned with their reputations in the community. The extent to which others trust them not to default may influence their long-term good. An agent must consider how defaulting on team-related commitments may impact its ability to collaborate in the future and, more generally, how team-related factors may affect its future expected outcomes.

We assume that each of the agents is self-interested and acts in an individually rational manner. Even when participating in a collaborative activity, an agent will aim to maximize its own outcome. Agents are also assumed to belong to a community of agents who periodically form teams to accomplish shared goals. Different agents in the community may participate on different teams at different times, and teams may vary in both size and duration. Even though a given team may exist only while engaged in a single group activity, agents in the community may have longer-term relationships. An

α_i: system maintenance of home PC

α_g: system maintenance of large group of workstations

β: upgrade operating system

γ: go to lecture by Nobel Prize winner

Individual context. You have a PC at home; you are the only user. You are committed to doing β in the context of doing α_i. A friend offers you a ticket so you can do γ.

Team context. You are a student employee of the systems administration group at your university and a member of the team doing α_g. You are committed to doing β in the context of doing α_g. A friend offers you a ticket so you can do γ.

Fig. 1. Intention-reconciliation scenarios from the systems administration domain, used to illustrate the differences between individual and team contexts

agent may want or need to participate with other agents in future group activities. Depending on the situation, team members may or may not know each other's identities and contributions to the team. In this work, we do not address the coalition formation problem, i.e., the process by which teams are formed. Furthermore, we use the term *team* to refer to a group of agents who have formed the intentions and beliefs required for collaborative activity. The term *group* refers to a collection of agents that may (or may not) be a team.

2.2 Sample Scenarios

To illustrate the problem of intention reconciliation in the context of teamwork, we will consider an example from one of the domains that our empirical system seeks to model: computer systems administration. Figure 1 sketches two scenarios involving tasks from this domain. In both scenarios, an agent has committed to spending a certain period of time upgrading an operating system (activity β). It is then presented with the opportunity to attend a lecture that occurs during that same period of time (activity γ). Thus, the agent must reconcile a prior intention to do β with a potential intention to do γ. In the first scenario, the prior intention is in the context of a purely individual activity; in the second, the intention is in service of a group activity.

In the individual context, the agent weighs the various costs and benefits of sticking with its original intention or dropping it in favor of the new opportunity. If, for instance, the agent can do the upgrade β the next day without having to drop any other commitments, then it will defer β and commit to going to the lecture. If deferring to the next day means the agent will have to give up going to a movie, then it must also decide whether it prefers the lecture to the movie. On the other hand, if doing β at the planned time is critical to some other activity (for instance, producing a tax return that is due that day), then the agent may decline the lecture ticket. In all these deliberations, only the individual's outcome and future schedule matter.

Similar considerations apply in the team context, but there are additional ones as well. Since the agent's involvement with the systems administration group is an ongoing one, it must consider how other team members will view its failure to honor its commitment to do β. The agent needs to consider the costs it may incur as a result of the team's reaction to its defaulting on a team-related task. In addition, the agent must weigh team-related costs (and benefits) with individual factors.

2.3 Social-Commitment Policies

In interacting with one another, and particularly in working together, we assume that agents in the community adopt, either explicitly or implicitly, what we term *social-commitment policies*. These policies govern various aspects of team behavior, including both rewards and penalties for individual acts in the context of group activities. For instance, they may specify such things as the distribution of benefits from a group activity, the penalty structures imposed on agents who default on commitments to a group activity, and what defines a fair distribution of tasks among agents. We could assume that these policies are agreed on by a team when it forms. However, it seems more natural and efficient to require that the community of agents embody these principles, because in computational settings we expect agent designers will build multiple agents that at different times come together to form different teams.

Social-commitment policies differ from the "social laws" used in other multiagent planning work (Shoham and Tennenholtz 1992). Social laws provide constraints on agents that allow their actions to be coordinated; these laws constrain the ways agents *do actions* so that their activities do not negatively interact. In contrast, social-commitment policies concern *rational choice* and the ways a society can influence an individual's decision making. As a result, social laws are by their nature domain-specific, whereas social-commitment policies affect decision making across domains and tasks.

2.4 Incorporating Social Factors in Decision Making

Social-commitment policies address the tension between what is best for the individual in isolation and what is best for the team. In this paper we assume agents assess outcomes on the basis of utility functions. Although team members may consider group utility, they do not become group-utility maximizers. By stipulating ways in which current decisions affect future utility as well as current utility, social-commitment policies change the way agents evaluate trade-offs. They provide a mechanism for constraining individuals so that the good of the team plays a role in their decision making. Rosenschein and Zlotkin (1994) have presented similar conventions in the context of negotiation between agents.

Social factors can also function in an additional way. If agents get part of their utility from the team, they have a stake in maximizing group utility. A larger group benefit means a larger share for each agent, and thus a larger individual utility. Therefore, when facing a choice, it may be useful for an agent to consider not only this single choice, but also the larger context of similar choices by itself and others. While being a "good guy" may appear suboptimal by itself, everyone's being a good guy when faced with similar choices may lead to optimal outcomes for everyone in the team. The team as a whole will benefit and each individual ultimately gains. For example, in the team-context scenario of Fig. 1, an individual member of the systems administration team might benefit from choosing to go to the lecture. But if everyone in the team made a similar choice, the group utility would suffer severely. Although such effects could occur within a single interaction (for instance, if the whole team defaults to attend the same lecture), more typically they occur over the longer-term (different members of the team default at different times in favor of such "outside" opportunities). The *brownie points model* described by Glass and Grosz (1999) provides one means of incorporating a good-guy factor into decision making. Policies that encourage good guy behavior are, however, susceptible to manipulation; the "free-rider" problem can arise. Although we recognize this aspect of good-guy behavior, we leave treatment of it to future work.

3 Empirical Framework

3.1 Why Simulations Are Needed

The intention-reconciliation problem outlined above does not seem amenable to a single, all-purpose, analytic solution. Large numbers of agents, the potentially varied capabilities of agents, complex task interactions, uncertainty about future interactions, and incomplete information about other agents all complicate the analysis. Various environmental factors such as the number of tasks scheduled concurrently (task density) also affect outcomes for individuals and teams.

We have thus constructed the SPIRE (SharedPlans Intention-Reconciliation Experiments) simulation system to study the ways in which various environmental factors and social-commitment policies can influence individual and team outcomes and to examine the effectiveness of different decision-making strategies in the face of such environmental and team-related factors. SPIRE is general enough to allow us to model agents from a large set of problem domains, including the two systems we have built based on a SharedPlans-based architecture: WebTrader (Hadad and Kraus 1999) and GigAgents (Grosz et al. 1999).

3.2 The Basic SPIRE Framework

In SPIRE, a team of agents $(G_1,...,G_n)$ works together on group activities, called GroupTasks, each of which consists of doing a set of tasks (task instances). Each task instance is of one of the types $D_1,...,D_k$ and occurs at one of the times $T_1,...,T_m$. For example, a GroupTask for a systems administration team that includes both people and software agents might consist of a week's work (with the times T_i being the 40 hours of the work week) doing tasks of the types $D_1,...,D_6$ listed in Fig. 2. Some task-types may have only one instance in the week (e.g., D_6: printer maintenance); others may have multiple instances (e.g., D_5: run and maintain backups). We currently assume that each task type can be performed by a single agent. Agents receive income for the tasks they do; this income can be used in determining an agent's current and future expected utility.

A SPIRE simulation consists of a sequence of GroupTasks. Since varying either the group activity or the team members would make it more difficult to identify sources of variation in the outcomes, we currently require that the same GroupTask be

D_1: read and reply to technical questions by e-mail or in person
D_2: upgrade hardware
D_3: restore deleted files from backups
D_4: check system security
D_5: run and maintain backups
D_6: printer maintenance (paper, toner, etc.)

Fig. 2. Examples of task types from the systems administration domain

done repeatedly by the same team. However, the individual tasks within the GroupTask will not necessarily be done by the same agent each time. SPIRE considers a given GroupTask to consist of a set of tasks with time constraints on the tasks and capability requirements for agents doing the tasks. To simplify the description, we will assume that a GroupTask maps to a "weekly task schedule."

In SPIRE, these weekly task schedules are represented as sets of pairs $<task_i, time_i>$, where $task_i$ is to be done at $time_i$. At the start of each week, a central scheduler takes the elements of the weekly task schedule and assigns them to agents to produce a weekly task-schedule assignment (WTSA).[1] Each agent has a set of task capabilities and a set of available times that constrain the scheduler's assignment of tasks. For instance, only some agents (e.g., humans) might be able to check for security breaks, and only others (e.g., software agents) might be able to run the backup program.

After the scheduler has assigned all of the tasks in the weekly task schedule, agents are chosen at random and given the opportunity to do one of a series of "outside offers." Outside offers correspond to actions that an agent might choose to do apart from the GroupTask. Each outside offer conflicts with a task in the WTSA; to accept an offer, an agent must default on one of its assigned tasks. The central question we investigate is how different strategies for reconciling conflicting intentions (given a particular configuration of social-commitment policies and environmental factors) influence both the rates at which agents default and their individual and collective incomes.

The income values of the outside offers are chosen randomly from a distribution with approximately the same shape as the distribution of task values in the WTS, and with a mean value that exceeds the mean value of the WTS tasks; thus agents have an incentive to default. If an agent chooses an outside offer, γ, it defaults on its originally assigned task β. If there is an available replacement agent that is capable of doing β, the task is given to that agent; otherwise, β goes undone.

The team as a whole incurs a cost whenever an agent defaults; this cost is divided equally among the team's members. The cost of a particular default depends on its impact on the team. At a minimum, it equals a baseline value that represents the cost of finding a replacement agent. If no replacement is available, the group cost is increased by an amount proportional to the value of the task.

3.3 Social-Commitment Policy in SPIRE

For the experiments in this paper, SPIRE applied a social-commitment policy in which a portion of each agent's weekly tasks is assigned based on how "responsible" it has been over the course of the simulation. Each agent has a rank that reflects the total number of times it has defaulted, with the impact of past weeks' defaults diminishing over time. The higher an agent's relative rank, the more valuable the tasks it receives. Since there is a greater cost to the team when tasks go undone, an agent's rank is reduced by a larger amount if it defaults when no one can replace it.

---

1. This central scheduler is used only for convenience. In many domains requiring cooperative agents, agents would most likely need to negotiate each week's schedule. Since this negotiation is beyond the scope of the current SPIRE system and we wish to study aspects of team-commitment scenarios that come after the initial schedule is made, we simplified this aspect of the problem.

SPIRE gives each agent an initial rank of 0, and it uses the following formula to update an agent a's rank at the end of week i:

$$rank_a(i) = (PDF) \cdot rank_a(i-1) - penalty\_sum_a(i) . \tag{1}$$

where *PDF*, the penalty-discount factor, is a constant in the range (0, 1) that causes the impact of previous weeks' defaults to lessen over time, and *penalty_sum* is the sum of the rank reductions that the agent incurred because of its defaults during week i.

The scheduler assigns N tasks per agent on the basis of the agents' ranks. If there is more than one agent with the same rank, the scheduler randomly orders the agents in question and cycles through them, giving them tasks one at a time. Any remaining tasks are assigned to agents picked at random. The strength of the social commitment policy can be varied by modifying the value of N.

3.4 Decision Making in SPIRE

In deciding whether to default on a task β so as to accept an outside offer γ, an agent determines the utility of each option. In the version of SPIRE used for the experiments in this paper, the utility that an agent receives from doing an action *act* in week i depends on two essentially monetary factors: current income (CI), and future expected income (FEI):

$$U(act, i) = CI(act, i) + FEI(act, i) . \tag{2}$$

Current income only considers the income from the task or outside offer in question, as well as the agent's share of the group cost if it defaults. Its value in the default and no-default cases is thus:

$$CI(\text{def}(\beta, \gamma), i) = value(\gamma) - \frac{group\_cost(\beta)}{n}$$
$$CI(\beta, i) = value(\beta) \tag{3}$$

where def(β, γ) represents the action of doing γ having defaulted on β, and n is the size of the team.

The income that an agent will receive in future weeks depends on its relative position in future weeks' rankings, because higher-ranked agents receive higher-valued tasks. We assume that agents do not know the ranks of other agents, nor the total number of defaults in a given week, but only their own relative ranking in both the current and the previous week. Therefore, an agent can only estimate its FEI, which it does by approximating its new position in the agent rankings both if it defaults and if it does not default, and estimating the assignments it would receive in each case (from the tasks assigned based on rank). By comparing the value of these task sets, the agent can approximate the impact that defaulting will have on its income in the following week.

An agent may also extrapolate beyond the following week when making its FEI estimate. Because the single-week estimate described above is inexact and is less likely to reflect reality for weeks that are further away, an uncertainty factor $\delta < 1$ can be used to discount FEI. Under this approach, if F is the original estimate of the following week's income, then the discounted estimate for the kth week after the current one is $\delta^k F$. The full FEI estimate in week i of an M-week simulation is thus:

$$FEI(act, i) = \delta F(act, i) + \delta^2 F(act, i) + \ldots + \delta^{M-i} F(act, i)$$
$$= (\delta + \delta^2 + \ldots + \delta^{M-i}) F(act, i)$$
$$= \frac{\delta(1 - \delta^{M-i})}{1 - \delta} F(act, i). \tag{4}$$

Note that the factor $(1 - \delta^{M-i})$ decreases as the simulation progresses, reflecting the fact that an agent has less to lose from defaulting when there are fewer weeks left in the GroupTask.

Since our current experiments do not consider any "good guy" factors, the utilities that an agent receives from defaulting and from not defaulting in week i of the simulation are given by:

$$U(\text{def}(\beta,\gamma), i) = CI(\text{def}(\beta,\gamma), i) + FEI(\text{def}(\beta, \gamma), i)$$
$$U(\beta, i) = CI(\beta, i) + FEI(\beta, i). \tag{5}$$

Agents default when $U(\text{def}(\beta,\gamma), i) > U(\beta, i)$.

In another paper (Glass and Grosz 1999), we model the possibility of agents being good guys—i.e., being willing to sacrifice short-term personal gain for the group good—by allowing agents to earn "brownie points" (BP) each time they choose not to default, and including an agent's BP level in its utility function.

4 Preliminary Results

In our pilot experiments with SPIRE, we made the simplifying assumptions that all agents are capable of doing all tasks and that all agents are initially available at all times. To maximize the contrast between "socially conscious" and "socially unconcerned" agents, we also made a relatively large number of outside offers and imposed relatively large rank deductions and group costs when agents defaulted. Figure 3 summarizes the settings used for the majority of these experiments; departures from these values are noted in each experiment's description.

52 weeks per simulation run

12 agents

20 task types (values=5, 10, …, 100)

40 time slots per week

10 tasks per time slot = 400 tasks per week, of randomly chosen types

10 tasks per agent per week assigned based on the agent's rank, the rest assigned randomly

250-350 outside offers per week:
• number & values chosen randomly
• possible values = task values + 95

initial agent ranks = 0

rank deductions:
• if replacement available, deduct 1
• if no replacement available, deduct 5

discount factor on prior deductions = 0.5

group costs from defaulting:
• baseline=(n/n-1)(max_task_value), where n = # agents
• if no replacement, add(4*task_value)

δ weighting factor for FEI = 0.8

Fig. 3. SPIRE settings used for most of the experiments in this paper. Departures from these values are noted in each experiment's description

The results presented below are averages of 30 runs that used the same parameter settings but had different, randomly-chosen starting configurations (the values of tasks in the weekly task schedule, and the number and possible values of the outside offers). In each run, the first ten weeks serve to put the system into a state in which agents have different ranks; these weeks are not included in the statistics SPIRE gathers.

4.1 Varying the Strength of the Social-Commitment Policy

For all of the experiments, we employed the social-commitment policy described in Sect. 3.3, in which agents are ranked and assigned tasks based on how often they have defaulted. In our first set of experiments, we varied the policy's strength by using different values for the number of tasks per agent, N, assigned on the basis of rank.

Results for $N = 0$, 5, 10, 15, and 20 are graphed in Fig. 4. As expected, the average number of defaults per week drops off as the value of N increases (Fig. 4, *left*). The $N = 0$ case (all tasks assigned randomly) is equivalent to having no social-commitment policy at all. Since defaulting has no effect on FEI in this case, agents are effectively "socially unconcerned" and consider only CI when deciding whether to default on a task. Because outside offers are almost always worth more than tasks—even with an agent's share of the group cost factored in—agents default on average over 90% of the time. Clearly, this situation is undesirable from the point of view of the team.

As N increases, the social-commitment policy drastically reduces the average number of defaults. While this result is unsurprising, it verifies that the FEI estimates made by the agents are reasonable, and it provides a concrete demonstration of how a social-commitment policy can affect the decision making of self-interested agents.

The impact of the social-commitment policy on both mean individual income (from tasks and offers) and group income (from tasks only) is shown in the right half of Fig. 4. Incomes are normalized by dividing by the income that would have been earned if the originally assigned tasks had all been completed. Negative income values can occur as a result of the shared group costs incurred when agents default.

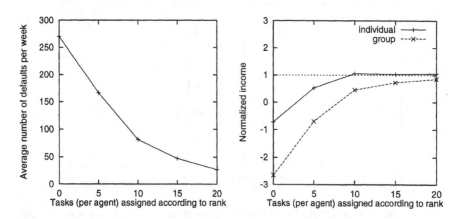

Fig. 4. Effect of the social-commitment policy on the average number of defaults per week (*left*) and on the normalized group income and normalized mean individual income (*right*). Incomes are normalized with respect to the amounts that would have been earned if the originally assigned tasks had all been completed

When all tasks are randomly assigned ($N = 0$), the high number of defaults results in a large loss of group task income, as well as added group costs. Therefore, the group task income is very low (approx −2.7, where 1.0 represents what would have been earned with no defaults). Mean individual income is also negative, but it is higher than group income because of the payments that agents receive for outside offers. This result illustrates that individually rational decisions can still lead to suboptimal outcomes for individuals, in this case as a result of shared group costs. Individuals consider group costs when reconciling their own intentions, but they fail to take into account the costs they will incur from defaults by other agents.

As the value of N increases and agents default less often, both group and individual incomes increase. For $N = 10$, 15, and 20, individual agents do slightly better than they would have if they had done all their assigned tasks. The "plateau" effect that occurs in this range comes from a balance between the value of outside offers and the group costs incurred from defaulting. Agents accept fewer outside offers (and thus lose the extra income that such offers bring), but they also incur lower group costs.

4.2 Varying the Weight Given to FEI

Our next set of experiments varied the δ value that agents use when they weight their single-week FEI estimates (F) to obtain estimates of FEI over the rest of the simulation (cf. Sect. 3.4). As the value of δ increases, so does the value by which F is multiplied, and FEI thus becomes a larger part of the agents' utilities. We therefore expected to see fewer defaults as δ increases. The results shown in the left half of Fig. 5 confirm this. In addition, both mean individual income and group task income again increase as the number of defaults decreases (Fig. 5, *right*).

δ values of 0.4 and 0.5 lead to particularly poor outcomes, since they never multiply the single-week FEI estimate (F) by more than 1, even when there are many weeks left in the simulation. δ values of 0.6, 0.7, and 0.8 are more effective, since for most of

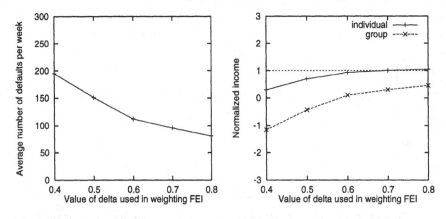

Fig. 5. Effect of the weight given to FEI on the average number of defaults per week (*left*) and on the normalized group income and normalized mean individual income (*right*). Incomes are normalized with respect to the amounts that would have been earned if the originally assigned tasks had all been completed. See Sect. 3.4 for a detailed explanation of the way in which the parameter δ is used

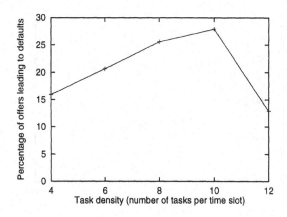

Fig. 6. Effect of task density on the percentage of outside offers that lead to defaults. There were 12 agents throughout, so 12 tasks/time slot is the maximum density

the simulation they multiply F by factors of about 1.5, 2.3, and 4, respectively (see the last line of equation (4)).

4.3 Varying the Task Density

The last of our pilot experiments varied an environmental factor, the number of tasks scheduled in each time slot (task density). Since a larger task density makes it more difficult on average for a defaulting agent to find a replacement, and since the group costs and individual rank penalty are larger when there is no replacement, we expected that there would be fewer defaults as task density increased. However, our results (Fig. 6) do not confirm this hypothesis. Instead, as task density increases, there is a gradual *increase* in the percentage of outside offers for which defaults occurred, with the exception of a drop that occurs at the maximum density of 12 tasks per time slot (with 12 agents). This increase occurs despite the fact that the percentage of offers for which no replacement is available also increases as the task density increases (Table 1).

We were puzzled by these results, until we realized that task density also affects the values of the tasks assigned based on rank, and thus the FEI estimates made by agents. For each of the task densities, we consistently scheduled 10 tasks per agent based on rank (120 tasks in all), and the tasks assigned during this stage of the schedul-

Table 1. Effect of task density on the average percentage of outside offers for which no replacement agent is available

Tasks density	Offers with no replacement
4	0.00%
6	0.02%
8	2.06%
10	39.88%
12	100.00%

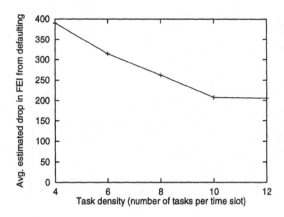

Fig. 7. Effect of task density on the average of the agents' estimated losses in future expected income as a result of defaulting on an assigned task

ing were always the most valuable tasks still available. However, as task density increases, so does the total number of tasks, and thus (on average) the number of tasks of each type. This means that the 120 tasks assigned according to rank tend to have an increasingly narrow range of values as task density increases. As a result, the effect of rank on the tasks an agent receives—and therefore on its FEI—is lessened. In the extreme case, if there were more than 120 tasks with the highest value, an agent's rank would have no effect on the value of the tasks it received.

To confirm this explanation, we analyzed data we collected regarding the agents' estimates of how much FEI they would lose by defaulting. We found that as task density increases, the average estimate of the drop in FEI caused by defaulting *decreases* (Fig. 7), suggesting that the tasks assigned based on rank are indeed drawn from more and more homogeneously valued pools of tasks. In the maximum density case, the fact that replacements are never available makes the average cost of defaulting large enough to outweigh this effect.

This experiment illustrates how a system like SPIRE can uncover unexpected interactions between parameters, enabling agent designers to find them in advance and adjust their designs accordingly.

5 Related Work

Kalenka and Jennings (1999) propose several "socially responsible" decision-making principles and empirically examine their effects in the context of a warehouse loading scenario. Our work differs from theirs in three ways: (1) their policies are domain-dependent and not decision-theoretic; (2) they do not vary environmental factors; and (3) they do not look at conflicting intentions or agents defaulting on their tasks, but at whether agents choose to help each other.

Sen (1996) also considers decision-making strategies that encourage cooperation among self-interested agents, but his work focuses on interactions between pairs of individual agents, rather than those between an individual and a team.

There is also a significant body of economics literature on rational choice and intention reconciliation (Iannaccone 1992; Holländer 1990; inter alia) that space limitations preclude our reviewing here.

6 Conclusions

We have developed an empirical framework that enables us to simulate the process of intention reconciliation in team contexts and to examine the impact of environmental factors and team norms as well as the effectiveness of various decision-making strategies in the face of these external factors. Our initial experiments confirm the reasonableness of our model and illustrate some of the issues involved in the problem we are trying to address.

In a related paper (Glass and Grosz 1999), we investigate agents who consider both their monetary interests and their reputation as team members when reconciling conflicting intentions. In future work, we intend to investigate the following classes of problems within the SPIRE framework: (1) the influence of information about other team members on the agents' behavior; (2) heterogeneous communities, including agents with different capabilities and time availabilities, and agents who embody different decision-making strategies (e.g., some may be good guys, others not); (3) teams with larger numbers of agents; (4) alternative social-commitment policies; (5) alternative intention-reconciliation strategies; and (6) the possibility of agents modeling and adapting to the team behavior of other agents.

Since intention reconciliation in realistic multi-agent contexts is an extremely complex problem, we believe a system like SPIRE is essential for obtaining the insights needed to design collaboration-capable agents (Grosz et al. 1999). Such agents will function not merely as tools but as problem-solving partners, working as members of heterogeneous teams of people and computer-based agents in our increasingly interconnected computing environments.

References

[Bratman 1987] Bratman, M.E. 1987. Intention, Plans, and Practical Reason. Harvard University Press, Cambridge, MA.

[Decker and Li 1998] Decker, K. and Li, J. 1998. Coordinated hospital patient scheduling. In: *Proceedings of ICMAS-98*, pp. 104-111.

[Doyle 1991] Doyle, J. 1991. Rational belief revision. In: *Proceedings of the Second International Conference on Knowledge Representation and Reasoning (KR-91)*, pp. 163-174.

[Glass and Grosz 1999] Glass, A. and Grosz, B.J. 1999. Socially conscious decision-making. Submitted to the Bar Ilan Symposium on the Foundations of Artificial Intelligence (BISFAI-99).

[Grosz and Kraus 1996] Grosz, B.J. and Kraus, S. 1996. Collaborative plans for complex group action. *Artificial Intelligence*, 86(2):269-357.

[Grosz and Kraus 1999] Grosz, B.J. and Kraus, S. 1999. The Evolution of SharedPlans. In Wooldridge, M. and Rao, A., editors, *Foundations and Theories of Rational Agency*. Kluwer Academic Publishers, The Netherlands, pp. 227-262.

[Grosz et al. 1999] Grosz, B.J., Hunsberger, L., and Kraus, S. 1999. Planning and acting together. *AI Magazine* (to appear).

[Hadad and Kraus 1999] Hadad, M. and Kraus, S. 1999. SharedPlans in electronic commerce. In Klusch, M., editor, *Intelligent Information Agents*. Springer Verlag.

[Holländer 1990] Holländer, H. 1990. A social exchange approach to voluntary cooperation. *American Economic Review*, 80(5):1157-1167.

[Horty and Pollack 1998] Horty, J. and Pollack, M.E. 1998. Option evaluation in context. In: *Proceedings of the 7th Conference on Theoretical Aspects of Rationality and Knowledge*, pp. 249-262.

[Iannaccone 1992] Iannaccone, L.R. 1992. Sacrifice and stigma: reducing free-riding in cults, communes, and other collectives. *Journal of Political Economy*, 100(2):271-291.

[Kalenka and Jennings 1999] Kalenka, S. and Jennings, N.R. 1999. Socially responsible decision making by autonomous agents. In: *Proceedings of the Fifth International Colloquium on Cognitive Science*, pp. 153-169.

[Kinny et al. 1994] Kinny, D., Ljungberg, M., Rao, A.S., Sonenberg, E., Tidhar, G., and Werner, E. 1994. Planned team activity. In Castelfranchi, C. and Werner, E., editors, *Artificial Social Systems, Lecture Notes in Artificial Intelligence (LNAI-830)*, pp. 227-256. Springer Verlag.

[Levesque et al. 1990] Levesque, H., Cohen, P. and Nunes, J. 1990. On acting together. In: *Proceedings of AAAI-90*, pp. 94-99.

[Rosenschein and Zlotkin 1994] Rosenschein, J.S. and Zlotkin, G. 1994. *Rules of Encounter: Designing Conventions for Automated Negotiation among Computers*. MIT Press, Cambridge, MA.

[Sen 1996] Sen, S. 1996. Reciprocity: a foundational principle for promoting cooperative behavior among self-interested agents. In: *Proceedings of ICMAS-96*, pp. 322-329.

[Sen et al. 1997] Sen, S., Haynes, T., and Arora, N. 1997. Satisfying user preferences while negotiating meetings. *International Journal on Human-Computer Studies*, 47(3):407-427.

[Shoham and Tennenholtz 1992] Shoham, Y. and Tennenholtz, M. 1992. On the synthesis of useful social laws for artificial agent societies. In: *Proceedings of AAAI-92*, pp. 276-281.

[Sycara and Zeng 1996] Sycara, J. and Zeng, D. 1996. Coordination of multiple intelligent software agents. *International Journal of Intelligent and Cooperative Information Systems*, 5:181-211.

[Tambe 1997] Tambe, M. 1997. Towards flexible teamwork. *Journal of Artificial Intelligence Research*, 7: 83-124.

A Similarity Evaluation Technique for Cooperative Problem Solving with a Group of Agents

Seppo Puuronen[1] and Vagan Terziyan [2]

[1] University of Jyväskylä, Department of Computer Science and Information Systems, PO.
Box 35, FIN-40351 Jyväskylä, Finland
sepi@jytko.jyu.fi
[2] Kharkov State Technical University of Radioelectronics, 14 Lenin Avenue,
310166 Kharkov, Ukraine
vagan@kture.cit-ua.net

Abstract. Evaluation of distance or similarity is very important in cooperative problem solving with a group of agents. Distance between problems is used by agents to recognize nearest solved problems for a new problem, distance between solutions is necessary to compare and evaluate the solutions made by different agents, and distance between agents is useful to evaluate weights of the agents to be able to integrate them by weighted voting. The goal of this paper is to develop a similarity evaluation technique to be used for cooperative problem solving with a group of agents. Virtual training environment used for this goal is represented by predicates that define relationships within three sets: problems, solutions, and agents. We derive and interpret both internal and external relations between the pairs of subsets taken of the three sets: problems, solutions, and agents. The refinement technique presented is based on the derivation of the most supported solution of the group of agents and refining it further using a multilevel structure of agents.

1 Introduction

Cooperative problem solving methods have been developed based on intelligent information agents' framework. Evaluation of distance or similarity is very important in cooperative problem solving with a group of agents. Distance between problems is used by agents to recognize nearest solved problems for a new problem, distance between solutions is necessary to compare and evaluate the solutions made by different agents, and distance between agents is useful to evaluate weights of the agents to be able to integrate them by weighted voting. The goal of this paper is to develop a similarity evaluation technique to be used for cooperative problem solving with a group of agents. Virtual training environment used for this goal is represented by predicates that define relationships within three sets: problems, solutions, and agents. We derive and interpret both internal and external relations between the pairs of subsets taken of the three sets: problems, solutions, and agents. The refinement technique presented is based on the derivation of the most supported solution of the group of agents and refining it further using a multilevel structure of agents.

We use an assumption that each agent has its competence area inside the domain area. In a way cooperative problem solving with a group of agents has much in common with the multiple expertise problem or with the problem of combining multiple classifiers in machine learning, data mining and knowledge discovery [3,4]. All three groups of problems solve the task by taking submissions from several sources and selecting the best one separately for every new case. In [14] we have suggested a voting-type technique and recursive statistical analysis to handle knowledge obtained from multiple medical experts. In [15] we presented a meta-statistical tool to manage different statistical techniques used in knowledge discovery.

Evaluation of distance or similarity between problems is used to recognize solved problems, which are the nearest neighbors of a new problem. Such distance, for example, is widely used to integrate multiple classifiers [12]. Distance between solutions is necessary when an agent learns based on virtual training environment to evaluate its individual solution relatively to previously made cooperative solutions (similar Cross-Validation Majority approach [6,8] is used to learn multiple classifiers). This distance helps to find out the areas of competence for agents (like in [7] to find out competence areas for every individual classifier from an ensemble). Distance between agents is useful for example to evaluate the weights of the agents to be able to integrate solution results by weighted voting (this has analogy with the classifiers' integration technique [1]).

There are many approaches to define distance between any two problems based on their numerical or semantic closeness. For example the semantic closeness between terms is a measure of how closely terms are related in the solution schema [13]. Distance metric used by Rada et al. [10] represents the conceptual distance between concepts. Rada et al. uses only the path length to determine this conceptual distance, with no consideration of node or link characteristics. Distance is measured as the length of the path representing the traversal from the first term to the second. Rocha [11] has suggested a method to "fuzzify" conversation theory, by calculating continuously varying conceptual distances between nodes in an entailment mesh, on the basis of the number of linked nodes they share. In order to measure the distance between two concepts in a mind, Jorgensen measures a distance between two concepts, which he calls *psy* [5]. It has been suggested to assign an arbitrary distance of n units to the separation between two concepts such as "Concept A" and "Concept B" and then ask a subject to tell us how far other concepts (C and D) are from each other in these units. Problem-based learning techniques typically handle continuous and linear input values well, but often do not handle nominal input attributes appropriately. To compute the similarity between two solutions also a probabilistic metrics of the PEBLS algorithm [2] can be applied. The distance d_i between two solutions v_1 and v_2 for a certain problem is:

$$d(v_1, v_2) = \sum_{i=1}^{k} \left(\frac{C_{1i}}{C_1} - \frac{C_{2i}}{C_2} \right)^2,$$

where C_1 and C_2 are the numbers of problems in the virtual training environment with selected solutions v_1 and v_2, C_{1i} and C_{2i} are the numbers of problems from the i-th group of problems, where the solutions v_1 and v_2 were selected, and k is the number of groups of problems.

The value difference metric was designed by Wilson and Martinez [16] to find reasonable distance values between nominal attribute values, but it largely ignores continuous attributes, requiring discretization to map continuous values into nominal values. As it was mentioned in the Wilson and Martinez review [16] there are many learning systems that depend upon a good distance function to be successful. A variety of distance functions are available for such uses, including the Minkowsky, Mahalanobis, Camberra, Chebychev, Quadratic, Correlation, and Chi-square distance metrics; the Context-Similarity measure; the Contrast Model; hyperrectangle distance functions, and others [16].

The present paper deals with the cooperative problem solving with virtual training environment and a group of agents. The agents make a virtual training environment that is then used for learning purposes. For virtual training environment representation, we use predicates that connect problems, solutions and agents. Each agent defines its selection concerning each problem-solution pair by a voting-type system supporting or resisting the use of a solution to solve the problem. The agent also has the option to refuse to vote in favor of either possibility. We apply our formalisms developed in [9] to define general framework of similarity evaluation between problems, solutions and agents to be used in the cooperative problem solving with a group of agents.

In chapter 2 we present the basic notation used throughout the paper and the problems to be discussed. The next chapter deals with finding the most supported relations among the agents. In chapter 4 we discuss the discovery of similarity relations between problems, solutions, and agents. Chapter 5 deals with a virtual training environment refinement using relations discovered. We end with a short conclusion in the last chapter.

2 Notation and problems

In this chapter we present the basic notation used throughout the paper and describe briefly the main problems discussed in the paper.

Virtual training environment created by a group of agents is represented by a quadruple $< D, C, S, P >$, where D is the set of the problems D_1, D_2,..., D_n in the virtual training environment, C is the set of the solutions C_1, C_2,..., C_m, that are used to solve the problems, S is the set of the agents S_1, S_2,..., S_r, which select solutions to solve the problem, and P is the set of semantic predicates that define relationships between D, C, S as follows:

$$P(D_i, C_j, S_k) = \begin{cases} 1, \textit{if the agent } S_k \textit{ selects solution } C_j \\ \quad \textit{to solve the problem } D_i; \\ -1, \textit{if } S_k \textit{ refuses to select } C_j \\ \quad \textit{to solve } D_i; \\ 0, \textit{if } S_k \textit{ does not select or refuse} \\ \quad \textit{to select } C_j \textit{ to solve } D_i. \end{cases}$$

We will consider three groups of problems that deal with processing virtual training environment based on a group of agents.

1. *Binary relations between the elements of (sub)sets of C and D; of S and C; and of S and C.* The value of the relation between each pair (C_j, D_i) of elements shows the support among all the agents for selection (or refusal to select) of the solution C_j to solve the problem D_i. This is called the total support. The value of the relation between each pair (S_k, D_i) of elements shows the total support which the agent S_k receives selecting (or refusing to select) all the solutions from C to solve the problem D_i. The value of the relation between each pair (S_k, C_j) of elements shows the total support which the agent S_k receives selecting (or refusing to select) the solution C_j to solve all the problems from D. We will refer to this first group of deriving relations as *deriving external similarity values.*

2. *Binary relations between two subsets of D; two subsets of C; and two subsets of S.* The value of the relation between each pair (D_s, D_t) of the two problems from D shows the support for the neighbourhood ("similarity") of these problems via the solutions, via the agents, or via both of these. The value of the relation between each pair (C_s, C_t) of the two solutions from C shows the support for the nearness ("similarity") of these solutions via the problems, via the agents, or via both of these. The value of the relation between each pair (S_s, S_t) of the two agents from S shows the support for the likeness ("similarity") of these agents via the problems, via the solutions, or via both of these. We will refer to this second group of deriving relations as *deriving internal similarity values.*

3. *Refinement of a virtual training environment.* This means the improvement of the virtual training environment for the cooperative problem solving problems based on internal and external similarity values and using the existing intersection between sets D and S. Such intersection reveals possibilities for some agents to select some other agents. In some cases, an intersection can be interpreted as a multilevel structure. For example, such a multilevel structure occurs when some agents select other agents, which select other agents, and so on.

3 Deriving external similarity values

In this chapter, we define first how the total support for binary relations is formed. We consider relations between any pair of subsets taken from different sets D, C, or

S. Then we introduce how the values describing this total support are standardized to the closed interval [0,1]. Next we study an evaluation of the quality of the agents. In section 3.4, we describe the use of threshold value to select the relations and we conclude this chapter by giving an example.

3.1 Total support of binary relations

The total support of the binary relations *DC*, *CD*, *DS*, *SD*, *CS* and *SC* is formed using the following formulas:

$$DC_{i,j} = CD_{j,i} = \sum_{k}^{r} P(D_i, C_j, S_k), \forall D_i \in D, \forall C_j \in C;$$

$$SC_{k,j} = CS_{j,k} = \sum_{i}^{n} DC_{i,j} \cdot P(D_i, C_j, S_k), \forall S_k \in S, \forall C_j \in C;$$

$$SD_{k,i} = DS_{i,k} = \sum_{j}^{m} DC_{i,j} \cdot P(D_i, C_j, S_k), \forall S_k \in S, \forall D_i \in D.$$

The definition of the value of the relation between each pair (C_j, D_i) of the elements of the sets *C* and *D* sums up the total support among all the agents for selection (or refusal to select) of the solution C_j to solve the problem D_i. If, for example, three agents select the solution C_j to solve the problem D_i, then $DC_{i,j}=3$.

The definition of the value for each pair (S_k, D_i) of the elements of the sets *S* and *D* and for each pair (S_k, C_j) of the elements of the sets *S* and *C* use the total support calculated above. The value of the relation (S_k, C_j) in a way represents the total support that the agent S_k obtains selecting (refusing to select) the solution C_j to solve all the problems. If, for example, agent S_k selects solution C_j to solve four problems from the environment, then $SC_{kj}=4$.

The value of the relation (S_k, D_i) represents the total support that the agent S_k receives selecting (or refusing to select) all the solutions to solve the problem D_i. If, for example, agent S_k uses two different solutions to solve the same problem D_i, then $SD_{k,i}=2$.

3.2 Standardizing total support of binary relations

The goal of standardizing external relations is to make the appropriate similarity values to be within the closed interval [0,1]. For this we use simple basic scheme:

$$\text{standardizing value} = [\text{value}] = \frac{\text{value} - \min(\text{value})}{\max(\text{value}) - \min(\text{value})}.$$

From the definitions presented in 3.1 it follows that the minimum and maximum values of total support in each relation are:

$$\max_{i,j} DC_{i,j} = \max_{j,i} CD_{j,i} = r; \ \min_{i,j} DC_{i,j} = \min_{j,i} CD_{j,i} = -r;$$

$$\max_{k,j} SC_{k,j} = \max_{j,k} CS_{j,k} = n \cdot r; \ \min_{k,j} SC_{k,j} = \min_{j,k} CS_{j,k} = n \cdot (2-r);$$

$$\max_{k,i} SD_{k,i} = \max_{i,k} DS_{i,k} = m \cdot r; \ \min_{k,i} SD_{k,i} = \min_{i,k} DS_{i,k} = m \cdot (2-r).$$

The transformation to the standardized values can be made using the following formulas (notice that we use brackets around the name of the standardized support array to distinguish it from the array with the basic support values):

$$[DC]_{i,j} = [CD]_{j,i} = \frac{DC_{i,j} + r}{2 \cdot r}; \ [SC]_{k,j} = [CS]_{j,k} = \frac{SC_{k,j} + n \cdot (r-2)}{2 \cdot n \cdot (r-1)};$$

$$[SD]_{k,i} = [DS]_{i,k} = \frac{SD_{k,i} + m \cdot (r-2)}{2 \cdot m \cdot (r-1)}.$$

3.3 Quality evaluation

The quality of each agent from the support point of view is calculated using the standardized total support values derived in 3.2. For each agent S_k, we define a quality value $Q^D(S_k)$ that measures the abilities of the agent in the area of problems, and a quality value $Q^C(S_k)$ that measures the abilities of the agent in the area of solutions:

$$Q^D(S_k) = \frac{1}{n} \cdot \sum_{i}^{n} [SD]_{k,i} = Q^C(S_k) = \frac{1}{m} \cdot \sum_{j}^{m} [SC]_{k,j}.$$

The above shows that the evaluation of an agent competence (ranking, weighting) does not depend on the competence area "virtual world of problems" or "conceptual world of solutions" because both competence values are always equal.

3.4 Selecting relations using threshold value

There are situations where it is reasonable to pick up the most supported relations as a cooperative result of the agents. We use a threshold value as a for calculating the cutting points used to select the appropriate relations. These cutting values are applied to the standardized support arrays. First we select the threshold value T that belongs to the closed interval [0,1] and then we calculate the cutting points and apply them to the standardized values of relations as follows:

$$\forall T (T \in [0,1]) \forall [A]_{s,t} ([A]_{s,t} \in [A] \in \{[CD]; [DC]; ...; [DS]\}) \exists$$

$$\exists \tilde{T}((\tilde{T} = \frac{T \cdot \sigma_{[A]}^2 + \mu_{[A]}}{\sigma_{[A]}^2 + 1}) \&$$

$$\& \begin{cases} ([A]_{s,t} \geq \tilde{T})) & \Rightarrow [A]_{s,t}^T = 1; \\ ([A]_{s,t} \leq 2 \cdot \mu_{[A]} - \tilde{T})) & \Rightarrow [A]_{s,t}^T = -1; \\ (2 \cdot \mu_{[A]} - \tilde{T} < [A]_{s,t} < \tilde{T})) \Rightarrow [A]_{s,t}^T = 0, \end{cases}$$

where: $\mu_{[A]}$ is the average and $\sigma_{[A]}^2$ is the standard deviation of the values of a matrix $[A]$;

We will use the operator $[A]^T$ for selection of the relations according to the threshold value T. This operator takes into account the distribution of the values.

4 Deriving internal similarity values

In this chapter we first define internal similarity values between the same type of subsets. Then we present the internal similarity value of each type: agent, solution, and problem in their own sections. An internal similarity value is based on an internal relation between any two subsets taken from the same set D, C, or S. An internal relation is derived using as an intermediate set one of the other sets or both of the other sets. We refer to the relation which has one intermediate set I as an I-based relation, and we refer to the relation with two intermediate sets I and J as an IJ-based relation.

In the following definitions we need parts of the relations SD, DS, SC, CS, DC, and CD. These parts are formed from the original relations by taking the appropriate subsets of values. For example, when we have two subsets S' and S'' of the set S, then $S'D$ and DS'' are:

$$\forall S'_{k'} \in S, \forall D_i \in D \exists S_k ((S_k \in S) \&$$

$$\& (S_k = S'_{k'}) \& (S' D_{k',i} = SD_{k,i}));$$

$$\forall S''_{k''} \in S, \forall D_i \in D \exists S_k ((S_k \in S) \&$$

$$\& (S_k = S''_{k''}) \& (DS''_{i,k''} = DS_{i,k})).$$

4.1 Internal similarity values for agents

Internal similarity values between any two subsets of the set S are derived using as an intermediate set the set of problems, the set of solutions, or both of these.

D-based similarity. Let S' and S'' be subsets of the set S. We define the D-based internal similarity value between S' and S'' as a value of the relation $S'S''^D$ is obtained by the following rule: $\forall S' \subset S, \forall S'' \subset S \Rightarrow S'S''^D = S'D \times DS''$, where $\times$ is the symbol of multiplication of the appropriate matrixes. It is obvious that $S'S''^D_{s,t} \equiv S''S'^D_{t,s}$.

To obtain standardized values we assume that $r \geq 2$ (there exist at least two agents). Then we calculate min and max values which are:

$$\min_{k',k''} S'S''^D_{k',k''} = \min_{k'',k'} S''S'^D_{k'',k'} = \sum_i^n (\min_{k,i} SD_{k,i} \cdot \max_{i,k} DS_{i,k}) =$$

$$= \sum_i^n (m \cdot (2-r) \cdot m \cdot r) = n \cdot m^2 \cdot r \cdot (2-r);$$

$$\max_{k',k''} S'S''^D_{k',k''} = \max_{k'',k'} S''S'^D_{k'',k'} = \sum_i^n (\max_{k,i} SD_{k,i} \cdot \max_{i,k} DS_{i,k}) =$$

$$= \sum_i^n (m \cdot r \cdot m \cdot r) = n \cdot m^2 \cdot r^2.$$

The standardized values of D-based internal similarity between agents are:

$$\left[S'S'' \right]^D_{k',k''} = \left[S''S' \right]^D_{k'',k'} =$$

$$= \frac{S'S''^D_{k',k''} + n \cdot m^2 \cdot r \cdot (r-2)}{2 \cdot n \cdot m^2 \cdot r \cdot (r-1)}, \forall S',S'' \subset S.$$

C-based similarity. We define the C-based internal similarity between any two subsets S' and S'' of the set S as value of the relation $S'S''^C$ is obtained by the following rule: $\forall S' \subset S, \forall S'' \subset S \Rightarrow S'S''^C = S'C \times CS''$. It is obvious that $S'S''^C_{s,t} \equiv S''S'^C_{t,s}$.

To derive standardized similarity values, we need min and max values which are:

$$\min_{k',k''} S'S''^C_{k',k''} = \min_{k'',k'} S''S'^C_{k'',k'} = \sum_j^m (\min_{k,j} SC_{k,j} \cdot \max_{j,k} CS_{j,k}) =$$

$$= \sum_j^m (n \cdot (2-r) \cdot n \cdot r) = m \cdot n^2 \cdot r \cdot (2-r);$$

$$\max_{k',k''} S'S''^C_{k',k''} = \max_{k'',k'} S''S'^C_{k'',k'} = \sum_j^m (\max_{k,j} SC_{k,j} \cdot \max_{j,k} CS_{j,k}) =$$

$$= \sum_j^m (n \cdot r \cdot n \cdot r) = m \cdot n^2 \cdot r^2.$$

The standardized values of C-based internal similarity between agents are:

$$\left[S'S''\right]^{C}_{k'',k''} = \left[S''S'\right]^{C}_{k'',k'} = \frac{S'S''^{C}_{k'',k''} + m \cdot n^2 \cdot r \cdot (r-2)}{2 \cdot m \cdot n^2 \cdot r \cdot (r-1)}.$$

DC- based similarity and *CD- based similarity.* We define the *DC*-based internal similarity between two subsets S', S'' of the set S as the value of the relation $S'S''^{DC}$ obtained by the following rule: $\forall S' \subset S, \forall S'' \subset S \Rightarrow S'S''^{DC} = S'D \times DC \times CS''$.

We define the *CD*-similarity $S'S''^{CD}$ using the following rule: $\forall S' \subset S, \forall S'' \subset S \Rightarrow S'S''^{CD} = S'C \times CD \times DS''$. It can be shown that $S'S''^{DC}_{s,t} \equiv S'S''^{CD}_{t,s}$.

4.2 Internal similarity between solutions

Internal similarity values between any two subsets of solutions are defined in a similar way as those between agents. We represent here only formulas for calculating main (not standardized) values of the appropriate relations.

S-based relation. We define the *S*-based internal similarity between any two subsets C' and C'' of the set C as the value the relation $C'C''^{S}$ which can be obtained as follows: $\forall C' \subset C, \forall C'' \subset C \Rightarrow C'C''^{S} = C'S \times SC''$.

D-based relation. We define the *D*-based internal similarity between any two subsets C' and C'' of the set C as the value of the relation $C'C''^{D}$ obtained by the following rule: $\forall C' \subset C, \forall C'' \subset C \Rightarrow C'C''^{D} = C'D \times DC''$.

DS- and SD-based similarity. We define *DS*- and *SD*-based internal similarity values between any two subsets C' and C'' of the set C to be obtained by the following rule:

$$\forall C', C'' \subset C \Rightarrow C'C''^{DS} = C'C''^{SD} =$$
$$= C'D \times DS \times SC'' = C'S \times SD \times DC''.$$

4.3 Internal similarity between problems

We define the internal similarity between problems in a similar way as the previous ones between agents and solutions. Here as in previous subchapter we present only formulas for calculating main (not standardized) values of the appropriate relations.

S-based similarity. We define the *S*-based internal similarity between any two subsets D' and D'' of the set D as the value of the relation $D'D''^{S}$ obtained by the following rule: $\forall D' \subset D, \forall D'' \subset D \Rightarrow D'D''^{S} = D'S \times SD''$.

C-based similarity. We define the *C*-based internal similarity between any two subsets D' and D'' of the set D as the value of the relation $D'D''^{C}$ obtained by the following rule: $\forall D' \subset D, \forall D'' \subset D \Rightarrow D'D''^{C} = D'C \times CD''$.

CS- and SC-based similarity. We define *CS-* and *SC*-based internal similarity values between any two subsets D' and D'' of the set D to be obtained by the use of the following rule:

$$\forall D', D'' \subset D \Rightarrow D'D''^{CS} = D'D''^{SC} =$$

$$= D'C \times CS \times SD'' = D'S \times SC \times CD''.$$

5 Virtual training environment refinement

In this chapter we first discuss a situation where the sets of problems and agents are not disjoint. It means that agents are considered themselves as problems for solution. Solution in such case can be thought as selection.

Let us suppose that there exists a nonempty set S^D that includes elements belonging to the intersection of the sets D and S: $S \cap D = S^D$. Thus some of the agents select some other agents through a common element which gives a possibility to define new connection from any problem D_i to any agent S_k (using the external relation between D_i and $S_{k'}$ and the external relation between $D_{i'}$ and S_k) which is obviously more informative than the direct external DS connection (3.1).

Such intersection reveals possibilities for some agents to select some other agents to solve the problem. In some cases, an intersection can be interpreted as a multilevel structure. For example, such a multilevel structure occurs when some agents select some other agents, which select some other agents, and so on. For such general case we define subsets $S^1, S^2, ..., S^w$ of the set S as follows:

$$S^1 = \left\{ S_k \in S | \exists D_i \in D \setminus S^D \,\&\, \exists C_j \in C \,\&\, P(D_i, C_j, S_k) \neq 0 \right\} \text{ and}$$

$$S^{a+1} = \left\{ S_k \in S | \exists S_q \in S^a \,\&\, \exists C_j \in C \,\&\, P(S_q, C_j, S_k) \neq 0 \right\}, a = 1, ..., w-1.$$

We have: $S^1 \cup ... \cup S^w = S$, and $S^a \cap S^{a+1}, a = 1, ..., w-1$ might be empty or nonempty. We say that an agent S_k belongs to the level a when it is included in the set S^a.

At each level of agents, it is possible to calculate the total support of binary relations, then standardized values, quality evaluation and use threshold value as presented in chapter 3.

We define a refined DC-matrix ($^*DC$) using this multilevel structure of agents. Refinement is made so that those solution results of agents in higher levels of the hierarchy have a greater effect on the resulting values of matrix $^*DC$. Let us suppose that we have the subsets $S^1, S^2, ..., S^w$ of agents at the levels $1, 2, ..., w$. Then the refined DC-matrix is obtained as follows:

$$^*DC_{i,j} = (DS^1 \times S^1 S^2 \times ... \times S^{w-1} S^w \times S^w C)_{i,j}, \text{ where:}$$

$$DS_{i,k}^1 = \sum_{j}^{m} (DC_{i,j} \cdot P(D_i, C_j, S_k)), \forall S_k \in S^1, \forall D_i \in D \backslash S^D,$$

$$S^a S_{i,k}^{a+1} = \sum_{j}^{m} (DC_{i,j} \cdot P(D_i, C_j, S_k)), \forall S_k \in S^{a+1}, \forall D_i \in S^a,$$

$$S^w C_{i,j} = \sum_{i, \forall D_i \in S^{w-1}}^{n} (DC_{i,j} \cdot P(D_i, C_j, S_k)), \forall S_k \in S^w, \forall C_j \in C.$$

It is possible to show that $^*CD_{j,i} = {}^*DC_{i,j} = (CS^w \times S^w S^{w-1} \times ... \times S^2 S^1 \times S^1 D)_{j,i}$.

6 Conclusion

The goal of this paper was to develop formal similarity evaluation framework to be used in cooperative problem solving with group of agents.

In this paper, we represent a virtual training environment by predicates defining relations between the elements of three sets: problems, solutions, and agents. This representation is directly applicable, for example, when virtual training environment is collected using a three-value voting technique. Each agent derives his comprehension of the use of each solution to solve each problem. Each agent can accept the use of the solution to solve the problem, refuse such use or be indifferent. The results of voting are collected into a basic predicate array. Discussion was given to methods of deriving the total support of each binary similarity relation. This represents the most supported solution result that can, for example, be used to evaluate the agents. We also discussed relations between elements taken from the same set: problems, solutions, or agents. This is used, for example, to divide agents into groups of similar competence relatively to the problem environment. Discussion was given also to refining virtual training environment when certain agents select some other agents. In this case we divide semantic predicates at several levels and use refined support arrays.

The results presented in this paper are mostly on a formal level. Further research with real examples is required in order to evaluate their usefulness in real environments. We also plan to generalize our basic voting setting into more general value settings.

Acknowledgment: This research has been partly supported by the grant from the Academy of Finland.

References

1. 1. Bauer, E., Kohavi, R.: An Empirical Comparison of Voting Solution Algorithms: Bagging, Boosting, and Variants. Machine Learning, Vol. 33 (1998).

2. Cost, S., Salzberg, S.: A Weighted Nearest Neighbor Algorithm for Learning with Symbolic Features. Machine Learning, Vol. 10, No. 1 (1993) 57-78.

3. Dietterich, T.G.: Machine Learning Research: Four Current Directions. AI Magazine, Vol. 18, No. 4 (1997) 97-136.

4. Fayyad, U., Piatetsky-Shapiro, G., Smyth, P., Uthurusamy, R.: Advances in Knowledge Discovery and Cooperative problem solving. AAAI/ MIT Press (1997).

5. Jorgensen P.: P Jorgensen's COM515 Project Page (1996) Available in WWW: http://jorg2.cit.bufallo.edu/COM515/ project.html.

6. Kohavi, R.: A Study of Cross-Validation and Bootstrap for Accuracy Estimation and Model Selection. In: Proceedings of IJCAI'95 (1995).

7. Koppel, M., Engelson, S.P.: Integrating Multiple Agents by Finding their Areas of Expertise. In: AAAI-96 Workshop On Integrating Multiple Learning Models (1996) 53-58.

8. Merz, C.: Dynamical Selection of Learning Algorithms. In: D. Fisher, H.-J.Lenz (Eds.), Learning from Data, Artificial Intelligence and Statistics, Springer Verlag, NY (1996).

9. Puuronen, S., Terziyan, V.: The Voting-type Technique in the Refinement of Multiple Expert Knowledge. In: Sprague, R. H., (Ed.), Proceedings of the Thirtieth Hawaii International Conference on System Sciences, Vol. V, IEEE Computer Society Press (1997) 287-296.

10. Rada R., Mili H., Bicknell E., Blettner M.: Development and application of a metric on semantic nets, IEEE Transactions on Systems, Man, and Cybernetics, Vol. 19, No. 1 (1989) 17-30.

11. Rocha L., Luis M.: Fuzzification of Conversation Theory, In: F. Heylighen (ed.), Principia Cybernetica Conference, Free University of Brussels (1991).

12. Skalak, D.B.: Combining Nearest Neighbor Agents. Ph.D. Thesis, Dept. of Computer Science, University of Massachusetts, Amherst, MA (1997).

13. Tailor C., Tudhope D., Semantic Closeness and Solution Schema Based Hypermedia Access, In: Proceedings of the 3-rd International Conference on Electronic Library and Visual Information Research (ELVIRA'96), Milton, Keynes (1996).

14. Terziyan, V., Tsymbal, A., Puuronen, S.: The Decision Support System for Telemedicine Based on Multiple Expertise. International Journal of Medical Informatics, Vol. 49, No. 2 (1998) 217-229.

15. Terziyan, V., Tsymbal, A., Tkachuk, A., Puuronen, S.: Intelligent Medical Diagnostics System Based on Integration of Statistical Methods. In: Informatica Medica Slovenica, Journal of Slovenian Society of Medical Informatics,Vol.3, Ns. 1,2,3 (1996) 109-114.

16. Wilson D., Martinez T., Improved Heterogeneous Distance Functions, Journal of Artificial Intelligence Research, Vol. 6 (1997) 1-34.

A Computational Model for a Cooperating Agent System

S. M. Deen
DAKE Group, Computer Science Department
University of Keele,
Keele, Staffs, ST5 5BG
England
Fax: +441782 713082
Email: deen@cs.keele.ac.uk

Abstract

This paper first describes a cooperation approach for a Cooperating Knowledge Based System, founded on an *engineering paradigm* (as against a *mentallistic* paradigm of DAI) that is meant to ensure termination of the execution process at user-defined recoverable points. The paper then develops an execution model, based on a highly distributed architecture with many operational primitives. The execution model forces the operations to terminate at the start of these primitives without forming any cycles, which are are avoided by rigorous control at each functional components within an agent. The model also supports rollback, redo, recovery and abort, and provides operational stability.

This model is intended to provide the theoretical foundation of a major international project in agent-based manufacturing,

Keywords: Computational model, Multi-agent System, Cooperating Knowledge Based System.

1. Introduction

Agent technology is a growing area of research and development, in which the Multi-Agent Systems (MAS) of DAI has distinguished itself by using a *mentallistic* approach for inter-system cooperation (and competition) among large grain autonomous agents for distributed applications. The area of our research, under the title of Cooperating Knowledge Based Systems (CKBSs) overlaps with that of DAI/MAS, except that we use an engineering (or database-oriented) approach. The objective in this approach is to provide a good solution for real-world distributed applications, using well-founded computer-science concepts, borrowing ideas from distributed databases. It is therefore important for us to ensure that our model provides termination with predictability. Our general model has been described in [2,3,34].

In this paper an agent is assumed to be an autonomous system, having a compulsory software and an optional hardware component. Structurally an agent has a head connected to its body by a communication link called the neck. Typically the head is largely software and is responsible for inter-agent activities (including communications), while the body (subdivided into functional components) provides the individualistic skill of the agent and may include hardware.

Generally we assume an agent to be characterised by a behaviour model, which in the case of a cooperating agent is complemented by a cooperation model, the behaviour of an agent to be displayed during execution, failure and recovery. During execution, an agent may offer options to choose from, and it may support invocation of special procedures on various execution states. On failure, an agent may or may not ask for its replacement (which may involve negotiation), depending on the nature of the failure and the behaviour of the agent. Equally a recovery will generally require rollback, and sometimes rescheduling (with negotiation). The behaviour of the agent will dictate how these activities will be carried out. In our approach we separate agent behaviour described above into two parts: self-invoked which the agent invokes automatically depending on its execution logic, and user-invoked which the user specifies in what we call a *Cooperation Strategy* of a task.

We assume all our agents to be implicitly cooperative - an agent will what it is asked to do unless it is busy or incapable. We shall describe later our cooperation model. The cooperation strategy is a user-defined specification of how a task will be processed (execution, failure and recovery) in a cooperation environment.

In this paper, we wish to develop a computational model for a cooperative process (in which a set of agents work together to solve a joint task), with a view to showing that the process will always terminate, if not successfully, then at user-defined recovery points. The plan of the paper is: In section 2 we shall describe our cooperation model, while in section 3 we shall present our operational framework. The execution model is given in section 4, followed by a discussion on the correctness of the model in section 5. However, we shall present below some related activities, largely from the domain of DAI multi-agent systems before we proceed to the next section.

Related Activities

Concepts of belief, desire and intention (BDI) as the basis of a single-agent architecture were introduced by Bratman et al [4, 5] and developed further by Rao and Georgeff [6,7]. These concepts are also employed in DAI/multi-agent architectures as reviewed below. The BDI scheme defines the internal processing of an agent through a set of mental categories, within a control framework for rational selection of a course of action, often with the added concepts of goals and plans.

The Speech-Act theory of Searle [8] encouraged multi-agent researchers [9,16,20] to develop inter-agent communications protocols, treating communication as a type of action to be incorporated to the planning and reasoning processes. Primitives inspired by the Speech-Act theory and used in many multi-agent prototypes include propose, refuse, oppose, respond, refute and inform. More recently DARPA has introduced a Lisp-based environment, with KIF (Knowledge Interchange Format) [10] and KQML (Knowledge Query Manipulation Language) [11], which has made an impact particularly in the United States. Y. Shoham's [12] Agent Oriented Programming Language (AOPL), apparently motivated by Searle's Speech Act theory, is a logic based instrument for multi-agent systems. Agents are specified with a set of capabilities, a set of beliefs and commitments and a set of commitment rules, the rules determining how an agent acts. However, Shoham's agents are unable to plan or to communicate requests for certain types of actions, and a major drawback of AOPL is its inability to execute the associated logic.

The Cosy architecture of Haddadi et al [13, 14] of Daimler-Benz is considered to be a hybrid BDI architecture, with five main components: (i) sensors, (ii) actuators, (iii) communications, (iv) cognition and (v) intentions. The cognition component is made up of four further components: knowledge base (for belief), script execution, protocol execution and reasoning (with deciding and reacting). Its communication protocols are a set of predefined dialogue trees. It has been applied to the simulation of some road traffic problems.

Mueller's INTERRAP model [15, 16] is built on a layered architecture, with hierarchical abstractions. The highest layer is the cooperation layer and the lowest is the world interface, with behaviour and plan based layers in between. The inter-agent communications are expressed through primitives, such as Inform, Announce, Reject, Accept etc, within logic expressions. The effectiveness of the model has been demonstrated in a simulated environment to resolve conflicts among forklift robots placing boxes on shelves.

The European ESPRIT programme supported two major projects on multi-agent systems: ARCHON [17] and IMAGINE [19] the first for application in complex systems such as power-plants and the second as a more general approach. The GRATE model [18] of Jennings, based on the ARCHON project, consists of two major layers: (i) cooperation and control layer and (ii) application domain layer. The behaviour of the cooperation layer is determined from the built-in knowledge held in the system, but does not address the issue of how to reconcile reactivity and deliberation. Domain dependent information includes self model and acquaintances models. As indicated above the model has been used in a number of simulated environments.

The MECCA architecture of Steiner et al [20] is an off-shoot of the IMAGINE project, in which this author was also a participant. Steiner divides an agent structurally into two parts: head and base (or body) as in our model. However Steiner's approach is AI-based, supporting four parallel processes in the agent head: goal activation, planning, scheduling and execution. A set of cooperation methods and cooperation primitives are defined as required for specific applications. An extended version of concurrent Prolog is seen as the basis of distributed processing in the model, presently upgraded with Java. The model has been applied to a simulated traffic control environment.

A different approach has been advocated by M. Singh [21], who employs a triplet of intention, know-how (ability plus knowledge) and communication, which he has formalised into a model of actions and time. According to this model, agents' intentions, along with their knowledge and know-how, constrain the actions they choose to perform. Agents that know how to achieve what they intend can succeed provided they (a) act on their intentions, (b) exercise their know-how, and (c) persist with their intentions long enough. The model is perhaps a shade too complex for effective implementation.

More recently FIPA (Foundation of Intelligent Physical Agents) [22], in which a number of DAI researchers (including Steiner of the MECCA Architecture [20] are involved), has proposed a detailed agent architecture, which includes an infrastructure, a communications facility, commands and languages. It uses the BDI concepts with some modification, such as a new concept of *uncertain*, and supports Speech-Act inspired primitives, mentioned above.

The architectures described above employ different interpretations of the basic BDI approach, sometimes referred to as the *folk psychological approach* (i.e. the ascription of mental propositions or intentionality to a computer system), which has been criticised as non-scientific by some researchers, such as Paul Churchland [23] and Patricia Churchland et al [24], who believe that much more research is needed on how the human-brain works before a viable approach can be developed in this area. As stated earlier, simulation of human behaviour and the thinking process is not our objective and therefore our approach is different from those above.

An IEC group has recently proposed a distributed architecture, based on what it calls Function Blocks, for distributed programmable controllers [27, 28]. This architecture is being adapted for agent-based manufacturing by the HMS project [29], and can be viewed as an implementation instance of our more formalised model [30].

There are a number of research papers available that address the area of agent-based manufacturing. Norrie et al [31] discussed some multi-agent facility for concurrent engineering, Parunak et al [32, 33] addressed the issues in agent-based manufacturing, and Jarvis et al [35] investigated quality control issues in holonic manufacturing.

2. Cooperation Model

We may define cooperation as the process in which agents carry out dependent activities of a joint task, also referred to as a global task. In turn, negotiation is a process by which agents agree on a mutually acceptable solution. The agents work together in what we call cooperation blocks, one such block for each joint task, each block having a coordinator and one or more cohorts. The coordinator supervises the execution of the joint task as a whole and selects other agents as its cohorts for their specific skills, perhaps through negotiation, say using a Contract Net protocol [25, 26]. Before selecting its cohorts, the coordinator has to decompose (unless already decomposed) its global task into lower tasks and perhaps into further lower tasks as appropriate. A cohort can in turn be a coordinator of a lower-level cooperation block, to solve its task as a joint task, with the help of other agents. The process can continue recursively.

2.1 Dynamic Constraints in Cooperation

Let us consider a global task $T = GT$ where G represents the global constraints applied to T in order to complete T. In a *trivial cooperation* a task T is decomposed into a set of lower tasks as:

$$T = T^0, T^1, \ldots, T^n \quad \ldots \ldots \text{Eqn (1)}.$$

where $T^i = G_i T_i'$, task T_i' to be executed by agent (i.e. cohort) A_i, using skill K^i, subject to the constraint G_i, except A_0 is part of the coordinator executing the residual global task T^0, subject to the residual global constraint G_0. The constraints $\{G_i\}$ are *static*: that is, they do not change dynamically; they are exclusive to each task T_i', and remain independent of the solutions of other tasks. Each cohort in general may come up with a number of possible solutions, the collection being referred to as its solution space. Any solution that satisfies the constraints $\{G_i\}$ is acceptable. Each cohort produces its solution independently of other cohorts. A common example is a distributed database query.

The principal characteristic of a *nontrivial cooperation* is the generation of dynamic constraints by agents during the execution of their tasks - the dynamic constraints produced by one agent are generally meant to be obeyed by other agents. Nontrivial cooperation is needed in solving complex problems. Consider a complex query for a customer to fly to New York for three days in the second half of June, by some preferred airlines, with a cheap ticket and preference to stay in a relatively inexpensive hotel close to Broadway, ideally on the 47th Street. The task can be solved by three agents: a coordinator and two cohorts, say, an air-travel database (agent) and a hotel database (agent). Each cohort may come up with a set of local solutions, but the solution of one cohort dynamically creates constraints on the other, since they have to match on the three days. This problem has:

P: Preferences
G: Global constraints (e.g., the second half of June)
S: Solution space
D: Dynamically generated constraints which forbids some solutions

We can describe such a task more generally as:

$$T = PGTD$$

where P represents the preferences and G the global (static) constraints that apply to T to produce **T**. The dynamic constraints D are generated during the execution. We can decompose it over n agents as before:

$$\mathbf{T} = T^0, T^1, \ldots, T^n \quad \ldots \ldots \quad \text{Eqn (2)}.$$

where $T^i = G_i P_i T_i' D_i$, G_i, T_i' and G_g have been defined earlier, P_i is the preferences for agent i, and D_i the dynamic constraints generated by *other agents* $\{T_j' \mid j <> i\}$ to be enforced on task T_i'.

Therefore, the solution produced in the solution space S_i of agent i must satisfy the global (i.e., static) constraints G_i and also the dynamic constraints D_i produced by the solutions in other agents. If there are preferences specified (as in this example), then the eventual solution should meet as many preferences as possible. Thus, because of the generation of associated dynamic constraints, the solution produced by one agent reduces the solution space of the other agents. In our example a globally acceptable solution must satisfy:

$$G_0 P_0 S_0 D_0 \ \ AND \ \ G_1 P_1 S_1 D_1 \ \ AND \ \ldots. \ \ AND \ \ G_n P_n S_n D_n$$

If this does not hold, then the agents must negotiate, giving up their preferences until a satisfactory solution is found. Say it is:

$$G_0 P_0' S_0' D_0' \ \ AND \ \ G_1 P_1' S_1' D_1' \ \ AND \ \ldots. \ \ AND \ \ G_n P_n' S_n' D_n'$$

In our model this is achieved by decomposing tasks into their lower-level tasks and by identifying their inter-dependencies, which are then incorporated in a user-defined and task-dependent *cooperation strategy* at the coordinator, describing how the agents involved should behave in the execution of a prescribed task. A distributed update under 2PC or 3PC will fall under nontrivial cooperation, where the outcome of each cohort (success/failure) generated during execution affects all others.

Observe that if we drop preferences and dynamic constraints, then a nontrivial cooperation becomes a trivial cooperation. The primary objective in a cooperation model is to provide an environment for nontrivial cooperation. Therefore in the rest of the paper we shall use the term cooperation to imply nontrivial cooperation, unless otherwise qualified. *We should restate here that it is the presence of dynamic constraints that makes a cooperation nontrivial*, not the presence of preferences as such, unless they generate dynamic constraints. Therefore we shall not focus on preferences below.

3. Operational Framework

We shall describe here agent classes, heterarchies of tasks, skills and events, and their representational schemes, which together provide an operational framework for a computational model.

3.1 Classification and Hierarchies

We assume several categories of agents [34], of which two are relevant to this paper:

> Coordinator agents
> Skill agents

In each category, there can be multiple classes; each class having a set of agents (called twins), which carry out identical activities, in the sense that one twin can replace another (say in the event of breakdown) although they may not be identical in content. Each class has associated with it a class minder agent, which is generally responsible for the scheduling of its twins and replacing the faulty agent by another as needed for fault recovery. Thus the minder acts as a supervisor of its twins. The skill agents in particular are grouped into many skill classes (possibly overlapping), each class representing a skill, backed by its twins and minder. In our jargon a skill K^i represents its class, each of its twins (such as A_i) having that skill to perform task T^i.

A task T^i can in general be decomposed into a heterarchy of lower-level tasks, each leaf in the heterarchy being an atomic task. Thus a task T_f can be resolved into its m lower tasks as:

$$T_f = T_{f0}, T_{f1}, T_{f2}, .. T_{fm}$$

where T_{f0} is the residual task of the parent T_f for consolidating the results from the child tasks $\{T_{f1}..T_{fm}\}$. We shall treat T_{f0} like any other lower tasks, except that *child dependency* (see later) will apply to it.

Correspondingly to the task heterarchy we shall assume a skill heterarchy, with atomic skills at the leaf levels. Likewise we shall assume the *body of the skill agent A_i* to consist of a heterarchy of functional components (*funcom*s for short), funcom F_i representing the kernel of the body (*body kernel*), which is the highest level funcom in an agent. Thus corresponding to any task T_f, we shall assume skill K_f and funcom F_f. The division of the agent body into funcoms permits the localisation of faults into small units and enhances choice and flexibility. However, the possibility that an agent body is made up of only one funcom (i.e the body kernel) is not excluded. We can also regard the agent head as being made up of one or more funcoms, not discussed here.

Parallelling skill classes at the skill agent level, we also assume each lower level skill class to have funcom twins and a class minder (i.e. a funcom minder agent). We shall denote agent minder with superscript, e.g. M^i for skill K^i (of agent A_i) and a funcom minder with subscript, say M_p, for skill K_p of funcom F_p, except for the highest funcom - the body kernel - which (along with the agent head) is supervised by the agent minder and is responsible for the execution-time management of its body constructed from its lower funcoms.

For generality, we shall assume that (i) each funcom requires hardware resources (which limits the number of twins in each funcom class), and (ii) funcom twins are allocated exclusively by their minders to each agent body for the duration of task T^i. We shall assume that the task heterarchy forms only a small subset of the skill hierarchy, such that the execution of task T^i requires only a very small subset of the skills available in K^i, and therefore only a small subset of the corresponding funcoms. Thus agent A_i will need only a small subset of funcoms for its task T^i. Note that we shall use level f below to imply any level, 1 to n, except where qualified otherwise.

3.2 Task Representations and Dependencies

To describe a task T_f (where f represents any level) we need three elements:

(1) *task scheme (TS)*, in which task **T** is described with its properties, constraints (and preferences if any). The constraints will include pre, post and end conditions described later.

(2) *a dependency scheme (DS)*, in which relevant dependencies are described, The dependency rules will contribute to pre, post and end conditions discussed later.

(3) *a dependency satisfaction rule (DR)*, which must be satisfied in the execution of the task.

If we consider the travelling example given earlier, the dependency scheme DS may state that the Air-Travel agent should send its results R_1 on dates to both the coordinator and the Hotel agent, and the Hotel agent should send its results R_2 to both the coordinator and the Air-Travel agent. But DR will be satisfied if:

(i) the Air-Travel agent sends its R_1 to the Hotel agent, or
(ii) the Hotel agent sends its R_2 to the Air-Travel agent, or
(iii) both of them send their results to the coordinator.

Therefore, DR will specify alternative solutions to choose from, some of which will be more efficient than others. Observe that if the task of the Air-Travel agent (and/or the Hotel agent) is decomposed into further lower level tasks, each lower task yielding say the result for each date, then the contents of both DR and DS will have to be decomposed appropriately for these lower tasks. DR can be expressed in any convenient logical form, e.g.. as:

DR: Dep_1 AND Dep_2 OR Dep_3 ... etc

where Dep_m is a Dep-id in the dependency scheme. So far as this paper is concerned, we assume that the user specify a suitable DS in the cooperation strategy in what we call trigger schemes [3], which is then converted into appropriate pre, post and end conditions for execution (see below).

Consider a parent task T_f and its child tasks $\{T_{f1} .. T_{fm}\}$. There is a parent child relationship implying a dynamic constraint that the parent cannot complete its task until the children have completed theirs. This we shall refer to as *children depen-dency*, which is applied to the residual parent task T_{f0} discussed earlier. Let us further consider the following cyclic dependency of dynamic constraints that holds on the children:

$$T_{f1} \rightarrow T_{f2} \rightarrow ....T_{fm} \rightarrow T_{f1}.$$

A common example of such cycles can be found in the application domain of cooper-ative design. This cycle can be broken if all m children send their unconstrained (i.e. before applying the dynamic constraints) results to the parent (the residual task T_{f0}), which can then apply the constraints. A more efficient technique will be the reduction of each task $T_{f1} .. T_{fm}$ into a task that produces only one solution (rather than many solutions, and worse still, all possible solutions) at a time and then it sends the result to T_{f0} for the constraints validation.

This demonstrates that a cycle can be broken, and hence we shall assume that the DS specified for a task T_f is non-cyclic.

3.3 Pre, Post and End Conditions

As implied earlier, these conditions may apply to any task T_f. We consider four types of precondition on any task T_f:

(1) System-dependent: The system must be available in a fault-free state before the task can start. If a funcom twin has broken down, the agent will attempt to get a replacement from the funcom minder.

(2) Task-dependent: Specific conditions that must be met for the successful com-pletion of this task, e.g, certain tools must be available before the task can begin. Again non-availability can lead to delays.

(3) Precedent-dependent: These are the precedent constraints, some of which may be derived dynamically by the system from the dependency scheme. If a

required input item (including a physical object) is not available, this can lead to delays and abort.

(4)   Child dependent: These constraints will apply to T_{f0}, which may also have other types of pre, post and end conditions like any other tasks.

A postcondition refers to the situation when a completed task must satisfy a validity condition, without which the result will be invalid. Such a condition could require the passing of an inspection check or meeting some preferences. If a post condition is not satisfied, the task (unless aborted) will require re-doing, which may cause a delay. The endcondition applies to a successfully completed task and includes the messages to be sent announcing the completion of the task.. There are two types of endcondition (i) compulsory (ii) interest. If the dependency rule requires a message to be sent to some other funcoms (for example the result of the hotel agent to the coordinator), then this is a compulsory endcondition, otherwise it is an interest endcondition. Any failure in a compulsory endcondition will trigger a resend of the message as part of task completion. On the other hand the failure of an interest endcondition can be ignored. Observe that while a failure of the post condition will require re-doing of the task, the failure of the endcondition requires the re-doing of only the endcondition itself.

Preferences are meaningful only when alternative choices are available on skills and their options. Once resolved over the lowest possible funcoms, then pre, post and end conditions can be used to ensure a proper execution of these preferences. As we do not cover preferences in the execution model, they will not be discussed in this paper any further.

4. Execution Model

We can view the execution model as a set of interacting agents, and interacting funcoms within agents, supervised by interacting minders, all in a dynamically changing environment. The agent interactions are established by cooperation blocks and funcom interactions by task hierarchies. So far the execution states are concerned we can consider the following activities:

Pre-execution Activities
    Task Decomposition
    Planning and
    Preliminary Scheduling
Execution-time Activities
    Task Execution
    Failure and Recovery
        Rollback and Redo
        Dynamic scheduling
        Abort and Termination

Planning, sometimes referred to as long-term scheduling is scheduling without specifying start and end times. If alternative decompositions are available, then planning and decomposition can be interleaved. However, task decomposition is essentially user-specified, and preliminary scheduling is the tentative or the initial schedule, which is expected to change. If the system gets into a cycle, or it malfunctions or breaks down, then the task can be aborted and then restarted from suitable restart points without any material side-effects. Therefore termination is always ensured, and hence we shall not discuss the pre-execution activities in this paper.

There are three areas of major interactions during execution: (i) among the funcoms, (ii) among the coordinator and cohorts, and (iii) among the minders, coordinators and twins. Of these (i) is much more complex; the other two are relatively straightforward and they follow the pattern set by (i). We shall therefore address only (i), and drop the other two.

4.1 Execution Scenario

The user selects a suitable agent (via a coordinator minder) to act as a coordinator of a task (say **T**). The coordinator decomposes the task using a user-specified decomposition strategy (unless the task is already decomposed) into Eqn (2) given earlier, along with the specification of the Dependency Scheme and the Dependency Rule. Using, say a Contract Net protocol, the coordinator forms a Cooperation Block for task **T** with cohorts from the agent minders in a Directory agent. The cooperation block is created through what we call a 3-Stage Coordination Protocol [3], consisting of an *Agreement, Interaction* and *Termination* stage, backed by a time-out mechanism.

We assume a general case in which each cohort allocated by an agent minder consists of only the head and the body kernel, which subsequently constructs its body with other funcoms from the relevant funcom minders. Observe that interactions with other agents (other skill agents, coordinators and minders) are always carried out by the agent head as requested by its body kernel. If some of the selection parameters of lower-level funcoms become known only during the execution time, then the relevant funcoms can be found only by dynamic scheduling, which we shall assume to be the norm. Thus each parent funcom will choose its children dynamically, but the negotiation with the respective funcom minders will be carried out by the agent head.

Observe that although the allocation of funcoms to a cohort is exclusive for the duration of a cooperation block, a child funcom can be shared by multiple parents in the same cohort. Therefore sometimes a funcom wanted by a parent might already exist in the body, and if so then the body kernel would not require the agent head to negotiate with the funcom minder. If a funcom malfunctions, this will be communicated, via the successive parents and the body kernel, to the agent head, which will then negotiate with the relevant funcom minder for the replacement of the faulty twin. In the event of a contention, a child funcom may use the hierarchical order (subject to the precedent constraints being satisfied) to select its next task for execution.

If a funcom fails during execution, the processing has to be rolled back, as if no work has been done by this funcom. Furthermore, if the processing involved physical operations on physical objects (e.g., welding two parts), then these physical objects may have to be thrown away, and replaced by undamaged ones. In that case the rollback may have to cascade upward to one or more higher level funcoms (ancestors), where the undamaged objects are available. This requires task T_p on physical object(s) to specify the relevant ancestor T_g as the rollback point. If a rollback is required at T_g, the restart will have to begin at T_f, where T_f is an ancestor of T_g.

Thus we should be able to define Rollback and Restart trees. If f and p are the roots of two rollback trees B_f and B_p respectively, then B_f subsumes B_p, if f is an ancestor of p. If B_p and B_q are two rollback trees then B_f will contain both if f is the common ancestor of of both p and q. These conclusions will be true if they were restart trees instead.

4.2 Funcom Architecture

The execution model of a funcom F_f has three components, (i) the execution process itself, (ii) input messages (MIN) and (iii) output messages (MOU) as shown in what we call a funcom diagram (Figure 1).

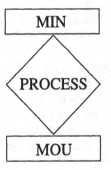

Figure 1: Funcom Diagram

The states of the execution process are captured in Event Indicator (EIN) described fully later. The execution process has two parts: (i) controller and (ii) executor. The controller reads the input messages from MIN and the execution states from EIN before determining the the next legally valid primitive to be executed, following *the Serialisation Rules* given later. The executor executes the next primitive (see below) and produces output messages for MOU, and changes the states in EIN, as the execution progresses. We may visualise that EIN, MIN and MOU are backed by three run-time tables called *white boards*, one for each. A MIN may receive messages from parents and ancestors, children and descendents, and neighbours; and conversely, MOU may send messages to all of them to appear in their respective MINs.

A funcom can serve multiple parents with appropriate entries in EIN, MIN and MOU, such that a task can be executed in the correct order determined by the precedent constraints and other rules. If a task is delayed, the funcom can start with any task that is available, subject to the precedent rules.

4.3 Funcom Activities and Primitives

The execution of any skill K_f for task T_f by a funcom F_f includes two types of activities: control activities and skill activities, the later includes lower-level skills where relevant. Therefore, the execution plan in a funcom F_f may incorporate the following activities.

Precondition (P)
Schedule (S) to schedule children
Do (D) to perform the skill activity
Postcondition (F)
Endcondition (E)
Termination (Ter) - termination of the task (1 for succ or 2 for fail)
Rollback (B)

Redo (R) - to redo any activity including D.
Abort (A)
Processing of information from MIN (Ii)
Generation of output information (Io)

An activity may have lower-level activities; the lowest levels will be referred to as the as *event primitives* and entered in EIN. The following activities in the above list are assumed to have lower levels, which constitute their event primitives:

S: has six primitives: Invite, Bid, Evaluate, Accept, Reject, Confirm
P: has four conditions defined earlier, each a primitive.
D: may have lower skills (each a primitive for this funcom), t1..tn.
B: may form a tree of several funcoms, B in each funcom being a primitive.

The successful execution of an event primitive is an event, registered as an EIN tuple, which may contain:

EIN [T-id, Par-id, Fun-id, Prim, Qual, Mf, V, Bt, Et, Dy]

where we have task-id (T-id), parent-id (Par-id), funcom-id (Fun-id), the current number of attempts V (for version), the state of system-malfunction (Mf), begin-time (Bt), end-time (Et), delay (Dy). Some primitives may require qualifier, e.g. the Redoing of say Invite (in scheduling) will have Redo as the primitive (Prim), and Invite as the qualifier (Qual).

We have assumed that a funcom schedules (S) its children before it starts on its D; alternatively the scheduling can be part of its D {t1 .. tn}. Observe that the scheduling will actually be carried out by the body kernel which will also create whiteboards for EIN, MIN and MOU. If the wanted funcom has already been acquired by the body kernel, then there will not be any need for negotiation with minders, and in that case the whiteboards will pre-exist. If the task T_f proceeds uninterrupted, it follows the path <P, S, D, F, E, Ter>, generating messages for Io as appropriate. If a message is produced during a primitive X, we assume it is written out to MOU as a primitive Io, following the execution of the primitive X.

There does not seem to be a situation where the MIN will bring new conditions for P, F and compulsory E. Thus only important messages in a MIN will be for A, B, R. However, P, F and E might receive via MIN some wanted data from other tasks to evaluate the conditions.

The MIN can be visualised to have a structure like this:

[Source, Destination, {Activity, Time1, Time2} ...]

where each activity triplet will have an activity from the list above, along with two Time parameters: Time1 is the time the message was sent, and Time2 is the time by which the message should be acted upon. There could be rules to determine validity of sources (funcoms) and destinations (funcoms) and message type, etc. The messages in the MIN may include messages for:

Information for: P, F, E, A, B, R, Dy, Mf

Requests for activity: D, E, B, R, A

Information on activities can be either (i) information required to execute an activity typically for P, F and E, or (ii) information on an activity that has occurred in another funcom. For instance if a lower task has been aborted, then this funcom will have to take some action, and must pass this information to its parent (see also later).

The MOU should have a similar structure:
[Destination, {Activity, Time1, Time2} ...]

4.4 Serialisation Rules

We present here some rules which serialise activities (including primitives) in a correct order. We assume:
An Abort never fails

A Rollback (B) never fails
All R must be preceded by B
Ii and Io never fail
All communications (MOU/MIN) are delivered via a failsafe mechanism.

Primitives Ii and Io can follow any primitive, although we have not considered how information travels from MOU to MIN, except for the assumption of a failsafe communication mechanism, which ensures an ordered delivery, although delays cannot be excluded. An Abort can follow any primitive. An R is often preceded by a B, and can be preceded by another R; R' below implies B precedes R, written as R' = <B,R>. We define below successor activities (or primitives) for three cases in order: $\{X \mid Y \mid Z\}$ (W), where X, Y and Z are the successor activities (or primitives) of activity (or primitive) W; X follows the successful completion of W, Y follows the failure of W due to time-out or due to too many attempts, and Z follows the failure of W due to other reasons, expressed as .

Activity S: successors $\{D \mid A \mid R'\}$ (S) === nAR' (S)
Activity P: successors $\{D \mid A \mid R\}$ (P) === nAR (P)
Activity D: successors $\{F \mid A \mid R'\}$ (D) === nAR' (D)
Activity F: successors $\quad \{E \mid A \mid R'\}$ (F)
Activity (D+F): successors $\quad \{E \mid A \mid R'\}$ (D+F)
Activity E: successors $\{Ter \mid A \mid R\}$ (E); successful Ter

Activity R: successors $\{n \mid A \mid R\}$ (R) === nAR
Activity B: successors $\{R \mid A \mid A\}$ (B)
Activity A: successors $\{Ter \mid - \mid - \}$ (A): unsuccessful, but a valid Ter
Activity Io: successor $\{n'\}$ (Io); n' is the next activity if Io was not there
Activity Ii: successor $\{s \mid n'\}$ (Ii); s selected from Ii, n' if Ii was not there.

where n is the next activity in the correct sequence. The successor activity of Ii is either the activity suggested by Ii (if the suggestion is accepted) or the next activity that would have been if Ii was not there; but in the case of Io, there is only one successor, the next activity that would have been if Io was not there. So each activity W (W <> {A, Ii, Io, B}) has successors of the form $\{n \mid A \mid R \}$ (W), or $\{n \mid A \mid R' \}$ (W). An actual sequence may differ from application to application.

Finally, a delayed funcom (as identified by the time parameters) can advise its parent, which in turn can revise its time parameters to the affected children - this can continue recursively to successive parents if needed, eventually to the coordinator via the agent head. This ability to manage delays may be viewed as part of user-controlled agent behaviour beyond the scope of this paper. However, in the absence of any delay management, an activity will fail if an input it is too late for the end time implied by the time-out .

5. Correctness of Execution

In a CKBS the concurrent tasks do not lead to lost updates, nor to corrupt knowledge states, since a task is assumed to be an action which does not change the state of global knowledge. Therefore concurrent activities do not concern us here; what is important is the execution of a task without lost actions and its correct termination. A task is terminated correctly, if it has been executed successfully or if it is left unfinished at some well-defined recovery points. A corollary to this is that the task execution should not lead to cycles. A second corollary is that the system must be stable in execution. We shall examine these issues below:

5.1 Execution Characteristics

In the execution model presented earlier, the following can be seen as the relevant characteristics:

(1) *Execution of an activity*: During the execution of an activity, it may succeed or fail. In case of failure, it can follow with R' or A. If successive attempts at R fail, then the task can be aborted. An abort will also follow if P or F cannot be met. A malfunction can cause an Abort. An abort is a controlled action, which is propagated via the successive parents to the root, when a human decision must be made. Thus the system will always remain under control. Since all activities are linked by child dependency (precondition), the loss of an activity will eventually show up at each parent.

(2) *Next Activity*: The next activity is well-defined, and as long as the specification is correct, the system will behave correctly. If the specification is wrong, then it will have contradictions, which will be detected in some stage of execution leading to Abort. The activities under EIN have well-defined execution order and hence have a valid specification; tasks under a parent also have a well-defined execution order enforced by precedent constraints under P. If tasks T_p and T_q are required to execute in that order, then it would imply that some results from T_p are needed by T_q. Therefore T_q will fail if the order is not obeyed, leading to an abort.

(3) *Interrupt from MIN*: The execution process checks information from MIN and accepts the execution of an activity if it is deemed valid, within the correct sequence. If R is accepted, it is preceded by B, without any side-effect. If Abort without rollback causes side-effects, then all Aborts can be changed to <B,A>. Therefore the multiplicity of information arriving at MIN for execution will not cause any uncontrolled behaviour.

(4) *Delays and Malfunctions*: If a required piece of information arrives late there could be several consequences. If it is precondition information, then the task can fail, but might succeed under a redo if the information arrives by then. A system of acknowledgements can be instituted to protect against such problems. If a request for R or A arrives late, there will be wasted activities. If a funcom malfunctions, then it is aborted and replaced by the minder with a twin. The task is rolled back and restarted, but without requiring the redo of the completed lower-level tasks.

(5) *Dynamic Decomposition of Tasks*: If tasks are dynamically decomposed by a funcom, they would be meant to be executed by children or by a lower-level cooperation block (which we have not considered so far). However, in either case there should not be any problem for correct execution.

(6) *Dynamic Constraints*; Observe that the structures (i.e., Dependency Scheme and the Dependency Satisfaction Rule) of the constraints are specified in a non-cyclic manner (section 3.2) during task decomposition, but their contents are generated dynamically.

(7) *Idempotent Redos*: This problem can arise only for S and D. Since these Redos are preceded by Rollbacks, the problem is avoided.

We may define a recovery point as a point wherefrom the system can be restarted after a failure; this in our model will be any state reached following a successful execution of any primitive. Obviously, this is the state a rollback will reach, but an abort might not unless accompanied by a rollback. Observe that the system defined above terminates on recovery points for automatic recovery, except for abort which requires human intervention.

5.2 Operational Stability

As indicated earlier, the execution model of our CKBS can be depicted as a network of interacting funcoms (Figure 2) and therefore it is important to demonstrate that the system behaviour is stable. The behaviour of a dynamic system is stable, if it is able to remain on course, despite deviations caused by the operational environment. This can be achieved, if each deviation as it occurs, triggers a proportionate counteraction, which bounces the system back onto its course. However no system can ever be fully stable, as there always will be circumstances beyond anyone's control. Therefore stability should be defined with respect to a given environment for which we assume that the deviations are caused only by the forces within the modelled system, not from outside it. That is, we ignore earthquakes, other disasters, failure of all related external systems, such as electricity supply, communication networks, computers, and other equipment not explicitly modelled in the operational environment.

An apt definition of stability is: *bounded input, bounded output.* To sustain stability, the system should not only produce only bounded outputs, but also reject all unbounded inputs, which we shall assume to be those coming from the external systems. An unstable system can lead to a catastrophe.

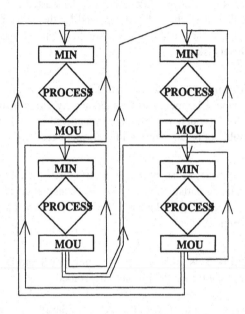

Figure 2: Interacting Funcoms

We claim the execution model presented in this paper is stable because of its execution characteristics (described above). In particular the execution, in the absence of any failure, proceeds always in the valid course. A deviation can be caused only by a failure or by an interrupt from MIN. All failures are strictly controlled, with rollback/redo and eventually abort, which bounces the execution onto the valid course. Only those interrupts (from MIN) that are valid are accepted for execution. A valid interrupt is designed to retain the valid course.

There is a parallel between neural networks and funcom networks (Figure 2). Many inputs arrive at a neuron, their contributions used to produce a result, which if exceeds a threshold, produces an output to other neurons, except that wild inputs can lead to wild outputs, eventually creating instability. However, in contrast a funcom accepts only valid inputs and produces only valid outputs, thus avoiding instability; on the other hand buffer overflows due to delay/malfunction/breakdown (if not modelled as part of the operational environment) can lead to chaos and thus instability.

6. Conclusion

We have presented the operational aspects of a multi-agent environment founded on an *engineering paradigm*, and shown that it not only ensures correct termination, but also provides stability. These are properties which are required for industrial applications, as evident from the needs of our partners in the HMS project.

We are aware that we have not provided any formal proof of correctness - a topic in which we are currently working on. A preliminary version of a theoretical foundation can be seen in [36].

Acknowledgement: Thanks to M. Fletcher and N. Thomas of the DAKE Group for comments and corrections.

References

[1]   C. Hewitt: "Open Information Systems Semantics for DAI", AI Journal, Jan 1991.

[2]   S. M. Deen: "An architectural Framework for CKBS Applications", IEEE Transactions on Knowledge and Data Engineering, Vol (8:4), Aug 1996, pip 663-671.

[3]   S. M. Deen: "A Database Perspective to a Cooperation Environment", Proc, CIA'97, edited by P. Kanzia and M. Klusch, Springer, 1997, pp 19-41.

[4]   M. E. Bratman: "Intentions, Plans and Practical Reason", Harvard University Press, 1987.

[5]   M. E. Bratman, et al: "Plans and Resource Bounded Practical Reasoning", Computational Intelligence, Vol (4:4), pp349-355, Nov 1988.

[6]   A. S. Rao and M. P. Georgeff: "Modeling Agents within a BDI architecture", KR'91, edited by R. Fikes and E. Sandewall, pp473-484, published by Morgan Kaufmann.

[7]   A. S. Rao and M. P. Georgeff: " BDI agents - from theory to practice", Proc. of the 1st Int Confc on Multi-agent Systems, San Francisco, 1995.

[8]   J. R. Searle: Speech Act, Cambridge University Press, 1969.

[9a]   A. Sehmi *et al*: "Support for Distributed Multi-Agent Systems", Proceedings of the Second International Working Conference on CKBS, Keele University, edited by S.M. Deen, published by the DAKE Centre, pp 357-376, June 1994, ISBN 0 9521789 2 3

[9b]   M. Fisher *et al*: "Specifying and Executing Protocols for Cooperative Action", Proceedings of the Second International Working Conference on CKBS, June, 1994 as in Ref [9a], pp 295-306.

[10]   M.R. Genesereth and R.E. Fikes: "Knowledge Interchange Format Reference Manual", Computer Science Department, Stanford University, June 92.

[11]   T. Finin and R. Fritszon: "KQML - A language for protocol and information exchange", Proc 13th DAI workshop, pp 127-136, Seattle, WA, USA.

[12a]   Y. Shoham: "Agent Oriented Programming", Artificial Intelligence, Vol: 60, pp51-92, 1993.

[12b]   M. P. Singh: "A Semantics for Speech Acts", Readings in Agents, Morgan Kaufmann, edited by M. N. Huhns and M. P. Singh, pp 458-470, 1997.

[13]   A. Haddadi: "A hybrid architecture for multi-agent systems', CKBS-SIG Proceedings, 1993, pp 13-26, editor S. M. Deen, published by the DAKE Centre, ISBN 0 9521789 1 5.

[14]   A. Haddadi: Communication and Cooperation in Agent Systems - A Pragmatic Theory, Springer 1996.

[15]   J. P. Mueller: "A conceptual model for agent interaction", Proceedings of the Second International Working Conference on CKBS, Keele University, edited by S.M. Deen, published by the DAKE Centre, pp 213 - 234, June 1994, ISBN 0 9521789 2 3

[16]   J. P. Mueller: The Design of Intelligent Agents, Springer, 1996.

[17]   N.R. Jennings: "The ARCHON Project and its Applications", Proceedings of the Second International Working Conference on CKBS, Keele University, edited by S.M. Deen, published by the DAKE Centre, pp 13-30, June 1994, ISBN 0 9521789

[18]   N. R. Jennings: Controlling cooperative problem solving in industrial multi-agent systems using joint intentions", Artificial Intelligence, vol (74:2), 1995.

[19]   H. Haugeneder: "IMAGINE: A Framework for Building Multi-Agent Systems", Proceedings of the Second International Working Conference on CKBS, Keele University, edited by S.M. Deen, published by the DAKE Centre, pp 31-64, June 1994, ISBN 0 9521789 2 3

[20]   A. Lux and D. D. Steiner: "Understanding Cooperation - An Agent's Perspectives", Readings in Agents, Morgan Kaufmann, edited by M. N. Huhns and M. P. Singh, pp 471-480, 1997.

[21]   M. P. Singh: Multi-agent Systems: A Theoretical Framework for Intentions, Know-how and Communications, Springer, 1994.

[22]   FIPA 97 Specification (version 2, 1998): Foundation of Intelligent Physical Agents. This is a non-profit-making organisation registered in Switzerland, at the time of writing, it had 35 corporate members from 12 countries. Address: www.cselt.stet.it/fipa

[23]   Paul M. Churchland: "On the ontological status of intentional states ... ", Behaviour and Brain Sciences, Vol (11:3), pp507-508, 1988.

[24] Patricia Churchland et al: "The Computational Brain", MIT Press, 1992.

[25] R.G. Smith: "The Contract Net Protocol: High Level Communication and Distributed Problem Solver", Readings in Distributed Artificial Intelligence, edited by A. Bond and L. Gasser, published by Morgan Kaufmann, pp 357-366, 1988.

[26] R. Davis and R.G. Smith: "Negotiation as a Metaphor for Distributed Problem Solving", Artificial Intelligence vol 20, pp 63-109, 1983.

[27] Function Blocks for Industrial Process-measurement and Control Systems, Part1: Architecture. Technical Report: International Electrotechnical Commission, TC65, WG6. ftp://ftp.ab.com/stds/ iec/tc65wg6/ document/pt1cd2.doc, 1997.

[28] J. Christensen: "Holonic Manufacturing Systems, WP1, D1.1",1998, ftp://hms@ifwpd7.ifw.uni-hannover.de/hms-wps/wp1-seng/html/t1/d11f.htm.

[29] HMS/IMS Programme: IMS (Intelligent Manufacturing Systems) is an international programme with the participation of major industries, universities and research institutes from six regions: Australia, Japan, EFTA countries, EU countries, Canada and USA, partially funded by the Governments. It is intended as a ten year pre-competitive research programme from about 1994. It has several projects, one of which is the Holonic Manufacturing Systems (HMS) for high-variety low-volume manufacturing in a largely un-manned environment. A holon is close to a CKBS agent. The author is a participant in this HMS project, which inspired some of the work presented here.

[30] Martyn Fletcher (Ed):HMS Project, EU Brite-Euram [BPR-CT-97-9000], WP1/Deliverables D1.1-1,and D1.1-2, Holonic Systems Architecture, Sept,1998, DAKE Group, Dept of Computer Science, University of Keele, Keele, England.

[31] S. Balasubramanian and D. Norrie: "A Multi-agent Architecture for Concurrent Concurrent Engineering" Concurrent Engineering:Research and Applications, Vol (4:1), March 96, pp7-16.

[32] H. Van Dyke Parunak et al: "The AARIA Agent Architecture":ICAA Workshop on Agent-Based Manufacturing, 1998

[33] H. Van Dyke Parunak: Practical and Industrial Application of Agent-Based Systems, 1998.

[34] S. M. Deen: "A Fault-Tolerant Cooperative Distributed System", Proc. of the 9th IEEE DEXA Workshop, Vienna, Aug 1998, Edited by R. Wagner, pp508-513.

[35] D. Jarvis et al.: "Quality Control Holonic Manufacturing Systems", Technical Report, CSIRO, Australia, 1998a (to be published).

[36] S. M. Deen and C. A. Johnson: "Towards a Theoretical Foundation for Cooperating Knowledge Based Systems", Proc of the 11th Int Symposium for Methodologies for Intelligent Systems (ISMIS99), June, 1999 (to appear)

Mobile Agents Behaviours: From Declarative Specificiations to Implemenation

C. Hanachi, N. Hameurlain, C. Sibertin-Blanc

University of Toulouse I,
Place Anatole France 31042, Toulouse, France.
{hanachi,nabil,sibertin}@univ-tlse1.fr

Abstract. We propose a method to derive Mobile Agents Behaviours from simple and easy to use declarative specifications. We use for that a manufacturing system route metaphor as a mean to express the mission of a mobile agent. The specification is expressed with a data-model and is automatically transformed into a two-component behaviour: a Task Net expressed with Petri Nets(PN) and an Intelligent PN Interpreter guaranteeing agent autonomy and flexibility.

1. Introduction

One of the challenging and emerging problems of Agent-based computing is to provide Software Engineering methods and solutions to address industrial applications [1]. Our work is a contribution to this new problematic since it proposes a method to generate automatically mobile agents behaviours in the context of Cooperative Information Gathering.

Mobile agents are considered as a promising technology for the implementation of *Information Gathering Systems* (IGSs) exploring the World Wide Web [11]. Roughly speaking, an IGS performs a user-defined task by executing the following process:
– it decomposes the user task in sub-tasks;
– *it builds a mobile agent to solve each sub-task;*
– it runs each agent that will make its trip and will return the expected results;
– it merges these results to build the final response.
This paper aims at providing a contribution to the second step of this process. More precisely, it provides *a method* to automatically build, from a simple, declarative and easy-to-use data model, a mobile agent able to achieve a given task.

The *data model* -inspired by the definition of "production routes" in manufacturing system- defines abstract trajectories in terms of operations to be achieved in order to produce the final product(s). This data model is stored in a *Routing Database* that records for each operation (resource discovery, translation, querying, ...) the type of resources needed (mediator, wrapper, dbms, ...) and the products handled or created (query, text, url, ...). The trajectory is called *abstract* because we do not give explicitly the address of the different sites (hosts) to visit nor the synchronization of the operations. Each agent will decide autonomously and in real time of its real behaviour and route.

Given a user task, *the generated behaviour* consists of two components :
- A *Task Net*, expressed in terms of Petri Nets, which describes "what must be done", i.e. the abstract trajectory.
- An intelligent *Petri Net Interpreter* which decides "how to do it", i.e. how to drive the execution of the Task Net.

The PN interpreter implements the intelligence of the agent since it decides, according to the current context, *what* operation to perform (in case of alternative among several enabled operations), *when* to perform an operation (in case of several possible schedules), and *where* to perform an operation that may be executed on several sites. With regard to the choice of the successive hosts and the moving of the agent over the network, the interpreter includes a specific "know-how": while operations are being executed on the current host, the agent concurrently identifies the future operations to be performed elsewhere and questions sites about their availability for these operations, in order to select the best next site. This interpreter is generic so that all agents have the same one. However, it calls reasoning functions which may accommodate for constraints or objectives of specific agents.

Let us precise that the use of Petri Nets guarantees some interesting advantages. It makes the expression of concurrent behaviour possible and it is well-suited to implement protocols needed by mobile agents to negotiate with hosts. Moreover, the models obtained could be directly executed by the interpreter or analyzed in order to check if they have the expected behaviour and/or good formal properties.

The main *advantages* of our approach are:
- Its simplicity for the designer since he only has to specify the tasks through the data model and possibly provides the criteria to be used to select the best sites. This saves the designer the work of drawing directly a Petri Net, which is a difficult task.
- The derived model is easy to understand in its graphical form, may be improved by the designer , and then analyzed and executed.
- It preserves the autonomy of each agent : actually, its route is not known in advance as the agent decides it in an opportunist way and in real time. However, its route remains task-driven.
- Numerous actions are performed concurrently and therefore improve the agent efficiency : while the host works for the agent, this latter anticipates the future by managing contracts to select the future hosts.

The remaining sections are organized as follows. Section 2 presents briefly Petri Nets and their uses in Multi-Agent Systems. Section 3 describes the Routing Database to generate the task-nets. Section 4 gives the algorithm that generates the task nets from the information recorded in this database. Section 5 describes the algorithm of the Intelligent Interpreter. Section 6 presents some related works.

2. Backgrounds on Petri Nets

2.1 Informal Presentation of Petri Nets

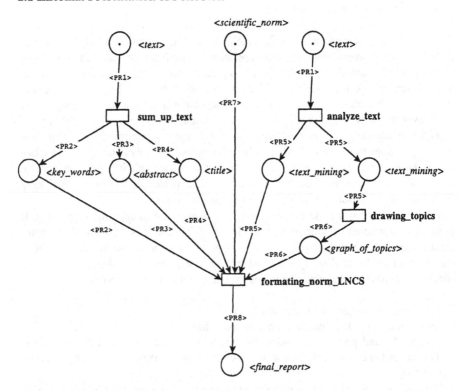

Fig. 1. An example of Petri Net.

Petri Nets have been created to model, analyze and validate parallel systems. They enable the expression of activities made of sequential, simultaneous or conflictual actions. They are widely used in industry because they provide a graphical and easy to understand representation and at the same time they have a rigorous and mathematic definition [13].

A Petri Net is represented by a directed bipartite graph with two node types : places and transitions. Graphically, we represent places by circles and transitions by rectangles. An arc can only connect a place to a transition or a transition to a place. In the first case, the place is called *an input place* and in the second case *an output place*.

Most of the time, a system is modeled as a set of resources and a set of operations consuming and producing resources. The resources are described by places and the operations by transitions. The number n of available resources in a place p is represented by n tokens (black dots) in p.

At a given time, *the state* of the system is defined by the distribution of tokens over places. *The dynamic* of the system is described by the execution of transitions which moves the tokens from input places to output places according to the two following rules:

1. A transition t is said to be *enabled* if each input place p of t has at least one token. An enabled transition may fire.
2. If a transition t *fires*, then t removes one token from each input place p of t and deposes one token on each output place.

Finally, we have to mention that there are several dialects of Petri Nets which differ from one another according to the type of the tokens used : atomic and indissociable values, tuples, objects , etc.

Example : The net of figure 1 highlights important features of the Agent's behaviour such as:

- *the sequence* of Operations e.g. drawing_topics is possible only if analyze_text has been previously performed.
- *the synchronization* between Operations e.g. formating_norm_LNCS could be executed only if all the needed Products are available.
- the available *parallelism* e.g. sum_up_text may be performed concurrently with analyse_text and drawing_topics.

2.2 Petri Nets and Multi-Agent Systems

The combination of Petri Nets and Multi-Agent Systems (MAS) is not new. Actually, Petri nets have permitted the modeling of agent conversations ([6], [9]), distributed planification [8], concurrent blackboard [7], prey-predator game [5], Shoam's Agent Oriented Programming paradigm [12], etc.

Some existing environments or agent specification languages already integrate Petri Nets. Thus, the Bric language [9], is based on colored Petri nets to define the basic components of a MAS. Moreover, there are remarkable Petri nets extensions (deontic [16], recursif[8], with data structures [20], with fuzzy markings [4], ...) which improve their expressiveness, make them flexible and therefore suited to MAS development.

3. The Routing Database

The purpose of this Database is to record information allowing the generation of a route for some tasks. The system administrator is responsible for entering the supported tasks and for providing the information needed to associate a route to each task. The structure of this database, given in Figure 2 according to UML notation [10], is inspired by the definition of "production route" in manufacturing system shop. Indeed, the moving of a part in a manufacturing system shop is comparable with the trip of an agent through the network.

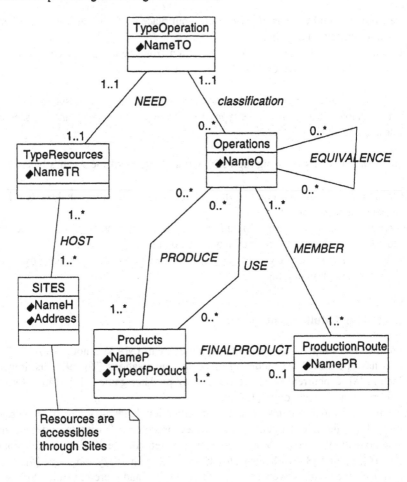

Fig. 2. The structure of the Routing Database

To each *Task* is associated both the set of Products that result from its achievement (the *final Products*) and the set of Operations that are needed to perform that Task (the *member* Operations). An *Operation* is an atomic action like to discover a resource, to translate a document, to query an information source, and so on. An Operation *uses* some Products as input and *produces* Products as a result, and two Operations may be defined as being *equivalent* if they use and produce the very same Products. A *Product* is an electronic object such as a text, a query, a translation or an url. A Product may be used by any many Operations, but it has to be produced by equivalent Operations; thus a given Product results from the occurrence of equivalent Operations. The achievement of an Operation *needs* some *Types of Resources,* or type of tools, such as compilers, wrappers or mediators. Finally, instances of these Resource Types are located on *Sites,* which are the nodes of the network. We say that a site *provides* an Operation if it is a host for the Resources needed by this Operation, and each Operation must have at least one provider.

From the structure of the Routing Database, the system administrator has only to enter on the one hand what can be done on the network (that is the execution environment) in terms of Operations, Products, Resources and Sites, and on the other hand Tasks that may be achieved in terms of their results (the final Products) and their requirements (the member Operations). Thus, the Database is a declarative description of the objectives that may be assigned to mobile Agents and of the context where they will work. It contains no information about the synchronization among the Operations of a Task; they will be inferred by the algorithm that generates the task net (see section 4.).

4. Automatic Generation of the Task Net

To build an Agent, the user just describes its actual task by giving:
- the name of the Task, which must appear in the Routing Database, and
- the set of initial Products needed to its achievement.

Then, the task-net of the Agent is automatically generated. It includes initial places for the Products supplied by the user to the agent, final places for the results supplied by the agent, one transition for each Operation that may take place during the achievement of the Task, while the other places and the arcs of the net express the scheduling constraints of the Task. Figure 1 has already shown an example of tasknet, where the user has to provide a text and a scientific norm and the Agent will progressively build a new document made of a title, keywords, an abstract, an analyze of this text and a graphic presentation of the topics involved in the text.

The algorithm that generates the Petri net of a Task is given in *Algorithm 1*. It first requires to identify all the Products involved in the Task, by using the sets of its final Products and of its member Operations. Each such Product falls into one of the three following classes:
- *final Products* that are associated to the Task and constitute its objectives; these Products must be produced by one member Operation (else the Task is not consistent).
- *intermediate Products* that are produced by one of the member Operations of the Task and used by one or several member Operations.
- *initial products* that are used by member Operations of the Task but are not produced by any such Operation.

```
ALGORITHM Generate_Behaviour
input The_Route : production_route
output PN : petri_net

/* Each operation becomes a transition*/
For each operation OP_i do
        create a transition t_i
End For

/* Treatment of the initial products*/
For each initial product PR_i of The_Route do
        For each operation OP_k using PR_i do
            identify the transition t_k corresponding to OP_k
            create a place p
            put a token referencing PR_i into p
            create an arc from p to t_k labelled by PR_i
        End For
End For

/* Treatment of the intermediate products*/
For each intermediate product PR_i of The_Route do
            identify the operation OP_c creating PR_i
            identify the transition t_c corresponding to OP_c
        For each operation OP_u using PR_i do
            identify the transition t_u corresponding to OP_u
            create a place p_iu
            create an arc from t_c to p_iu labelled by PR_i
            create an arc from p_iu to t_u labeled by PR_i
        End For
End For

/* Treatment of the final products*/
For each final product PR_f of The_Route do
            identify the operation OP_c creating p_f
            identify the transition t_c corresponding to OP_c
            create a place p_f referencing PR_f
            create an arc from t_c to p_f labeled by PR_f
End for
Integrate_alternative_operations (see algorithm 2.)

END ALGORITHM.
```

Algorithm 1. Generation of the agent behaviour.

Once the Products of a Task are known, the algorithm is based on the following principles:
- Each member Operation gives rise to a transition.
- Each Product used or produced by a member Operation gives rise to a place intended to bear a token referencing this Product.
- The connection between places and transitions depends on the class of the Product: initial, intermediate or final.

- The Operations equivalent to a member Operation are integrated into the Petri net (see details in *Algorithm 2*).
- Finally, the initial marking is build by putting into the initial places of the net references towards the user-supplied initial products.

```
ALGORITHM Integrate_alternative_operations

        For each operation OP_i of The_Route do
                For each operation OP_j equivalent to OP_i do
                    create a transition t_j corresponding to OP_j
                    For each input place p of t_i do
                    identify the label l of its arc
                    create an arc from p to t_j labeled by l
                    End For
                    For each output place p of ti do
                    identify the label l of its arc
                    create an arc from t_j to p labeled by l
                    End For
                End For
        End For
END ALGORITHM.
```

Algorithm 2. Integrating alternatives operations in the task net PN

Once the task net is built, the consistency of the task can be checked, namely the fact that the task-net includes no dead transition and that the final marking may be reached from the initial one whatever sequence of (sets of) Operations occurs (thus the agent will provide the results in any case).

With regard to the storing of this net, the use of a dynamic data structure (including many pointers) would make difficult the allocation of the agent when it moves on a site. It turns out that a Petri net may be stored within a static data structure compatible with a generic interpreter [17].

5. The Petri Net Interpreter

While the task-net of an Agent defines what it has to do, its interpreter defines how it will perform this task. Therefore, the interpreter defines the semantics of the task-net in as much as it determines which behaviour is caused by the execution of the task-net.

An Agent runs its interpreter as soon as it arrives at a site, and this run stops when the Agent leaves the site. Thus *the Agent's activity* is totally controlled by the interpreter, which has to:

1. manage the execution of transitions (operations) which may occur on this site,
2. collect information from other sites about their availability to execute the next operations to be done by sending out Requests For Proposals (RFP),
3. select the next site to visit,

4. make the Agent move to this site.

Our generic interpreter synchronizes these four tasks. In addition, it makes use of two reasoning functions to solve the conflicts among enabled transitions and to choose the next site. A general algorithm of the interpreter is given in *Algorithm 3* and the following of this section explains its principles. In addition, we provide a more detailed algorithm in [2].

ALGORITHM Interpreter

```
/*local execution and requests for proposals addressed
to external sites */
Repeat

    -Execute the enabled transitions in the order de-
    fined by the selection-transition function.

    -Send requests for proposals(RFP) to external sites
    about their availability to execute the next opera-
    tions not supported by the current site.

Until      (no transition in progress) and
           (no enabled transition supported by the
           current site)

/* treatment of the answers to the RFP*/
Repeat
   treat the answers to the RFP
Until no answer is expected

S:=select_site /*select the best next site*/
moveto(S) /*move to the next site*/
```

END ALGORITHM.

Algorithm 3. The algorithm of the interpreter

First of all, the interpreter is a sequential process; indeed, a concurrent interpreter would bring no performance improvement and would raise issues with regard to concurrent accesses to the task-net marking. However, the interpreter accommodates to the capability of a site to concurrently execute several operations; in this case, it triggers the execution of an enabled transition without waiting for the completion of transition occurrences that are currently in progress.

When an Agent arrives at a site, it triggers the execution of the transitions which may occur on this site according to the current marking of the task-net. Moreover, if some transitions become enabled after the completion of these transition occurrences, their execution is also triggered. Thus, an Agent leaves a site only when no more transition may occur on this site; doing so, it does not move to another site when this move can be avoided. In addition, it leaves only after the completion of the current execution, and thus remains at the site as long as some transition is in progress; doing so, it can keep the result of each transition occurrence.

When several transitions may occur, the interpreter has to choose which one will occur first (in case of independent transitions, the other ones will occur afterwards; in case of alternative transitions, the selected transition prevents the other ones to occur). Thus, each Agent must be provided with a *select_transition* function that returns one transition among the currently enabled ones. To solve conflicts caused by independent transitions, the select_transition function can order transitions according to the amount of work required (or the length of time needed by the site) to execute their operation. To solve conflicts caused by alternative transitions, the function can either use this ordering or use a priority associated to equivalent operations. Each Agent can have its own policy to solve conflicts, according to specific aims or constraints. Indeed, the select_transition function can account for Agent-related knowledge, and some Agent classes may be provided with a specific version of this function.

Before leaving, an Agent has to select the next site it will move to. To make a choice, it needs to know to what extent other sites are available for carrying out the next transition's operations. Thus, for each transition which may occur once the work on the current site will be finished, the Agent has to question the sites providing the transition's operation (a site *provides* an operation if it has the resources needed by this operation). The sooner the Agent sends the questions, the sooner it receives the answers and can accordingly select the next site. Thus the Agent has better to question a site as soon as it knows that some transition will become enabled, even if this transition is not yet actually enabled. In other words, an Agent collect information about the available sites in advance, and can build a plan of the operations to be done. So the question arises how many steps the Agent looks ahead, that is: how long is the plan? The proposed algorithm looks one step ahead. Indeed, it would be risky to assume that sites are able to foresee their workload a long time ahead; it is likely that Agents receive inaccurate information if they issue questions too early. In addition, the conflicts among transitions and among sites make the number of plans to grow exponentially with their length; thus long-term plans would cause a communication overhead.

Looking one step ahead means that, as soon as an Agent has started the execution of some transitions, it is able to compute the transitions which will become enabled when these executions finish. That is, an Agent is able to compute the next enabled transitions before the completion of the previous transition occurrences. A simple and efficient way to provide Agents with this ability is to consider *future-tokens*, which stand for forecoming tokens (see [2] for more details about this notion).

Once an Agent has collected information about the availability of sites for carrying out the next operations, it has to select the site where it will move to thanks to the *select_site* function.

6. Related works

[14] has precisely defined the problematic of Cooperative Information Gathering (CIG) and has explained the reasons why it requires a multi-agent approach.

Sycara is one of the first to take into account a software engineering dimension in the development of CIG systems. Actually, [19] presents a framework called RETSINA devoted to CIG and based on reusable components. RETSINA has been used to implement the WARREN system which tracks and filters financial information sources to manage financial portfolio.

The introduction of mobility in CIG is new. [11] justifies the interest of mobile agents for CIG in the context of the project MIAOW (Mobile Information Agents on the Web). [15] has developed a mobile agent system called MAMA where focus is put on security aspects.

From a software engineering point of view, [18] is the closest work to ours. It takes a declarative specification of the desired interactions of a MAS and automatically enact them. The differences with our work lie on the facts that this approach is based on Temporal Logic, focuses on the coordination of the whole system and finally does not address the mobility.

7. Conclusion

This paper provides a method to generate automatically mobile agents devoted to Information Gathering through the web. The advantages of our approach are its simplicity for the designer, the guarantee of the autonomy of each generated agent, and its operational semantics based on Petri nets.

It is clear that there are still a number of issues which require further investigations. The next problem we intend to address is to improve the generation process in order to generate several mobile and cooperating agents for a given task.

References

1. AgentLink News 2, ISSN 1465-3842, January 99.
2. N. Hameurlain, C. Hanachi, C. Sibertin-Blanc, "Petri Net approach to build and execute missioned mobile agents"; Workshop on Application of Petri Nets to Intelligent System development, within ICATPN, June 21-25 1999, Williamsburg, USA.
3. H. Bachatène, P. Estraillier, "A modular design based on stepwise refinements of coloured petri nets", Proceedings of the Second Conference Annual Software Engineering, Research Forum (SERF), Melbourne, USA, november 1992.
4. J. Cardoso, "Sur les Réseaux de Pétri avec marquages flous", PHD thesis of University of Toulouse III, France, 1990.
5. W. Chainbi, C. Hanachi, C. Sibertin-Blanc, "*The Prey-Predator game : A petri-Net solution*", Computational Engineering in Systems Applications (CESA), Symposium on Discrete Events and Manufacturing Systems, Lille-France, July 9-12, 1996.

6. E. de B. Costa, A. Perkusich, A. A. Jatobé, "Petri Net Modeling of the cooperative Interaction in a Multi-Agent Based Intelligent learning Environment", CESA 96, IEEE-SMC, Lille, France.

7. D.S. Devapriya, B. Descottes-Genon, P. Ledet, "Distributed Intelligence Systems for FMS Control Using Objects Modelled with Petri Nets", IFAC symposium on Distributed Intelligence Systems, Arlington, Virginia, USA, 13-15 August 1991.

8. A. El Fallah-Seghrouchni, S. Haddad "A formal model for coordinating plans in multiagent systems", Proceeding of Intelligent Agent Workshop, Augustin technology Ltd., Oxford Brooks University, UK, november 1995.

9. J. Ferber, "Les systèmes Multi-Agents : Vers une intelligence collective", InterEditions, Paris, 1995.

10. M. Fowler, K. Scott, "UML Distilled, Applying the Standard Object Modelling Language". Addison-Wesley 1997.

11. A. Ghemeyer, J. Muller, A. Schappert, "Mobile Information Agents on the web"; in Proceedings of Second International Workshop on Cooperative Information Agents, LNAI 1435, Paris, France, 1998.

12. D. Moldt, F. Wienberg, "Multi-Agent-Systems based on coloured Petri Nets", Proceedings of the 18th Internat. Conf. on Application and Theory of Petri Nets, Toulouse, France, June 1997.

13. T. Murata, "Petri Nets: Properties, Analysis and Applications"; in Proceedings of the IEEE, vol 77, n° 4, April 1989.

14. T. Oates, M.V.N. Prasad, V.R. Lesser, "Cooperative Information-Gathering: a distributed problem solving approach"; in IEE Proceeding of Software Engineering, vol. 144. Pages 72-87. Black Bear Press.

15. A. Corradi, M. Cremonini, C. Stefanelli, "Melding Abstractions with Mobile Agents"; Proceedings of Second International Workshop on Cooperative Information Agents, LNAI 1435, Paris, France, 1998.

16. J-F. Raskin, Y-H. Tan, L. W. N. Van der Torre, "Modeling Deontic States in Petri Nets "; Proceedings of the Seventh Dutch Conference on Artificial Intelligence (NAIC95), Eramus University, Rotterdam, 1995.

17. C. Sibertin-Blanc, "An overview of SYROCO"; in Proceedings of the Tool Presentation Session, 18th International Conference on Application and Theory of Petri Nets, Toulouse (F), June 23-27 1997.

18. M. P. Singh, "A customizable Coordination Service for autonomous agents"; in Proceedings of 4th International Workshop on Agent theories, Architectures, and Languages, Providence, Island, USA, 1997.

19. K. Sycara, D. Zeng, "Multi-agent Integration of Information Gathering and Decision Support"; in Proceedings of ECAI'96. Pages 549-553 of: W. Wahlster (ed), Wiley Pubs.

20. C. Sibertin-Blanc, "High-level Petri Nets with Data Structures", in 6th European Workshop on Application and Theory of PN, Helsinki, Finland, June 1985.

Maintaining Specialized Search Engines through Mobile Filter Agents

Wolfgang Theilmann, Kurt Rothermel

Institute of Parallel and Distributed High-Performance Systems, University of
Stuttgart, D-70565 Stuttgart, Germany,
[theilmann|rothermel]@informatik.uni-stuttgart.de

Abstract. Information Retrieval in the World Wide Web with general
purpose search engines is still a difficult and time consuming task. Specialized search tools have turned out to be much more effective and useful
in certain domains. However, their ideas are often trimmed to one special
domain so they cannot be applied to set up series of specialized tools. In
addition, they tend to induce a tremendous load on the network.

This contribution reports our approach for designing specialized search
engines, so-called domain experts. These experts gather the documents
relevant for their domain through mobile filter agents. We show the effectiveness of domain experts with a case study in the domain of scientific
articles. Finally, we demonstrate that the filter agents' mobility can cause
a significant reduction of the induced network load.

1 Introduction

With the invention of the World Wide Web the Internet has become a very
popular forum for publishing documents. In summer 1997, there were already
more than 150 million Web pages distributed on around 650,000 sites [4]. The
great challenge for current and future research in information retrieval (IR) is
to help people profit from this immense database.

General purpose, robot-based search tools (such as [1]) are comprehensive
but imprecise. Manually generated directories (for example [12]) are precise but
cannot keep up with the fast evolution of the Web. Specialized automatic search
tools seem to be a promising synthesis of the former approaches because they
can achieve both, a comprehensive and within a certain domain precise index.

However, the construction of such search tools is very difficult. As we will see
in the next section there are three major problems, which have to be tackled:

1. The scope problem, i.e. how to determine whether an arbitrary document is
   relevant for the special scope of the search engine.
2. The location problem, i.e. how the relevant documents existing in the World
   Wide Web can be efficiently located.
3. The generality problem, i.e. whether it is possible to apply the techniques
   from one search engine to create a new one for another domain, and if yes,
   how much human effort is needed for this application.

To sum up these issues we can conclude that the challenge of research about specialized search engines is to find frameworks for such engines which enable the fast construction of effective and efficient tools for various domains.

After discussing the related work in Section 2 we present our approach of such a framework (Section 3) together with a validation of this approach in two terms: We demonstrate the effectiveness of the approach with a case study in the domain of scientific articles (Section 4). In addition, we show that the technology of mobile agents[1] can be successfully employed in order to achieve a rather efficient service (Section 5). We finish with some conclusions in Section 6.

2   Related Work

Many approaches have been undertaken to improve effectiveness and efficiency of general purpose search tools, for instance hierarchical distribution of indexes or automatic subject assignment (according to a given schema). A discussion of them can be found in [10].

2.1   Specialized Search Engines

We will compare the most important related approaches according to the major issues identified in the previous section.

The *Ahoy!*-system [9] locates personal homepages. An email address services and an institutional database are used as crossfilter for result items retrieved from general purpose search engines. An internal database is used to store successfully determined homepages. An interesting feature of the *Ahoy!* framework is the learning component that learns typical URL patterns of institutions and personal homepages. These patterns are successfully used to guess URLs in the case that the other search methods fail. The *Ahoy!*-system is a very effective and efficient search tool for its domain. However, it is rather difficult to apply the used techniques to other domains since the tool depends on specialized external information services. In addition, the application of the URL pattern learning component to other domains seems to be less promising than it is for the homepage domain.

In order to constrain the scope of search engines [5] suggest the definition of *digital neighbourhoods*. A neighbourhood can be based (1) on the geographic position of Web servers, (2) on a distance metric between IP-addresses, (3) on the hypertext-distance (i.e. length of the shortest path between two pages) and (4) on a similarity function that compares the content of two pages. While methods (1-3) seem to be of limited value it remains unclear how (4) shall be efficiently realized without periodically scanning the whole Web.

A framework for specialized crawlers is presented by [7]. New, personal crawlers are formulated by the specification of the two functions *visit(Page p)* and

---

[1] Mobile agents are program entities which can decide autonomously to transfer themselves to a remote server and to continue their exectution there.

shouldVisit(*Link l*). Reusable classifier components shall ease this formulation. It seems questionable whether the function *shouldVisit* can be sufficient to constrain the scope of crawlers for arbitrary domains. Crawlers can be relocated on remote servers, too. However, this is only a technical feature because no mechanisms are implemented which decide in which situation it might be useful to ship the crawler code on a remote server.

The *Nordic Web Index* [2] is a regional search service for the nordic European countries. This service uses the DNS toplevel domain as filter policy. Documents from the domains *.com, .org* are not included into the index.

2.2 Searching for Scientific Articles

Several tools have been developed for the automatic searching for scientific articles. In [8], the search is completely based on a bibliography server. An additional institution service is used to determine the Internet hosts which correspond to institution names extracted from the found bibliographic entries. The institution's Web server, the author's homepage and the respective articles are then discovered by an online search and by applying various heuristics.

External information sources (a bibliography server, a search tool for personal homepages and a general purpose search engine) are also heavily exploited by [6]. Queries have to contain at least one of the authors' names. Results of the external information sources are used for an online search starting at the author's and the departmental homepage.

We differ from these two approaches as our search service does not rely on special external services (except for a general purpose search engine). In addition, we construct a local database of articles once found which reduces network load and latency for future queries significantly. Finally, our approach is more general as we do not assume that articles have to occur in the neighbourhood of a personal or departmental homepage.

A database of articles is constructed by [3]. The user can either browse this database by links to *citing* or *cited* articles or can perform a search for keyword specified articles or for articles similar to a given article. Title, author, abstract and citation information is automatically extracted from a given article. However, the problem of article acquisition and article recognition is poorly addressed.

2.3 Employment of Mobile Agents

Though mobile agents have often been suggested to perform specific search tasks on remote servers their benefit has rarely been quantified for Internet scenarios. One reason for this lack of quantification is that most of the approaches (for example, [11] or [7]) are based on the assumption that every Web server also provides a platform for hosting agents. This is obviously not the case for the Internet of today. In contrast to such approaches we already profit from a small number of agent platforms distributed over the world.

3 The Framework of a Domain Expert

3.1 Overview

A domain expert is supplied with domain specific knowledge (strategies, algorithms etc.), which enables it (among other things) to decide on its own whether a document belongs to its domain or not.

Domain experts automatically build up a specialized index. In contrast to traditional indexes, this index is based not only on keywords contained in the indexed documents, but also comprises meta descriptions of documents that are expressed implicitly, for instance in the document's structure or environment. In the context of scientific articles, a meta description could be the information that a certain set of keywords is part of a single reference.

The construction of this index happens in the following way: At the beginning of its life cycle a domain expert has its domain specific knowledge but does not know any document that belongs to its domain. The expert expands its document knowledge by *learning* from a traditional search engine. In this phase the expert is already able to answer user queries. An incoming query is forwarded to a search engine. The resulting URLs are taken as a first hint pointing to interesting documents. The expert sends out mobile filter agents in order to scan the remote documents (described by the URLs) and to decide which documents shall be registered in the expert's document knowledge base. The acquired knowledge is used to answer the query.

Later on, as the document knowledge of the domain expert grows it becomes more and more *autonomous*, i.e. independent of traditional search engines. It is able to answer the majority of user queries directly by inspecting its document knowledge base. A search engine is just queried to check whether new documents have been published or whether old documents have been updated. Mobile agents are sent out only if new or modified documents have been found by the search engine. This is expected to happen only seldom in the autonomous phase.

Finally, a domain expert tries to discover new documents *proactively* without the context of a previous user query. This can be done in several ways:

- The environment of an interesting document (i.e. documents on the same Web server) can be examined for other possibly interesting documents.
- Relevant documents already found can be processed for further hints, such as URLs, a person's name, names of conferences etc. These hints can be exploited to find other interesting documents.
- External knowledge bases can be queried to acquire new or additional knowledge.

After acquiring enough hints the domain expert generates a proactive internal query. This query is then processed by the filter agents like an ordinary user query.

3.2 Filter Agents

Filter agents perform the analysis of a document in three steps. First, the document is transformed into a sequence of simple tokens. These tokens are still specific for the document type (e.g. html-tokens can be a markup token like "<H1>" or a simple text token). Second, the type specific tokens are converted into a sequence of tokens which contains exactly the information which is relevant for the final filtering process. These simple mechanisms allow to decouple the filtering process from the distinct document types and minimize the effort needed to adopt the filter agent to new types.

The final step of the document analysis consists of the core filter process. It results in a rating that represents the confidence in the respective document being relevant for the expert's domain. A certain tolerance threshold bounds the range down to which ratings (documents) are accepted. The agents return the ratings, the accepted documents and some meta descriptions of accepted documents (which they gained through their analysis) to the domain expert. The expert possibly performs a further analysis of the documents and integrates them into its document knowledge base.

A detailed discussion of the framework of domain experts can be found in [10].

4 A Case Study in the Domain of Scientific Articles

In order to validate our approach of domain experts we implemented a prototype expert that is able to recognize scientific articles (publications)[2]. Currently, this *publication expert* is bound to articles written in English and available in HTML-format.

We have to emphasize that our filter algorithm is not meant to compete with other AI research about filtering (e.g. learning approaches). Instead, we only want to show the feasability of Web-filtering and its benefit for the user. Therefore the following description of the filter technique is kept very brief.

4.1 Filter Algorithm

The domain specific tokens (compare to Section 3.2) generated by the filter agent consist of simple keywords extended by three attributes: a *markup level* (e.g. determined by the used markup tags, font style or size), a *cut level* that describes the degree to which a token is separated from its predecessor token (e.g. by paragraph or section separators like "<P>" or "<H1>" or by a horizontal rule) and an *alignment level* (the justification). We want to stress that these attributes are independent of the specific document format, i.e. markup and cut level are simply expressed through numbers that are to be interpreted relative to each other.

Based on these domain specific tokens the filter algorithm tries to identify certain structure elements that are typical for scientific articles. Such elements are the article's title, the author names, the abstract, the division of the text into certain sections, citations of other articles and a part containing the references.

---

[2] For the ease of writing/reading this paper we use the concepts *scientific article* and *publication* as synonyms.

In order to assess the element candidates we characterize each candidate by some structure element attributes (the number of words, the position in the text, the markup level, etc.). The attribute values vary from one document to the other but, in general, they always remain within a range typical for scientific articles. In order to provide a robust and fault tolerant recognition algorithm we describe valid/typical parameters for the structure element attributes through fuzzy sets. This enables us to rate any candidate for a structure element and therefore we can compare different candidates and select the best fitting (best rated) one. Finally, the ratings of the best candidates are combined with fuzzy algebraic operations to an overall rating that represents the confidence in the document being a scientific article.

For each accepted document the domain expert stores the document's keywords together with the information to which part of the document the respective keywords belong to, i.e. title, author and address part, abstract, introduction, main text or references part (including an item number for the single reference).

4.2 Experiments

Our experiments for evaluating the effectiveness of the publication expert are targeting (1) an analysis of the recognition quality and (2) a comparison between the expert's results and results that can be achieved by traditional search methods.

In order to have a document test set that reflects the enormeous variety of documents existing in the WWW we decided to base our experiments on search queries which we submit to a general purpose search engine and for which we consider the resulting list of URLs. Of course, this limits the size of the document test set since we have to classify each document manually. The alternative of using classified document collections (for instance, the online proceedings of a conference) seemed to be of limited value because such collections tend to have a rather uniform structure/layout.

We present the results for three queries (described in Table 1) which may occur in the context of a search for publications. The query syntax corresponds

no	query	#answers	#valid links	#publications
1	+"mobile agent" +"information retrieval"	200	160	22
2	+multicast	200 (>10.000)	127	29
3	+"software engineering" +"petri net" +invariant	113	66	4

Table 1. Some test queries.

to the AltaVista-syntax, i.e. the '+' enforces the occurrence of the respective keyword or phrase. The table shows for each query the number of result items returned by AltaVista, the number of valid links to an HTML-document and the number of scientific articles found on these pages by a manual analysis. For the second query, we only considered the first 200 answers.

Figure 1 provides an evaluation of the recognition quality for queries #1 and #2. The x-axis of the graphs describes the tolerance threshold down to

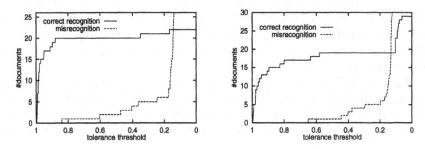

Fig. 1. Recognition quality for queries #1 and #2.

which rated documents are recognized as being scientific article. Decreasing the threshold always increases the number of correctly recognized and misrecognized articles (those that are considered as publications but which are not). We can see that the recognition for the first query is both, effective and robust. With a high threshold of 0.87 already 20 articles are correctly recognized without any misrecognition. A threshold of 0.4 still only leads to 4 misrecognitions.

For query #2 there are some lately recognized articles (only for a threshold < 0.1). A manual analysis brought out that these result from documents (Internet-RFCs - request for comments) which have an HTML-frame but for which the body contains simple ascii-text. Therefore it is not surprising that these documents have not been recognized since we have not yet implemented the second step of tokenization of ascii-texts (compare to Section 3.2). The other articles are recognized very well.

The left side of Figure 2 shows the recognition quality for query #3. Once more, the recognition algorithm turns out to be robust. Misrecognitions do rarely occur if the threshold is higher than 0.4. The second target of our experiments was to compare the expert's results with traditional search methods, i.e. a general purpose search engine. A user of such a tool has to provide his query with some keywords which are supposed to appear in the requested articles. He is not able to look for the keywords *scientific article* or *publication* as these words do not appear explicitly in scientific articles. However, a smart user might extend his query by the keywords *abstract* and *references* because these are more likely to occur in a scientific article than in an arbitrary document. We call these two query types the *simple* and the *smart* query type. Note that the result set is always the same for the simple and the smart query type because we do not enforce the occurrence of the additional keywords for the smart query type. The only difference consists of the result items' order.

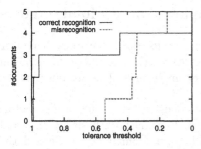 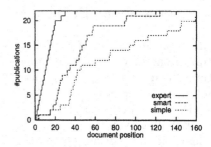

Fig. 2. Recognition quality for query #3 and "speed" of publications' presentation for query #1.

For each query we compared the results of both of the query types with the result of the publication expert which postfilters the results from AltaVista. Since we have ordered lists for the expert's result items (ordering according to the relevance rating) and for the items from AltaVista (directly returned as ordered list) we can examine the "speed" with which the relevant documents (i.e. publications) are presented to the user. The right side of Figure 2 provides a comparison of the presentation speed for the results of query #1. We can see that the publications are more or less equally distributed among the returned result items for the simple query type. Their presentation happens slightly earlier for the smart query type. In contrast, the expert presents nearly all publications in the leading positions. For example, the user has to walk through more than 80 result items from the smart query until he finds the twentieth publication. The expert presents these 20 publications in the 20 leading positions. Due to space limitations, we cannot show presentation speed results for queries #2 and #3. However, they are quite similar.

4.3 Discussion

The experiments show that even with a handmade and naive algorithm an effective and robust recognition of scientific articles can be achieved. We have also shown the immense benefit a user can have through the use of the publication expert (in comparison to the use of general purpose search engines). An additional, useful feature of the publication expert is that it allows to restrict queries to specific document parts, for example the abstract or the references part. This feature is directly enabled by the recognition algorithm which extracts the specific structure elements from the analysed documents.

A crucial point for the construction of domain experts will be the amount of human effort required for the implementation of the domain specific parts of a domain expert, most of all of the domain dependent filter function. The source code of the filter function for scientific articles consists of about 1000 lines. We expect that standard filter components will ease this effort for future domain experts. However, there will also remain a certain part that has to be manually coded/implemented.

5 Notes about Efficiency: Employment of Mobile Agents

An important aspect of specialized search services is the amount of network traffic/load they cause. Some proposed services (such as [8]) perform a crawling through large parts of the Internet for every single query. It is obvious that such solutions do not scale.

Domain experts will be efficient (in terms of network load) for various reasons: First of all, they use an existing search engine thus having a basis for the search. This avoids a reindexing of the whole Web for every domain expert. Second, they store the knowledge, once gained, in an internal knowledge base. By this, many queries can be answered just by inspecting the internal knowledge base. The only situation in which a domain expert wastes significant network resources occurs when it analyses remote documents. In order to reduce the network load required for this analysis we employ mobile agent technology[3]. This technology enables us to send the filter function to the respective data servers and to perform the filter process locally.

In this section, we explain the strategies for the employment of mobile agents and present some results about the reduction of network load that can be achieved by this technology.

5.1 Dissemination of Mobile Agents

In contrast to other approaches we do not assume the availability of agent platforms on every Web server. Instead, we can already profit from a small set of available agent platforms. We send the filter agents (in parallel) to those platforms which are most *closely* connected to the data servers that contain the documents to be analysed. Figure 3 shows a possible result of such a dissemination process. In this example two remote agent platforms are used to analyse

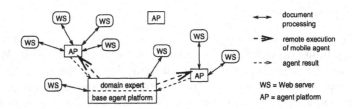

Fig. 3. Example for a dissemination process.

a certain set of Web servers. Two Web servers which have no closely connected agent platform are examined directly from the domain expert which is also the base agent platform from which the agents are sent out.

---

[3] Our agent model simply requires the agent's ability to perform a remote execution, i.e. to copy (replicate and transfer) its code on a remote server and to start it there with some arguments.

Currently, we explore techniques for a scalable acquiring, representing and updating of information about network distances in the Internet and for computing dissemination schemas for arbitrary scenarios.

5.2 Measuring Network Load

In the following we define network load as the amount of data that is transmitted across a network weighted by some kind of network distance. We based our experiments on two distance metrics which are easy to acquire and which do not induce a heavy network load. The first metric is the number of hops (network routers) existing on a path between two hosts. The second used metric is the round trip time (the time needed to transmit a simple datagram packet to a remote host and back).

The following equations show how the overall load for the traditional client server approach (in which all documents have to be downloaded to the domain expert) and for the agent approach is computed. In order to simplify the equations we define WS as the set of Web servers which contain the considered set of documents and AP as the set of agent platforms involved in a single scenario. $|*, *|$ denotes the distance between two hosts.

$$client\_server\_load = \sum_{ws \, \in \, WS} |ws, \, base\_platform| * data\_amount(ws)$$

$$agent\_solution\_load = \sum_{p \, \in \, AP} |p, \, base\_platform| * (agent\_size + result\_size(p))$$

$$+ \sum_{ws \, \in \, WS} |ws, \, closest\_agent\_platf(ws)| * data\_amount(ws)$$

$$load\_reduction = 1 - agent\_solution\_load/client\_server\_load$$

5.3 Experiments

Our experiments were performed on the basis of four hosts, one in Germany (Stuttgart), two in the USA (Berkeley, Boston) and the final one in Australia (Perth). We measured network distances (number of hops and round trip time) between these hosts and the Web servers resulting from our test queries in Section 4. The size of the filter agent's code is 16 kByte. The amount of data sent back from the remote filter agents to the domain expert is 2 bytes for every analysed document (the rating) plus the document itself for the accepted documents (we set the tolerance threshold to 0.5). The evaluations always assume the host in Stuttgart as the base platform and consider the availability of one to three additional remote agent platforms. We ordered the document's Web servers according to their minimum distance to an agent platform (either base or remote platform). Load reductions are always computed relative to the number of top ordered Web servers by applying the above formulas to the respective sets of top ordered servers.

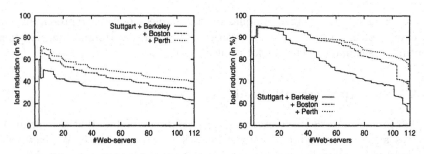

Fig. 4. Network load reduction based on #hops (left) and round trip time (right).

Figure 4 shows the reduction that can be achieved in the scenario of query #1. The 160 documents were distributed among 112 Web servers. The left graph shows the achieved reductions if we take the number of hops as distance metric. We can see that the overall reduction (the rightmost value) is rather low for the case of one remote platform (about 23%) and significantly higher in the case of three remote platforms (39%). We can also state that in the latter case the top 20 ordered Web servers (roughly one fifth of the set of servers) can be examined with network costs reduced by 60%. This allows the rough extrapolation that we can achieve 60% reduction if we have five times more agent platforms effectively distributed across the Internet.

Similar conclusions can be drawn from the right graph which presents the reductions for the case of distances measured by round trip time. An interesting observation is that the load reduction for this distance metric is much higher than for the other one (#hops). For instance, the analysis of the top 20 Web servers wastes only 6% of the network load which is needed for the traditional client server analysis. The reason for the higher reductions can be found in the higher standard deviation of round trip times. The round trip time of a remote connection is about 100 times higher than for a local one. In contrast, the number of hops varies just about a factor of 5-10. For this, the benefit of local examination is much higher in the case of round trip time metric than for the hops metric.

Several repetitions of the above measurements and an evaluation for the scenarios of query #2 and #3 proved reductions of the same order of magnitude as above.

6 Conclusions

Our contribution has shown a way to construct specialized search engines which satisfy the three major issues, identified in Section 1. We demonstrated the effectiveness through a case study in the domain of scientific articles. We also validated that the technology of mobile agents can be successfully employed in order to reduce the network load (caused by the process of acquiring knowledge about documents in the Web). Finally, we showed that the approach can be applied for every domain for which it is possible to implement a recognition algorithm.

Future work concentrates on mechanisms for an optimal dissemination of the mobile filter agents and on the improvement of our framework.

Acknowledgements

The experiments in the last section of this article would not have been possible without various people who helped us to perform measurements from their location. We are indepted to Nikolaos Radouniklis (Univ. of California at Berkeley), Rumen Stainov (Boston University), Thomas Bräunl (Univ. of Western Australia) and Riccardo Bettati (Texas A&M University).

References

1. AltaVista: URL: http://altavista.digital.com
2. A. Ardö, S. Lundberg: *A regional distributed WWW search and indexing service - the DESIRE way.* Proc. of 7th Int. World Wide Web Conf. (WWW7), Brisbane, Queensland, Australia, April 14-18, 1998
3. K.D. Bollacker, S. Lawrence, C.L. Giles: *CiteSeer: An Autonomous Web Agent for Automatic Retrieval and Identification of Interesting Publications.* Proc. of 2nd Int. Conf. on Autonomous Agents, Minneapolis, USA, May 10–13, 1998
4. D. Brake: *Lost in Cyberspace.* New Scientist, 28 June 1997, URL: http://www.newscientist.com/keysites/networld/lost.html
5. P. Falcão Gonçalves, A.C. Salgado, S. Lemos Meira: *Digital Neighbourhoods: Partitioning the Web for Information Indexing and Searching.* Proc. of 9th Conf. on Advanced Information Systems Engineering, Barcelona, Spain, June 16–20, 1997
6. Y. Han, S.W. Loke, L. Sterling: *Agents for Citation Finding on the World Wide Web.* Department of Computer Science, University of Melbourne, Australia, Technical Report 96/40, 1996
7. R.C. Miller, K. Bharat: *SPHINX: A Framework for Creating Personal, Site-Specific Web Crawlers.* Proc. of WWW7'98, Brisbane, Australia, April 14–18, 1998
8. A. Monge, C. Elkan: *The WebFind tool for finding scientific papers over the worldwide web.* Proc. of Int. Congress on Computer Science Research, Tijuana, Baja California, Mexico, November 27–29, 1996
9. J. Shakes, M. Langheinrich, O. Etzioni: *Dynamic Reference Sifting: A Case Study in the Homepage Domain.* Proc. of WWW6'97, Santa Clara, California, USA, April 7–11, 1997
10. W. Theilmann, K. Rothermel: *Domain Experts for Information Retrieval in the World Wide Web.* Proc. of 2nd Int. Workshop on Cooperative Informative Agents, Paris, July 4–7, 1998, LNAI 1435, Springer, 1998, pp. 216–227
11. J. Yang, P. Pai, V. Honavar, L. Miller: *Mobile Intelligent Agents for Document Classification and Retrieval: A Machine Learning Approach.* Proc. of 14th European Meeting on Cybernetics and Systems Research, Vienna, Austria, April 14–17, 1998
12. Yahoo!: URL: http://www.yahoo.com

Execution Monitoring in Adaptive Mobile Agents

Walter Vieira[(1)(2)]   L. M. Camarinha-Matos [(1)]

[(1)]Universidade Nova de Lisboa, DEE, Quinta da Torre, 2825-Monte Caparica, Portugal
[(2)]Instituto Superior de Engenharia de Lisboa, DEEC, Portugal
{wv, cam}@uninova.pt

Abstract. Remote operation of equipment is progressively gaining importance due to its large range of potential application areas such as hazardous environments, spatial vehicles, remote telescopes, remote manufacturing systems, virtual laboratories, etc. The traditional approaches based on remote procedure calling mechanisms reveal several difficulties when dealing with non-ideal networks that exhibit high delays and poor availability and reliability. The authors have proposed a solution for remote operation and supervision based on adaptive mobile agents which has important advantages for this kind of networks. In this paper further work is described concerning the inclusion of execution monitoring capabilities in the mobile agents.

1 Introduction

In the last years considerable research effort has been put on issues related to remote operation and remote supervision what is due to the many potential applications, ranging from machines operating in hazardous or inaccessible environments to spatial vehicles operating with large autonomy. There has been also a considerable growth in the number of applications that make use of the Internet for a wide range of domains (remotely operated robots and telescopes, manufacturing systems, virtual laboratories, etc.).

The traditional approaches taken in tele-robotics and tele-supervision assume a set of pre-defined services which a remote user can activate in a closed loop control way on simple machine and sensorial environments. This approach becomes inappropriate when there is a need to achieve remote operation of complex machinery or sensorial environments with high levels of flexibility, as in such cases it is not possible to stand on a set of pre-defined services and on simple monitoring/recovery procedures. Things become more complicated when dealing with large or variable time-delays and low availability of the communication channels, which turn remote closed loop control impracticable, and require that more sophisticated and more reliable solutions be found to adequately face these difficulties, allowing the increase of the autonomy of the equipment being operated, yet preserving a high degree of flexibility.

The mobile agents paradigm [5] reveals interesting characteristics when these issues are considered [2], because: i) moving the code to the places where the machines and sensors are located enables real-time response without strong dependency on network reliability and delays; ii) since new mobile agents can be built and sent for remote execution whenever needed, higher levels of flexibility are achieved.

Flexibility may be further increased if we take into account that in many situations the same execution plan can be executed using different resources (machines), which is a very important aspect when we consider remote operation of many heterogeneously equipped execution environments. In order to take advantage of this possibility, in this paper a solution is proposed based on mobile agents that carry general execution plans, which must be refined/adapted when the agents reach their target places.

Plan adaptation issues were considered in [2], while in this paper the focus is put on issues related to execution monitoring of the adapted plans and error recovery.

Execution monitoring [11] and error recovery in the context of mobile agents is difficult since the exact configurations of the execution environments are not known in advance. Proposed solutions must be general enough to deal with this uncertainty and also must reveal enough effectiveness to be of practical interest.

The rest of this paper is structured as follows: in section 2 some relevant issues related to the application of mobile agents in remote operation are discussed; section 3 describes an application scenario where remote operation based on adaptive mobile agents has been tested; in section 4 the proposed solution to execution monitoring in mobile agents is presented; finally, in section 5 some conclusions are presented and areas where further work is needed are pointed out.

2 Mobile agents for remote operation

One popular solution for remote operation assumes low level services available in the remote place being high level tasks composed of a sequence of calls to these services by means of the traditional remote procedure calling (RPC) mechanism, as is illustrated in Fig. 1. This solution is very flexible in what concerns functionality, since clients can easily achieve new functionality by composition of the low level commands the remote place recognizes. However, it is extremely dependent on the characteristics of the communication links, such as availability, reliability and delays.

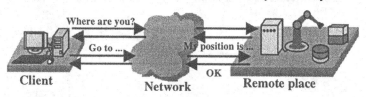

Fig. 1. Remote operation based on low-level commands

One possible solution for the network dependence is to increase the intelligence of the remote places, by implementing there high level commands which, when activated from the client side, execute almost entirely in the remote place (see Fig. 2). However, this solution is quite limited in what concerns flexibility, since it implies that any change in functionality requires the corresponding update of all remote places where that changed functionality has to be implemented.

Mobile agents allow a solution where flexibility and network independence are conciliated. In this solution, remote places still implement a set of low level services but are augmented with the capability to run mobile agents. In the client side, mobile agents are implemented according to the desired functionality and sent to the remote places where they run independently of the characteristics of the network. Intelligent recovery strategies may be implemented in the agents, since they carry the overall execution plan.

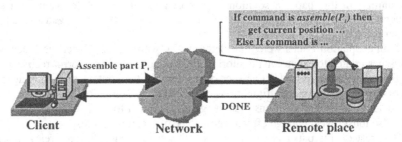

Fig. 2. Remote operation with high-level commands

It is consensual that often the same desired functionality can be achieved using quite differently equipped execution environments. The concept of device driver popularized within the operating systems arena is paradigmatic of how this characteristic can be favorably used. However the concept of device driver is very limited in the extent of this exploitation. When one considers systems with planning skills [12] more effective strategies can be devised by thinking of plan refinement techniques that allow the adaptation of high level abstract plans to the specific capabilities of the execution environments. Essentially, a set of planning operators mirroring the functionality of the device drivers may be used to refine an abstract execution plan in order it can be executed with the specific capabilities (functionality) of each execution environment, thus allowing the same abstract plan to be executed using quite different sets of resources.

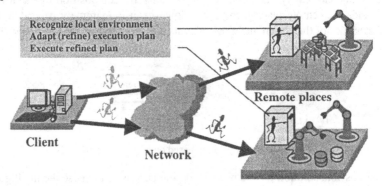

Fig. 3. Remote operation based on adaptive mobile agents

The solution proposed in this paper is based on adaptive mobile agents with the ability to adapt the abstract plans they carry to the local execution environments, as illustrated in Fig. 3.

3 An application scenario

The concepts described in the previous section have been tested in a prototype system (called MobCare) to support elderly living alone at home, which is a multi-agent system [14] structured around a set of places interconnected through the Internet, as illustrated in Fig. 4. At the heart of a MobCare system we have the home places (HP) which are located at the homes where elderly people (the users) live. HPs may include a set of sensors (temperature, humidity, etc.), measurement devices (blood pressure, body temperature, etc.) and a set of robotized home appliances. This equipment may be operated both locally, by local monitoring agents, and remotely, from social care centers (care center places - CCP), health care centers (health center places - HCP), or from relative's jobs (relative's places - RP). Other places that may exist in a MobCare environment are leisure places which the user may visit to participate in some social activity (leisure places - LP), and commerce places which give support to some electronic supported trade (commerce places - CP). A more complete discussion of the MobCare system can be found in [3].

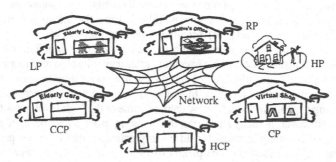

Fig. 4. Structure of a MobCare System

For illustration purposes, in this paper only interaction between CCPs and HPs are considered. Mobile agents are sent from CCPs to run in HPs. For example, a mobile agent could be sent to a HP to help the user in some food preparation. This agent would carry an abstract plan considering abstract actions such as *set the table, warm-up the meal, serve the meal*, etc. When in the destination HP, the agent would adapt its abstract plan to the local capabilities of the HP. For example, would the HP have a robotized microwave and the agent could perform the action *warm-up the meal* almost entirely automatically. Otherwise, if only a conventional gas-stove were present the agent would have to resort to a set of help messages sent to the user using some local capability (voice synthesizer, color lights, bell, TV screen, etc.).

4 Execution monitoring in adaptive mobile agents

Execution monitoring and error recovery in automation have been addressed by several authors [6], [8] but, very often, the proposed solutions have focused on very restricted domains (one such domain is execution monitoring and error recovery in flexible assembly cells [8]). The reason for that is that the delimitation of the application domain allows the enrichment of the knowledge about the domain and, so, eases the definition of execution monitoring and error recovery strategies.

In the work described in this paper, the restricted domain assumption does not hold, and, therefore, several difficulties arise: i) a solution is searched for a very wide range of applications; ii) the actual composition of the execution environments is not known in advance; iii) the agents must run with a high degree of autonomy.

As a consequence, an approach based on general monitoring and recovery methods and on an appropriate generation of annotated plans in order to help the execution monitoring and error recovery was adopted. A hierarchical plan structure was considered, since it allows the specification of monitors at various levels of detail which is very appropriate for complex domains. Furthermore, the hierarchical approach is a powerful mean to structure interesting monitoring strategies that range over a set of low level actions (for example, if some condition has to be verified during the execution of a set of actions, an action may be defined in the upper level which abstracts those lower level actions, and a monitor may be associated to the higher level action to observe the maintenance condition during its execution).

The following types of monitors are considered: i) effect monitors check the expected effects upon termination of the actions; ii) maintenance monitors are used to guarantee the maintenance of some conditions during the execution of an action (either primitive, or abstract); iii) time-out monitors may be used to define some upper bound limit on the duration of an action; and iv) failure monitors are activated if a child of one abstract action fails execution after trying its recovery methods.

At a first glance one could think of complex autonomous mobile agents to manage the adaptation mechanism referred to in the previous sections. These agents would have planning capabilities which allow them to achieve the high level goals they carry with them. However, in many situations, the planning process may be so complex that full automated planning systems would be impracticable due to either performance insufficiency or the associated complexity of the considered domain. For example, in complex domains, rich execution monitoring strategies may better be achieved with mixed initiative off-line planners than with local (and so limited in scope) planners embedded in the agents.

In the approach taken in this work the mobile agents carry with them high level abstract plans obtained a priori, which are refined according to the capabilities found in each place visited by the agents. Finally the resulting refined plan is executed.

The abstract plans may have special annotations (generated automatically or with the user support) intended to guide the local plan refinement process, the local execution monitoring process, or the local error recovery process.

Previous work related to plan refinement in mobile agents was described elsewhere [2]. Basically, a least commitment strategy of the kind found in partial order causal link (POCL) [15] planners is followed. Each abstract action is refined according to the capabilities found in the local environment and the obtained refined sub-plan is merged with the current refined plan.

Plan representation

In the POCL abstract plan carried by the agent, two types of abstract actions (AA) exist: i) high level abstract actions (HLAA) whose refinements are specified in terms of other abstract actions, and ii) low level abstract actions (LLAA) that must be refined locally in each site visited by the agent. A third type of action is generated by the refinement process which corresponds to executable procedures using local capabilities and are called executable actions (EA). Fig. 5 depicts a simplified version of the object model of the actions considered in an agent's plan, using the Unified Modeling Language (UML).

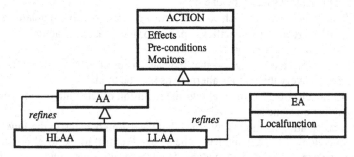

Fig. 5. Types of actions during execution of the agents

Currently, JAVA mobile agents (implemented in previous work [3]) act as shells which transport the abstract plans.

An abstract plan specification always begins with one action (either an HLAA or an LLAA), whose refinement methods determine the agent's behavior. The refinement procedure is recursively applied starting in the initial action until a plan composed only of executable actions is obtained.

For the specification of the abstract plans, a preliminary version of a plan representation language, called mobile agents abstract plan language (MAAPL), was defined. An excerpt of its syntax in EBNF is shown in Fig. 6.

```
<plan spec> ::= <action spec>+
<action spec> ::= action (<action name>,<type>,<parameters>,<priority>,<pre-conditions>,<effects>,
                          <refinement>,<effect monitors>, <maintenance monitors>,
                          <time-out monitor>,<fail monitor>)
<effect monitors> ::= EFFECT (<set of effect monitors>) I default
<effect monitor> ::= (<effect condition>,<recovery method>)
< maintenance monitors> ::= MAINTAIN (<set of maintenance monitors>) I nil
< maintenance monitor> ::= (<state condition>,<recovery method>)
<time-out monitor> ::= TOUT (<time>,<recovery method>) I nil
<fail monitor> ::= FAIL (<child action name>,<recovery method>) I nil
<recovery method> ::= RETRY I REDO I FAIL I ...
<refinement> ::= <unconditional refinement> I TEST (<set of selections>)
<unconditional refinement> ::= EXECUTE (<function>) I PLAN <partial order> I
                          CHOICE (<set of partial orders>) I ADAPT (<adaptation method>)
<selection> ::= (<state condition>,<unconditional refinement>)
<partial order> ::= <set of action names> <set of ordering constraints> <set of causal constraints>
<ordering constraint> ::= (<action name>,<action name>)
<causal constraint> ::= (<action name>,<condition>,<action name>)
<adaptation method> ::= STRIPS I LIBRARY I POCL I ...
```

Fig. 6. Excerpt of the preliminary syntax of MAAPL

As can be observed in Fig. 6, a plan specification is composed of one or more occurrences of action specifications, being the first the action where the abstract plan begins. Action specifications necessarily include a name that identifies the action within the plan, a type used during plan refinement, a priority which is used to decide what action is first selected for execution in case there are several actions enabled for execution, lists of pre-conditions and effects in STRIPS-like form, and a refinement strategy.

The refinement strategy may be one of:

- EXECUTE (<function>)in which case the action corresponds to a standard service.
- PLAN <partial order> that specifies a partial order of abstract actions at a lower level that implement this action.
- CHOICE (<list of partial orders>) that indicates a set of alternative partial orders. During error recovery the various alternatives may be tried.
- TEST(<list of selections>) which allows the inclusion of alternative branches in the plan depending on some state conditions.
- ADAPT (<adaptation method>) specifies that the action belongs to the lowest level of abstract actions (LLAAs) and has to be adapted/refined to the local environment in order to be executed. The <adaptation method> specifies the strategy that must be used for adaptation of the action to the local environment.

Optionally, action specifications may include a set of monitors of the following types:

- *Effect monitors* specify monitors that verify the achievement of the effects of actions upon their completion. A set of monitors may be specified, being each one a pair composed of a condition on the effects of the action and a recovery method which indicates one of the available recovery strategies. Currently, the following recovery strategies are considered: i) RETRY for retrying the action with the current refined plan, ii) REDO for trying an alternative refinement, and iii) FAIL for gracefully failing the action, and propagate error recovery to the upper level. Inclusion of other recovery strategies is planned for the future.
- A set of *maintenance monitors* may be specified, each one being a pair composed of a world state condition that must be maintained during the execution of the action, and a recovery method. The maintenance condition must be one of the pre-conditions (possibly a static pre-condition) of the action where the monitor is defined. Currently, only the FAIL recovery method is available for these monitors.
- A *time-out monitor* runs if the maximum allowable action's duration is exceeded.
- A *fail monitor* specifies what recovery method must be used when the named child action fails after trying all its applicable recovery methods.

During the agent's execution, the actions appearing in a MAPPL specification correspond to either LLAAs (those which mention an ADAPT clause in the <refinement> component) or HLAAs. As said before, EAs are obtained at run-time as a result of the refinement of LLAAs. During execution, EAs use the effect list as a set of expected conditions to be verified after their completion; for the LLAAs the effects specify the desired effects after execution of all the actions belonging to the corresponding refined sub-plans; the effects of HLAAs specify the desired observations after completion of all the abstract actions corresponding to the chosen refinement branch. The effects of both HLAAs and LLAAs are subsets of the effects produced by the successful execution of the corresponding refined sub-plan. During plan refinement, pre-conditions of LLAAs (like their effects) are passed to the refinement process [2] where they are used to obtain the refined sub-plans. In the case of EAs, pre-conditions are used only during execution to test real world state conditions that have to be hold in order the execution of the action may be initiated.

Plan execution and monitoring

Fig. 7 depicts the general architecture of the proposed adaptive mobile agent with execution monitoring capabilities.

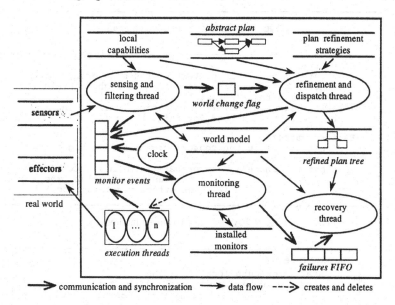

Fig. 7. Architecture for execution monitoring in mobile agents

EAs are executed as concurrent threads and interface with the local environment via a set of effectors. They call local procedures determined by the capabilities they are associated with. It is assumed that the local execution environment is equipped with adequate monitoring and error recovery mechanisms at the execution level. If execution of an EA fails, sufficient information for characterizing the failure is obtained from the local environment. This information may be used by the high level error recovery procedures.

The sensing and filtering thread is a high priority thread that runs periodically and is responsible for maintaining an updated persistent world model. It is assumed that the time elapsed between two consecutive cycles of this thread is small enough to guarantee that no significant real world transient changes are lost. Whenever this thread perceives a world state change it notifies the monitor thread and the refinement and dispatch thread, by signaling the event FIFO and the world change flag (a binary semaphore), respectively.

The refinement and dispatch thread runs in two phases: i) in phase one it refines the carried abstract plan; ii) in phase two it acts as a dispatcher, scheduling next EAs for execution. When all pending EAs are waiting for the completion of precedent actions, this thread blocks in the world change flag to wait for a world change. The refinement and dispatch thread behavior is illustrated in Fig. 8.

```
Refinement and dispatch Thread:
  Refine abstract plan //creates the refined plan tree
  Do forever
    Reset world change flag
    if there is one action ready for execution
      action.setStatus(waiting_exec)//waiting for exec
      sendMonitorEvent(start(action))//sign. mon. thr.
    else
        block in the world change flag
```

Fig. 8. Refinement and dispatch tread

```
EA.start()
  // note: runs in the context of the monitoring thread
  father.start() // propagate start to higher levels
  install monitors // install action's monitors
  setStatus(executing) // this action is executing
  start execution thread for this action

EA.terminate()
  // note: runs in the context of the monitoring thread
  remove monitors
  father.terminate() // propagate termination to higher
                     // levels (uninstall maint. mon.,
                     // check effect monitors, etc.)
```

Fig. 9. EA's start and terminate methods

```
EA.execThread:
    stat ← execute local function
    SendMonitorEvent(terminate(action,stat))
                    // signals the monitoring thread
```

Fig. 10. EA's execution threads

The result of the refinement process is a refined plan tree where the hierarchical plan is represented along with the corresponding annotated information. The nodes of this tree correspond to actions, being its leaves the primitive executable actions (EAs). Each node maintains information about its monitors, its pre-conditions and its expected effects. The nodes of the refined plan tree are defined according to a class hierarchy that resembles shown in Fig. 5. All classes in this hierarchy have the methods *start()* and *terminate()* (Fig. 9). EAs also have a corresponding execution thread (Fig. 10).

The higher level abstract actions (HLAAs) propagate their maintenance monitors to the lower levels. To achieve this, the corresponding nodes in the refined plan tree keep track of the number of children they have. When the first child executes the father's method *start()*, the father's monitors are installed; when the last child executes the father's method *terminate()*, the father's monitors are uninstalled.

The monitoring thread (see Fig. 11) waits in the monitor events FIFO for the following types of events: i) clock events implying checking the installed time-out monitors; ii) start action events, in which case the method *start()* of the started action is activated and all its corresponding monitors installed; iii) terminate action events, in which case the method *terminate()* of the terminating action may be activated, after error checking is done and error recovery launched if appropriate; iv) world state change events in which case the maintenance installed monitors are checked.

```
Monitoring thread:
  Do forever
      ev ← wait for next monitor event
      case ev of
        clock: check time-out monitors
        world state: check maintenance monitors
        start(action): action.start
        terminate(action,stat):
          if correct termination (action,stat) then
            //test for normal termination incl. eff. mon.
            action.terminate()
            action.setStatus(success)
          else
            action.setStatus(error)
            signal recovery event to the recovery thread
```

Fig. 11. Monitoring thread

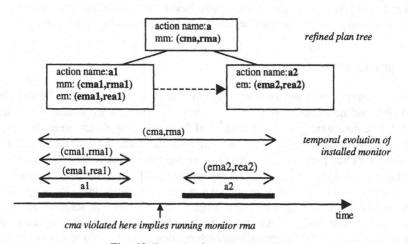

Fig. 12. Example of monitors' installation

Fig. 12 gives an idea of the process of installation of monitors. As can be observed, when action **a1** starts, its own monitors are installed as well as the maintenance monitor of action **a**. During execution of action **a1**, these are the installed monitors. When **a1** terminates, its own monitors are uninstalled, but the maintenance monitor of action **a** remains active (note that besides the pause after execution of **a1**, action **a** is still executing). Starting of action **a2** installs its own monitor, and the rest of the execution will be done under the supervision of the maintenance monitor of action **a** and the effect monitor of action **a2**.

When errors are detected , the recovery thread is activated by the monitoring thread via events placed in the failures FIFO. These events include the classification of the occurred error and the identification of the related monitor. If the recovery method involves plan refinement, this is processed as in the refinement of the initial abstract plan, i. e., the refinement of one LLAA is done by considering its pre-conditions as the initial world state and its effects as the goals. The refined recovery plan is then merged with the current refined plan, in order to substitute the actions belonging to the failed part of the old plan. If after the merging of the recovery plan with the existing plan, some actions in the recovery plan have pre-conditions not satisfied by the current world model state, nor by any other action in the refined plan, the execution of the dispatch thread is suspended, and a patch plan is tried to achieve these pre-conditions. This patch plan is obtained by calling one of the planners available for plan refinement, having as goal the conjunction of the failed pre-conditions, and as initial state the current world model state, from where the conditions which appear in the effects of any EA still executing are removed. The patch plan is then executed in order to achieve the missing pre-conditions.

If the recovery strategy corresponding to one action at some level doesn't work, that action is terminated and the corresponding fail monitor of its parent action (in the upper level) is tried. If the recovery procedure doesn't work at all, the plan execution fails.

This recovery scheme may be very effective in those domains where actions don't interact too much and the frequency and consequences of errors are moderate, although some problems may appear if these conditions don't hold. Nevertheless, it is a simple strategy appropriate for integration within lightweight mobile agents.

5 Conclusions

Remote operation and supervision is a very active area of research. Conciliating flexibility and network independence is a very important factor to consider in this area. Some disadvantages of the traditional RPC based approach were discussed. Following previous work done by the authors in this area, the concept of adaptive mobile agents was presented as a mean to cope with these disadvantages. Contrary to several other systems described in the literature [1], [7], [9], [10], these agents don't have a deep knowledge of their execution environments, which turns the adoption of very specific execution monitoring strategies very difficult. A solution based on mobile agents that carry off-line generated high level abstract plans annotated with execution monitoring and error recovery information at the various levels of the plan hierarchy was presented. These carried plans are adapted by the agents to the actual execution environments they find in each place they visit. Since the high level plans may be generated off-line by mixed initiative planners, very effective monitoring strategies can be incorporated.

Following these principles, an architecture for execution monitoring in adaptive mobile agents was presented which relies on the monitoring strategies defined in the abstract plans carried by the agents. This architecture is based on a set of concurrent fixed specialized execution threads for plan refinement and action dispatching, execution monitoring, error recovery, and maintenance of the world model. Besides these fixed threads, an execution thread is dynamically created for each primitive action being executed by the agent. These concurrent execution characteristics turn the system more appropriate for practical applications than other execution control systems based on sequential execution of the agents' actions [4], [7], [13].

There remain some open issues related to the integration of the described plan language (MAAPL) with other components of the mobile agents. The use of MAAPL in conjunction with the language JAVA has many advantages, but also has some weak points. On the other hand, MAAPL could be improved in order to incorporate some of the more traditional mechanisms of programming languages (use of variables, control cycles, etc.). Future work has to be done to decide what solution is better. Another aspect where more research is needed is related to the use of local diagnosis capabilities in order to improve the error recovery strategies implemented in the mobile agents.

Acknowledgements

This work received partial support from the PRAXIS XXI program of the Portuguese Ministry for Science and Technology.

References

1. Bonasso, R., Kortenkamp, D., Miller, D., Slack, M.: Experiences with an Architecture for Intelligent, Reactive Agents, J. of Experimental and Theoretical AI, Vol. 9, No. 1 (1997)
2. Camarinha-Matos, L. M. Vieira, W.: Adaptive Mobile Agents for Telerobotics and Telesupervision, in: Proc. of the IEEE Int. Conf. INES'98 (1998) 79-84
3. Camarinha-Matos, L. M. Vieira, W.: Using multiagent systems and the Internet in care services for the ageing society, in: L. M. Camarinha-Matos, H. Afsarmanesh and V. Marik (eds.), Intelligent Systems for Manufacturing: multi-agent systems and virtual enterprises, Kluwer Academic Publishers (1998) 33-47
4. Firby, R.: Adaptive Execution in Complex Dynamic Worlds, PhD thesis, Yale University, tchnical report YALEU/CSD/RR #672 (1989)
5. Fuggeta, A., Picco, G. P., Vigna, G.; Understanding Code Mobility, IEEE Trans. on Software Engineering, Vol. 24, No. 5 (1998) 346-361
6. Gini, M.: Towards Automatic Error Recovery in Robot Programs, Proc. of the 8th Int. Joint Conference on AI (1983) 821-823
7. Haigh, K., Veloso, M.: Interleaving Planning and Robot Execution for Asynchronous User Requests, Autonomous Robots, Vol. 5, No.1 (1998) 79-95
8. Meijer, G. R.: Autonomous Shopfloor Systems: a Study into Exception handling for Robot Control, PhD thesis, University of Amsterdam (1998)
9. Miller, J. P.: The design of Intelligent Agents: a layered approach, Springer-Verlag, (1996)
10. Pell, B., Gat, E., Keesing, R., Muscettola, N., Smith, B.: Plan Execution for Autonomous Spacecraft, working notes of the AAAI-96 fall Symposium on Plan Execution (1996)
11. Veloso, M., Pollack, M., Cox, M.: Rationale-Based Monitoring for Planning in Dynamic Environments, 4th Int. Conf. on AI (1998)
12. Weld, D.: Recent Advances in AI Planning (to appear in AI Magazine, 1999)
13. Wilkins, D., Myers, K., Lowrance, J., Wesley, L.: Planning and Reacting in Uncertain Environments, J. of Experimental and Theoretical AI, Vol. 7, No. 1 (1995) 197-227
14. Wooldridge, M., Jennings, N.: Agent Theories, Architectures and Languages: A Survey, In: Wooldridge, M., Jennings, N. (eds): Intelligent Agents, Lecture Notes in Artificial Intelligence, Vol. 890, Springer-Verlag, Berlin Heidelberg (1995) 1-39
15. Young, R., Pollak, M. Moore, J.: Decomposition and Causality in Partial-Order Planning, Proc. of the 2nd International Conference on AI planning Systems (AIPS) (1994) 188-193

Mobile-Agent Mediated Place Oriented Communication

Yasuhiko Kitamura[1], Yasuhiro Mawarimichi[1], and Shoji Tatsumi[1]

Department of Information and Communication Engineering
Faculty of Engineering, Osaka City University
3-3-138 Sugimoto, Sumiyoshi-ku, Osaka 558-8585, Japan
{kitamura, ym, tatsumi}@kdel.info.eng.osaka-cu.ac.jp
http://www.kdel.info.eng.osaka-cu.ac.jp/~kitamura/

Abstract. When we communicate with others in a most primitive way like face-to-face conversation, we normally gather at a common physical place. This physical constraint has been recognized as an obstacle against free communication. To relax this constraint, modern communication systems like post, telephone, and the Internet have been invented. Now we are building a free society with no border on the Internet by using the electronic communication tools to enjoy free communication with people all over the world. On the other hand, in this network society, we face many serious problems like spam mail and malicious access to information resources. We believe that one reason causing these problems is that current communication technologies neglect roles of physical place in primitive communication. Implicitly, a place defines who is allowed to enter it and who is not.

In this paper, we propose the Agent Mediated Communicator (AMC) which creates virtual places for electronic communication on the Internet. Communication on the AMC is mediated by mobile agents and is achieved as interactions among agents and services in a place. When we start a communication with a person, we send a mobile agent to his/her place. Before the agent enters the place, it is authenticated and can enter only when it is allowed. Multiple agents can enter in a single place and they are visible to others. We can install various communication tools called services in a place like E-mail, Talk, Chat, BBS, WWW and so on. To show an example of look and feel of AMC, we developed a prototype of AMC based on a mobile agent platform IBM Aglets.

Place oriented communication by AMC has the following implications.
- It gives a simple and clear security model for communication.
- It gives a platform of communityware where people with a common interest can communicate with each other to create a community.
- It gives an information network platform which is easily adaptable to current physical social systems because our physical society can be viewed as a society consisting of mobile agents.

1 Introduction

When we communicate with others in a most primitive way like face-to-face conversation, we normally gather at a common physical place. This physical constraint has been recognized as an obstacle against free communication. To relax this constraint, modern communication systems such as post, telephone, and so on have been invented and widespread over the world. By using mail and telephone, we can easily communicate with people who live in distant places.

Information network technology such as the Internet succeeds in alleviating the constraint dramatically. We can exchange messages with people on the other side of the earth in a moment by E-mail and can gather and offer various information from and to the world through the WWW. Now we are building a free society with no border on the Internet by using these communication tools to enjoy free communication with people all over the world.

On the other hand, we face many serious problems in this network society. We are annoyed with uncomfortable incoming mail called spam or junk mail everyday. Our personal information, which is open to the public on the WWW, might be used for an unintended purpose by others. Group communication on a BBS (Bulletin Board System) could be threatened by anonymous malicious posting. Nowadays it is quite difficult to solve these problems just by appealing to the network users to keep "netiquette" as social rules.

We believe that one reason causing these problems is that current communication technologies that support our network society neglect roles of physical place in primitive communication. In our daily life, when we talk with others, we usually consider the place. We usually greet friends or colleagues in a corridor, an elevator, and almost everywhere. For a business or research discussion, we usually do it in a meeting room that is separated from others to avoid interventions. When we talk about private matters, we may use a private room to keep the talk secret from others. Implicitly, a place defines who is allowed to enter it and who is not. A person who is not allowed are refused to enter it, or asked or forced to be out when he/she has already been there. Hence, we choose an appropriate place depending on the contents or participants of communication.

In this paper, we propose the Agent Mediated Communicator (AMC) which creates virtual places for electronic communication on computer network. Communication on the AMC is mediated by mobile agents and is achieved as interactions among agents and services in a place. When we start a communication with a person, we send a mobile agent to his/her place. Before the agent enters the place, it is authenticated, and can enter it only when it is allowed. Multiple agents can enter in a common single place and they are visible to others and can interact with each other. We can install various communication tools called services in a place. Services such as Chat or BBS are shared by multiple agents in the place. Place oriented communication supported by AMC has the following implications.

- It gives a simple and clear security model for communication.
- It gives a platform of communityware where people can communicate with each other to create a virtual community.
- It gives an information network platform which is easily adaptable to current physical social systems because our physical society can be viewed as a society consisting of mobile agents.

In Section 2, we show the basic components of AMC and a prototype implemented by using a mobile agents platform called IBM Aglets. In Section 3, we discuss the above implications in more detail and conclude in Section 4.

2 Agent Mediated Communicator

2.1 Overview

In Fig. 1, we show an overview of AMC (Agent Mediated Communicator).

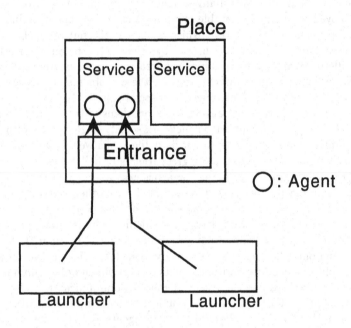

Fig. 1. Overview of AMC.

AMC consists of mobile agents, places, and launchers. An agent is a surrogate of its user with his/her profile information and moves from the user's launcher to designated places.

A place accepts agents and offers communication services to them. The Entrance is a persistent service and gives authentication to an agent that tries to enter the place. Once the agent is allowed to enter the place, it can invoke or use service programs like Mail, Talk, BBS, Chat, WWW, and so on, available there. Multiple agents can enter the same place at the same time. They are visible to others and can interact with each other.

In AMC, we have two ways to establish communication. For example, here we show two ways of mailing as shown in Fig. 2. In one-way mailing (Fig. 2(a)), we send an agent with a message from our launcher to a designated place and post the message in the Mailbox service. This is similar to the current E-mail system except the agent is required to be authenticated to enter the place.

In two-way mailing (Fig. 2(b)), we send an agent from our launcher to a designated place to invoke the Envelope service there. Then, the Envelope service creates an Envelope agent with an envelope that moves to our launcher. At our launcher, the Envelope agent starts an envelope program and we put our message in the envelope. Finally, the agent returns to its home place and posts our message in its Mailbox.

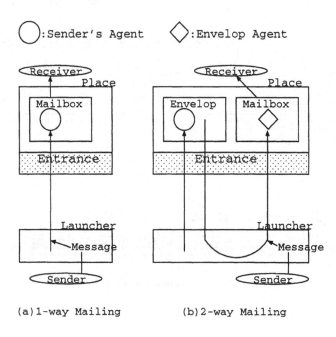

(a)1-way Mailing   (b)2-way Mailing

Fig. 2. Two ways of mailing.

Group communication services such as Chat and BBS can be implemented by using the two-way method because they need a client-server setup for bilateral message exchange. In the place, a service starts a server program that stores messages. When an agent requests to use the service, the service creates an client agent that moves to a launcher where the request agent is originated and starts its client program to read and write messages from and to the server. One advantage of this method is its easiness of version-up of client and server programs because client programs are transferred by client agents. Another advantage is the visibility of agents. Because agents are visible to others in the place, they can recognize not only who writes messages but also who can read them. Hence, we can use this mechanism to create an active community sharing a common interest or to monitor malicious inspections from anonymous agents.

2.2 Prototype System

We developed an AMC prototype by using a mobile-agent platform IBM Aglets [3]. At this moment, we have not implemented the authentication mechanism.

A place is managed by a window shown in Fig. 3 with the following functions.

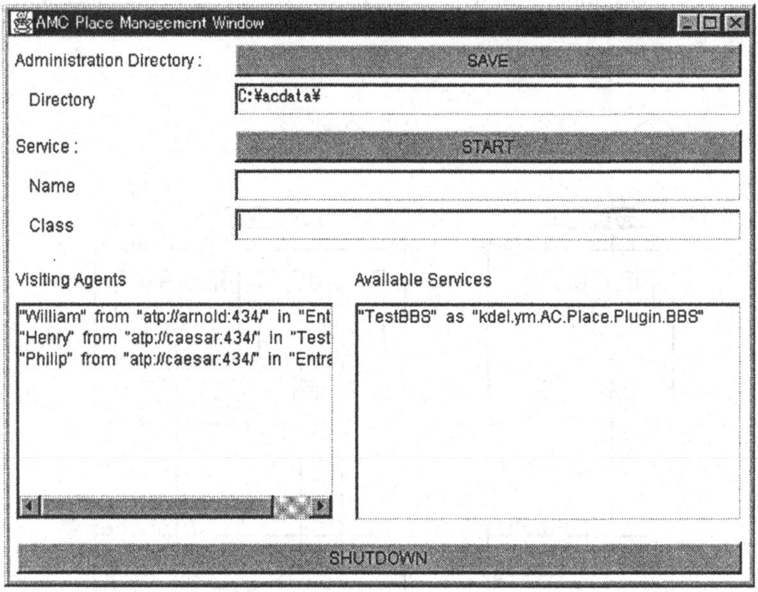

Fig. 3. Place management window.

Administration Directory specifies a directory where the configuration and logs of services offered in the place are stored.

Service starts a new service program at the place by specifying the name and the Java class and clicking the START button.

Visiting Agents lists visiting agents; name, originated address, and service being offered at the place.

Available Services lists available services at the place.

Shutdown terminates the place.

In Fig. 3, agent Willy from launcher arnold and agents Henry and Philip from launcher caesar are at this place and receives Entrance and TestBBS services. At the place, a service TestBBS is available. Entrance service is a default and persistent service, so it is not shown in the list.

A launcher is managed by a window shown in Fig. 4 with the following functions.

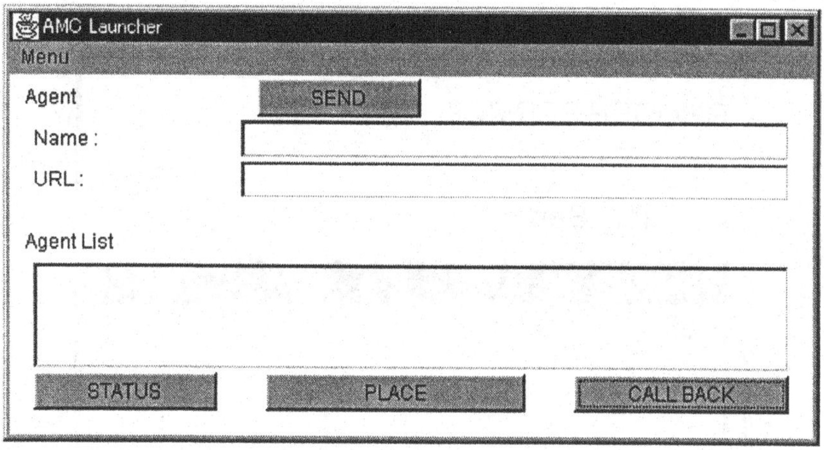

Fig. 4. Launcher management window.

Agent creates an agent with a specified name and sends it to a specified URL by clicking the SEND button.

Agent List lists agents being sent from the launcher and at remote places. By clicking buttons, we can send commands to the agents. "STATUS" shows the current status of service that the agent is offered. " PLACE" shows other agents at the visiting place. "CALL BACK" calls back the agent from the place and terminates it.

When we send an agent to a place, by default the agent invokes its Entrance service. The service creates an Entrance agent and sends it back to our launcher to open a window shown in Fig. 5. Then, we can choose services through this window.

Agents in the visiting place are displayed through a window shown in Fig. 6 by clicking the "PLACE" button of launcher management window. We can interact with other agents by clicking the following buttons.

TALK starts a talk to the designated agent.
INFORMATION shows the user profile of the designated agent.
CLOSE closes the window.

Here we show how to use a BBS service at a remote place. First we send an agent from our launcher to a place where a BBS service is available. When it succeeds to enter the place, a window shown in Fig. 5 appears. We choose TestBBS, then a BBS agent comes from the place to our launcher. It starts a BBS client program, a window in Fig. 7 opens, and a connection between the client at our launcher and the server at the remote place is established. By specifying our name and message in NAME and MESSAGE boxes respectively and clicking the WRITE button, the message is sent to the BBS service and forwarded to the other connected agents.

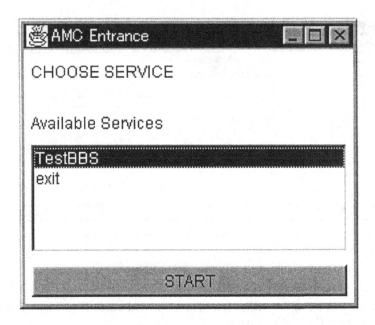

Fig. 5. Entrance window.

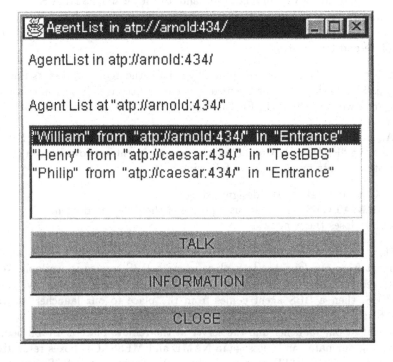

Fig. 6. Agents at a place.

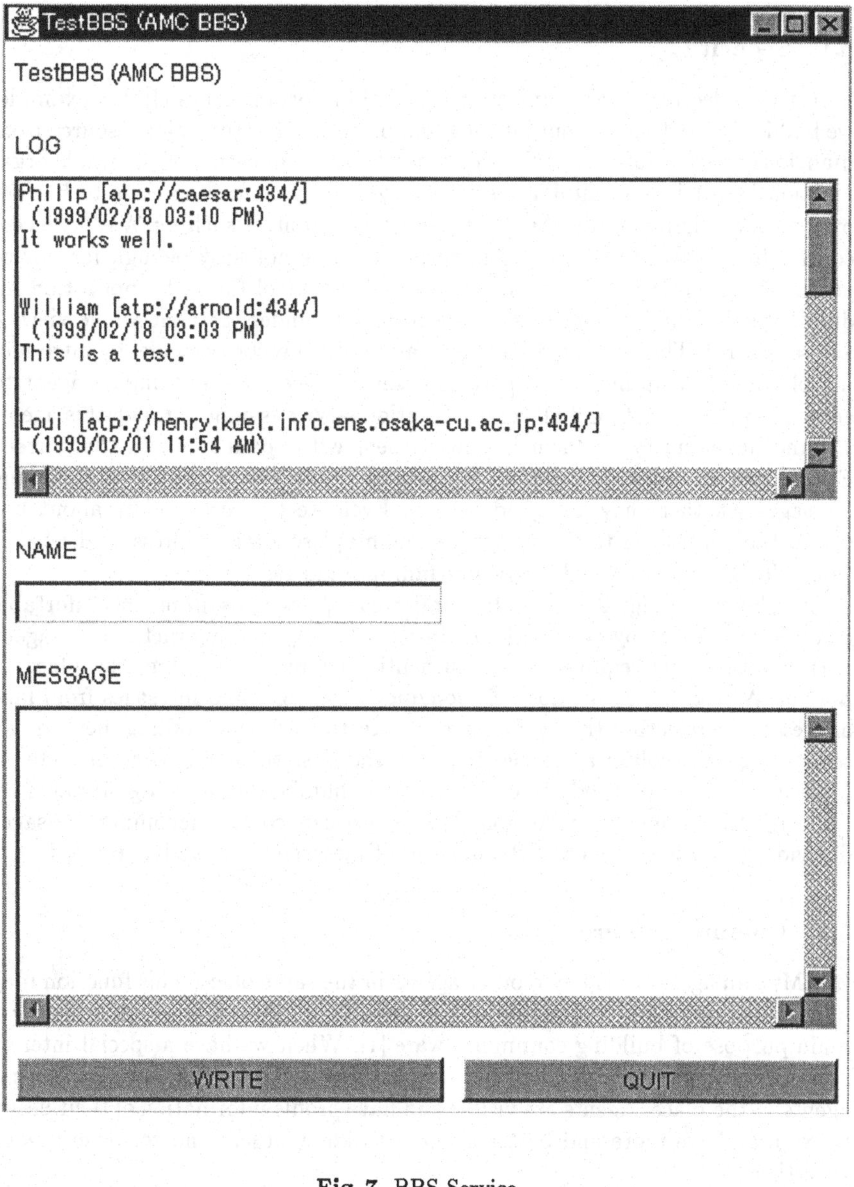

Fig. 7. BBS Service.

3   Implications of Place Oriented Communication

With AMC, we bring back roles of place to electronic communication on computer network and propose "place oriented communication (POC)." POC has several implications as follows.

3.1   Security

Security in electronic communication is one of important issues [4]. For example, we build a firewall around our intranet and protect our information resource from malicious access. However, a firewall controls communication of the whole organization but it is not suitable for a user to flexibly control accesses to his/her own resource individually. Application oriented control such as WWW access control by password or access configuration file is not easy enough for novice users. Moreover, if we have to configure access control for each application individually, it would be tiring and too complex to understand the whole view of access control. The AMC gives a simple and unified security model by introducing places into communication. We can control access by allowing an agent to enter the place or not, and all communication service is done through this agent.

Another security problem is how to deal with spam mail. In the current E-mail system, once our address is open to public, we cannot stop incoming messages whether they are good or bad. Even we try to complain about uncomfortable messages to the sender, he/she may use a fake address, and what is worse, he/she may pretend to use our familiar address.

As shown in Fig. 2, the AMC mailer can protect us from uncomfortable incoming messages by two methods. In the one-way mailing method, an agent with a message is required to be authenticated before it enters the place to post it. We can filter out most of anonymous messages and messages from fake addresses by rejecting the agents to enter. In the two-way mailing method, we send an agent to collect a message from its sender, so the sender can not pretend. Moreover, by this method, we can control the number of incoming messages by limiting the number of collection. Hence, we can control incoming messages depending on the origins and the number of messages that we like to read.

3.2   Communityware

In AMC, an agent is visible to other agents in the same place. This function may be useful to create a community of people with a common interest, which is a main purpose of building communityware [1]. When we have a special interest in some topic, we open a place and invite others with the same interest to send agents to the place. Agents are visible and have profile information of their users, so we may have more and better chances to know others and to make friends with them.

In the place, agents store and exchange information concerning the common interest. The current WWW technology is suitable for distributing knowledge, but we believe the AMC helps to collect and accumulate knowledge through interactions among agents. For example, we can install a special service for developing a software product like Linux where we need many developers to collaborate. The service provides a testbed and developers send agents with software modules to check whether they work together properly.

3.3 Adaptability to Physical Social System

As the Internet spreads out over the world, we are going to create a network society with no border. It is said that our social regulation system such as laws cannot catch up with the advancement of the technology. Here we quote an example from an article on E-commerce [2].

> For example, does clicking Accept using a mouse in New York to download a new Netscape browser constitute a binding contract of adhesion? If so, where is the contract considered valid – in New York where the click occurs or in California where the server is located? If a dispute arises, what state has jurisdiction?

Current electronic contract on the Internet loses the concept of place. In our physical world, a contract between two parties are often made through human agents and one of them may go to an office of the other party to put his/her signature on documents. The AMC based on mobile agents can naturally model this process.

The above problem shows that there is a gap between the physical society where place has a meaning and the network society where it loses its meaning, and how to narrow this gap will be an important issue. Our solution to this issue is by an approach from the technology side. We believe that it is better to build a network society that is a natural extension of the physical society than an isolated one. The AMC can help to build such a network society because our physical society can be viewed as consisting of places and agents.

4 Conclusion

We proposed the Agent Mediated Communicator (AMC) which is a communication platform consisting of places and mobile agents. We developed a prototype system by using a mobile-agent platform IBM Aglets. In addition, we mentioned its implications from security, communityware, and its adaptability to physical social systems.

In this paper, we just proposed initial ideas of place oriented communication by AMC. Our future work is to add an authentication function to AMC and to develop various services to show its advantages. We also should consider the connectivity to current communication tools like E-mail, WWW, and so on and incorporate them into the AMC platform.

By incorporating mobile agents, we may introduce another security issues like kidnapping, analyzing, and converting agents, so we need to study more about these issues.

Acknowledgement

This work is partly supported by IBM Tokyo Research Institute.

References

1. Toru Ishida (Ed.): Community Computing: Collaboration over Global Information Networks, John Wiley and Sons (1998)
2. Ajit Kambil: Doing Business in the Wired World, IEEE Computer, 30(5) (1997) 56–61
3. Danny B. Lange and Mitsuru Oshima: Programming and Deploying Java Mobile Agents with Aglets, Addison Wesley (1998)
4. Rolf Oppliger: Internet Security: Firewalls and Beyond, Communications of the ACM, 40(5) (1997) 92–102

Agents and Electronic Commerce: Mechanisms and Protocols (Abstract)

Michael P. Wellman

University of Michigan, Ann Arbor, MI 48109-2110 USA
wellman@umich.edu
http://ai.eecs.umich.edu/people/wellman

Abstract. Design mechanisms; analyze protocols.

In research on agents and electronic commerce, how one applies terminology is perhaps the best way to describe one's perspective on fundamental technical issues. The following is adapted from an online glossary created for the "Michigan Adaptive Resource eXchange" (MARX) project.[1]

1 Terms

Agent. A locus of decision making in a system of multiple decision-making entities. We attribute to the agent autonomy over its decisions, and typically, "agent attitudes" such as preferences, beliefs, intentions, and capabilities. The term is generic in that it can apply to humans, computational processes, or organizations. The attribution of agent attitudes includes an assumption of conformance to some rationality principle, dictating that the agent's behavior will be consistent with its beliefs and preferences in some way. We expressly avoid the senses of this term having to do specifically with: "personal" assistance to human users, mobile or transportable code, objects with their own threads of control, or unaccountable claims of "intelligence".

Electronic Commerce. Commercial activity that is automated in some way. Current usage includes fairly straightforward automation of communication functions. We might distinguish more fundamental automation, for example involving computational agents or mediated negotiation mechanisms (see below). "Automated commerce" would probably be a more suitable term.

Mechanism. Short for *resource allocation mechanism*. A mechanism comprises the rules of a resource allocation process, specifying (1) system messages and (2) resource allocations, as a function of messages (or entire message patterns) from mechanism participants (agents). A mechanism is the part of a complete protocol governing the behavior of the mediator. A strict requirement is that it can be specified without reference to agents' private information. Therefore, it does not define agent-specific behavior.

---

[1] http://ai.eecs.umich.edu/MARX/glossary.html

Mediated. A mechanism is mediated if there is some entity (the *mediator*, or *institution*), distinct from the participants, that manages the communication and implements the mechanism rules.

Protocol (general). A joint (communication) protocol defines for each participant, its allowable actions (messages) as a function of its local state. Notes: (1) Allowable messages might be specified at varying levels (syntax, semantics). (2) Local state may be influenced by messages received.

Resource allocation protocol. A joint communication protocol consisting of a resource allocation mechanism, along with (optionally) specification of allowable agent behavior.

2 Discussion

The realm of electronic commerce present researchers several distinct design problems, differing in the scope of control of the designer. Specifically, the designer may control the behavior of agent(s), mediator(s), or both. In the case where everything is under the control of the designer, we might question the autonomy (and hence the *agency*) of individual "agents". Thus, we consider the standard designer roles to be limited to either agent or mechanism.

Of course, the outcomes of any mechanism depend on what the agents do, so the mechanism designer must consider how the mechanism rules will influence agent behavior. (Agent designers must similarly account for the behavior of other agents.) Thus, in research on e-commerce mechanisms, one should include models of the agents, while recognizing that these are ultimately outside the designers' control. In other words, the scope of analysis comprises the entire *protocol.* Although conclusions about properties of mechanisms are unavoidably relative to *some* assumptions about agents, we can evaluate alternative mechanisms according to the realism or robustness of agent assumptions necessary to support desirable properties.

Agent researchers differ in the sorts of assumptions that they are willing to make about agent behavior. For self-interested agents, we typically appeal to some rationality criterion, and consider a model more plausible to the extent that it does not require agents to be apparently irrational (a matter of degree, not an absolute), or to have either too much or too little knowledge of its environment. Perhaps the ideal situation–not generally achievable—is when we can support a desired outcome through dominant strategies.

Much research proceeds under an assumption that agents are "cooperative", although it is not always perfectly clear what this means for the agents' autonomy or privacy of information. Indeed, it seems difficult to draw a precise line between multiple cooperative agents, and distributed implementation of a single agent. If there is a distinction, understanding it is crucial in evaluating the plausibility of particular models of agent behavior.

The Role of Agent Technology in Business to Business Electronic Commerce

Mike P. Papazoglou

Tilburg University, INFOLAB
PO Box 90153, NL-5000 LE Tilburg
The Netherlands
mikep@kub.nl

Abstract. The purpose of business-to-business electronic commerce is to improve the way businesses trade by creating a secure networked environment in which businesses may exchange information, knowledge, goods and services. However, interoperability of the diversity of systems for tele-cooperation and global electronic commerce is not an easy task to achieve. The diversity of information systems generates incompatibilities which need to be surmounted before advanced business-to-business electronic commerce applications are developed.
Agent-oriented technology can help eliminate some of these problems by facilitating the incorporation of reasoning capabilities within the business application logic and by enabling the inclusion of learning and self improvement capabilities at both infrastructure and application levels. In this paper we discuss agent-oriented support for business-to-business electronic commerce and introduce three different categories of information agents based on their functionality and competence.

1 Background

Until the massive growth of the World Wide Web, business-to-business electronic commerce was limited to functions appropriate for expensive proprietary WANs and a lot of custom software. However, the rapid growth of the Internet, electronic network systems including EDI systems, and the penetration of ISDN (Integrated Services Digital Network)-based applications, where access speeds can be pushed up to 128,000 bits per second, have demonstrated the enormous potential of new global networking possibilities and are opening up new opportunities for business. The growth of the Internet is fueling this process and is stimulating an ever increasing number of businesses to participate in Electronic Commerce world-wide. For example, innovative companies with good partner relationships are beginning to share sales data, customer buying patterns, and future plans with their suppliers and customers.

1.1 Problems with Current Electronic Commerce Solutions

The Internet has become a tool used to reduce transaction costs, shorten product cycles, expand markets, and provide rapid response to the customer's changing needs. However, interoperability of the diversity of systems for tele-cooperation and global electronic commerce is not an easy task to achieve. The vigorous development of the underlying technologies and infrastructure generates diversity and incompatibilities which need to be surmounted before advanced business-to-business electronic commerce becomes a fact.

These new realities of business to business electronic commerce have created new imperatives for business information systems. Today's business systems must provide tighter links with business partners and suppliers so that islands of disparate information can be integrated into a meaningful whole. They must be able to cope with the overwhelming complexity of distributed technology and an inter-enterprise information base. They must be open to survive a network-centric business ecosystem which consists of collaborating enterprises that have entered into alliances and shared technology investments in order to be successful in the market place. Business systems must be knowledge-based if they are to cope with the incompleteness and ambiguity of real business processes and workflows. And they must be adaptive to meet the needs of an ever changing market to guarantee increased productivity and improved customer service.

1.2 Enabling Technologies

Business objects are the key building block in the re-engineered (process-oriented) enterprise as they can realize domain business processes and default business logic that can be used to start building applications in these domains. The combination of business objects with distributed object computing sets the foundation for both enterprise and inter-enterprise computing that is essential to the open processes and distributed workflow applications of electronic commerce. Business-objects provide pre-assembled business functionality that can be used to bring together and customize applications. They provide a natural way for describing application-independent concepts such as customers, products, orders, bills, financial instruments and temporal information, such as a quarterly earnings period or annual tax cycle. Business-objects add value to a business by providing a way of managing complexity and giving a higher level perspective that is understandable by the business [1], [2]. They achieve this by packaging together essential business characteristics such as business procedures, policy and controls around business data. However, business objects provide standard solutions and are in no position to express advanced concepts such as rules, constraints, goals and objectives, roles and responsibilities.

"Intelligent" business agents are the next higher level of abstraction in model-based solutions to business to business electronic commerce applications. This technology allows the development of rich and expressive models of an enterprise and lays the foundation for adaptive, reusable business software. Agent-oriented technology can be leveraged to enhance enterprise modeling as well as to offer new techniques for developing intelligent applications and infrastructure services. By building on the distributed object foundation, agent technology can help bridge the remaining gap between flexible design and usable applications. Agents support a natural merging of object orientation and knowledge-based technologies. They can facilitate the incorporation of reasoning capabilities within the business application logic (e.g. encapsulation of business rules within agents or modeled organizations). They permit the inclusion of learning and self improvement capabilities at both infrastructure (adaptive routing) and application (adaptive user interfaces) levels [3]. Unlike objects, information agents can participate in high-level (task oriented) dialogues through the use of interaction protocols in conjunction with built-in organizational knowledge. In many cases, the need for communication is greatly reduced, as within these high-level dialogues, complex packets of procedural and declarative knowledge as well as state information may be exchanged in the form of mobile objects.

In this paper we sketch a vision of how agent-enabled business to business electronic commerce could provide an unprecedented level of functionality to people and enterprises. However, before we discuss the role of agent-oriented technology for business to business electronic commerce in detail, we have to describe what wee mean by such terms as 'information agent' and 'agent-based systems' as key concepts in agent-oriented computing lack universally accepted definitions.

The agent metaphor due to it suitability for open environments has recently become popular with distributed, large-scale, and dynamic nature applications such as electronic commerce and virtual enterprises. Information agents can be thought of as active objects with special properties tailored to distributed and open environments. For the purposes of this paper, the key aspects of agents are their autonomy their abilities to perceive reason and act in their surrounding environments, as well as to cooperate with other such agents to solve complex problems [4]. An essential quality of an information agent is its dimension of "intelligence". Intelligence is the amount of learned behavior and possible reasoning capacity that an agent may possess. At the most basic level, the agent may follow a set of rules that are pre-defined by the user. The agent can then apply these rules for instance to the Internet at large. The most intelligent agents will be able to learn. They will also be able to adapt to their environment, in terms of user requests and the resources available to the agent. All of this interaction will benefit the user by providing better information, yet will be invisible to the user.

This paper is organized as follows. In the following section we present a high-level view of an integrated enterprise framework which will be used as a vehicle to discuss agent support for business to business electronic commerce. Section-3 describes the essential characteristics of agents for electronic commerce and categorizes agents in terms of their functionality and capabilities. Sections 4, 5 and 6 discuss in some detail the different types of agents required to support business to business activities and applications. Finally, section-7 presents our summary.

2 A Layered Approach to Electronic Commerce

Figure-1 illustrates an integrated value chain enterprise framework for model-ing business applications and for developing and delivering enterprise solutions [5]. This enterprise framework consists of business components, processes, and workflow applications defined within a specific "vertical" industry, e.g., finances, manufacturing, telecommunications, transportation, etc. The upper two layers in the enterprise framework provide the core business process objects and workflow applications that can be easily combined and extended to offer a complete cross-organizational business solution. At the next level business objects can be used as a basis for building interoperable business solutions. Although interoperation in this environment is achieved mainly at the workflow and business process level, cross-enterprise applications may script together business objects from different organizations. This allows business objects to effectively reuse legacy systems in the form of legacy (wrapped) objects. In this way legacy systems that are critical to business objectives can participate in the distributed object environment. The lowest layer provides the infrastructure and services that are required to built industrial-strength applications in distributed, multi-platform environments.

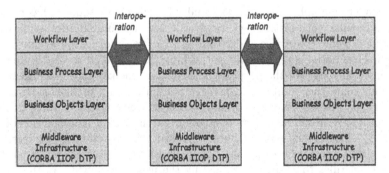

Fig. 1. The Integrated Enterprise Framework.

Workflow support for integrated value chains provide the infrastructure to allow business processes to cooperate and execute distributively across enter-prise boundaries. Workflow components will necessary be disparate, they will either be adapted from existing proprietary workflow products or will be newly developed specifically for the distributed business infrastructure. The purpose of the distributed workflow infrastructure is to allow the disparate workflow components to interoperate over enterprise-wide networks and deliver consistent workflow functionality. For example, an order activity in a production planning process may start an appropriate order entry process at a closely aligned parts supplier. This type of cooperation can only be achieved if the workflow systems of the cooperating companies are loosely coupled. This results in the elimina-tion of supply chain discontinuities that produce delays and waste. Distributed workflows are normally built on a distributed object network infrastructure [6], [7]. This enables a business to change its organizational structure and processes independently of another.

In situations like these information agents provide a natural framework of executing workflow scenarios involving business objects and their interactions. A network-centric business ecosystem[1] possesses the capability of breaking apart a complex workflow enabled application, comprising business processes and objects, to the level of specialized information agents. Subsequently, the information agents plan for the efficient fulfillment of parts of the application, using a montage of legacy and current generation systems information sources, e.g., modern databases and ERP packages, through coordinated interaction and exchange of information. Information agents make certain that the cooperating application components (legacy and business objects) understand the format of the application that they are sharing and the rules governing its exchange.

3   Agents for Business to Business Electronic Commerce

A promising approach to dealing with business to business electronic commerce applications is to compose business objects and enact workflows by providing an execution environment realized by means of an organized collection of cooperating information agents [8], [9]. Agent-enabled electronic commerce computing is concerned with combining appropriately information agents (both humans and computers) working cooperatively over space and time to solve a variety of complex problems in medicine, engineering, finance, banking, commercial enterprises and so on by providing the semantic support infrastructure for high-level elements such as business objects, business processes and workflows. In this new computing paradigm, the classical client/server model is extended to a more dynamic and versatile architecture.

To accomplish a complex task, an information agent uses an incremental processing style, which might include recruiting other agents in the process of task execution in a dynamic and opportunistic way. This agent capability assumes that an information agent can invoke the functionality of other such agents, see figure 2. In each vertical domain tackled by a network-centric business ecosystem, there is:

- *distribution of data:* purchase information, product order information and invoices.
- *distribution of control:* each individual business process is responsible for performing a set of tasks, e.g., order processing or goods shipping.
- *distribution of expertise:* a business process's knowledge, e.g., order handling, is quite different from that of another, e.g., request for tender.
- *spatial distribution of resources:* a legacy information system may be responsible for providing information and functionality about purchase requisitions

---

[1] A business ecosystem is an interacting community of business partners, leveraging brand and growing ubiquity of the Internet to gain mutual business advantage.

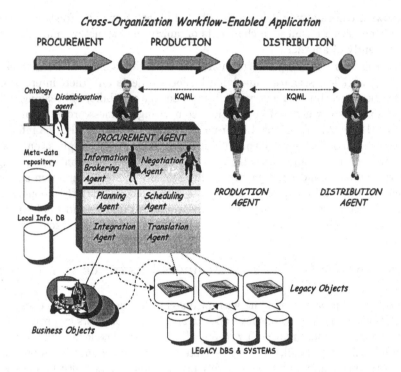

Fig. 2. Connecting Workflows and processes and business objects to information agents.

while a remote ERP package may provide financial or accounting activity services.

3.1 Types of Agents

In a multi-agent electronic commerce environment it is necessary to organize agents into different categories depending on their functionality and competencies. Here we may be able to distinguish between three forms of agents: *application*, *general commerce activity* and *system-level* agents.

Application Agents: these agents typically support users in effectively performing complicated tasks – e.g., medical diagnosis, engineering design, banking decision making – efficiently using the most appropriate information and computing resources (be they processing, knowledge and/or data) available in large computer networks. We refer to such types of agents as application agents. A business to business electronic commerce application is a networked system that comprises a large number of application agents, each having a particular narrow area of specialization, e.g., tender, order handling, goods processing, etc, that work cooperatively to solve a complex problem in a vertical domain. Application agents should be in a position to dynamically change their role in the client/server relationship: at times they may function as recipients of information services, from other application-supporting agents, and at other times they will serve as providers.

General Commerce Activity Agents: these are agents which provide the general functionality that is required by application agents to solve a variety of complex electronic commerce problems. Such general functionality agents may include search agents that navigate effectively through fragmented on-line electronic information and services in order to find trading partners and items of interest; negotiation agents that negotiate on behalf of a buyer or a seller; billing agents; marketing agents to market product and services on the Internet and so on.

System-level Agents: these types of agents are responsible for realizing the technical infrastructure that makes it possible to develop business to business applications. System-level agents exist on top of the distributed objects infrastructure, implemented in CORBA IIOP, which provides objects with transparent access not only to other application objects but also to such facilities as transaction processing, permanent object-storage, event-services and the like. For example, distributed workflow managers are a special type of system-level agents, which may track business transactions across unit, company and enterprise boundaries. As part of a multi-agent system, workflow agents can capture and apply semantic constraints among processes spanning diverse departments and organizations in order to enact distributed workflows, see Figure-2.

Workflow agents must also possess the ability to assemble information services on demand from a montage of networked legacy applications and information sources comprising business objects and possibly ERP package applications. In such situations workflow agents may rely on another type of agent, the wrapping agent, which can help synthesize legacy objects out of a large number of related heterogeneous legacy systems after discovering the appropriate information sources; applying syntactic/semantic-reconciliation and translation between diverse data representations; solving ontological mismatch problems; aligning functionality and rectifying data inconsistencies; and partially integrating the data and functionality.

3.2 Characteristics of Information Agents

Information agents in a network-centric business ecosystem are "coarse" in that they comprise a number of modular pieces of software that combine several competencies. Each information agent is essentially another active information source, however, it draws on already existing information repositories and applications and combines them with organizational and business model components. Through this approach, inter-networked information systems move from a passive information supplying role to more pro-active, agile systems that can reason about their functionality and competence.

Each agent is specialized to single area of expertise and provides access to the available information sources in that domain. This results in the formations of clusters (or groups) of information sources around domains of expertise handled by their respective information agents. Figure-2 shows three types of agents, namely procurement, production, and distribution, that are involved in distributed workflow electronic commerce application that spans diverse organizations. The expertise model of an information agent does not need to contain a complete description of the other agents capabilities, but rather only those portions which may directly relevant when handling a request that can not be serviced locally [8]. This approach provides conceptual simplicity, enhances scalability and makes interactions in a large collection of information sources become tractable.

In general we require that intelligent agents for electronic commerce possess the following distinguishing characteristics:

Self-Representation Abilities One of the most challenging problems to be addressed by business to business electronic commerce environments is the development of a methodology that opens up the general process of constructing and managing business objects based on dispersed and pre-existing networked information sources. Activities such as object integration, message forking to multiple object subcomponents, scheduling, locking and transaction management are until now totally hidden and performed in an ad hoc manner depending on the application demands. What is needed is the ability to work with abstractions that express naturally and directly business and system aspects and then combine these into a final meaningful implementation.

Such ideas can benefit tremendously from techniques found in reflection and meta-object protocols. The concepts behind meta-object protocols may be usefully transferred to cooperating systems at the systems level. For example, at the systems level core cooperative tasks, carried out in an ad-hoc manner up to now, can be performed using meta-level facilities. These can be used to separate implementation, e.g., issues relating to distribution of control and resources, from domain representation concerns and to reveal the former in a modifiable and natural way [10]. Therefore, information agents may provide a general coordination and policy framework for application construction and management of legacy and business objects, one that allows particular construction and management policies to be developed and applied in a controlled manner. This results in self-describing, dynamic and reconfigurable agents that facilitate the composition (specification and implementation) of large-scale distributed applications, by drawing upon (and possibly specializing) the functionality of already existing information sources.

Agent Communication Languages and Protocols In order to perform their tasks effectively, information agents depend heavily on expressive communication with other agents, not only to perform requests, but also to propagate their information capabilities. Moreover, since an information agent is an autonomous entity, it must negotiate with other agents to gain access to other sources and capabilities.

To enable the expressive communication and negotiation required, a number of research efforts have concentrated on knowledge sharing techniques [11]. To organize communications between agents a language that contains brokering performatives can be particularly useful. For example, the Knowledge Query and Manipulation Language (KQML) [12] can be used to allow information agents to assert interests in information services, advertise their own services, and explicitly delegate tasks or requests for assistance from other agents. KQML's brokering performatives provide the basic message types that can be combined to implement a variety of agent communication protocols. This type of language can be used for both communication and negotiation purposes and provides the basis for developing a variety of inter-agent communications protocols that enable information agents to collectively cooperate in sharing information.

4 Application Agents

Business to business electronic commerce can be in a wide range of industry sectors and a wide range of application areas including retail, finance, publishing, telecommunications, engineering design and so on. An interesting consequence of electronic commerce is that companies are turning to alliance building strategies to strengthen and extend their value/supply-chains. Alliances play a vital role in many value chain strategies. Alliances play a vital role in many value chain strategies. The code-sharing practice typical of airlines is a good illustration. Airline companies use these arrangements to extend their own routes and offer seamless services to passengers. They also form alliances with car rental companies and hotels so that passengers can make flight, car rental and hotel arrangements in one business transaction. The business landscape is rapidly changing into a dynamic field where companies with complimentary capabilities and common interests can coalesce to win competitive advantage. This leads to a phenomenon known as *integrated value chains* [5].

Integrated value chains are a fertile ground for agent technology due to its suitability for problem solving in open and dynamic distributed environments. Agents can help transform closed trading partner networks into open markets and extend such applications as production, distribution, inventory management functions across entire value chains spanning diverse organizations. Figure-3 shows an example of such an integrated value chain employing various types of application agents such as inventory, production, and distribution agents which need to collaborate to implement a business ecosystem. Each application agent has a unique area of specialization. Figure-2 shows how such specialized application agents collaborate as part of a distributed workflow application that implements a typical range of cross-organizational activities. This figure also shows how application agents, such as the procurement agent, lean on general commerce activity agents to accomplish their functions. General commerce agents

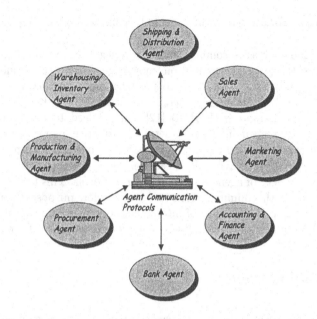

Fig. 3. Integrated value-chain applications involving information agents.

are also implemented by drawing on the functionality of system-level agents such as planning, scheduling, disambiguation, translation and wrapping agents.

5 General Commerce Activity Agents

The activities and functions of electronic commerce need certain basic information agent support that is likely to become the basis for developing standard digital agents for electronic commerce. General commerce agents perform a large number of general commerce support activities that can be customized to address the needs of a particular business organization. Such basic agents include: information brokering agents, negotiation agents, billing agents, marketing agents, legal agents that advise on issues surrounding privacy, taxes, export controls, etc, and so on. Several representative key digital agents for electronic commerce are listed below.

5.1 Information Brokering Agents

An important characteristic of an information agent its the ability to act as an information broker in order to discover the appropriate information sources and support services (i.e., wrapper enabled services) in order to fulfill an organizational requirement or a user's needs. Information brokers for electronic commerce provide facilities such as locating information on Web sources or other information agents that are required to solve a common problem, e.g., sales and distribution processing, by name (white pages), by capabilities (yellow pages), content-based routing or problem decomposition. The term broker agent may be perceived as synonymous to what is also known in the literature as a match-making agent. Brokering agents, in general, maintain information about other agents in a business ecosystem. An agent must have a model of its own domain of expertise, the *agent expertise model*, and a model of the other agents that can provide relevant information the agent *awareness model* [13]. These two models constitute the knowledge model of an agent and are used to determine how to process a request that comes for example from an integration module.

Brokering agents use distributed information resource discovery and retrieval facilities to assist service providers list and publish their services, and help seekers to find services and information of interest. These information facilities cover an agent's ability to maintain, update and access distributed directory services (listing products and business services). They also cover more advanced navigation services such as maintaining hyper-links, advanced keyword and context search engines and Web crawlers – another form of agent – that can explore and index information sources and services of interest.

Currently there is widespread interest in using ontologies as a basis for modeling an agent's expertise model [14], [15], [16]. An ontology can be defined as a linguistic representation of a conceptualization of some domain of knowledge. This ontology consists of abstract descriptions of classes of objects in a vertical domain, relationships between these classes, terminology descriptions and other domain specific information and establishes a common vocabulary for interacting with an information agent and its underlying information sources. Electronic commerce applications are based on the existence of standard ontologies for a vertical domain that establish a common terminology for sharing and reuse. Such ontologies can be used for disambiguating terms and translating between local systems that use different terminology to describe product and services in a vertical domain. The brokering agent uses the terms in the ontology to make assertions that will assist it in accomplishing its mission. For instance, the information broker uses a standard terminology in order to describe products in a particular domain which is used to map between diverse company descriptions of a product in order to support queries that ask for products providing a certain characteristics. In this way consistent business semantics can be provided across different market domains and segments. Without ontology-based consistent business semantics, processes and workflows cannot be shared across multiple, disparate, and distributed organizations.

Both expertise and awareness models may be expressed in some concept representation language such as, for example, Loom [17], or KL-ONE [18] and be formalized by using concept lattices [19] (a formal method based on a set-theoretical model for concepts and conceptual hierarchies). An example of the use of concept oriented languages for building ontologies for cooperating database systems can be found in [16].

5.2 Marketing and Advertising Agents

Agents can look for opportunities to create or target communities of interest. These communities act as central marketplaces where businesses can deposit or find authoritative information and conduct transactions with suppliers. These central market places are forums for providing information about companies and products, as well as gathering market data.

Agent technology can also be used to facilitate sellers to locate potential buyers or new markets. Information agents can help to solve this problem by acting as a virtual salesperson for an enterprise. Sellers will also be able to create personal agents to provide expert advice, thus helping to troubleshoot common customer problems. This has a distinct advantage in small organizations where there may not be a large budget for product support staff.

In general this category may contain a variety of agents each of which may perform a specific activity such as [20]:

- engaging information brokering agents to search and browse electronic directories and catalogs on the network;
- enabling personal agents for various purposes on behalf of one or many buyers and/or sellers;
- buyer agents sending electronic requests for proposal and seller agents responding with various offers;
- seller agents advertising their products and services; and
- electronically navigating network accessible services and selecting the most appropriate ones by employing an information push methodology.

5.3 Personal Agents

Personal agents are the ones that work directly with users to help support the presentation, organization and management of user profile, requests and information collections. A personal agent gives its user easy and effective access to profile (preference) related specialized services and information widely distributed on the Web. For example, marketing on the Internet will be affected by two types of agents, demand agents and decision agents. Demand agents work in the interest of the provider. Demand agents are trained with product knowledge. They represent the products and services and transfer that information to the decision agent. Decision agents work for the consumers. The consumer trains them to search for products and services that are represented by the demand agents. They make recommendations based on the preferences of the consumer. The demand and decision agents work together. The decision agents interact with the demand agents to gather information requested by the user. The demand agents are able to tell their providers the current demand of products by using information gathered from their interaction with the decision agents.

Agents can be be trained to give a product awareness through brokering agents, help consumers locate a product by brand names, or track the demand of a product. A business could even train an agent to alert them when their market share changes. Another useful aspect of information agents is that demand agents can learn from decision agents. For example, a demand agent can learn how close their product was to meeting the needs of the decision agent. In this fashion, valuable market research can be collected in an automated manner. It would seem that the information collected in these transactions between demand and decision agents would have a higher level of validity, unless the decision agent was directed with acquired information that was incorrect.

5.4 Negotiation and Contracting Agents

Buyer and seller agents may also elect to negotiate the terms of an electronic commerce transaction as regards to exchange and payment. The process of negotiation can be stateful and may consist of a "conversation sequence", where multiple messages are exchanged according to some prescribed protocol. Terms may, for instance, cover delivery, refund policies, arranging for credit, installment payments, copyright or license agreements, usage rights, distribution rights, etc. These terms can be standardized for commodity use or customized to suit more unique individual situations. Negotiation protocols can be structured by making use of formalized conversations, such speech acts [21]. These may, for example, be developed in KQML which provides the means to define formalized negotiation messages describing offers, rejections, propositions, acceptance of terms and the like.

Electronic contracts link cash flows to the exchanges of products, goods, and services rendered. Contracts include instructions regarding the handling, routing, scheduling, storing and workflow of the contract itself and of the objects contained or referenced by the contract. Contract instructions can address liabilities, acceptance forms of payment, terms of payment, billing and payment instructions, delivery instructions, return policies, methods of dispute resolution, and so on [20]. Contracts can be negotiated including prices, terms of payment, penalties, necessary documentation, credit checks or required insurance, or collateral or margin. Given such advanced characteristics and functionality it is only natural to consider the use of agent-oriented technology in support of electronic commerce contracts.

6 Agent System Level Support

The basic system support for electronic commerce comprises a host of critical middleware communications, program-to-program, and data management services. These facilities are realized through distributed objects which set the foundation for both enterprise and inter-enterprise computing. CORBA's Object Request Broker (ORB) is the foundation for distributed object computing as it functions as a communications infrastructure, transparently relaying object requests across distributed heterogeneous environments. CORBA 2.0 defines a backbone protocol specified to allow interoperability among different ORB implementations by means of the Internet Inter-ORB Protocol (IIOP). IIOP specifies a series of messages for communication between ORBs and maps them to

TCP/IP services. CORBA services are combined with TP-monitors to support large numbers of users requesting concurrent access to transaction programs and services, e.g., database, security, workflow; balance local and distributed loads to optimize performance; and efficiently synchronize data updates to multiple databases during transaction using standard protocols [22]. At the lower level distributed TPs create a logical ensemble of interactions ensuring that the business transaction is secure and reliable, and is completed with integrity. They are also able to run nested transactions that can span many resources while allowing failures to be trapped and retried using an alternative method which still allows the main transaction to succeed. These facilities can form a natural framework to support the distributed computing infrastructure.

These low system services are designed to absorb complexity in the operational and development environment so that applications appear to be transparent, local, and fully resourced. However, there is advanced system functionality that is required to achieve interoperation of open market business processes and workflow applications and provide support for such tasks as translation, partial integration and semantic reconciliation, advanced functionality for electronic commerce transactions, security support and so on. Agent solutions are thus deployed as an extension of the distributed object foundation and may assist in accomplishing the following systems-related tasks.

6.1 Planning and Scheduling Agents

In a multi-agent planning approach to cooperation, a multi-agent plan is formed that specifies the future actions and interactions for each agent [23]. Typically, in electronic commerce applications an agent may act as the group planner for a cluster of agents surrounding an application agent, e.g., procurement agent. The planning agent forms a plan which it uses to coordinate the other agents. In case that two application agents need to interact they do so by means of their planning agents. Because the plan that is constructed by a planning agent is based on a global view of the problem, all important interactions between the agents can predicted.

The plan specifies how agents coordinate in a a multi-agent planning system and also identifies all actions and interactions of agents. The strength of this approach is that a plan for agent interaction is formed for a given predictable situation. In this way agents can cooperate effectively in a given situation. However, in dynamic situations plans need to change over time. In such situations the multi-agent planning approach would be less effective.

To work cooperatively in dynamic situations, planning agents require the ability to cooperate with other agents despite having inconsistent views of planned actions and interactions. Moreover, they should be able to form plans and communicate these plans to other agents as problem solving proceeds. In such situations it would be beneficial for agents to participate in task-oriented dialogues through the use of interaction protocols in conjunction with built-in organizational knowledge. To be able to reason under uncertainty agents must rely on AI technologies of fuzzy systems, neural networks and genetic algorithms.

6.2 Translation and Partial Integration

One of the principal characteristics of information agents is that they have the ability to act as a translation agent by homogenizing heterogeneous legacy information systems (e.g., older generation databases and programming applications) and provide an abstraction of these in the form of a wrapped legacy objects. A translation module provides data presentation facilities to reduce client complexity and conversion of data between incompatible data representations, formats and languages. The translation/wrapper information agent provides the appropriate interface code (and translation facilities) which allows an existing information source to conform to the conventions of an organization. Standard ontologies provide the basis for rectifying terminology mismatches. Mismatches can be dealt with by means of a common ontology and translators that provide mappings to the terms used in the interfaces of the related business objects.

In the value-chain workflow application in Figure-3 information that may be acted upon by the various application agents may originate from different wrapping agents that provide such services as:

- entry to an enterprise resource planning (ERP) system checking inventory for the products described in the procurement order;
- entry to a distribution/shipping company system using customer address an delivery condition information to schedule a delivery;
- a bank system using company provided financial information to authorize a transaction.

Once diverse representations originating from heterogeneous information systems have been homogenized the following step is to selectively combine semantically interrelated legacy data into cohesive legacy objects. These legacy objects are then combined with business objects in the enterprise framework. These virtual business objects provide the connections to underlying legacy data and functionality. Thus the integration agent is another important type of an information agent which provides consolidated access to distributed data and services by aggregating various types of data and functions, see figure 2.

The translation and integration agents provide the core support facilities for building new workflow-based applications by mapping services into a collection of host distributed information systems and applications, see figure 2.

6.3 Agents and Electronic Commerce Transactions

A key activity in electronic commerce is the collection, management, analysis, and interpretation of the various commercial data to make more intelligent and effective transaction-related decisions. Examples include collecting business references, coordinating and managing marketing strategies, determining new product offerings, granting/extending credit, and managing market risk. Performance of these tasks requires involving sophisticated agent and collaborative computing technologies to support distributed workflow processes.

When applied to electronic commerce transactions, information agents could simplify the processing, monitoring and control of transactions by automating a number of activities. Agent support for business to business electronic commerce transactions may, for example, include controlling the workflow governing a set of electronic transactions or monitor and enforce the terms and conditions of electronic contracts. Some of these issues are covered in the following.

Workflow activities can be supported by another kind of agent, the workflow agent. Local workflow agents can collaborate with remote workflow agents to support distributed workflow applications. Workflow implementations of business processes can be not only transactional processes, or classical transactions, but also non-transactional processes. Transactions as activity implementations frequently appear when the business model represents one of the core business processes (order entry, etc.) of an enterprise. Non-transactional activity implementations are frequently found within support processes (travel expense accounts, etc.). Transactions in the business to business electronic commerce are usually long lived propositions involving negotiations, commitments, contracts, floating exchange rates, shipping and logistics, tracking, varied payment instruments, exception handling and customer satisfaction. *Business transactions* have two basic distinguishing characteristics. Firstly, they extend the scope of traditional transaction processing as they may encompasses classical transactions which they combine with non-transactional processes. Secondly, they group both classical transactions as well as non-transactional processes together into a unit of work that reflects the semantics and behavior of their underlying business task. In addition to these basic requirements business transactions are generally governed by contracts and update accounts and may include the exchange of bills and invoices, and exchange of financial information services. As a consequence, business transactions must provide modeling support and mediate communication, interaction, and coordination among collaborating people and business activities within and between organizations. Hence, business transaction characteristics are better addressed by a process-centered approach to transaction management that supports long-lived concurrent, nested, multi-threaded activities [24], [7], [25].

Business transactions exhibit two broad phases: *construction* and *enactment*. Construction involves the collection of information based on catalogues and brokerage systems to locate sources; agreement leading to terms and conditions through *negotiation* mechanisms; and engagement resulting in a formal contract. Enactment involves deployment across the group of participants in the transaction; service execution in the the context of the contract and management of exceptions; and termination involving validation and closing the contact across all participants. In the world of electronic commerce, traditional; database transactions are replaced with long lived, multi-level collaborations. It is thus not surprising that they require support for a variety of unconventional *behavioral* features which are summarized in the following:

1. *General purpose characteristics:*
   (a) who is involved in the transaction;

(b) what is being transacted;
(c) the destination of payment and delivery;
(d) the transaction time frame;
(e) permissible operations.
2. *Special purpose characteristics:*
   (a) links to other transactions;
   (b) receipts and acknowledgments;
   (c) identification of money transferred outside national boundaries;
3. *Advanced characteristics:*
   (a) the ability to support reversible (compensatible) and repaired (contingency) transactions;
   (b) the ability to reconcile and link transactions with other transactions;
   (c) the ability to specify contractual agreements, liabilities and dispute resolution policies;
   (d) the ability to support secure EDI, e.g., SET [26], transactions that guarantee integrity of information, confidentiality and non-repudiation;
   (e) the ability for transactions to be monitored logged and recovered.

An important requirement of business transactions which deserves mentioning is *business commitments*. Business commitments comprise the "glue" that binds businesses and other organizations at their boundaries. A business commitment is the result of an agreement between business parties, that may bring about contractual agreements. Business commitments, viz. contracts, mandate certain outcomes that are to be produced by the business. They have a strong recursive element that says that agreements are composed of more granular agreements such as terms, conditions and obligations, viz. conditions of fulfillment and conditions of satisfaction. It is important for a distributed workflow application to be able to express varying types and extents of business commitments. It is therefore convenient, as shown in [27], to represent such commitments as special purpose transactions including their own semantics and communication protocol. Termination of these contracts may be a long lived activity as these may include ongoing service agreements with online customer service delivery and other complex aspects of overall customer relationship management. Such activities can also be overseen by specialized information agents.

6.4 Security Agents

Consumer concern about security of business conducted over the Internet is a very important issue facing electronic commerce. Protecting financial data in transit, communications and securing the entire electronic commerce transaction process are a critical concern. Thus electronic commerce business to business communication need to be guarded by specially designed information agents that provide the security services required for the conduct of electronic commerce. Agents can, for example, be used to collect commercial data only from trusted and controlled sources. Moreover, trusted regulation servers, also maintained by agents, can help information agents determine how much faith they can put in information from various sources.

Agent support for secure electronic commerce can be segmented into five distinct categories [28]: authentication, authorization, data integrity, confidentiality, and non-repudiation, each of which requires specialized agent support:

Authentication agents can be used to identify the source of a message sent over the Internet, because the receivers want to know and verify the identity of the person who originated the message.

Authorization agents may control access to sensitive information once identity has been verified. Thus, certain transactions may need to be partly accessible to certain parties, while the remainder of the transaction is not. These tasks can be coordinated by the transaction workflow and authorization agents. Authorization is meant to limit the actions or operations that authenticated parties are able to perform in a networked environment.

Secure transactions should guarantee that a message has not been modified while in transit. This is commonly known as *integrity* and is often accomplished through digitally signed digest codes. Transactions should also guarantee *confidentiality*. Confidentiality refers to the use of encryption for scrambling the information sent over the Internet and stored on servers so that eavesdroppers cannot access the data. This is also known as "quality privacy", but most specialists reserve this word for the "protection of personal information" (confidential or not) from aggregation and improper use.

Non-repudiation is of critical importance for carrying out transaction over the Internet. It consists of cryptographic receipts that are created so that the author of a message cannot falsely deny sending a message. Again these tasks fall well within the premises of agent technology.

7 Concluding Remarks

The growth of the Internet is stimulating an ever increasing number of businesses to participate in Electronic Commerce world-wide. For example, innovative companies with good partner relationships are beginning to share sales data, customer buying patterns, and future plans with their suppliers and customers. However, interoperability of the diversity of systems for tele-cooperation and global electronic commerce is very complicated task. The vigorous development of the underlying technologies and infrastructure generates diversity and incompatibilities which need to be surmounted before advanced business-to-business electronic commerce applications become feasible.

Agent-oriented technology can help eliminate some of these problems by enabling the development of "Intelligent" business agents, which are the next higher level of abstraction in model-based solutions to business to business electronic commerce applications. This technology allows the development of rich and expressive models of an enterprise and lays the foundation for adaptive, reusable business software. Agent-oriented technology can be leveraged to enhance enterprise modeling as well as to offer new techniques for developing intelligent applications and infrastructure services. By building on the distributed object foundation, agent technology can help bridge the remaining gap between flexible design and usable applications.

Information agents for business to business electronic commerce applications should possess self-representation capabilities as as well as the ability to utilize expressive communication languages and protocols to cooperate with other agents, not only by performing requests, but also by propagating agent information capabilities. Moreover, since an information agent is an autonomous entity, it must negotiate with other agents to gain access to other sources and capabilities.

In a multi-agent electronic commerce environment it is necessary to organize agents into different categories depending on their functionality and competencies. We may be able to distinguish between three forms of agents: application, general commerce activity and system-level agents. Application agents typically support users in effectively performing complicated tasks – e.g., pharmaceutical applications, medical diagnosis, engineering design, banking decision making – efficiently using the most appropriate information and computing resources available in large computer networks. General commerce agents provide the general functionality that is required by application agents to solve a variety of complex electronic commerce problems. Finally, system-level agents are responsible for realizing the distributed infrastructure, e.g., extensions of CORBA and business objects, that makes it possible to develop business to business applications.

References

1. F. Manola et al. "Supporting Cooperation in Enterprise Scale Distributed Object Systems", in M.P. Papazoglou and G. Schlageter, editors, *Cooperative Information Systems: Trends and Directions*. Academic Press, London, 1998.
2. M.L. Brodie. "The Emperor's Clothes are Object-Oriented and Distributed", in M.P. Papazoglou and G. Schlageter, editors, *Cooperative Information Systems: Trends and Directions*, Academic Press, 1998.
3. F. Farhoodi, and P. Fingar. "Competing for the Future with Intelligent Agents", http://www.trcinc.com/news/iagents/, 1998.
4. N.R. Jennings, and M. Wooldridge. "Applications of Intelligent Agents", in N.R. Jennings and M. Wooldridge, editors, *Agent Technology, Foundations, Applications and Markets*, Springer-Verlag, 1998.
5. M.P. Papazoglou. "Integrated Value Chains and their Implication for Business Objects and Legacy Systems", J. Chen and Y. Kambayashi, editors, *Procs 2nd Conf. On Cooperative Database Systems*, Springer-Verlag, 1999.
6. S. Paul et. al. "Essential Requirements for a Workflow Standard", OOPSLA'98 Business Object Workshop III, http://www.jeffsutherland.org/oopsla97/, Atlanta, October 1997.
7. M.T. Schmidt. "Building Workflow Business Objects, Object-Oriented Programming Systems Languages Applications", OOPSLA'98 Business Object Workshop IV, http://www.jeffsutherland.org/oopsla98/, Vancouver, Ca., October 1998.
8. M.P. Papazoglou, and S. Laufmann, and T.K. Sellis. "An Organizational Framework for Cooperating Intelligent Information Systems", *Int'l Journal of Cooperative Information Systems*, 1(1), 1992.

9. C.A. Knoblock, and Y. Arens, and C.N. Hsu. "Cooperating Agents for Information Retrieval", *Procs of 2nd Int'l Conf. on Cooperative Information System*, May 1994.

10. D. Edmond, and M.P. Papazoglou. "Reflection is the Essence of Cooperation", in M.P. Papazoglou and G. Schlageter, editors, *Cooperative Information Systems: Trends and Directions*, Academic Press, 1998.

11. R. Patil et al. "The DARP Knowledge Sharing Effort", *Procs. of the 3rd Int'l Conference on Principles of Knowledge Representation and Reasoning*, Morgan-Kaufmann, 1992.

12. T. Finin, and Y. Lambrou, and J. Mayfeld. "KQML as an Agent Communication Language", in J. Bradshaw, editor, *Software Agents*, AAAI/MIT Press, 1995.

13. M.P. Papazoglou, and W.J. van den Heuvel. "From Business Processes to Cooperative Information Systems: An Information Agents Perspective", in M. Klusch, editor, *Intelligent Information Agents*, Springer-Verlag, 1999.

14. G. Wiederhold. "Interoperation, Mediation and Ontologies", *Procs Int'l Workshop on Heterogeneous Cooperative Knowledge-Bases*, Tokyo, 1994.

15. S. Milliner, and A. Bouguettaya, and M.P. Papazoglou. "A Scalable Architecture for Autonomous Heterogeneous Database Interactions", *Proceedings of the 21st VLDB Conference*, Zurich, Sept. 1995.

16. V. Kashyap, and A. Sheth. "Semantic Heterogeneity in Global Information Systems: the Role of Metadata Context and Ontology", in M.P. Papazoglou and G. Schlageter, editors, *Cooperative Information Systems: Trends and Directions*, Academic Press, 1998.

17. R. McGregor. "The Evolving Technology of Classification-Based Knowledge Representation Systems", in J.F. Sowa, editor, *Principles of Semantic Networks*, Morgan-Kaufmann, 1990.

18. R.J. Brachman, and J.G. Scholze. "An Overview of the KL-ONE Knowledge Representation System", *Cognitive Science*, 2(9), 1985.

19. R. Wille. "Concept Lattices and Conceptual Knowledge Systems", in F. Lehmann, editor, *Semantic Networks in Artificial Intelligence*, Pergamon Press, 1992.

20. National Information Infrastructure: Electronic Commerce in the NII. http://nii.nist.gov/pubs/pubs_list_and_abstract.html

21. M. Merz, et. al. "Supporting Electronic Commerce Transactions with Contracting Services", *Int'l Journal of Cooperative Information Systems*, 4(7), 1998.

22. J.M. Andrade et. al. "The Tuxedo System", Addison Wesley Publishing Co., Reading Mass., 1996.

23. E.H. Durfee. "Coordination of Distributed Problem Solvers", *Kluwer Aacademic Publishers*, Boston, 1988.

24. M.P. Papazoglou, and A. Delis, and A. Bouguettaya, and M. Haghjoo. "Class Library Support for Workflow Environments and Applications", *IEEE Transactions on Computer Systems*, 46(6), June 1997.

25. F. Leymann, and D. Roller. "Workflow-based Applications", *IBM Systems Journal*, 36(1), 1997.

26. M.S. Merkow, and J. Breithaupt, and K.L. Wheeler "Building SET Applications for Secure Transactions", *J. Willey & Sons*, New York, 1998.

27. E.M. Verharen, and M.P. Papazoglou. "Introducing Contracting in Distributed Transactional Workflows", *HICSS-31: Hawaii Int'l Conf. on System Sciences*, IEEE Computer Science Press, Jan. 1998.

28. N.R. Adam et. al. "Electronic Commerce: Technical, Business and Legal Issues", *Prentice-Hall*, 1998.

An Agency-Based Framework for Electronic Business

Larry Kerschberg and Sonali Banerjee

Center for Information Systems Integration and Evolution,
Department of Information and Software Engineering,
School of Information Technology and Engineering
George Mason University, MSN4A4, Fairfax, Virginia, 22030-4444, USA
http://cise.krl.gmu.edu/
{kersch, sbanerje}@gmu.edu

Abstract. This paper presents an overview of current trends in Electronic Business (E-business), and how an enterprise can use the Electronic Marketspace for strategic advantage. The role of cooperative information agents is discussed within the context of E-business. An agency-based framework is presented for E-business in the class of logistics and supply systems. Such systems are enjoying wide acceptance in commercial and military application domains, as witnessed by the phenomenal growth in Internet stocks for companies such as Amazon.com. We also show how agent-based systems provide scalable, configurable and evolutionary solutions for such applications.

1 Introduction

The rapid strides made in computer science and information technology have enabled business organizations to reach new customers and open new markets in an Electronic Marketspace. The Internet and World Wide Web facilitate searching for and sharing information, sharing crucial business data, and building better business-to-business relationships.

Electronic commerce is a more cost-effective way of doing business than building new stores or warehouses and hiring more people to run them. It has streamlined processes, simplified sharing of critical data and lowered organizational barriers—reaching beyond a company's walls and into the operations of its customers, suppliers and business partners. Shopping in an interactive world provides more options, customized goods and services based on user preferences, a record of previous activity as well as customer-based feedback, permits customers to "try before they buy," and even involves them in product design and delivery.

Internet technology can deliver what the customer wants - timeliness, accuracy and lower cost. Customers previously had to call a customer service representative, while now orders can be taken and tracked online, and a customer's credit status can be verified online. This provides a tighter *integration* between consumers and producers, thereby eliminating the traditional middleman, and replacing him by the *infomediary*, as witnessed by "business portals" such as Yahoo!

The Internet provides a new medium and mechanism to establish business associations, collaborations, and alliances. One might say that the Internet and Web are about *leveraging relationships for strategic advantage*, as witnessed by the recent mergers and acquisitions, such as AOL, Netscape and Sun Microsystems, @Home and Excite, Yahoo!, Geocities, and Broadcast.com, AT&T, TCI, and MediaOne, etc. This new medium, called the Electronic Marketspace, enables an entirely new range of entrepreneurial possibilities, with future enterprises providing valued-added cooperative, end-to-end virtual and real services.

Cooperative information agents will play a major role in the Electronic Marketspace. We now discuss some possible roles for such agents. Subscriptions to information sources such as online investing, auctions, and brokerage services, allow people (or agents) of similar interests to meet, discuss, provide recommendations and suggestions, negotiate and conduct business. Moreover, monitoring services provide alerts, based on user-specified critical events, conditions, or new information and knowledge, pertinent to a user's decision-making criteria. Users get immediate feedback and triggered alerts, so that the end-to-end experience is perceived to be of higher quality, because a *relationship of trust* is being established. The quality of the product, commodity, or service, as well as the information, knowledge, communication, delivery mechanisms is perceived to be of high quality because of the ongoing interactive and evolutionary nature and mutual nurturing of the customer-to-business or business-to-business relationship. Quality of service issues will play a large role in creating "brands" in Electronic Business.

Electronic business, or E-business, has brought about changes in marketing strategies. E-business is a new vehicle for building relationships of mutual benefit between businesses, with their customers, and their suppliers. Information can be easily sifted, facts checked immediately and third party evaluations obtained rapidly. This brings to the forefront the quality of goods and services provided. Brands can be established or destroyed very quickly, and this is less biased by the size of the business or the amount of money it can invest on advertisement and marketing. Marketing itself is more narrowly targeted with highly customized products and services, as for example the customer profiles maintained by Amazon.com to recommend new books to returning customers. Continuing with the Amazon.com example, customers register their payment and delivery preferences, thereby enabling "One-Click Shopping", whereby the shopping basket is checked out, order tracking number assigned, and periodic status reports sent (the date the order was filled and the date it left the warehouse) via email. The Electronic Marketspace raises customer expectations regarding quality-of-service issues; issues such as the quality of the customer shopping experience, product and service quality, web site performance, and content management, will be receiving increasing attention.

Today E-business is having an impact on the way companies do business. These impacts involve the re-engineering of existing business processes, such as marketing, order processing, billing, payment, inventory and delivery, to support distributed solutions across the enterprise and throughout the entire supply chain. E-business enables not only business transactions, but also information exchange. E-Business has also raised business-to-business commerce to unprecedented levels. In 1998, Cisco Systems transacted about US$5 Billion of business through its Web site, and Boeing provides seven-days-a-week, 24-hours-a-day parts ordering for the world's airlines through its site.

In general, an E-business framework has a number of major functions or components:

Day to Day Operations
- interactive business and financial transactions including e-forms, email and electronic faxes;
- electronic cataloguing;
- order placing;
- order fulfillment and shipping;
- logistics and electronic order-tracking services;
- automatic invoicing and payment services;
- electronic funds transfer; and
- the exchange of multimedia information and product designs, such as CAD/CAM drawings, photos, and schematics.

Long Term Operations
- vendor registration and contracting;
- demand forecasting and order scheduling;
- advertising of products and services;
- data mining of consumer information and transactions; and
- customer profiling and customization of advertisements to have a more effective impact on prospective customers.

A fully-automated demand-driven inventory management and just-in-time delivery system can be achieved by integrating these components with guaranteed overnight (or on-time) delivery. The advent of the Internet, its popularity and accessibility, has increased radically the number of organizations doing business electronically and has brought about increased competition and made global commerce a reality.

Today virtually every major information technology supplier is involved in electronic business. Apple, Boeing, IBM, HP, Cisco, Compaq, Microsoft, Oracle, SAP, and Sun Microsystems are some of the giant E-business facilitators that offer a wide range of products and services. The advent of the service-based approach to E-business promotes the formation of *virtual enterprises*, capable of providing specialized services within a broader end-to-end virtual and real environment. An example is the use of overnight and guaranteed delivery services such as FedEx and UPS to ship products from warehouses to customers.

A more striking shift is occurring at the physical level of enterprise cooperation. Recently Dell Computer, Inc. announced plans to build a factory employing 3,000 people, adjacent to the airport at Nashville, Tennessee, home of FedEx's hub. Clearly, this *strategic* decision by Dell to co-locate with FedEx so as to be closer to a world-class overnight delivery service, indicates the need to reduce the time between when an on-line order is taken and the time the computer is shipped to the customer. In addition, FedEx is expanding its reach deep into the supply and manufacturing chains of companies like Fujitsu and Hewlett-Packard, for whom it is now assembling computers from parts delivered just-in-time to FedEx's Nashville facility, and then shipping them to customers. FedEx is also handling computer repair for these companies.

In this paper we present an agency-based architecture for an Electronic Marketspace for logistic applications, and more specifically, study the role of intelligent software agents in facilitation, negotiation, brokerage, monitoring, alerting and performance verification, for a federation of customers, producers, catalog curators, and contracting agents. This framework and architecture is modular, scalable, and should foster the creation of virtual enterprises, in this and similar application domains. Section 2 examines the role of agents in electronic business. Section 3 discusses agent architectures and compares single versus multiagent schemes. Section 4 depicts our agency-based architecture for a class of logistics applications. Section 5 presents conclusions and suggestions for future research. Appendix 1 presents a table describing the many commercial, research and prototype software for agent specification, configuration and deployment.

2   The Role of Agents in Electronic Business

An agent is a program regulating a certain aspect of its environment. Autonomous agents are self-starting mechanisms with specific goals [28]. An intelligent agent is an attempt to model a software agent [23] after human cognitive behavior.

Agents are useful in electronic business because they are goal-driven adaptive problem solvers, and therefore act as proactive catalysts'. They can make contact, establish connections, negotiate and facilitate interactions. They can disseminate information to a wide audience or automatically target information to those with special interests [43]. Intelligent autonomous software agents may be used to filter information [39], integrate information from heterogeneous sources [30, 31], automate stereotypical behavior and regulate transactions for efficient business interactions [27]. The use of agents removes the need of having the user initiate all tasks explicitly and to monitor all events.

An agent could provide a common interface for the entire business process. Agents can be configured automatically with appropriate knowledge bases (ontologies), task-specific information, negotiation and communication protocols for its mission. The advantage of using agents for E-business is that they are scalable, modular, robust, composable and configurable. This enables the application system requirements for a particular enterprise to be built (and altered) fairly rapidly. The agent system would provide the infrastructure needed for a seamless connection of enterprises and would serve as an 'engine" or "shell" for transactions between databases involved in the different commerce applications.

Using agents for E-business increases productivity by allowing processes to be done concurrently and autonomously. The increased throughput becomes critical to performance with greater proliferation of business on the Internet. Furthermore, by modeling software agents to behave like human agents, consumer resistance to change from traditional to virtual environments is likely to be overcome.

Most enterprises have legacy systems and also access information on the Internet. E-business requires access to diverse data residing in multiple, autonomous, heterogeneous databases and the integration of that data into coherent information that can be used by the enterprise. The problem is complicated by the fact that the data may by multimedia with diverse temporal and spatial granularity [58, 59, 63, 64] and stored in diverse formats [62]. The semantics of the data may conflict across multiple sources and the data may be of uncertain quality, and the reliability of the source may be questionable. Cooperative information agents can play a major role in the intelligent integration of information and its associated problems mentioned above.

3   Agent Architectures

In this section we discuss several agent architectures, and discuss their pros and cons vis-a-vis E-business. First we examine single-agent systems, then multiagent systems. We introduce *agencies* of agents. Also examined are federated architectures and research issues of agent coordination and communication.

3.1   Single Agent System

An agent system may consist of a single agent or multiple agents. To many people a single agent approach is more intuitive than multiagent approaches. Although it might seem that single agent systems should be simpler than multiagent systems, the opposite is in fact true. Distributing control among multiple agents allows each agent to be simpler. No one agent has to be able to complete a given task on its own. A single agent could very well turn out to be more complicated than a multiagent system if its tasks are complex. Single agent systems should be reserved for domains that require centralized control. To perform more complex tasks, agents may be organized as part of a community of cooperative problem solvers.

Multiagent systems have several agents who model each other's goals and actions. There may be direct interaction among agents in a multiagent environment. This interaction could be viewed as environmental stimuli or may be direct agent interaction (communication) separate from the environment. From an agent's perspective, multiagent systems differ from single agent systems most significantly in that other agents can determine the environment's dynamics. In addition to the uncertainty that may be inherent in the domain, other agents affect the environment in unpredictable ways.

3.2   Multiagent Systems

A single agent to model E-business transactions would be very complicated and would unnecessarily burden the agent. Having multiple agents could speed up a system's operation by providing a method for concurrent processing. Since the domain is easily decomposed into components— several independent tasks that can be handled by separate agents— it could benefit from a multiagent architecture. Furthermore, the parallelism can help deal with limitations imposed by time-bounded reasoning requirements. While parallelism is achieved by assigning different tasks or abilities to different agents, robustness is a benefit of multiagent systems that have redundant agents.

If control and responsibilities are sufficiently shared among different agents, the system can tolerate failures by one or more of the agents. Another reason for choosing a multiagent system architecture is scalability. Since they are inherently modular, it is much easier to add new agents to a multiagent system than it is to add new capabilities to a monolithic single agent system. Systems, whose capabilities and parameters are likely to change over time, or across agents, can also benefit.

From a programmer's perspective the modularity of multiagent systems can lead to simpler programming. Rather than tackling the entire task with a centralized agent, programmers can identify subtasks and assign control of those subtasks to different agents. The problem of splitting a single agent's time among different parts of a task is also solved. We conclude therefore that a multiagent architecture is more amenable to the needs and requirements of the E-business domain.

There are several forms of organizations of multiple agents, namely:

- Homogeneous non-communicating agents.
- Heterogeneous non-communicating agents.
- Communicating agents with any degree of heterogeneity.

Each multiagent organization introduces new issues and complications. If a task can be accomplished with non-communicating agents, then adding communication only makes the system more complicated. The type of multiagent system to be used depends on the characteristics of the domain. The simplest possible system that is effective within the domain should be used. Relevant domain characteristics include: the number of agents; the amount of time that may be allocated; whether or not new goals arrive dynamically; the cost of communication; the cost of failure; user involvement; and environmental uncertainty. Decker distinguishes three different sources of uncertainty in a domain [17]: the transitions in the domain itself might be non-deterministic; agents might not know the actions of other agents; and agents might not know the outcomes of their own actions.

Multiagent Homogeneous System without Communication

The simplest multiagent system consists of homogeneous non-communicating agents. All agents have the same internal structure including goals, domain knowledge, and possible actions. They also have the same procedure for selecting among their actions. The only differences among agents are their inputs, the actual actions they take and possibly their location. Although the agents have identical capabilities and decision procedures, they may have limited information about each other's internal state and sensory inputs. Thus they may not be able to predict each other's actions. Several information retrieval and information filtering agents (Meta-crawler, Copernic, etc.) have this kind of architecture.

Multiagent Heterogeneous System without Communication

Heterogeneous agents in a multiagent domain add a great deal of potential power, but at the price of added complexity. Agents might be heterogeneous in any of a number of ways, from having different goals to having different domain models and actions. An important aspect of heterogeneous agent systems is whether agents are *benevolent* or *competitive*. Even if they have different goals, they may be co-operative towards each other, or they may actively attempt to inhibit each other. An agent can serve its own self-interests by establishing a reputation for being cooperative. When working on a task with another cooperative agent, the two can benefit from a sense of trust for each other. Cooperation is also an issue when certain resources are required simultaneously by the competing agents. Designers of multiagent systems having limited resources must decide how the agents will share those resources. In another paper in these proceedings, we present novel ways that agencies can negotiate for constrained resources in an optimal fashion.

With heterogeneous agents, the problem of modeling others is very complex. The goals, actions, and domain knowledge of the other agents may be unknown and thus will need to be modeled. Without communication, agents are forced to model each other strictly through observation.

Multiagent Heterogeneous System with Communication

The full power of a multiagent system can be realized when agents are given the ability to communicate with one another. With the aid of communication, agents can coordinate much more effectively. Communication also helps with resource allocation bottlenecks by allowing the heterogeneous agents to post constraints to each other's blackboards and schedulers, thus allowing them to coordinate without the aid of a centralized agent.

When agents have similar goals, but different abilities, they can be organized into a team or "agency." Each agent then plays a separate role within the team. With such a benevolent team of agents that are heterogeneous with respect to their abilities, one must provide some method for assigning different agents to different roles. This assignment might be obvious if the agents are very specialized.

Since e-business benefits from software agents that are specialized to perform particular tasks, cooperation is required for successful of the job at hand. A heterogeneous multiagent system is therefore, probably the best architecture for e-business. The different agents in the system may be organized into "agencies" in order to accomplish complex tasks. The agencies may be established ones that are organized along functional lines, or they may be formed dynamically.

Agency Organization

There are several possible organizational structures for heterogeneous multiagent systems such as:

- Uncoordinated teams ? where a matchmaker is queried about potential agents that can perform a task and then the request is sent to an agent selected at random.
- Economic markets ? where agents bid for tasks based on some pricing function that may include its current load, resources required in order to perform the task, and are selected based on price, reliability and other utility characteristics.
- Federations ? where agents give up individual autonomy to a centralized facilitator or broker that handles requests.
- Dynamic Teams ? where agents form teams based on some input parameter for the duration of a single task.

This is not an exhaustive list. Studies in organizational theory indicate that no one structure can be said to be 'best" for all organizations. The structure must adapt to the task environment based on the uncertainty associated with input and output measurements, causal relationships in the environment, time lapse between decision and feedback, etc.

3.3 Federated Architectures

A federated approach using cooperating agents rather than a monolithic system is more amenable to the needs of both information integration and electronic business [30, 31]. Agents are mobile, and can act autonomously, communicate, cooperate, adapt and reason based on rules and knowledge [24]. Thus, a system of trustworthy cooperating information agents, each having the requisite knowledge to perform its tasks within the larger problem-solving framework [17, 18, 42], would provide a flexible architecture for E-business. The approach proposed in this paper is to build a federation of configurable intelligent agents, which provide services, such as catalog access, consumer report information, product query formulation, facilitation, brokerage, negotiation, contracting, mediation, information integration and source wrapping, to enable the enterprise to realize its E-business goals. The agents in a federation may cooperate with each other and function as an agency, with agents being autonomous but sometimes surrendering autonomy in order to collaborate efficiently.

In an environment where we have multiple agents concurrently performing multiple tasks, we require a mechanism by which we can regulate the sequence in which tasks are performed so as to optimize productivity. This requires us to determine how to model an agent's activities and how to detect dependencies between those activities.

3.4 Research Issues in Multiagent Systems

Problem-solving should be a cooperative endeavor in Multiagent Systems [7, 41]. Multiple copies of knowledge and data, possibly in differing formats, may have to be maintained by the system. There are several facets to the heterogeneity of information in systems: syntactic, control and semantic. Syntactic heterogeneity refers to the myriad of knowledge representation formats, data definition formats to represent both knowledge and data. Control heterogeneity arises from the many reasoning mechanisms for intelligent systems including induction, deduction, analogy, case-based reasoning, etc. Semantic heterogeneity arises from disagreement on the meaning, interpretation and intended use of related knowledge and data. The advantage of different knowledge representations and information about the same thing being represented in different ways in the knowledge database is that such alternative views are helpful in creativity while syntactic differences can be resolved by translation agents given the computational equivalence of the representation formalisms.

Agent Coordination

A crucial problem in agent-based systems [6, 32] is to coordinate autonomous cooperating agents that are working towards common and/or individual, and possibly conflicting goals [10, 15, 17, 28, 29, 44]. In multiagent environments, the need to coordinate agents may arise from several reasons [28]: 1) to manage dependencies among agents' actions; 2) to adhere to and maintain global constraints; and 3) to facilitate problem solving in cases where no one agent has sufficient competence, resources or information to solve the entire problem. Coordination is the process of managing dependencies between activities in order to avoid conflicts while having maximum concurrency [8, 9, 17, 28, 29, 44, 46, 45]. Coordination involves task decomposition, resource allocation, synchronization, group decision making, communication and the preparation of common objectives.

The major coordination issues are: distributed planning [20], coalition formation [33-36], negotiation mechanisms [3, 7, 16, 37, 47] and the protocols [7, 56] by which agents can coordinate and manage commitments [28]. There are two approaches to coordination: implicit and explicit coordination [8, 9, 21, 55].

Agent coordination and control [5, 19, 24, 25, 38, 42] may be accomplished through:

a) mediated means using planning algorithms and load balancing [13, 14, 48],

b) reactive means based on the perception of the various autonomous agents [11, 12],

c) proactive means by the spontaneous formation of coalitions with the autonomous agents themselves taking the initiative [33-36, 41], or

d) competitive means which are market based [60].

Controls may be enforced through role-based access control mechanisms [1, 2, 50-52], by task reassignment, agent adaptation and evolution [18, 22, 26, 40, 49], or agent termination. These decisions may be made by monitoring resource consumption, by means of a cost/benefit optimization model [4, 57], or may be based on performance criteria.

Agent Communication

With the aid of communication, agents can freely exchange information in order to help them coordinate much more effectively. Communication costs arise due to limited bandwidth, the consumption of reasoning time, and the time required for the communicative acts. There is a tradeoff between lower communication costs and better decisions. With communicating agents, systems can become arbitrarily complex and highly controlled. Of course this may cause communication bottlenecks and performance may be prohibitively low.

From a practical point of view, the communication might be broadcast or posted on a "blackboard" for all to interpret, or it might be targeted point-to-point from one agent to another specific agent.

In all communicating multiagent systems, and particularly in domains that include agents built by different designers, there must be some set language and protocol for the agents to use when interacting. Independent aspects of protocols are information content, message format, and coordination conventions. Among many others, existing language protocols for these three levels are: KIF for content [23], KQML for message format and COOL for coordination. There has been a lot of research done on refining these and other communication protocols.

Communication capability of agents may be considered as an "action" or speech acts [13]. When an agent transmits information to another agent, it has an effect just like any other action would have. Thus, within a planning framework, one can define preconditions and post-conditions (effects) for communicative acts. When combined with a model of other agents, the effect of a communication act might be to alter an agent's belief about the state of another agent or agents. Agents can learn to choose among a set of social behaviors that include broadcasting and listening.

When agents communicate, they may decide to cooperate on a given task or for a given amount of time. Such commitments to each other involves agreeing to pursue a given goal, possibly in a given manner, regardless of the cost to the agent. Commitments can make systems run much more smoothly by providing a way for agents to "trust" each other. Therefore, plans can be formed which depend on the timely completion of specific tasks by different agents that are specialized in the performance of the given task.

4   The Agency-Based Electronic Marketspace

We propose an agency-based architecture for the Electronic Marketspace. The architecture consists of a collection of cooperating multi-layered agencies, each consisting of cooperating agents. This system is designed to eliminate the need for large warehouses of food, clothing and pharmaceuticals for the different supply sites of the supply chain organization, and rather to have selected prime vendors bid on orders, negotiate special terms and deliver goods directly to customers. The enterprise has both in-house transportation facilities for routine/bulk transportation between physical stores as well as negotiated contracts with external commercial transportation services for rapid transportation of specific products to individual customers. The aim here is to maintain optimal enterprise-wide inventory levels.

Since customer satisfaction has strategic implications, it is very important to closely monitor transactions. In order to ensure that customers do not go elsewhere because of inventory shortages, it becomes necessary to track the supply of critical items, and to be able to take necessary corrective action in a timely fashion. This is done automatically by the deployment of special agents, called sentinels that monitor the system, inform logisticians and decision-makers, and trigger alternative contingency plans to take care of a possible crisis [4, 53, 54, 61]. Figure 1 provides an overview of the Electronic Marketspace architecture.

Each agent-based subsystem, called an *agency*, may be considered a federation of agents, each with specific goals and a specific functional role in the Marketspace. Therefore, each agency can be considered as a collection of cooperating autonomous agents with particular expertise. The following discussion outlines the constituent agents and the role they play.

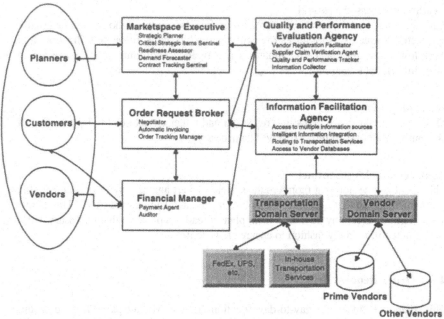

Fig. 1. Agency Architecture for the Electronic Marketspace

4.1 Marketspace Executive

This agency handles planning and monitoring of the Marketspace. It ensures that probable crisis situations are detected early and avoided by taking suitable action. This also acts as an interface for the organization's planners and strategists who are aware of the long term goals, expectations and strategies.

Strategic Planner

Strategic planning is performed within the interface Marketspace Executive agency. It allows planners to: provide domain knowledge, define long term plans and system objectives, define rules and constraints, identify critical items and situations to be monitored, define the cause-effect relationships, establish rules and courses of action for the sentinels, and obtain reports on all aspects of the system at any time. The desired features of the interface would be to provide heuristic support for all information searching scenarios and providing suggestions for building better queries.

Critical Strategic Items Sentinel

This agent is actually a collection of sentinels operating concurrently, continuously monitor the state of the system, tracking the critical and strategic items.

Readiness Assessor Sentinel
This agent ensures that strategic plans can be fulfilled by the in-house and externally contracted resources. It monitors the activities within plans, resource utilization, and workflow, ensuring that crisis situations are avoided and contingency plans are in place for critical situations.

Demand Forecaster
This agent breaks down plans into resources and materiel that need to be provided. It also builds the contract terms that will be necessary.

Contract Tracking Sentinel
This agent is a demon that monitors the system to alert against any deviation from the contracts made so that necessary alerts are flagged and triggers are fired. This allows the system to detect any deviation from plans already in place so that necessary action can be taken in a timely fashion to ensure crisis control.

4.2 Order Request Broker

This agency handles the day-to-day functions of the Marketspace. It ensures that transactions run smoothly without interruptions, and takes corrective action to handle inconsistencies. This also acts as an interface for the organization's operators who perform the individual transactions by providing optimized customer order - broker mapping, suggestion on building better queries to the user, improving overall order fulfillment and delivery turn around time, and by allowing the creation of personalized user profiles. This agency may be considered to have the following agents:

Negotiator
This agent would not only provide optimized broker-supplier associations, but also would negotiate with a registered supplier to issue a contract in accordance with the specifications and terms specified by the customer.

Automatic Invoicing
This agent is the supply receiver and payment requester. It consults a database containing records of contracts made and supplies obtained against these contracts. It acknowledges the receipt of merchandise based on UPC (bar) code scans and a contract identification code that indicates the partial or complete fulfillment of a particular contract. Upon receipt of merchandise it sends a request for payment to the appropriate agent in the financial broker.

Order Tracking Manager
This agent takes over the contract after the negotiator has completed negotiations, tracks progress made, and maintains contact with the supplier to ensure that the contract will be fulfilled according to schedule. In case of any problem indicated by

the supplier, this agent sends the pertinent information to the sentinel tracking contract terms in the Marketspace executive and the quality and performance tracker in the quality and performance evaluation agent.

4.3 Financial Broker

An issue vital to the electronic commerce architecture is a secure payment scheme. There are a number of institutions and organizations involved in research to develop not only a secure form of payment, but also to make the Internet a secure place for business transactions. Some of the major institutions include CyberCash, DigiCash, and First Virtual Bank. Besides the security issues that need to be addressed, a viable interface has to be developed to make payments for purchases with a pay-on-delivery paradigm in mind. This would involve automated invoicing, electronic transfer of funds and auditing of transactions. The financial broker is the agency that handles the financial transactions of the organization. It consists of the following agents:

Payment Agent

This agent removes the need for invoices to be prepared and approved. When the automatic invoicing agent acknowledges the receipt of merchandise corresponding to a particular contract, funds are automatically transferred to the supplier account and a record of the financial transaction is sent to the auditor. Depending on the contract terms, the payment may be made incrementally as items are delivered or deferred until the order is completed.

Auditor

This agent maintains records of all the financial transactions and performs audits.

4.4 Quality and Performance Evaluation Agency

This agency provides not only the "yellow pages" of registered vendors of the organization, but also tracks performance of the vendors, builds a level of confidence in different suppliers, verifies supplier claims and obtains referrals. The agency consists of the following agents:

Vendor Registration Facilitator

This agent enables new vendors to make their services available to the client. The agent serves as a broker and establishes the logistics between the vendor and the customer.

Supplier Claim Verification Agent

The services that this agent should provide include the verification of supplier authenticity by obtaining and checking references. Small contracts in non-critical areas may be recommended (to the negotiator in the order request broker) by this agent in order to build trust in a newly registered vendor.

Quality and Performance Tracker

This agent provides services that include: monitoring the performance of suppliers on their extant contracts, assessing the end-to-end performance of the supply chain, and updating the knowledge stored in the meta-database. Information is collected on user preferences, vendor performance, and services rendered. Data mining techniques can be used to extract relationships between the orders, suppliers, clients and information obtained from the order request broker. This information can be used to provide evaluations of vendor performance, which, in turn, can be used by the negotiator in the order request broker when selecting a vendor for a new contract.

4.5 Information Facilitation Agency

This agency handles access to data in enterprise-wide information sources, facilitates searching these databases, and accesses external Web-based data sources. Requests for special transportation services and vendor information are handled by this agency. In addition, information integration, fusion and filtering are provided by this agency.

4.6 Information Interchange among Agents

Information required by the different agents in order for them to perform correctly comes from various sources. The information exchange takes place by sending messages from one agent to another. The flow of information is critical to the agent performance. In table 1 we summarize the information flow among agents.

Table 1. Information Interchange among agents

Source of Information	Information Description	Receiver of Information
Customer, Strategic planner	Order info (requisitions, priorities, etc.)	Marketspace Executive Negotiator, Supplier Claim Verification Agent
Customer	Order ratification	Negotiator
Supplier Claim Verification Agent, Vendor Database – Established contracts	Supply Sources	Readiness Assessor, Strategic Planner, User
Readiness Assessor	Recommended alternative sources of supply prioritized to meet user order criteria.	Strategic Planner
Vendor Database, Vendor Meta-Database	Historic contract and vendor performance information	Strategic planner, Demand Forecaster
Order Request Broker	Contract and vendor performance information	Strategic Planner, Quality and Performance Tracker, Vendor database

Vendor Database	Historic vendor performance measures and risks. Vendor's expected contract performance parameters.	Readiness Assessor
Quality & Performance Tracker	Dynamic, real-time vendor performance estimates as well as uncertainty /confidence levels, Tradeoff relationships between vendor cost/price and performance	Readiness Assessor
Demand Forecaster	Demand data over the course of the planning scenario, Demand priorities established	Strategic planner
Strategic Planner Negotiator Readiness Assessor	Customer ordering criteria Real-time requisitions Subset of established business relationships that meet legal and regulatory conditions	Negotiator
Negotiator	Running contracts	Order Tracking Manager, Quality and Performance Tracker, Automatic Invoicing
Automatic Invoicing	Partial fulfillment of contract	Payment Agent Quality and Performance Tracker, Order tracking Manager
Demand Forecaster	Estimated risk of completing the transaction	Strategic Planner
Readiness Assessor	Best supply support alternative for demand, Prioritized list of alternative supply support, Measure of fit with customer ordering criteria	Strategic Planner
Order Tracking Manager	Deviation from schedule, Delays in delivery, Incomplete fulfillment of contract	Quality & Performance Tracker
Payment Agent	Record of funds transferred	Auditor
Vendor	Electronic Catalog Payment methods	Vendor Registration Facilitator
Supplier Claim Verification Agent	New supplier information	Readiness Assessor Vendor Database
Readiness Assessor Strategic Planner	Information about unconventional requirements	Information Facilitation Agency

5. Conclusions and Future Research

This paper has presented our ongoing research on the role of cooperating information agents in E-business. We have presented some of the impacts and benefits of moving the enterprise into an E-Business framework. The issues of agent coordination, control and evolution have been discussed within a multiagent systems framework. Much research needs to be done in the areas of agent communication, workflow, condition monitoring via sentinels, and agent negotiation to make such an architecture a reality.

We have presented an agency-based architecture for an Electronic Marketspace which is appropriate for the class of logistics and supply chain systems. By identifying the components, or agencies, of such systems, we hope to focus on the types of agents needed within each agency, and then examine negotiation, coordination and control mechanisms, within and among agencies, needed to realize enterprise-wide goals and objectives. We are presently beginning to construct a software prototype of the agency concept.

Acknowledgements

This research was sponsored in part by the Defense Advanced Research Projects Agency, Advanced Logistics Program, under contract number N00600-96-D-3202.

References

1. Bertino, E., Ferrari, E., Atluri, V.: A flexible model for the specification and enforcement of role-based authorizations in workflow management systems. 2nd ACM Workshop on Role-Based Access Control. Fairfax, VA (1997)
2. Biddle, B. J.: Role theory: concepts and research. Kreiger Publishing (1979)
3. Boehm, B., Bose, P., Horowitz, E., Le, M.J.: Software requirements negotiation and renegotiation aids: a theory-W based spiral approach. International Conference on Software Engineering (1995)
4. Brodsky, A., Kerschberg, L., Varas, S.: On Optimal Constraint Decomposition in Distributed Databases. Center for Information Systems Integration and Evolution, George Mason University, Fairfax, VA, Technical Report October (1997)
5. Brown, A. W.: Control Integration Through Message Passing in a Software Development Environment. Carnegie Mellon University, Pittsburgh, CMU/SEI-92-TR-35, December (1992)
6. Brown, D. C., Lander, S. E., Petrie, C. J.: Special Issue on The Application of Multiagent Systems to Concurrent Engineering. Concurrent Engineering: Research and Applications. vol. 4 (1996)
7. Bussmann, S., Miller, J.: A Negotiation Framework for Cooperation. Proceedings 1992 of the Special Interest Group on Cooperating Knowledge Based Systems (CKBS-SIG 1992). Dake Center, University of Keele (1992) 1-17
8. Chaibdraa, B.: Interaction between Agents in Routine, Familiar and Unfamiliar Situations. International Journal of Intelligent & Cooperative Information Systems. vol. 5 (1996) 1-25

9. Chaibdraa, B., Desharnais, J., Lizotte, S.: A Cognitive Map Formulation for Relationships between Agents. University of Laval, SteFoy, PQ, Canada, DIUL-RR- 9505, (1995)

10. Cohen, P. R.: Pulling Together or Pulling Apart? A Survey of the Eighth National Conference on Artificial Intelligence. AI Magazine, vol. 12, (1991) 16-41

11. Cohen, P. R., Levesque, H. J.: Persistence, Intention and Commitment.: Morgan Kaufman (1987)

12. Cohen, P. R., Levesque, H. J.: Intention is Choice with Commitment. Artificial Intelligence (1990)

13. Cohen, P. R., Levesque, H. J.: Communicative Actions for Artificial Agents. ICMAS '95 (1995) 65-72

14. Cohen, P. R., Perrault, C. R.: Elements of a Plan Based Theory of Speech Acts. Cognitive Science. vol. 3 (1979)

15. Crowston, K. G.: Towards a Coordination Cookbook: Recipes for Multi-Agent Action. MIT, Cambridge, MA, CCS TR#128, Sloan WP# 3416-91, (1991)

16. Davis, R., Smith, R.: Negotiation as a Metaphor for Distributed Problem Solving. Artificial Intelligence. vol. 20 (1983) 63-109

17. Decker, K. S.: Environment Centered Analysis and Design of Coordination Mechanisms. Ph.D. Thesis, Department of Computer Science. Amherst, MA,: University of Massachusetts, (1995)

18. Decker, K. S., Sycara, K.: Intelligent Adaptive Information Agents. Journal of Intelligent Information Systems. vol. 9 (1997) 239-260

19. Dix, A., Finlay, J., Hassell, J.: Environments for Cooperating Agents: Designing the Interface as Medium. HCI Group, University of York, June (1992)

20. Durfee, E.H.: Planning in Distributed Artificial Intelligence. In: O'Hare, G. M. P., Jennings, N. R., Eds.: Foundations of Distributed Artificial Intelligence. Wiley InterScience (1996)

21. Ephrati, E., Pollack, M.E., Sigalit, V.: Deriving Multi-agent Coordination through Filtering Strategies. Fourteenth International Joint Conference on Artificial Intelligence (IJCAI-95). Montreal, Canada (1995) 679-685

22. Gaines, B.R.: Knowledge Management in Societies of Intelligent Adaptive Agents. Journal of Intelligent Information Systems. vol. 9 (1997) 277-298

23. Genesereth, M., Ketchpel, S.P.: Software Agents. Communications of the ACM. vol. 37 (1994) 48-53

24. Guha, R.V., Lenat, D.B.: Enabling Agents to Work Together. Communications of the ACM. vol. 37 (1994) 126-142

25. Hewitt, C.: Viewing Control Structures as Patterns of Passing Messages. Artificial Intelligence. vol. 8 (1977) 323-364

26. Imam, I., Kerschberg, L.: Adaptive Intelligent Agents. Journal of Intelligent Information Systems. vol. 9 (1997) 211-214

27. Jajodia, S., Kerschberg, L.: Advanced Transaction Models and Architectures. Norwall, MA: Kluwer Academic Publishers, (1997)

28. Jennings, N. R.: Coordination Techniques for Distributed Artificial Intelligence. In: Georgeff, M. P., Jennings, N. R., Eds.: Foundations of Distributed Artificial Intelligence. Wiley InterScience (1996)

29. Kamel, M., Ghenniwa, H.: A Quantitative Analysis of Coordination Complexity for DAI Systems. Canadian Workshop on Distributed Artificial Intelligence. Banoe, Alberta, Canada, (1994)

30. Kerschberg, L.: Knowledge Rovers: Cooperative Intelligent Agent Support for Enterprise Information Architectures. In: Kandzia, P., Klusch, M., Eds .: Cooperative Information Agents, vol. 1202, *Lecture Notes in Artificial Intelligence*. Springer-Verlag, Berlin (1997) 79-100

31. Kerschberg, L.: The Role of Intelligent Agents in Advanced Information Systems. In: Small, C., Douglas, P., Johnson, R., King, P., Martin, N., Eds .: Advanced in Databases, vol. 1271, *Lecture Notes in Computer Science*. Springer-Verlag, London (1997) 1-22

32. Klein, M.: Computer Supported Conflict in Concurrent Engineering: Introduction to Special Issue. Concurrent Engineering: Research and Applications. vol. 2 (1993) 145-147

33. Klusch, M.: Using a Cooperative Agent System FCSI for a Context-Based Recognition of Interdatabase Dependencies. Workshop on Intelligent Information Agents, CKIM Conference. Gaithersburg, MD (1994)

34. Klusch, M.: Utilitarian Coalition Formation Between Information Agents. In: Kirn, S., O'Hare, G., Eds.: Cooperative Knowledge Processing. Springer-Verlag, London (1996)

35. Klusch, M., Shehory, O.: Coalition Formation Among Rational Information Agents. Seventh European Workshop on Modelling Autonomous Agents in a Multi-Agent World (MAAMAW-96). Eindhoven, Netherlands (1996) 204-217

36. Klusch, M., Shehory, O.: A Polynomial Kernel-Oriented Coalition Algorithm for Rational Information Agents. Second International Conference on Multi-Agent Systems. Kyoto, Japan (1996)

37. Kraus, S., Wilensky, J., Zlotkin, G.: Multiagent Negotiation Under Time Constraints. Artificial Intelligence (1995) 297-345

38. Kue-Chu, L., Mansfield Jr., W.,H, Sheth, A.P.: A Framework for Controlling Cooperating Agents. IEEE Computer (1993) 8-16

39. Lai, K.-Y., Malone, T. W.: Object Lens: Letting End-Users Create Cooperative Work Applications. Proceedings of CHI'91 (1991) 425-426

40. Laird, J.E., Pearson, D.J., Huffman, S.B.: Knowledge-Directed Adaptation in Multi-Level Agents. Journal of Intelligent Information Systems. vol. 9 (1997) 261-276

41. Lux, A., Bomarius, F., Stiener, D.: A Model for Supporting Human Computer Cooperation. AAAI Workshop on Cooperation among Heterogeneous Intelligent Systems (1992)

42. Maes, P.: Designing Autonomous Agents: Theory and Practice from Biology to Engineering and Back. Special Issues of Robotics and Autonomous Systems. Cambridge, MA, London, England: The MIT Press, (1990) 194

43. Maes, P., Darrell, T., Blumberg, B., Pentland, A.: The ALIVE System: Wireless, Full-Body Interaction with Autonomous Agents. ACM Multimedia Systems (1996)

44. Malone, T. W., Crowston, K. G.: The Interdisciplinary Study of Coordination. ACM Computing Surveys. vol. 26 (1994) 87-119

45. Prasad, B.: Concurrent Engineering Fundamentals. Integrated Product Development (1996)

46. Prasad, B.: Concurrent Engineering Fundamentals, II. Integrated Product and Process Organization (1996)

47. Rosenschein, J. S., Zlotkin, G.: Rules of Encounter: Designing Conventions for Automated Negotiation among Computers. Cambridge, MA,: MIT Press (1994)

48. Rosenschein, S., Kaelbling, L.P.: The Synthesis of Digital Machines with Provable Epistemic Properties. Conference on Theoretical Aspects of Reasoning about Knowledge (1986) 83-98

49. Rus, D., Gray, R., Kotz, D.: Transportable Information Agents. Journal of Intelligent Information Systems. vol. 9 (1997) 215-238

50. Sandhu, R.: Role hierarchies and constraints for lattice-based access controls. In: Bertino, E., Ed.: Proc. Fourth European Symposium on Research in Computer Security, *Lecture Notes in Computer Science*. Springer-Verlag, Rome, Italy (1996)

51. Sandhu, R., Bhamidipati, V.: The URA97 model for role-based administration of user-role assignment. In: Lin, T.Y., Qian, X., Eds.: Database Security XI: Status and Prospects. North Holland (1997)

52. Sandhu, R., Coyne, E., Feinstein, H., Youman, C.: Role-based access control models. IEEE Computer, vol. 29, (1996) 38-47

53. Seligman, L., Kerschberg, L.: Federated Knowledge and Database Systems: A New Architecture for Integrating of AI and Database Systems. In: Delcambre, L., Petry, F., Eds.: Advances in Databases and Artificial Intelligence, Vol. 1: The Landscape of Intelligence in Database and Information Systems, vol. 1. JAI Press (1995)

54. Seligman, L., Kerschberg, L.: A Mediator for Approximate Consistency: Supporting "Good Enough" Materialized Views. Journal of Intelligent Information Systems. vol. 8 (1997) 203 - 225

55. Shoham, Y., Tennenholtz, M.: On the Synthesis of Useful Laws for Artificial Agents Societies. Tenth National Conference on Artificial Intelligence. San Jose, CA, (1992) 276-281

56. Sichman, J.S., Demazeau, Y.: Exploiting Social Reasoning to Deal with Agency Level Inconsistency. First International Conference on Multi-Agent Systems. San Francisco, CA (1995)

57. Varas, S.: On Optimal Constraint Decomposition, Monitoring, and Management in Distributed Heterogeneous Environments. Doctoral Dissertation in Information Technology. Fairfax: George Mason University, (1998)

58. Wang, X.S., Bettini, C., Brodsky, A., Jajodia, S.: Logical Design for Temporal Databases with Multiple Temporal Types. ACM Transactions on Database Systems (1997)

59. Wang, X.S., Jajodia, S., Subrahmanian, V.S.: Temporal Modules: An Approach toward Federated Temporal Databases. Information Sciences. vol. 82 (1995) 103-128

60. Wellman, M.: A Market Oriented Programming Environment and its Application to Distributed Multicommodity Flow Problems. JAIR. vol. 1 (1993) 1-23

61. Widom, J., Ceri, S.: Active Database Systems: Triggers and Rules for Advanced Database Processing. : Morgan Kaufmann Publishers, Inc., (1995)

62. Wiederhold, G.: Foreword to Special Issue on the Intelligent Integration of Information. Journal of Intelligent Information Systems. vol. 6, 2/3 (1996) 93-97

63. Wiederhold, G., Jajodia, S., Litwin, W.: Dealing with Granularity of Time in Temporal Databases. In: Anderson, R., others, Eds.: Lecture Notes in Computer Science, vol. 498. Springer-Verlag (1991) 124-140

64. Wiederhold, G., Jajodia, S., Litwin, W.: Integrating Temporal Data in a Heterogeneous Environment. In: Tansel, A.U., Jajodia, S., others, Eds.: Temporal Databases: Theory, Design, and Implementation. Benjamin/Cummings (1993) 563-579

Appendix 1: A Survey of Agent Frameworks

Legend: The Type column denotes C for commercial product, R for research, and P for Prototype, respectively.

Agent System/URL	Type	Organiza-tion	Language	Description
Agent Building Environment http://www.net working.ibm.co m/iag/iagsoft.ht m	C	IBM	C++, Java	IBM's Agent Building Environment (ABE) is a toolkit for building applications based on intelligent agents. The intelligent agent watches for a certain condition, decides what to do based on a set of rules, and triggers an action as a result. The architecture for the agent is based on reasoning engine and adapters. "Adapters" or interfaces allow the agent to interact with the rest of the world.
Agent Building Shell (ABS) http://www.ie.u toronto.ca/EIL/ ABS-page/ABS-overview.html	R	U. of Toronto	COOrdina tion Language (COOL)	This provides several reusable layers of languages and services for building agent systems: coordination and communication languages, description logic-based knowledge management, cooperative information distribution, organizational modeling and conflict management. The approach is being used to develop multiagent applications in the area of manufacturing enterprise supply chain integration.
Agent Development Environment (ADE) http://www.gen sym.com/	C	Gensym		ADE provides a predefined class hierarchy of agents and agent parts, an agent communications "middle-ware" infrastructure, and a graphical language for designing and developing agent behavior based on the Grafcet standard. It takes advantage of the powerful capabilities of Gensym G2's application development environment on which it is built.
Agent TCL http://www.cs. dartmouth.edu/ ~agent/	R	Dartmouth University	Tcl (Tool Command Language)	Agent Tcl is a tool for developing transportable agent systems. Agent Tcl supports message passing. Agents can clone themselves and the system provides rudimentary security features. The agents migrate from machine to machine using the jump command. Each agent on a particular machine has a unique integer ID and a unique symbolic name. Migrating agents are encrypted and authenticated using Pretty Good Privacy (PGP). Access restrictions are imposed on the agent based on its authenticated identity. Safe Tcl enforces the access restrictions.
AgenTalk	C	NTT & Ishida Lab, Kyoto University.	LISP	AgenTalk is a coordination protocol description language for multiagent systems. It allows coordination protocols to be defined incrementally and to be customized to suit application domains by incorporating an inheritance mechanism.

AgentBuilder http://www.age ntbuilder.com/	C	Reticular Systems, Inc.	Java	AgentBuilder is an integrated tool suite for constructing intelligent software agents. AgentBuilder consists of two major components - the Toolkit and the Run-Time System. The AgentBuilder Toolkit includes tools for managing the agent-based software development process, analyzing the domain of agent operations, designing and developing networks of communicating agents, defining behaviors of individual agents, debugging and testing agent software. Agents constructed using AgentBuilder communicate using the Knowledge Query and Manipulation Language (KQML) and support the performatives defined for KQML.
Agentx http://www.iks. com/	C	Interna-tional Know-ledge Systems	Java	Agentx is a set of lightweight, high performance, and scaleable distributed computing libraries for the Java programming environment. The libraries were designed to provide object request broker facilities that were easier to use, faster, more compact and highly functional, than the RMI libraries bundled with the Sun JDK or generally available Java based CORBA implementations. Objects can move around on the network, attach themselves to a host, and begin independent execution of their program code.
Aglets http://www.trl.i bm.co.jp/aglets /	C	IBM Japan	Java	An aglet is a Java object that can move from one host on the Internet to another. That is, an aglet that executes on one host can suddenly halt execution, dispatch to a remote host, and resume execution there. When the aglet moves, it takes along its program code as well as its state (data). A built-in security mechanism makes it safe for a computer to host untrusted aglets.
Architecture type-based Development Environment (ADE) http://samuel.cs .uni-potsdam.de/soft /taxt/	R	U. of Potsdam Dept. of Computer Science	Java	Software agents and agent systems are modeled using object-oriented design thus allowing explicit modeling of agent interactions and a large number of property classes. The software architecture acts as a system of components whose interactions are realized via connectors. Theoretical fundamentals for the implementation of computer-independent platforms for agent programming have been found. The advantages of a substantiated methodology of an architecture type-based approach are lost while transforming them onto existing platforms.
Bee-gent http://www2.to shiba.co.jp/bee gent/index.htm	R	Toshiba Corpor-ation	Java	Bee-gent is purely an agent system. The applications are agents and all messages are carried by agents. "Agent Wrappers" are used to agentify existing applications, while "Mediation Agents" support inter-application coordination by handling all communications. The mediation agents move from the site of an application to another where they interact with the agent wrappers. The agent wrappers themselves manage the states of the applications they are wrapped around, invoking them when necessary.
Bond Distributed Object System http://bond.cs.p urdue.edu/	R	Purdue University	Java	The Bond distributed object system provides a message oriented middleware environment for developing distributed applications. Bond uses the KQML language for object communication. The agent framework of the Bond system simplifies the task of developing agents by allowing the programmer to concentrate on the specific strategies of a new agent. Bond agents have the intrinsic capability to be controlled remotely and to cooperate with each other. The task of an application programmer is limited to specifying the agenda, the finite state machine of the agent, and the strategies associated with each state.

Cable http://public.lo gica.com/~grac e/Architecture/ Cable/public/	R	Logica Corpor- ation	Agent Definition Language, C++	Cable can be used to develop and execute distributed applications that are based on the metaphor of multiple, cooperating intelligent agents. Cable provides the user with an Agent Definition Language (ADL), for defining agents, and a parser known as the Scribe, for compiling agent definitions written in ADL into agent applications. Agents are developed using ADL and C++. ADL allows developers to use Cable without worrying about underlying detail, providing a language with a level of abstraction close to that of the agents with which an application is designed. Inter-agent communication over a local area network is handled using ORBIX, an implementation of the CORBA 2.0 standard.
Concordia http://www.mei tca.com/HSL/P rojects/Concor dia	R	Mitsubishi Electric	Java	CONCORDIA is a framework for development and management of network-efficient mobile agent applications for accessing information on any device supporting Java. With Concordia, applications can: process data at the data source, process data even if the user is disconnected from the network, access and deliver information across multiple networks (LANs, Intranets and Internet), use wire-line or wireless communication, support multiple client devices, such as Desktop Computers, PDAs, Notebook Computers, and Smart Phones.
Cybele http://www.i-a-i.com/projects/ cybele/index.ht ml	R	Intelligent Automa-tion, Inc.	unknown	This supports rapid development by providing infrastructure for agent-based applications: (i) Agent creation and deployment over a network of varied platforms, (ii) a message addressing scheme for agent communication which is independent of the location of a sending or receiving agent, (iii) the accumulation of messages intended for a currently busy recipient agent,. (iv) the proper conversion of message data across platforms, (v) multicasting, broadcasting, and peer-to-peer messaging, and (vi) the migration of agents across processors for performance optimization and/or fault tolerance.
DECAF Agent Framework http://www.cis. udel.edu/~grah am/DECAF/	R,P	University of Delaware	Java	DECAF (Distributed Environment Centered Agent Framework) allows rapid development of agents by building an operating environment that provides an interface, internal agent scheduling and monitoring in a fashion similar to operating system primitives. The agent developer does not need knowledge of any of this structure and can thus focus on development of the agent itself. The basic DECAF architecture has been built using the Java programming language.
dMARS http://www.aaii .oz.au/proj/dM ARS-prod-brief.html	R	Australian Artificial Intelli-gence Institute Ltd.	C, C++	dMARSTM designed for rapid configuration and ease of integration with the issues of robustness, efficiency and user-extensibility in mind, is an agent-oriented development and implementation environment for building complex, distributed, time-critical systems. This product is based on Procedural Reasoning System (PRS) developed by SRI International (California). It provides a sophisticated suite of graphical tools for development and debugging and takes advantage of the latest research into multiagent, real-time reasoning.

Grasshopper http://www.ikv. de/products/gra sshopper/	C	IKV++	Java	Grasshopper built on CORBA, complies to the Mobile Agent System Interoperability Facility (MASIF) standard and provides the integration of traditional client/server paradigm and mobile agent technology. The agent applications are open towards other agent environments and allows one to build agent-enabled distributed applications which take advantage of local high-speed communication and local high-speed data access.
Gypsy http://www.inf osys.tuwien.ac. at/Staff/lux/Gy psy/	R	Technical University of Vienna	Java	Gypsy is a flexible environment for mobile agent programming intended for application in Internet information retrieval, Internet commerce, mobile computing, and networks network management.
iGENTM http://www.chii nc.com/ginaho me.htm	C	CHI Systems	C/C++	iGENTM is a toolkit and workbench based on a programmable model of human expertise. It includes high-level agent-building tools for the development of intelligent applications.
Infospiders http://www-cse.ucsd.edu/us ers/fil/agents/a gents.html	R	UC San Diego - Computer Science Dept.	unknown	InfoSpiders (aka ARACHNID: Adaptive Retrieval Agents Choosing Heuristic Neighborhoods for Information Discovery) features an artificial life inspired model using endogenous fitness for information retrieval in large, dynamic, distributed, heterogeneous databases, such as the WWW. A population of agents is evolved under density dependent selection for the task of locating information for the user.
Intelligent Agent Factory http://www.bitp ix.com/iaf/iafin tro/iafintro.htm	C	Bits & Pixels	Java	The Intelligent Agent Factory has agents that are controlled with rules written in Jess (CLIPS), a forward-chaining system. Agents and rules are generated from simple specifications of workflows.
Intelligent Agent Library http://www.bitp ix.com/busines s/main/bitpix.ht m	C	Bits & Pixels	Java	The Intelligent Agent Library provides extensive facilities for agent communications for building large agent assemblies. There is a KQML-based agent framework and many examples illustrating agents that perform activities for web-enabled applications. The library also supports mobile agents.
JACK Intelligent Agents http://www.age nt-software.com.a u/jack.html	C	Agent Oriented Software, Ltd.	JACK Agent Language	JACK provides the architecture and capability for developing and running software agents in distributed applications. JACK Agent Language is an extension to Java and provides all the features of the Java language.
JAFMAS http://www.ece cs.uc.edu/~aba ker/JAFMAS	R	University of Cincinnati	Java	JAFMAS provides a framework to structure ideas into multiagent systems with a set of classes for agent deployment. It directs development from a speech-act perspective -supports multicast and directed communication, KQML or other speech-act performatives; gives an analysis of multiagent system coherency and consistency; and provides a good comparison of agent tools with particular emphasis on mobile agents.
JATLite http://java.stanf ord.edu/java_a gent/html/	R	Stanford University	Java	JATLite provides a basic infrastructure in which agents register with an Agent Message Router facilitator using a name and password, connect/disconnect from the Internet, send and receive messages, transfer files, and invoke other programs or actions on the various computers where they are running. JATLite facilitates construction of agents that send and receive messages using KQML.

Jumping Beans http://www.JumpingBeans.com/	C	Ad Astra Engineering, Inc.	Java	Jumping Beans allows a Java application software to move from one host to another along with the executable, data, state, resources and other essential information so that can execute on hosts that did not have the application previously installed.
Kafka http://www.fujitsu.co.jp/hypertext/free/kafka/	C	Fujitsu	Java	Kafka is an extendable, flexible Java class library based on Java's RMI and designed for constructing multiagent based distributed applications.
Kasbah http://ecommerce.media.mit.edu/Kasbah/index.html	R	MIT	unknown	Kasbah is an agent-mediated electronic commerce system. A user wanting to buy or sell a product or service creates an agent, give it some strategic direction, and send it off into the agent marketplace. Kasbah agents pro-actively seek out potential buyers or sellers and negotiate with them on their creator's behalf. Each agent's goal is to make the "best deal" possible, subject to a set of user-specified constraints, such as a desired price, a highest (or lowest) acceptable price, and a date to complete the transaction.
Knowbot System Software http://www.cnri.reston.va.us/home/koe/	R	CNRI	Python	Knowbot is a mobile agent system intended for use in widely distributed systems such as the Internet. The design of the Knowbot architecture allows agents of several programming languages to interoperate.
LALO http://www.CRIM.CA/sbc/english/lalo/	R	CRIM	LALO	LALO is an Agent Oriented Programming (AOP) language and environment for the defining and creating extensible multiagent systems including reactive agents and deliberate agents. The inter-agent communication language used is KQML. A program written in LALO is translated into C++ source code, and then compiled with a C++ compiler.
LiveAgent http://www.agentsoft.com/	C	AgentSoft Ltd.	Java	LiveAgent Pro automates Web activity by creating Internet/Intranet scripts using a recording environment (like a high-level macro recorder or automated testing tool). A developer performs a sequence of Web operations in the browser, and those actions are automatically saved by LiveAgent Pro as a script or "agent". The completed script can then be run by the user or scheduled for automatic launching.
Microsoft Agent http://www.microsoft.com/workshop/imedia/agent/default.asp	C	Microsoft	Active X	Microsoft Agent uses animated characters characters as interactive assistants to introduce, guide, entertain, or otherwise enhance their Web pages or applications in addition to the conventional use of windows, menus, and controls. This enables the incorporation of speech recognition so applications can respond to voice commands. Characters can respond using synthesized speech, recorded audio, or text in a cartoon word balloon.
Mobiware Middleware Toolkit http://comet.columbia.edu/mobiware/	R	Columbia University	Java	Mobiware is a set of open programmable interfaces and algorithms for adaptive mobile networking, built on CORBA and Java distributed object technology. It runs on mobile devices, wireless access points and mobile-capable switch/routers.

MOLE http://www.inf ormatik.uni- stuttgart.de/ipvr /vs/projekte/mo le.html	R	University of Stuttgart	Java	This is a mobile agent with mechanisms for migration and communication.
Multi-Agent Modeling Language (MAML) http://www.sysl ab.ceu.hu/mam l/	R	Central European University	MAML	MAML can be used to develop models, run simulations, search in parameter space, and analyze results. It has a graphical user interface, support work through the web, and is aimed to support scientists who are not experts in programming.
MultiAgent Systems Tool (MAST) http://www.gsi. dit.upm.es/~ma st/	R	Technical University of Madrid	C++	MultiAgent Systems Tool is a general purpose distributed framework for the cooperation of multiple heterogeneous agents. The MAST architecture consists of two basic entities: the agents and the network through which they interact.
Odyssey http://www.gen magic.com/tech nology/odyssey .html	C	General Magic	Java	Odyssey is a set of Java class libraries to support development of distributed, mobile applications. Odyssey agents are Java threads. They are created by subclassing the Odyssey agent class or the Odyssey worker class.
Open Agent Architecture TM http://www.ai.s ri.com/~oaa/	R	SRI Internation al		Open Agent ArchitectureTM (OAA) is a framework for integrating a community of heterogeneous software agents in a distributed environment. In this framework, an agent is defined as a software process that registers its services in an acceptable form, speaks the Interagent Communication Language (ICL), and shares functionality common to all OAA agents (e.g. the ability to install triggers, manage data in certain ways).
ProcessLink http://cdr.stanfo rd.edu/Process Link/	R	Stanford University		This consists of generic agents and a message protocol. It allows the "wrapping" of legacy software to provide the coordination functions and send messages conforming to a defined interaction semantics.
RETSINA http://www.cs.c mu.edu/~softag ents	R	Carnegie Mellon University		RETSINA is a reusable agent. Each RETSINA agent has four reusable modules for communicating, planning, scheduling and monitoring the execution of tasks and requests from other agents. A RETSINA agent is distinguished according to the kind of task it performs (i.e. interface, task, information and middle agents).
Sodabot http://www.ai. mit.edu/people/ sodabot/sodabo t.html	R	MIT Artificial Intelligenc e Lab	unknown	Sodabot is is essentially an agent operating system. A new programming language was designed around human-level descriptions of agent activity. Using this language, users can implement a wide-range of typical software agent applications, e.g. personal on-line assistants and meeting scheduling agents.
Swarm http://www.san tafe.edu/project s/swarm/	R	Sante Fe Institute	C	Swarm is the simulation of collections of concurrently interacting agents.

Via: Versatile Intelligent Agents http://www.kinetoscope.com/via/default.htm	R	Kinetoscope	Java	Via contains tools for creating agent tasks, logic, and user interfaces into existing applications, Web sites and intranets. It also includes advanced features for supporting system-wide distribution, persistence, and scalability
Voyager http://www.objectspace.com/	C	Object Space	Java	Voyager combines the power of mobile autonomous agents and remote method invocation with complete CORBA support and distributed services such as directory, persistence, and publish subscribe multicast.. Agents are modeled as autonomous objects and Voyager allows construction of remote objects, sends messages and moves objects between applications so that agents can move themselves and continue executing as they move. In this way, agents can act independently on the behalf of a client, even if the client is disconnected or unavailable.
Zeus http://www.labs.bt.com/projects/agents/research/collaborative.htm	R	British Telecommunications Labs	Java	Zeus is a collaborative' agent building environment and component. Each ZEUS agent consists of a definition layer, an organizational layer and a co-ordination layer. The definition layer has a programming interface and represents the agent's reasoning and learning abilities, its goals, resources, skills, beliefs and preferences. The organization layer describes the agent's relationships with other agents. The co-ordination layer describes the co-ordination and negotiation techniques the agent possesses. Communication protocols are built into the co-ordination layer and enable inter-agent communication.

Secure Agent-Mediated Auctionlike Negotiation Protocol for Internet Retail Commerce

X.F.Wang[1], X.Yi[2], K.Y.Lam[1], C.Q.Zhang[3], E.Okamoto[2]

[1]School of Computing
National University of Singapore
E-mail: wangxiao@comp.nus.edu.sg
and
[2]Japan Advanced Institute of Science and Technology, Japan
[3]Deakin University, Australia

Abstract. With the proliferation of retail commerce on the Internet, mobile agents play more and more important roles in automating information brokering and negoiation for online shopping. However, due to the limited computing resources and security concerns, current first-generation shopping agents have limited capacities to conduct commercial bargaining. On the other hand, though auctions appear promising to solve these difficulties with their fairness and openness features, they suffer from the problems such as reversed consumer-buyer relation and low performance. In this paper, we propose a secure agent-mediated auctionlike negotiation protocol which combines togather the favorable features of traditional English auction and mobile agent scheme. Its features lie at: (1) auctionlike scheme is implemented which keeps the dominant equilibrium in the English auction and rationalizes consumer-seller relation in the retail commerce. (2) security for negotiation agents is guaranteed which makes tampering on agent body easy to detect. (3) flexibility during the trading is achieved by combining information gathering and negotiation together while few communications are needed.

1 Introduction

Online marketplaces open a new area for retail commerce. They offer traditional merchants an additional channel to advertise and sell products to customers, thus potentially increasing sales. Forrester Research estimates that online retail sales will reach 17 billion USD by 2001[1]. Moreover, online markets are also more efficient than their physical-world counterparts thus lowering transaction costs for both merchants and consumers.

Consumer Buying Behavior (CBB) marketing research shows negotiation is an important stage for retail commerce. It's the stage where the price or other terms of the transaction are determined [2]. To automate online negotiation, intelligent agent is the best candidate. The personification and autonomy features enable agents to simulate the process as it happens already between humans, and hence human negotiating strategies and approaches may be easier to translate into it [2]. Mobile agents further extend trading services to weak, mobile consumers and are promising to improve the flexibility, reliability and efficiency of negotiation protocols at the same time. In addition, since retail shopping always combines brokering and negotiation process together, mobile agent, as an important online information collector, is deemed as mediator to conduct automatic negotiation naturally.

Although great research efforts have been invested to the agent-mediated automatic negotiation [9][10][11], current first-generation shopping agents possess only limited bargaining capacities. The reasons come from two aspects. Firstly, automatic negotiation is a difficult procedure which needs complicated computing to infer rival's strategies. Whereas mobile agents have only limited computing resource. This makes them hard to compute rival's strategies while easy to be computed. Under the Internet retail scenario, online merchants usually have more resource than the shopping agents who are, therefore,at significant disadvantages. Secondly, mobile agents depend on server environment to run. Thus they have to expose codes and data to the hosts. In the hostile environment, this makes them vulnerable to information stealing and tampering from malicious hosts, which in turn jeopardizes mobile agents' qualifications as online negotiators.

As a special negotiation type, auction exhibits certain characteristics which fit well with intelligent mobile agents. In English and second-price auctions, bidders have dominant strategy which is open to all the participants. That means all the bidders are free from the intentions to infer rivals' strategies thus saving the computing resource as well as ensuring the fairness during the negotiation. From auctioneers' point of view, they want to maximze their payoff. Difference from other negotiation type, during auction, they may not at a disadvantage if the bidders divine their stragies [3]. Sometimes, the auctioneers even want to make the strategies publicly known to push up the final bid. This greatly reduces the confidential information that needs to protect during the trading. With such a open, simple and fair negotiation scenario, mobile agents can fully take advantage of their beneficial features to play active roles in automating the Internet trading.

However, current implementation of auction to the Internet retail commerce has exposed some of its unfavorable features. Guttman and Maes [4] point out these problems such as irrational consumer-seller relations and low performance. The introducing of centralized salesroom scheme also brings in new security concerns for mobile agent bidders, which actually impairs the advantages of auction itself.

Nowadays, consumers are much more in the driver's seat in the online market than in the physical-world market largely due to the dramatic reduction of search costs [5]. This increases the competition among retailers and forces them to positively differentiate themselves in value dimensions other than price. However, instead of merchants competing for consumer patronage, online retail auctions force consumers to compete with one another for a specific merchant offering. This brings in the "winner's curse", which pushes up the winning bid above the product's market valuation. On the other hand, retailers often care less about profit on any given transaction and care more about long-term profitability. Customers' loss through "winner's curse" actually destroys the relationship between retailers and customers, thus damaging the retailers' benefits in the long run.

Furthermore, the traditional online auctions have long delay between starting auctions and purchasing the product. This retards a large number of impatient or time-constrained consumers. In fact, the English and Yankee auction protocols are usually implemented over the Internet for several days. The passive role auctioneer plays makes thing worse: he has to wait for a critical mass of bidders to complete auction rather than actively search for potential bidders. This exacerbates time consuming during the auction. Since only the highest bidder(s) of an auction can purchase the auctioned good(s), the rest of the bidders (the majority) have to endure the long fruitless delays. Unlike the vendue of works of art, this is quite annoying in retail commerce

To improve auction performance, some people suggest to dispatch agent bidders to a centralized salesroom to conduct the auction locally. However, this causes security concerns. In order for an agent to run, it must expose its data and code to the host resources. Therefore, if the auctioneer conspires with the owner of the salesroom, he can manipulate the auction to his advantage. This results in the bidding agents to suffer losses.

In this paper, we propose a Secure Agent-Mediated Auctionlike Negotiation protocol which can fully preserve the favorable features of traditional auction while effectively solve its defects towards Internet retail commerce. The protocol enables mobile agents to carry out secure, rational and high performance retail negotiation in the chaotic and uncertain Internet environments. Its features lie at: (1) auctionlike scheme is implemented which keeps the dominant equilibria in the English auction and rationalizes consumer-seller relation in the retail commerce. (2) security for negotiation agents is guaranteed which makes tampering on agent body easy to detect. (3) flexibility during the trading is achieved by combining information gathering and negotiation together while few communications are needed.

The rest of the paper is organized as follows: Section 2 describes the main ideas and procedure of proposed agent-mediated negotiation protocol; Section 3 makes a detailed analysis and evaluation on the protocol; Section 4 concludes the whole paper.

2 Secure Agent-Mediated Auctionlike Negotiation Protocol

The whole agent-mediated Internet trading architecture on which the proposed negotiation protocol grounds can be illustrated in the following figure:

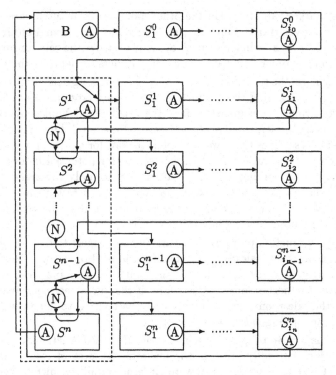

Fig.1: The Agent-mediated Internet Trading Architecture

In the above architecture, B denotes a buyer; S_i^j stands for a seller on Internet; A represents the intelligent trade agent and N acts as the auctionlike negotiation process.

We will present the negotiation protocol in following subsections.

2.1 Commercial actors in the protocol

There are three commercial actors in the proposed negotiation protocol. We describe them as following:

Buyer: When a buyer has intention to purchase products or service on the Internet, he sends an agent out to trade on his behalf. The buyer has a private catalogue which can supply a trade agent initial routing list including some recommended merchants and public catalogues. After completing the purchase, the buyer will evaluate the satisfaction of the overall buying experience and update a recommended vendor list correspondingly. They also can contact each other to exchange merchant information. Moreover, the buyer software (we call it agent home) has security mechanism which can authenticate incoming agents, check the validation of trading results and even conduct investigation to dig out the malicious hosts.

Trade agent: Based on his domain knowledge and buyer profile, a trade agent automatically gathers information about merchants who can provide targeted products or services. He should be able to identify similar offerings different merchants can provide and then conduct auctionlike negotiation among them. During the negotiation, the agent takes a role similar to an auctioneer and is responsible for controlling the process of negotiation. According to the buyer's requirements, the agent can decide the number of the bidders given he can find enough candidates. He is also cautious enough to avoid the actions which can arouse retailers' cheating incentives.

Seller: The seller compete each other for the low price they can provide for the same products or services. Actually, since the major portion of the proposed protocol is carried out by mobile agents, the seller need not to have specific negotiation software for the trading. This makes it possible for them to accommodate several other kinds of negotiation protocols at the same time. Besides negotiation, the seller sometimes may provide trade agents with certain commercial information. However, the agent will not take it until they trust the reliability of the information. In addition, the seller should have security mechanism to authenticate incoming agents, encrypt outgoing agents and record down some non-repudiation information such as agent's incoming and outing nodes, time stamp, his signature on the information provided to the agent. Once buyer detects any illegal actions after agents return, he may launch an investigation and then, any seller who cannot provide corresponding nonrepudiation evidence will be deemed as malicious breeder.

2.2 Trading procedure

Start Trading. The trading procedure starts when buyer sends a trade agent out to purchase specified products or services. Just before this, buyer will supply the agent with an initial routing list including several recommended merchants and public catalogues. Moreover, he must indicate to agent his reserve price, i.e, initial minimum bid (MB) and minimum bid decrement (MBD).

Referring to the agent-based Internet trading architecture in Figure 1, the trade agent A starts its purchasing trip over Internet from the buyer B, then one after the another roams a series of seller servers $S_1^0, S_2^0, \cdots, S_{i_0}^0 (i_0 \geq 0), S^1$ according to his routing list. We suppose the first i_0 servers do not have the required products or services to sell and Server S^1 is the first one which can meet purchase requirements with the price lower than MB. Then the agent replaces MB with S^1's price, duplicates itself, keeps his copy in current server and continues to roam to the seller according to the routing list.

Bidding Procedure. From the routing list of the agent, the agent chooses an un-passed seller and roams into the server. Note that if the routing list runs out, the agent will browse online catalogues to select new seller servers and add them to his routing list.

We assume the agent further roams a series of seller servers $S_1^j, S_2^j, \cdots, S_{i_1}^j$ $(1 \leq j \leq n - 1, i_1 \geq 0), S^{j+1}$ as shown in Figure.1. These servers can be divided into two types. One type belongs to the sellers which can not meet purchase requirements or further lower the MB. This is called Type I server. Another type consists of all servers whose owners have the targeted products or service to sell and are capable of lowering MB. The server of this type is called Type II server.

For a Type II server, a negotiation procedure should be carried out between him (also called bidding server BS) and Server S^j (called waiting server WS) for the sale. The agent who stays in the waiting server is called waiting agent (WA) and the agent who bids in the bidding server is called bidding server (BA). After negotiation, there are two possible results. One result is that the waiting server is still the winner of this competition. We call this negotiation result as Result I. Another result is that the bidding server beats the waiting server and become the new waiting server. This negotiation result is called Result II.

Among the series of seller servers $S_1^j, S_2^j, \cdots, S_{i_1}^j, S^{j+1}$, only Server S^{j+1} is supposed to be a Type II server and the negotiation result between Server S^{j+1} and Server S^j is Result II. For other servers, even if they are Type II servers, the negotiation result between them and Server S^j is definitely Result I.

The negotiation process between BS and WS(S^j) is performed in the following procedure:

1. The bidding agent (BA) sends the start-negotiation request to the waiting agent (WA). It includes BS's current bid which must be lower than current MB by integral times of MBD and some authentication information (from the routing agent or the BS, we will discuss it in next section).

2. The WA authenticates the request. If correct, it passes the new bid to WS and then continues the following procedure. Otherwise, it ignores the request.

3. The WS checks current bid and makes its decision about whether to further lower the sale price or give up. If the decision is lowering price, the WS gives its new bid according to the bidding regulation(new bid must be lower than the current bid by integral times of MBD), and then WA replies the BA with bidding response. If the decision is giving up, the procedure goes to 5.

4. BA notifies BS of new bid. Then the BS has to make a decision on whether to further lower the sale price or give up. If it lowers price, the BS renders another bid to BA who sends the bid to WS through WA. Then the procedure goes to execute 3. If it gives up, the procedure goes to 6.

5. Because the WS fails to further lower the price, it has to send a failure notification to the WA. The notification must include the BS's final bid and bear the WS's digital signature. WA sends the notification to the BA who passes it to BS after authentication. BS also signs on the notification and return to BA. BA keep a copy of dually signed notification for himself and sends it back to the WA who will authenticate it and then reserves it as nonrepudiation evidence. Both BA and WA replace the MB with the final bid. After that, WA becomes BA and leaves former WS to resume his information brokering task while BA has to stay in the new WS as a new WA. Thus this round negotiation is ended.

The negotiation process of the above case can be illustrated in the following figure:

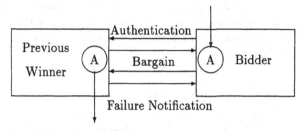

Fig.2: The negotiation process for Result II

6. Because the BS fails to lower the price, it sends a signed failure notification including WS's final bid to BA. BA notifies WA of BS's decision. The latter checks the signature of the notification and then passes it to WS. WS dually signs on the notification and return to WA. WA keep a copy for himself and send the notification back to BA. After checking the signature, BA leaves the current server and roams to the next merchant according to the routing list. Both BA and WA have to update MB before the end of this round.
In this case, the negotiation process can be illustrated in the following figure:

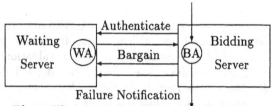

Fig.3: The negotiation process for Result I

In order to guarantee trade agent's security during trading, every server agent visited may preserve some nonrepudiation evidence for the agent such as coming and outgoing nodes, the signed confirm notification from next server, etc. Therefore, once some illegal actions on agent are detected, servers can use these information to prove their innocence.

Return of Trade Agent. Buyer can take control of the trading process by pre-setting termination conditions on the trade agent. These conditions usually include two aspects. One is the scale of the auction, i.e, the number of bidders agent should visit. The other is agent's lifetime. Therefore, once agents visited enough bidders or their lifetimes were expired, they must return to the buyer.

Once termination conditions are met, both BA and WA must return to buyer. Just before leaving, WA may conduct some additional trading actions such as completing some early steps of payment protocol since the last WS is obviously the final winner.

After having received BA and WA, the buyer checks final price and signatures on the notification of final round negotiation. If no problem is found, the buyer contacts the merchant for the payment and delivery. Otherwise, he will not trust the trade agent and launches an investigation to dig out the malicious server. To some weak user such as mobile users, they may simply discard the agent and restart the trading process.

3 Analysis and Evaluation

In this section, we will analyze and evaluate the proposed protocol from the viewpoints of auction theory, performance/flexibility and security.

3.1 Fair, Open and Rational Negotiation Protocol

To analyze auction model, McAfee and McMillan [6] starts from four assumptions:

1. All the bidders are risk-neutral, as is the seller.
2. The independent private-values model holds.
3. The bidders are symmetric.
4. The final payment from the winning bidder to the seller depends on the bid alone.

The first assumption indicates bidders' risk attitudes. The second supposes bidders' valuation model. There are two types of valuation models [7]. One is the Independent Private-Values Model: bidder i's valuation v_i is drawn from a distribution F_i, and the draws are statistically independent; the other is the Common-Value Model: the item being bid for has a single objective, but unknown value V and bidders's valuations v_i are independently drawn from publicly known $G(v|V)$. The third supposes bidders' valuations are drawn from the same distribution. The last decides winning bidder's final payment.

Once all these assumptions hold, the model is called as the "benchmark model" [6].

In the proposed auctionlike negotiation protocol, the retailers take similar roles as bidders. Thus, we can suppose they are risk-neutral. Since all the retailers know quite well about the cost of the products/service they want to sell, their value models are independent private ones. In the retail marketplace, the costs of certain products/services are usually drawn from the same bell-sized distribution (Normal Distribution). This manifests that all the retailers in the proposed protocol are symmetric. The last assumption obviously holds for the retail commerce.

From the above explanation, we know that the agent-mediated auctionlike protocol naturally satisfies the assumptions of the "benchmark model". Therefore, the protocol can be analyzed with the same method as for the traditional auction.

Consider all the merchants attending negotiation with the proposed protocol. Their costs for the products/services can be presented as $c_1, \cdots, c_n$ which are drawn independently from a Normal Distribution G with a density function g. Suppose c_1 is the lowest cost, c_2 is the second lowest, etc. The sequence is arranged in a non-decreasing way. In statistical terminology, c_i is called the $i - th$ order statistic, $i = 1, \cdots, n$. During the negotiation, merchants with different costs may bid in a random sequence. However, the one whose cost is c_1 will definitely win at last. The bidder with cost of c_2 will drop out of the bidding as soon as the descending price breaks his bottom line. Thus the lowest-cost individual wins the bidding and pays a price equal to the cost of his last remaining rival. The payoff the winner can obtain is $c_2 - c_1$. McAfee and McMillan [6] proved that the expected value of this payoff is given by the expectation of $\frac{G(c_1)}{g(c_1)}$. Thus the expectation of the final bid will be $c_1 + \frac{G(c_1)}{g(c_1)}$

Due to uncertainty about rivals' valuations, the best strategy for a merchant to obtain such payoff is to keep lowering down current bid by a small unit (i.e., one MBD) until the price gets down to his cost. This helps to avoid the possible losses coming from the over-depreciation. Obviously, the strategy is dominant in the SAMAN protocol. Even in the cases of risk-averse bidders, the conclusion still holds [6].

The above analysis shows that the proposed protocol is strategical analyous to a descending English auction. With the dominant equilibrium, all the participants are free from the intentions to couter-speculate others' strategies. Thus the computing resources are saved during the negotiation and the fairness of the traditional English auction is fully preserved.

From the buyer's point of view, he wants to get the item at as low price as possible. This intention is publicly known by all the parties involved. During the negotiation, mobile trade agents are similar to auctioneers. They need not to bring with themselves any negotiation information except the reserve price which actually, will be open to all the merchants to incur a bidding process. That means mobile agents have little confidential information needs to protect in the protocol. This openness feature effectively mitigates the security concerns in the trading.

Compared to current online retail auctions, the auctionlike protocol enables buyers to act as auctioneers and has merchants to compete each other for sell. This elimiates the "winner's curse" problem thus rationalizing the relation between the consumers and retailers in the retail commerce. Buyers can expect economic rent through revelation of their valuations. From the analysis above, we can see that the competition between merchants can reduce the bid to the second-last bidder's cost. Thus buyers can get the product or service at low price. On the other hand, sellers are also benefited from the negotiation in the long run. Just like what is mentioned in the introduction, retailers often care less about profit on any given transaction and care more about long-term profitability which actually depends on consumers' satisfaction. The interests retailers give to the customers will pay back by repeat purchases and additional purchases through direct referrals. Even for the losers in a specific trading round, their behaviors will also be recorded by the trade agents. Through purchase evaluation, they have the opportunities to be re-patronized in the future.

Although the proposed protocol is for price competition, the same scheme can be extended to multi-dimentional bargaining. That means, the merchants can compete on other qualities (such as brand, service and delivery) of certain product according to consumers' preferences. In this case, it is important for merchants to exhibit their features to every buyer regardless of whether he would make a purchase with them in current trading round. This is because the consumers may come back in the future once they find a matchup between the merchant's features and their needs. Therefore, it is definitly to merchants' benefits to participate such negotiation. The protocol gives them chances to establish their positive reputation.

The above discussions justify the secure agent-mediated auctionlike negotiation protocol as a fair, open and rational negotiation protocol for the Internet retail commerce.

3.2 Performance and flexibility

The proposed auctionlike negotiation protocol is asynchronous. Under Internet scenario, this feature makes the protocol exhibit better performance than traditional online auction. During English auction process, bidders need to connect to the remote server to send their bids. After that, they must contact the server again to get current bid and then based on it, prepare for their next bid. Thus every bidder need to communicate twice to change price by one unit following the dominant strategies in English auction. Although bidders can send agent to remote server to bid on their behalf, their valuations may leak out in this way because agent data are open to the server. For the proposed protocol, in every round of negotiation, two bidders in fact directly send bids to each other, thus their every communication message can lead to a unit decreasing of the price (except the failure notification and its reply). Therefore the communication load during the auction can be greatly reduced and system performance are improved in the proposed protocol.

Another benefit asynchronous protocol brings in is flexibility. In traditional online auction, a big problem is the long delay between starting auctions and purchasing the product. The reason is the auctioneer needs to wait for a critical mass of bidders to boost the bid. In the proposed protocol, the trade agents act as mobile auctioneers. Rather than wait passively for the incoming bidders, mobile agents are able to actively seek the potential bidders through information gathering. This shortens the delay during the auction. On the other hand, buyer also can control the negotiation delay through setting the termination conditions which includes agent lifetime and number of the merchants agent needs to visit. Buyers in a hurry may let agent return early with somewhat higher purchase price while patient ones may give agent enough time to locate an optimal bargain. The auction process therefore can cater to buyers' different requirements.

Mobile agent-mediated negotiation also has advantage in compatibility. Since major portion of the protocol is executed by agent, merchants need not prepare special modules for the protocol except some softwares to accommodate agent. Therefore, from merchants' viewpoint, they need not pay much extra expense to adopt the proposed protocol if they already took other kinds of agent-mediated negotiation protocols. In addition, the maintenance and upgrade of the protocol become easy since most modification can be made on trade agents' side.

3.3 Security issues

In order for mobile agent to run, he has to expose his codes and data to the host environment which supplies the means for agent to run. The host can always scan the agent for information and alter agent state and code. Thus the mobile agent is unprotected from the host.

Current consensus is that is computationally impossible to protect mobile agents from malicious hosts. Instead of tackling the problem from a computational (difficult) point of view, current research [8] is looking at sociological means of enforcing good host behavior.

In the proposed auctionlike protocol, trade agent acts as auctioneer. Just as analyzed before, auctioneer in a traditional English auction has nothing to conceal from bidders. Actually it may be in his benefit to open his valuation to get better payoff. Therefore, the trade agents in the protocol have no confidential information to protect from host's scanning.

On the other hand, the malicious merchants also have little opportunity to tamper with trade agents without being detected. Since there are always a WA residing in the current winner's server, the malicious actions to delete the winner's information from BA's data are easy to be detected. The winner may want to change the MB to get higher payment. However, his signature on the failure notification carried by BA will reveal this illegal action. Another kind of attack is to modify agent's routing list, thus leading the trade agent to "barren land" where he can hardly find any ideal bidders. The WS may have the intention to do this. To protect such an attack, we let the agent start information brokering only from the loser's server. The winner has to keep the agent until the end of the trading or his changing to the loser. Since loser gets no payoff while he has the risk to be detected if he tampers with the agent (remember servers must preserve nonrepudiation evidence in case of buyer's investigation), it is in his benefit to keep good behaviours.

4 Conclusion

Mobile agents have great potentials to provide high performance, flexible and reliable automatic negotiation services to both online and mobile consumers once certain obtstacles (such as security and resource limitation) are overcome. Although auctions possess characteristics which supply soluations to these difficulties, as retail negotiation protocols, they suffer from other problems such as irrational consumer-seller relation and low performance. To make full use of the favorable features of auctions while adapt them to cater for the requirements of the retail commerce, we proposed a secure agent-mediated auctionlike negotiation protocol. The protocol successfully inherits the openness and fairness features of English auctions and take advantage of them to overcome most of obstacles to the mobile agent based negoatiation such as security and resource limitation. On the other hand, it also renovates traditional online auctions by rationalizing the consumer-seller relation and imporving the system performance and flexibility. The analysis in the paper manifest that the proposed protocol not only provides mobile agents with a reliable platform to exhibit their benefits but introduces a novel approach to the Internet retail negoatiations. Actually, it enables the personal purchase auctions with minimal expense over a maximal merchant space. The retailers will also get their payoff from the protocol by the additional opportunties to promote their products/services and particularities in business.

We have developed a prototype system for the proposed protocols using Java and IBM Aglet. Futher improvements will be made based on experimental results.

References

1. Forrester Research Report. On-Line Internet Spending. 1997.
2. Robert H.Guttman and Pattie Maes, Agent-mediated Integrative Negotiation for Retail Electronic Commerce. Proceedings of Workshop on Agent Mediated Electronic Trading (AMET'98), Minneapolis, Minnesota, USA. May 1998
3. Carrie Beam, Arie Segev, J.George Shanthikumar. Electronic Negotiation through Internet-based Auctions. CITM Working Paper 96-WP-1019, available at http://haas.berkeley.edu/citm/wp-1019-summary.html
4. R.Guttman and P.Maes. Cooperative vs. Competitive Multi-Agent Negotiations in Retail Electronic Commerce. Proceedings of the Second International Workshop on Cooperative Information Agents(CIA'98), Paris, France, July 3-8, 1998.
5. E.Schewartz, Webonomics. Nine Essential Principle for Growing Your Bussiness on the World Wide Web Broadway Books, 1997
6. McAfee, R.P. and J.McMillan. Auction and Bidding, Journal of Economic Literature, 1987, 699-738.
7. Sanjiv Ranjan Das, Rangarajan K. Sundaram, Auction Theory: A Summary with Application to Treasury Markets. Working Paper 5873. National Bureau of Economic Research.
8. N.Borenstein. Email with a Mind of its Own: The Safe-Tcl Language for Enabled Mail. IFIP WG 65 Conference, Barcelona, May, 1994, North Holland, Amsterdam, 1994.
9. Zlotkin, G. and Rosenschein, J. S. (1989), "Negotiation and Task Sharing among Autonomous Agents in Cooperative Domains", Proceedings of the 11th IJCAI, Detroit, Michigan, 912-917
10. D.Zeng and K.Sycara, Bayesian Learning in Negotiation. *Working Notes of the AAAI 1996 Stanford Spring Symposium Series on Adaptation, Co-evoluation, and Learning in Multiagent Systems* .
11. Sandholm, T. 1993. An Implementation of the Contract Net Protocol Based on Marginal Cost Calculations. Eleventh National Conference on Artificial Intelligence (AAAI-93), Washington DC, pp. 256-262.

Semantic Information Brokering
How Can a Multi-agent Approach Help?

Amit Sheth, Vipul Kashyap[1], and Tarcisio Lima[2]

Large Scale Distributed Information Systems Lab.
University of Georgia, Athens GA 30602 USA
{amit, kashyap, tarcisio}@cs.uga.edu
http://lsdis.cs.uga.edu

Abstract. The challenge of information overload in dealing with ever increasing variety and size of digital data on the Web is now receiving serious attention of the researchers. The information brokering architecture provides one approach to addressing issues at data, information and knowledge levels. While reasonable progress has been made in achieving system interoperability as well as syntax and structure level interoperability of data and information systems, the semantic level is the key to a more satisfactory solution. This paper discusses whether a multi-agent approach can help achieve semantic information brokering by supporting three of the capabilities needed: (a) extract and use semantic metadata descriptions from the underlying data; (b) handle information requests independent of the structure, format and media of the underlying data; and (c) share, exchange, and interoperate across collections of knowledge represented using multiple domain specific ontologies.

1 Introduction

We are witnessing today an explosive growth in the creation of digital data, facilitated by affordable multimedia systems and capture devices. The data is managed by autonomous repositories (often seen as parts of Web sites), and vary in formats and representation from structured (e.g., relational databases) to semi-structured (e.g., e-mail, newsgroups, HTML pages) and unstructured (e.g., image data) formats. Excellent and near-ubiquitous connectivity afforded by the Internet, the web, and distributed computing infrastructures (resulting in a computing and information systems infrastructure referred to as the Global Information Infrastructure – GII), has lead to easy access to a large number of autonomous and heterogeneous information sources. However, easy potential access has not necessarily translated into effective use or user productivity. Data is accessible using a variety of forms (browsing, keyword, and attributed-based queries). Access to this huge variety and size of data, contrasted with dominance of relatively low precision access techniques and tools as well as the uses

---

[1] Currently at Telcordia Technologies, E-mail: kashyap@research.telcordia.com

[2] Also at Computer Science Department, Federal University of Juiz de Fora, MG, Brazil

that go beyond original intent, has lead to the well recognized problem of information overload.

For over two decades interoperability has been crucial for modern information systems. Starting from earlier research in federated databases, the need to consider the three dimensions of distribution, heterogeneity and autonomy has been well-recognized [25]. The scale and variety of issues involved has made it necessary to achieve a better understanding of interoperability concerns. One perspective, in the form of the types of heterogeneity, we need to deal with and the corresponding levels of interoperability issues is presented in Figure 1 [23]. With the benefit of past and current research, increasing complexity and variety of issues involved in dealing with information overload, the focus on interoperability is decidedly shifting from system, syntax, and structure to semantics [23]. As we move from managing data to information and, in future, knowledge, along with supporting increased specialization of work performed by knowledge workers, the need for achieving semantic interoperability has become more crucial than ever.

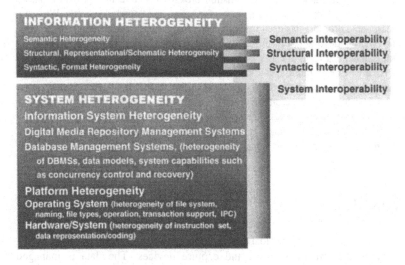

Fig. 1. A taxonomy of heterogeneity and interoperability

We propose an information brokering architecture emphasizing the strategies for achieving semantic interoperability to deal with the vexing information overload problem. Furthermore, we present a potential application for agent technology in this context. Increasing specialization of work forces people to work in an independent manner – a requirement that is readily reflected in a multi-agent system. The modular, autonomous, cooperative, and distributed nature of a multi-agent system also mirrors closely with the availability of information on the GII. However, to be able to perform semantic information brokering, agents need to be more "intelligent" especially in the areas of sharing, exchanging, and interoperating across different knowledge collections or domain specific ontologies.

Section 2 presents the issues related to information heterogeneity, the current trend of globalization in current information systems and their impact on information overload. We define and discuss our information brokering architecture in Section 3. The relevance and potential applicability of multi-agent systems in supporting semantic information brokering is discussed in Section 4. An example from our current work in supporting semantic interoperability in a Digital Earth prototype system is also given. Section 5 discusses the conclusions and future work.

2 Information Overload: Impact of Heterogeneity and Globalization

The information overload created by the necessity of keeping track of the various data types, representation formats, and query languages is further compounded by the trend of globalization in current and future information systems, participation of a broad variety of users – both naïve and specialized – with use of data well beyond the original intention of their collections, and so on. This section provides a brief overview of the sources of information overload and key techniques or capabilities that can help alleviate the problem.

2.1 Impact of Heterogeneity on Information Overload

Many types of heterogeneity are due to technological differences. For example, differences in hardware and operating system platforms. Researchers and developers have been working on resolving such heterogeneity for years. We refer to these as *system heterogeneities*. Differences in machine-readable aspects of data representation, formats and storage for digital media may be referred to as *syntactic heterogeneity*. We consider representational heterogeneity involving schematic mismatches and differences in data modeling constructs as *structural heterogeneity*. Differences in meaning are dependent on the vocabulary and terminology used to express the information and the contexts in which it is interpreted. They are referred to as *semantic heterogeneity*. Interoperability issues that deal with semantic heterogeneity are receiving increasing importance lately (e.g., see [19]). We now discuss common types of structural and semantic heterogeneities and how they contribute to information overload.

Differences in Structure. Different data models provide different structural primitives. For example, object oriented data models support inheritance while relational data models do not (data model heterogeneity). Even if the data model is the same, similar information content may be represented differently in different schemas (schematic heterogeneity). When retrieving information from systems using different structures to represent and store data, an *information overhead* related to keeping track of these differences and reconciling them is imposed upon the user.

Differences in Query Language. Different languages were used to manipulate data represented in different data models. Even when two DBMSs support the same data model, differences in their query languages (e.g., QUEL and SQL, or different versions of SQL) contribute to the heterogeneity. In this case the information overhead imposed on the user is related to keeping track of the appropriate languages and operations to be used when retrieving information from a given information system.

Semi-structured or Unstructured Data. Increasingly, the data available on the GII is unstructured and in some cases semi-structured. Examples of unstructured data are images, free text and video data. Some textual data such as an HTML page or a bibliographic entry comes in a semi-structured format. Data guides and document type definitions expressed as grammar rules have been proposed to model semi-structured data. The definition and use of wrappers and translators typically handle this type of data. In this case the information overhead to the user is related to keeping track and defining the appropriate wrapper and translator to retrieve information from a semi-structured or unstructured data source.

Media Heterogeneity. Information sources often store data corresponding to different media such as text and image. Often a response to an information request requires correlation of information stored in different media. For example, it may be necessary to correlate the area and population characteristics of a region (textual data) with the land cover and relief characteristics (image data). In this case the information overhead is related to the user extracting the relevant information (i.e., keeping track of the relevant text and image processing methods) and the actual correlation of the various characteristics of the region.

Terminology (and Language) Heterogeneity. A user has to choose different ontologies and vocabularies (e.g., an LCC based ontology for querying bibliographic data, FGDC for geo-spatial data, an ontology based on DDC or UDK) depending on which ontology or vocabulary has been used by the information source to describe its information content. There is an information overhead to the user related keeping track of the appropriate vocabulary and (re-)formulation of the information request to get at the information stored in a given source.

Contextual Heterogeneity. The same information request can retrieve different types of information depending under which contextual assumptions it is interpreted in. In current information systems results are retrieved under all possible interpretations of the request. A large proportion of the result returned is based on contextual interpretations that are completely irrelevant to the information request, thus leading to information overload on the user.

2.2 Impact of Globalization on Information Overload

Whereas a significant amount of information overload is introduced by structural and semantic heterogeneity especially due to the various types of digital data, the trend for globalization has increased the complexity of information overload. The scope of the problem has increased from tens to hundreds of databases to millions of information sources on the GII. We now discuss the main effects of globalization and their impact on information overload.

Information Resource Discovery. Due to the presence of millions of information sources on the GII, it is no longer feasible to expect the user to determine and keep track of the repositories relevant to his information request. It may also be the case that an information request may not be completely satisfied at an information source or that one or more sources may contain information similar to, though not exactly the same, as that required by the request. This is the information resource discovery problem.

Modeling of Information Content. Modeling of information at different levels of abstraction, e.g., information may be modeled at a more general level in one information source compared to another. Also, information modeled at one source may not be modeled in another. This introduces an information overhead on the user related to keeping track of the level of abstraction at which the results returned. The user also has to keep track of which information is modeled at which source. Given the millions of information sources, the number of possibilities related to a GII request may be overwhelmingly large.

Querying of Information Content. A typical scenario on the GII is the distribution of information required to satisfy a request across a wide variety of sources. It is crucial to be able to identify the subset of relevant information at a source and to combine partially relevant information across different sources

Information Focusing. This is the process of identification and retrieval of a subset of required information at an information source. In a typical scenario on the GII, different information sources would provide relevant information to a different extent. The most obvious choice of the source from which information will be retrieved is the one which returns most (or all) of the relevant information. In that case the user will have to keep track of which source has the most relevant information.

Information Correlation. This is the process of combining partially relevant information from different repositories to return a more precise and complete answer to the information request. In a typical scenario on the GII, there will be a combinatorial number of possibilities to be considered for determining the most precise and complete combination of partial information. Given the huge number of information sources, there will be an exponential number of possibilities, leading to an enormous information overhead.

3 Information Brokering: Handling the Information Overload

Our approach to dealing with information overload on the GII is to propose an *information brokering* architecture that allows for a study of a broad variety of interdependent issues, followed by recognition and use of the existing research and technologies that provide building blocks for addressing syntactic, schematic and struc-

308

tural issues, while addressing the new ways to address the difficult problem of semantic heterogeneity.

Information brokering can be viewed as interplay across the three dimensions illustrated in Figure 2. This representation facilitates a pedagogical discussion of the information brokering architecture. A minimal definition of an information brokering architecture on the GII is **an architecture that guides creation and management of information systems and semantic-level solutions to serve a variety of information stakeholders (participants), including** *providers, facilitators, consumers,* **and the business involved in creating, enhancing and using of information.** Semantics is an important aspect of this architecture, which is reflected in explicit attention to understand and exploit the meaning and use of data as well as in understanding participants' needs, intentions and understanding of information (not data). To a certain extent, this architecture borrows from, and builds upon, the federated database and information systems architectures and the mediator architecture [26].

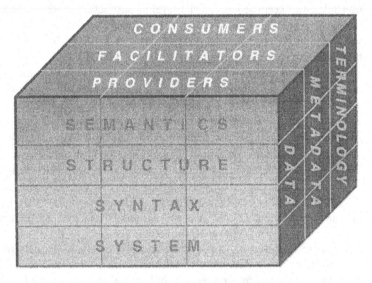

Fig. 2. Dimensions of information brokering

We first discuss and identify the key players on the GII and define information brokering based on the interchange of information between them. We then present the different levels of brokering that should be enabled by an information brokering architecture and discuss the role of *facilitators* in enabling the brokering.

3.1 Stakeholders and Beneficiaries in Information Brokering

The key players on the GII are the *information providers* which export information, *information consumers* which use information, and the *information facilitators* who help to match the consumers requests with the information exported by the providers (Figure 3)[3].

Information Providers. The GII consists of the millions of data/information repositories made available through information systems provided by various information providers. Examples of data/information repositories are newswires, corporate statistics, etc. and may be represented as structured (e.g., databases), semi-structured (e.g., HTML pages), or unstructured data (e.g., text files).

Information Consumers. Millions of consumers utilize services and information made available by the numerous information providers on the GII. These consumers might be individual users (or their agents) on workstations or application programs running on many machines at the same time.

Information Facilitators. The information consumer on the GII would be deluged by a variety of information available (information overload) from the millions of information providers. Information facilitators enable **brokering** between the information consumer and provider that may be defined as:

- Arbitration between the information consumers and providers for resolving the *information impedance*, i.e., the differing worldviews of the consumers and providers.
- Dynamic re-interpretation of information requests for determination of relevant *information services* and *products*.
- Dynamic creation and composition of *information products* after suitable assembly or correlation of *information components* available from the various providers, or other value addition activities.

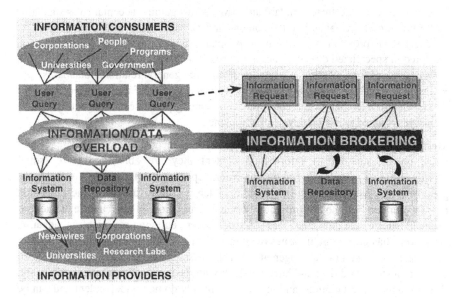

Fig. 3. Information brokering – stakeholder perspective

---

[3] Organizational (including ownership), financial and business, legal and other issues are relevant but we will not discuss them here.

3.2 Levels of Information Brokering

We view the information on the GII at three levels – *data*, which comprises of the data represented in a variety of syntactic representation stored in information sources connected to each other over a network; *metadata* which may be thought of as information/data about the data and used to capture information content; and *semantics*, which are best captured using standard terminologies and domain ontologies and are used to specify metadata descriptions capturing information content. Brokering at the data level, and partially at the metadata level has made excellent progress primarily due to the development and use of widespread standards [20]. However, current R&D challenges involve investigating issues in semantic brokering using domain specific metadata, terminologies, and context.

Data Brokering Standards-Based Interoperability. One of the oldest approaches to achieving interoperability among heterogeneous components is to agree on a standard that achieves a limited amount of homogeneity among them. The key reason for the success of these standards has been that they were compelling and easy to use and fulfilled an important need at the right time. Some examples are:

- The TCP/IP and HTTP protocols have become the de-facto standard for transmission of data over a network. These protocols support the transmission of data packets over the network.
- Other protocols like CORBA/IIOP and Java/RMI support the transmission of data objects and are gaining fast acceptance in the Internet community.
- HTML is also a de-facto standard and XML is fast gaining acceptance as standards for markup of textual and digital content, and for semi-structured data.
- The LDAP protocol has become a popular standard for accessing information stored in specialized directories or databases. The JDBC protocol on the other hand is a standard for accessing information from more general relational databases.
- Protocols such as OKBC and standards such as KQML/KIF are being proposed for knowledge interchange and communication among processes and agents, but have not yet reached sufficient levels of acceptance.

Metadata-Based Brokering. At a very broad level, metadata may be distinguished based on the amount of information content they are able to capture (some classifications of metadata based on this criteria appears in [4]). Along this spectrum, great progress has been made in enabling interoperability based on metadata that capture limited or no information content and those that capture structural characteristics of the data. Database schema is a very common source of metadata. A lot of work has been done in issues relating to the use of these metadata for resolving schematic and structural heterogeneity [2, 13]. These techniques have, however, been focused on structured data and have not dealt with the issues of semantics adequately. Data formats, representations and media are typically domain independent and can be automatically characterized by structural and media-specific metadata.

Further progress in achieving interoperability at this level has been achieved through the use of models for metadata (also called meta-models), or standards or specifications for metadata. Some well-accepted metadata standards or specifications for domain independent metadata are the Dublin Core and Warwick frameworks. These capture rather limited information and consequently have limited value in achieving interoperability. However, domain specific standards, such as geo-spatial standards and specifications (e.g., FGDC, OGIS, and SDTS) provide a more meaningful level of interoperability at this level when multiple information providers subscribe to the same metadata standard or specification. In a GII however, it is not only possible but likely that different providers in the same domain subscribe to different metadata standards or specification, once again leaving complex interoperability challenges. As domain specific metadata bring more semantics to the information they help model, we need to resort to the semantic interoperability level to address the challenges [12]. It is unlikely to that we can device a fully automatic approach for achieving such interoperability, and involvement of domain experts or more comprehensive representation of context will be needed. The techniques, however, should be designed in a manner to minimize the participation with the optimal utilization of the domain knowledge of the experts. A context sensitive approach for defining and using these mappings can be found in [11].

Semantic Information Brokering. The critical issue in capturing the information content to perform semantic information brokering is the terminology used to characterize the information content. It may be noted that domain specific metadata and their mappings to structural and media specific metadata discussed in the previous section are necessarily constructed by using terms specific to an information domain. These domain specific terms are provided by the domain experts responsible for the construction and mapping of the metadata descriptions. This leads us into the issue of semantic heterogeneity where the heterogeneity may stem from the following factors:

- The use of different terms to describe similar information (synonymy) and the use of similar terms to describe dissimilar information (homonymy).
- The use of different modeling choices for describing similar information. For example, describing a student using the concept *student* as opposed to the concept *graduate-student*.
- The use of different metadata expressions describing similar information.
- Different context relevant to creation of data and information requests.

Here we propose an approach[4] that has its roots in the standardization approach used for data brokering. We propose the re-use of standardized terminologies captured as domain specific ontologies. A domain specific ontology may be defined as the specification of a representational vocabulary for a shared domain of discourse which may include definitions of classes, relations, functions and other objects [5]. Metadata descriptions can then be constructed from ontological concepts. Some well-known ontologies/thesauri that attempt to capture and represent a global collection of knowledge are the Cyc [15] and WordNet ontologies [18]. Attempts have also been made to use a common domain ontology for information gathering within the context

---

[4] This approach addresses only some aspect of the above, and does not integrate with a capability to address context differences (see [10] for efforts in this area).

of an information domain [1, 16]. However, we recognize that it is not practical to design a common ontology satisfying the needs of the various user communities. Thus we need to support multiple ontologies and contexts within and across different domains of information. Concepts in these ontologies may differ in the ways enumerated above. Also, there might be multiple information contexts within the same domain ontology. True semantic interoperability requires interoperation across multiple ontologies and contexts. Some initial approaches to define and specify contexts and use them for information integration and brokering are presented in [10, 21, and 6]. As far as supporting interoperation across ontologies is concerned, techniques need to be developed to characterize overlaps across different ontologies and use them to merge different overlapping ontologies. The merged ontologies may then be used to reformulate the metadata descriptions across different ontologies. These reformulations would also typically result in change in semantics. Techniques for measuring the extent of changes also need to be developed. An initial attempt at handling this difficult problem is the OBSERVER system [17].

3.3 The Role of Facilitators on the GII

We discussed above the three levels at which information brokering may be performed on the GII. We now identify the ways *information facilitators* can help enable the various brokering functions and capabilities discussed in the previous sub-section.

- The facilitator constructs and designs multimedia views using metadata descriptions from standardized terminologies available to the consumers. These descriptions enable the consumers to retrieve and search for relevant information with greater precision.
- The facilitator maintains and stores associations between the digital data exported by the providers and the metadata descriptions designed by it. These associations enable the providers to increase the likelihood of the consumers "discovering" the information exported by them. These associations also help broker between the different worldviews of the providers and the consumers.
- The facilitator thus acts as a bridge between the providers and the consumers and also enables a transition from the structural aspects to the semantic aspect of the information.

A multitude of terminologies may be used on the GII to characterize information exported/requested by the providers and consumers. **Domain specific ontologies** are used to characterize vocabularies and terminological relationships between them for interoperation. This helps reduce information overload by: (a) precise specification of the information domain of the information request; and (b) efficient and precise semantic interoperation as the number of terminological relationships between terms across ontologies is typically an order of magnitude smaller than the number of terms in all ontologies [17]. Some of the services the facilitator can offer are to:

- provide a collection of standard terminologies captured as domain specific ontologies to the consumer, who can choose and align himself to the one closest to his worldview. These collections can also be used by the providers to construct appropriate metadata descriptions.

- support the interoperation across multiple domain specific ontologies. A facilitator[5] maintains the inter-ontological terminological relationships across the different ontologies. It thus provides a service to both the consumers and providers, as they can introduce new ontologies into the system. The facilitator is responsible for "incorporating" the new ontology by maintaining the terminological relationship between the new and the existing ontologies on the GII.
- support the transformation of information requests across different ontologies in a manner that minimizes the loss of information. Thus the consumer's specification of an information request using ontologies of his choice is reformulated by a facilitator for other ontologies used by the information sources, thus retrieving more relevant information.

An information facilitator thus helps enable *semantic interoperability* across the different world views/ontologies supported by the consumers and the providers. The key objective of this approach is to reduce the problem of knowing the structure and semantics of data in the huge number of information sources on the GII to understanding and navigating a significantly smaller number of world views and ontologies.

3.4 Relating Information Brokering to Other Approaches

Approaches for interoperability across information systems were proposed in the context of database management systems in 1980s. They focused on issues related to the distribution, heterogeneity, and autonomy of information in the context of providing integrated access to databases. A federated architecture was proposed for interoperation across a set of databases [25]. A federated schema designed after integration of the schemas of the component databases is used to interoperate across the different systems. A drawback with this approach has been a relatively static nature of the integration and the inability of the approach to scale beyond tens of information systems.

Mediator approaches propose a more dynamic approach for integration of information. Wiederhold [27] defines a mediator as "a software module that exploits encoded knowledge about some sets or subsets of data to create information about a higher layer of applications". One interesting class of mediators have been those used to encapsulate and fuse information in semi-structured data sources using (multimedia) views and object templates (see [26] and [23] for examples). One shortcoming of the mediator approach is that the information model is typically implicit in the definition of the mediator. While the federated database architecture distinctly focused on data representation through different types of schemas, mediator architecture focus on software modules that perform value added activities, but kept the information model hidden.

---

[5] Any time we mention a facilitator, an alternative of cooperative agent based realization may be considered.

Given a large number of user communities on the GII, there is an urgent need to make the information model explicit and also support multiple information models belonging to the user communities. Although the mediator concept remains a viable component of information brokering, the latter recognizes additional dimensions of the problem space, and a presents a multi-layer approach for a more comprehensive solution to the challenges in GII that covers both data/information/knowledge (as emphasized in the federated database architecture) and software perspectives (as emphasized in the mediator architecture).

4 Appropriateness of Multi-agent Systems

There has been a lot of research in identifying and describing essential features of multi-agent systems from different perspectives [14, 7]. The various features of multi-agent systems make them an appropriate choice for implementing information brokering techniques on the GII, especially relevant is the fact that agents can also be mobile. However, in order to implement semantic interoperability and brokering, there are certain deficiencies. Some extensions to agent functionalities so as to enable them to support semantic information brokering over the GII are to:

- capture, view and interrogate the semantics of the underlying (multimedia) data. Thus, an information agent should be able to extract, associate semantic metadata descriptions or design mappings from the data, either automatically or in collaboration with other agents and humans. It should also be possible to represent and reason about the context in all aspects of information management, including data creation and information processing.
- request information without regards to the underlying data type, structure, format or media in which the information may be represented or stored. This is important in reducing the information overload on the user, as he doesn't have to keep track of the various possibilities. An information agent should have the capability of interpreting an information request in different ways depending on which media the information may be potentially stored in.
- support interoperation across multiple standard terminologies or domain specific ontologies. This helps reduce information overload on the user, as he can choose the one closest to his needs. The information agent should be able to identify related ontologies, reformulate information requests according to the new terminology and minimize the loss of information while retrieving information corresponding to another terminology.

We now discuss possible use of a multi-agent system architecture for information brokering with the help of an example.

4.1 Agents for Media Independent Correlation of Information

One of the key capabilities for semantic information is to be able to support correlation of information at a higher *level of abstraction*, and *independent of the medium of representation of the information* [8 and 22]. We need to model *domain specific* metadata for multimedia documents. Such metadata should necessarily be media-independent though they may be mapped to the associated documents via media-dependent attributes.

Example: Let us consider a City Council making decisions over the planning of a new landfill. Landfills are a common practice worldwide and by far the most com-

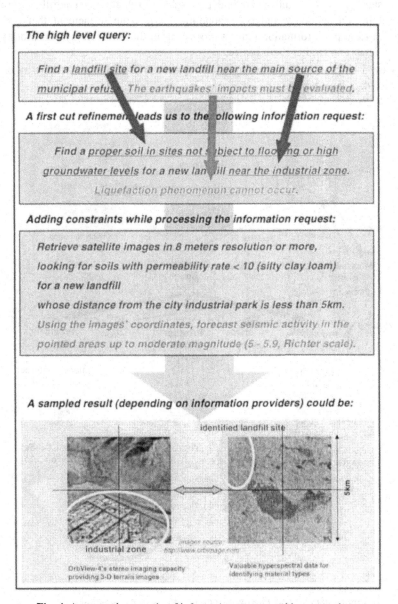

Fig. 4. An example scenario of information request and its processing

mon waste disposal method in the United States, probably accounting for more than 90 percent[6] of the nation's municipal refuse. Our example scenario comes in support of one of the suggestions for Digital Earth scenarios sampled by the "First Inter-Agency Digital Earth Working Group" [9], an effort on behalf of NASA's inter-agency Digital Earth Program. This is a simplified yet coherent hands-on learning interaction exercise with the Digital Earth. It should be refined through actual experience.

The starting point would be to find the best location for the landfill. Figure 4 shows a high-level query and corresponding intermediate refinement that occurs during an example information request processing in the InfoQuilt system prototype being applied to a Digital Earth project.

Figure 5 shows a relevant subset of the system architecture that primarily deals with metadata level issues.

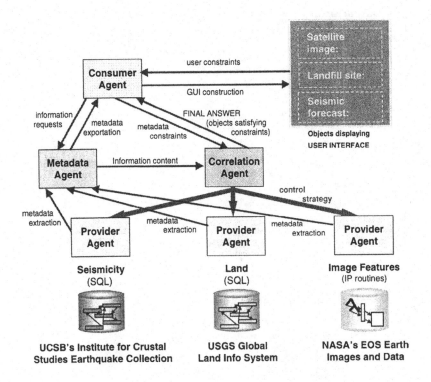

Fig. 5. Agents for media independent correlations

One of the challenges in GII is that information providers are autonomous and data change at different repositories independently. There are numerous issues related to keeping metadata consistent as the data change, as well as there are changes at system (e.g., new host of a site), syntax (e.g., change in data format) and structure (e.g., change in the Web site). Prototype systems such as VideoAnywhere [24], InfoSleuth [3] and InfoQuilt demonstrate implementations of fully distribute system consisting of autonomous agents.

Some of the agent interactions in processing the above information request are as follows:

Provider agents. They interact with the sources (including Web sites and databases), extracting relevant metadata, e.g., *aerial videography* for *industrial zones* and *landfill sites* or *soil* features.

Metadata agent. In cooperation with the provider agents and the consumer agent, keeps the metadata consistent to the level desired by the system and the information requests. It provides mapping from its own metadata, e.g., *distance* and *area* in addition to the schema metadata exported by the provider agents managing the structured databases, e.g., *seismicity* and *land,* that are sent to the consumer agent. A metabase is updated using metadata sent asynchronously by multiple provider agents. It also associates and utilizes symbolic metadata descriptions to capture the information content that is sent to the correlation agent.

Correlation Agent. It performs functions similar to some of the mediators [25] and InfoSleuth's broker and task planning and execution agents [3], and adds reasoning to support terminological differences related to the use of multiple ontologies [17]. It determines the order of computation of the metadata constraints (the control strategy) based on the information content received from the metadata agent and the metadata constraints, from the consumer agent. For example, it may decide to compute metadata from structured data before image data as computations on structured data are cheaper and the results can be used to reduce expensive image processing, e.g., *forecasting seismic activity* is a compute intensive task that should be done only after the prospective landfill areas are determined. The objects satisfying the constraints are then sent to the consumer agent.

Consumer Agent. It specifies relationships between the metadata descriptions by specifying an information request that is queried to the metadata agent, determining the exported metadata used to construct the user interface. It accepts constraints from the user, e.g., *image resolution > 12* or *soil permeability rate <10,* which are mapped to constraints on the metadata. It fuses the different media type objects received from the correlation agent and presents the final answer in a comprehensive GUI, using appropriate media.

4.2 Agents for Inter-Ontology Interoperation

We believe that it will be necessary to support multiple, independently created and managed ontologies that capture the terminologies of different and sometimes overlapping domains. Ontologies can be used by consumer agents to assist a in constructing information requests. Alternatively a facilitator can use multiple ontologies in the process of defining a media-independent information correlation[7]. For our scenario ontologies for earth science, soil science, water science, and space science are used (along with several domain-independent ontologies). Fragments of a relevant subset of ontologies are shown in Figure 6. In this case, it will no longer be feasible for the user to repeatedly specify the same information request using different but related ontologies. Thus inter-ontology interoperation is a critical requirement for semantic information brokering.

We now discuss the functional extensions to agents in order to support semantic information brokering that involves support for multiple ontologies. A typical agent interaction is described below and illustrated in Figure 7. Relevant capabilities of some types of agents are discussed next.

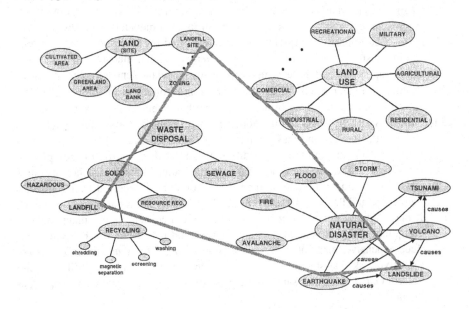

Fig. 6. Subsets of the ontologies used in the example scenario

Ontology Agent. Manages the domain ontologies that capture standardized terminologies. This includes providing ontological elements and the interrelationships between them and perform inferences on ontological expressions. A first very simple terminological example from our scenario relates ontology for *waste disposals* with *municipal refuse* in the information request.

Integration Agent. Keeps track of inter-ontological relationships between terms across different ontologies. These interrelationships enable the semantic inte-

---

[7] This concept is being extended to that of Information Landscapes (Iscapes) in a Digital Earth prototype being jointly developed with the Univ. of California, Santa Barbara at the Digital Library II effort.

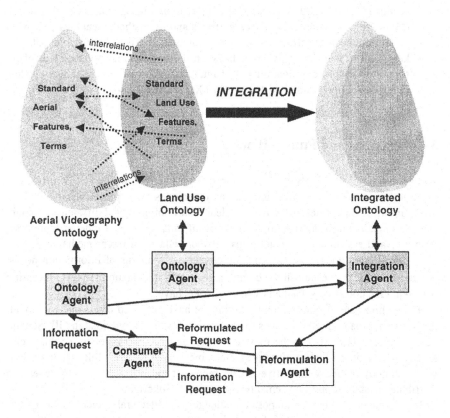

Fig. 7. Agents for inter-ontology interoperation

gration of ontologies, which is a crucial capability required for semantic information brokering. For our scenario, integrating *aerial-videography* with the process of *land use classification* is identified as an interesting example, leading to the gathering of ground-truth satellite image interpretation and post-classification land-cover mappings, a key point for solving the information request at hand. Much of the work to date has been limited with the simpler type of relationships, such as synonyms, hypernyms, and hyponyms [17]. However, support of more complex relationships is needed.

Reformulation Agent. Reformulates an information request expressed in a particular ontology into another information request using terms from another related ontology. The reformulation leads to a loss of information, the characterization of which is an important capability [17]. In our information request example we need to deal with *magnitude measures* of earthquakes. However, the metadata we have in the related ontology expresses *intensity measures*. Both describe earthquakes quantitatively but have different meanings. *Magnitude* measures the energy released at the source of the earthquake using a logarithmic scale (the Richter scale) that runs from 1 to 9. *Intensity* measures the strength of shaking produced by the earthquake at a certain location with gradations from I to XII (Mercalli scale). Based on observed effects and no mathematical basis, intensity is determined from effects on people, structures and natural environment. The key point is that the equivalence between these measures produces loss of information in the sense that quakes of intensities II to III are roughly equivalent to quakes of magnitude 3 to 4, and XI to XII are about 8 to 9.

5 Conclusions and Future Work

The only way to effectively deal with information overload in the GII is to increasingly address the semantic-level issues. Key techniques to support semantics include use of multiple ontologies as the basis to deal with terminological difference, domain specific metadata to bring data to the level of information, media-independent correlations to address semantic relationships between data of different media and types, use of profiles to understand information consumers' patterns of information needs, and use of context to establish the common ground in information request processing between what consumers want and what providers have.

The architecture of information brokering we have proposed offers one way to address a very broad variety of issues to deal with information overload in GII. Semantic information brokering is the most important and novel component of this architecture which uses techniques such as those mentioned above. Multi-agent systems with autonomous and cooperative agents represent an attractive way to develop a distributed system supporting semantic information brokering.

In this paper, we have juxtaposed challenges, architectural principles for understanding various dimensions of the problem, and potential of applying multi-agent technologies. A host of fundamental and practical issues need to be addressed, including effective human participants in addressing semantic problems, representation and reasoning of complex information in context sensitive manner, effective ways to discover interontological relationships and using them in reasoning to support semantic interoperability, issues of management (including performance and quality of service issues), making agents increasingly more cooperative and intelligent to deal with semantics, and so on. Some of these are being addressed at the LSDIS lab as part of its InfoQuilt system and Digital Library-II efforts.

References

1. Y Arens, C Knoblock and W Shen, Query Reformulation for Dynamic Information Integration. In Wiederhold G (Ed.) *Intelligent Integration of Information*. Kluwer Academic Publishers: 11-42, 1996.
2. C Batini, M Lenzerini and S Navathe, A Comparative Analysis of Methodologies for Database Schema Integration. *ACM Computing Surveys* 18(4): 323–64, 1986.

3. R. Bayardo, W. Bohrer, R. Brice, A. Cichocki, G. Fowler, A. Helal, V. Kashyap, T. Ksiezyk, G. Martin, M. Nodine, M. Rashid, M. Rusinkiewicz, R. Shea, C. Unnikrishnan, A. Unruh, D. Woelk, Semantic Integration of Information in Open and Dynamic Environments, ACM SIGMOD '97, May 1997.

4. S Boll, W Klas and A Sheth, Overview on Using Metadata to Manage Multimedia Data. In Sheth A, Klas W (Eds.) *Multimedia Data Management: Using Metadata to Integrate and Apply Digital Media.* McGraw-Hill Publishers: 1–23, 1998.

5. T Gruber, The Role of a Common Ontology in Achieving Sharable, Reusable Knowledge Bases. *Proceedings of the 2nd International Conference on Principles of Knowledge Representation and Reasoning, Cambridge:* 601-602, 1991.

6. R Guha, Contexts: A Formalization and Some Applications. *Technical Report STAN-CS-91-1399-Thesis*, Department of Computer Science, Stanford University, 1991.

7. M Huhns and M Singh, *Readings in Agents.* Morgan Kaufmann, 1998.

8. R Jain, InfoScopes: MultiMedia Information Systems. In B. Furht (Ed.) Multimedia Systems and Techniques. Kluwer:217-254, 1996.

9. R. Kahn et al., Digital Earth User Scenario Suggestions, First Inter-Agency Digital Earth Workshop, Greenbelt, MD, June 1998. http://digitalearth.gsfc.nasa.gov/Scenarios199806.htm, accessed on April 29, 1999.

10. V Kashyap and A Sheth, Semantics Based Information Brokering. *Proceedings of the 3rd International Conference on Information and Knowledge Systems*: 363-370, 1994.

11. V Kashyap and A Sheth. Schematic and Semantic Similarities between Objects in Databases: A Context-Based Approach. *The Very Large Databases Journal* 5(4):276-304, 1996.

12. V. Kashyap and A. Sheth (authors) *Semantic Information Brokering across Heterogeneous Digital Data: A Metadata-based Approach.* Kluwer 1999 (to appear).

13. W Kim, I Choi, S Gala and M Scheevel. On Resolving Schematic Heterogeneity in Multidatabase Systems. *Distributed Parallel Databases International Journal* 1: 251-279, 1993.

14. M Klusch (Ed.) *Intelligent Agents: Agent-Based Information Discovery and Management on the Internet.* Springer-Verlag 1999.

15. D Lenat and R Guha, *Building Large Knowledge Based Systems: Representation and Inference in the Cyc Project.* Addison Wesley, 1990.

16. A Levy, D Srivastava and T Kirk, Data Model and Query Evaluation in Global Information Systems. *Intelligent Information Systems* 5(2): 121-143, 1995.

17. E Mena, V Kashyap, A Illarramedi, A Sheth, 1998 Domain Specific Ontologies for Semantic Information Brokering on the Global Information Infrastructure. *Proceedings, International Conference on Formal Ontology in Information Systems (FOIS '98),* Trento:269-283.

18. G Miller, WordNet: A Lexical Database for English. *Communications of the ACM.* 38(11), 1995.

19. A. Ouksel and A. Sheth, Eds., Special Section on Semantic Interoperability in Global Information Systems, SIGMOD Record, Volume 28, Number 1, March 1999.

20. A Paepcke, C Chang, H Garcia-Molina and T Winograd, Interoperability for Digital Libraries Worldwide. *Communications of the ACM* 41(4): 33-43, 1998.

21. E Sciore, M Siegel and A Rosenthal, Context Interchange Using Meta-Attributes. *Proceedings of the 1st International Conference on Information and Knowledge Management (CIKM),* 1992.

22. K Shah and A Sheth, Logical Information Modeling of Web-Accessible Heterogeneous Digital Assets. *Proceedings of the Forum on Research and Technology Advances in Digital Libraries* (ADL'98), Santa Barbara, CA: 266-275, 1998.

23. A Sheth, Changing Focus on Interoperability in Information Systems: From System, Syntax, Structure to Semantics. In M F Goodchild, M J Egenhofer, R Fegeas and C A Kottman (Eds.) *Interoperating Geographic Information Systems*. Kluwer 1999.

24. A Sheth, C Bertram, and K Shah, VideoAnywhere: A System for Searching and Managing Distributed Video Assets, SIGMOD Record, March 1999.

25. A Sheth and J Larson, Federated Database Systems for Managing Distributed, Heterogeneous and Autonomous *Databases, ACM Computing Surveys* 22(3):183-236, 1990.

26. G Wiederhold (Ed.) *Intelligent Integration of Information*. Kluwer 1996.

27. G Wiederhold, Mediation in the Architecture of Future Information Systems. *IEEE Computer Magazine*, 25(3): 38-49, March 1992.

Arbitration and Matchmaking for Agents with Conflicting Interests

Thomas Tesch   Peter Fankhauser

GMD-IPSI Integrated Publication and Information Systems Institute
German National Research Center for Information Technology
Dolivostraße 15, D-64293 Darmstadt, Germany
{tesch,fankhaus}@darmstadt.gmd.de
http://www.darmstadt.gmd.de/oasys

Abstract. The exchange of goods and services among software agents requires reliable and fair brokering mechanisms to match trading parties and to mediate among their conflicting interests. Available trading models for electronic market-places are fixed price selling, bilateral multi-step negotiations, and various forms of auctioning. These models demand trading parties to evaluate appropriate interest matches on their own and encourage them to pretend inexact interests to their advantage. We introduce an arbiter as intermediary that finds buyers and suppliers with best matching interests. The intermediary uses matching and arbitration protocols that ensure better overall benefit than random matches, avoid advantages for agents that manipulate their interests (lies), preserve the mutual privacy of interests of the trading parties, and, if desired, their anonymity. We analyse the protocols with respect to their applicability under various conditions, investigate their robustness with different utility distributions by simulations, and describe which forms of interest manipulations can be avoided.

1 Introduction

The exchange of goods and services among software agents requires reliable and fair brokering mechanisms to match trading parties and to mediate among their conflicting interests. Available trading models for electronic marketplaces are fixed price selling, bilateral multi-step negotiations, and various forms of auctioning. These models demand trading parties to evaluate appropriate interest matches on their own and encourage them to pretend inexact interests to their advantage and to the disadvantage of their trading partners. We introduce a trustbroker as intermediary that finds buyers and sellers with best matching interests. The intermediary uses matching and arbitration protocols that ensure better net benefit than random matches, avoid advantages for agents that manipulate their interests (lies), preserve the mutual privacy of interests of the trading parties, and, if desired, their anonymity. We analyse the protocols with respect to their applicability under various conditions, investigate their robustness with different utility distributions by simulations, and describe which forms of interest manipulations can be avoided.

The paper is structured as follows. In Section 2, we review which properties electronic trading models should employ, and discuss their popular representatives paying attention on their applicability to matchmaking. We introduce three arbitration schemes in Section 3, discuss their net benefit in various settings, and their robustness against fraud. In Section 4, we investigate how simple two-party arbitration can be combined with matchmaking. We show by simulations how matchmaking schemes increase the net benefit. Additionally, we investigate their robustness against interest manipulations. In Section 5 we summarize our results, and outline future work.

2 Trading Models for Electronic Commerce and Related Work

Goods and services are exchanged between trading parties using a variety of trading models. Apart from fixed price selling, more flexible trading forms such as auctioning, bilateral negotiations, and matchmaking are becoming increasingly popular because the Internet can reduce certain types of frictional costs and time incurred in these forms. This trend is illustrated by services like Priceline.com, BidOnline.com, Acses.com etc.

Different trading models may be compared along the following desiderata [Tyg98]:

- *Mechanism design*: a trade model should be designed on economic principles such that fair outcomes are achieved for both parties[RZ94]. This includes robustness against manipulations, i.e., participants should have incentives to act as they truly value the deal in question.
- *Privacy of interests*: participants want to keep their true interests private. This seems paradoxical but is required to avoid that detailed preferences in a deal become available to the opponents giving them rise to profitable exploitation.
- *Anonymity of identities*: for certain trades, participants want to stay anonymous. Anonymity, in addition to protecting the privacy of interests, also saves the identities of the participants.
- *Efficient execution*: trading schemes should ensure a decision on the deal in as few steps as possible.

2.1 Fixed Price Selling

Fixed price selling is the most popular trading form in business to consumer commerce. The supplier associates with each offered good/service a fixed price. Buyers make a take-it-or-leave-it decision. Especially in small or highly individualized markets the model results in overcalculated offers (market based greedy lies), i.e., participants have no incentive to trade with their true values in the deal. In most cases privacy is preserved, that is, the mutual interests in a trade are only partially known by the trading partners through the acceptance of certain price. Falsification of one's true valuations is an inherent and important bargaining strategy in the model. Anonymity can be achieved with advanced payment schemes as they become available on the Internet [BGK95].

Beside the limitations with respect to the economic design, fixed price selling puts additional burden on the consumers to identify trading partners with matching interests and to compare the different offers. The providers, on the other hand, have additional costs to analyse the market situation in order to fix the price such that their gain is maximized.

2.2 Negotiations

To overcome the lack of flexibility of fixed-price selling, it is often preceded by bilateral negotiation. Such schemes involve two parties that bargain on a deal. Negotiations appear in business to business commerce for rather individualized and high value transactions. Usually both parties have conflicting interests, start with offers calculated to their own advantage and proceed until an agreement is reached. They obviously have no incentive to communicate their true interests in the deal, and thus, privacy of interest is a major concern of each negotiation strategy.

Game theorists have investigated negotiations schemes assuming public information, i.e., the utilities of both parties are published before the negotiation starts [ZR89]. In environments where published interests cannot be verified, the protocols allow for lies. Fairness for bilateral negotiations has been discussed in [RZ94,Rai82]. Extensions of negotiation protocols for bounded rationality and incomplete information environments are proposed in [SL95b].

2.3 Auctions

Another trading model for matching the interests of autonomous agents, which is more robust against manipulations than negotiations, are auctions. Auctions consider asymmetric situations between one auctioneer who wants to sell an item for the highest possible price, and many bidders who want to acquire the item for the lowest possible price. Traditional auctions address transactions with items of limited availability like antiques, second-hand goods, or flights with expiry dates. In a traditional first-price open-cry auction (english auction), the dominant strategy for the bidders is to bid up to their true value which, in economic terms, maximizes the consumer surplus. This scheme suffers from an enormous amount of interests becoming public. For a first-price sealed-bid auction, the bids depend on what each bidder beliefs of the opponent bidders forcing buyers and sellers into price-wars. Privacy of bids is only guaranteed among the bidders. The Dutch auction is a decreasing price auction that maximizes privacy, but is auctioneer friendly since it guarantees the purchase at the highest possible price. All schemes provoke various manipulations [GMM98,GM98b] like fake bidders (shills), sellers acting as auctioneers, or coalition formation by bidders [SL95a].

The Vickrey auction [Vic61,San95] is a non-discriminative auction scheme where the winning bidder pays the price of the second highest bid. This policy creates disincentive for speculative bidding and maximizes consumer surplus because bidders are best-off to submit bids reflecting their true valuation of the item being auctioned. But also for the widely used Vickrey auction it has been shown that bidding the truth is not always the dominant strategy for an agent [San95].

In contrast to fixed price selling and bilateral negotiations, the 1:n situation between auctioneer and bidders can filter out buyer/seller pairs with fewest conflicting interests.

2.4 Arbitration and Matchmaking

An alternative to bilateral negotiation is arbitration. The basic idea of arbitration schemes [LR89] is the introduction of a neutral third instance acting as arbiter. Buyers and suppliers report their interest in a bargaining situation to the arbiter which then selects an optimal and fair compromise. Arbitration schemes provide privacy of interests and anonymity of identities among the participants if the arbiter acts as a trustbroker, i.e., there is no need that the participants publish their interests to each other.

As detailed in the next Section, also arbitration can suffer from manipulations. To avoid fraud, the arbiter usually has to invest significant effort into researching the true interests of agents for a particular market. As an alternative, in this paper we introduce arbitration policies which increase the robustness against manipulations.

For typical bargaining situations one finds often opposing interests between buyers and suppliers. In contrast to auctions that only optimize deals in one dimension (usually the price), arbitration can find compromises on multiple dimensions [GM98a,GMM98]. Additionally, as further detailed in Section 4, arbitration schemes can be very effectively combined with matchmaking. Thereby, the asymmetric 1:n business relationship considered by auctions can be generalized to n:m relationships between arbitrary many buyers and suppliers.

3 Arbitration Protocols

3.1 Setting

For the subsequent considerations we assume the following setting. A population of bargaining agents are carrying out trades. A trade involves a pair of agents which need to reach an agreement among a number of alternative transactions, the *negotiation set*. We assume that each transaction in the negotiation set consists of complete exchanges, e.g., delivery and payment. Each agent associates with each transaction a certain utility which expresses its gain when the alternative is carried out. Usually these utilities are in conflict, i.e., the agents do not agree about the best alternative. The agents report the negotiation set together with the utilities to the arbiter. The task of the arbiter is to resolve the possibly conflicting interests among the agents and to decide which alternative is chosen. This should be accomplished in such a way that the net benefit which is the sum of the utilities gained by the agents is maximized.

In formal terms, for each trade at timestamp $t \in \mathbb{N}$ among n alternative transactions $a_{i,t}$ with $i = 0, \ldots, n_{t-1}$, we assume utilities $u_{i,t}$ for one agent, and $v_{i,t}$ for the other agent. Alternatives with high utilities are preferred. To make the utilities of agents comparable, they are normalized such that $\sum u_i = \sum v_i = 1$.

To illustrate this abstract setting, consider the following example: two types of agents, chip manufacturers, and chip resellers, want to trade electronic circuits. For this purpose, they have agreed on a predefined transaction template which allows to specify the number of pieces to be exchanged(100,500,1000), the delivery period (1 day, 2-5 days, 5-10 days), and the price per item (low, medium, high). This simple example already spans a negotiation set of 27 alternative transactions. Manufacturers with large capacities are usually interested in transactions with high number of pieces, long delivery periods, and high prices. The resellers on the other hand, have highly varying demands depending on current end-user demands, ongoing technology developments, and activities of competitors etc. In general, both types of agents have conflicting interests that need to be resolved. The goal of our approach is to resolve these conflicts such that the overall gain of all agents is maximized, agents are best off to know and announce their true utilities, but do not need to make their true utilities mutually known.

3.2 Lies

The game-theoretic approach to this setting is best exemplified by Nash's arbitration scheme[Nas50]. This scheme simply selects from the negotiation set the alternative where the product of the agents utilities is maximal. Under the assumption that both agents report their true utilities it provides pareto-optimal outcomes [Nas50]. An alternative to product maximization is the selection of the maximal sum which achieves a better overall gain [1].

Both solutions suffer substantially from the underlying assumption of public and true utilities. However, utilities are inherently private. Thus, agents can lie to their advantage by reporting falsified utilities to the arbiter. Nash's scheme provokes counter speculations and the maximal sum is vulnerable to exaggerated preferences.

More generally, lies can be classified along three dimensions. Lies exploiting knowledge about the utilities of opponents are *informed*; in contrast manipulations that are independent from the opponents utilities are *uninformed*. The second dimension of lies describes whether preferences are increased or decreased. *Greedy lies* exaggerate the utilities of the better alternatives, whereas *cautious lies* simulate little care by lying utilities closer to $\frac{1}{n}$. The third dimension considers the effect of a lie on the own gain and on the opponent's gain. A lie that successfully increases an agent's gain is a *beneficial lie*. Lies that damage the opponent more than the lying agent are called *malevolent lies* in contrast to *suicidal* or *altruistic lies* that have only harmful effects on the manipulator.

In the following we discuss various arbitration schemes which do not rely on public true utilities, and thus can avoid certain classes of lies.

3.3 Preference Selection

A straight forward way to avoid manipulations is to reduce the degree of freedom in reported utilities. This can be achieved by discretizing the utilities, taking only their relative rank into account. More formally, a unique rank $0 < r_i \leq n$ is associated with each alternative a_i, such that if $u_i < u_j$ then $r_i < r_j$, and if $u_i = u_j$, and $i < j$ then $r_i < r_j$. The scheme tries to compromise conflicting preferences by selecting the alternative with the maximum sum of ranks.

Other than schemes relying on a public true utility, this scheme avoids simple uninformed lies because every lie has to alter the relative ranking, and thus usually damages the lying agent. However, as exemplified in [FT99], beneficial informed lies are possible.

For agents with strong preferences and high conflict rates, the preference selection suffers from its ordinal treatment of utilities which forces them into evenly distributed ranks (see Section 3.6).

The relatively low gain of the preference selection scheme is compensated by its ability to arbitrate without taking past behaviour of agents into account. Therefore, it is especially useful in domains which are characterized by fragile business relationships (infrequent agent interactions) where the participants are unable to determine their exact utilities or have limited market knowledge.

---

[1] This approach violates Nash's symmetry axiom [Nas50,LR89], and thus is often regarded as unfair for individual decisions. But for sequences of decisions, this is less important because the utilities tend to be distributed symmetrically in the long run.

3.4 Deterministic Selection

Much better overall performance can be achieved if the exact utilities are taken into account rather than their abstraction in an ordinal ranking. But this gives rise to very simple greedy lies, where both agents exaggerate the utilities of their preferred alternatives. To avoid such manipulations, the deterministic protocol attaches costs to each utility announcement. This is accomplished as follows.

Each agent gets a weight, which determines its degree of influence on the decision of the arbiter. At each step the arbiter adjusts the individual weights according to the agents' expected gain. When the expected gain of the first agent is higher than the gain of the second, the first agent's weight is increased, otherwise it is decreased.

Formally, this scheme is implemented as follows. Agent1 holds weight w, agent2 $1 - w$; w is initiallized with $\frac{1}{2}$ such that both agents start with equal influence. Given n alternatives with utilities u_i, and v_i as defined above, the alternative with maximal $u_i^{w^s} v_i^{(1-w)^s}$ is selected. The exponent s allows to adjust to which degree the weights are considered for the arbitration. After each step, the weights are adjusted according to the expected gain. Given weight pairs $w[t], 1 - w[t]$ in round t, the subsequent weights $w[t + 1]$ are calculated by

$$w[t + 1] = w[t] + w[t](\sigma_v^2 - \sigma_{max}^2) - (1 - w[t])(\sigma_u^2 - \sigma_{max}^2)$$

where σ_u^2 is the standard deviation of utilities u_i, and σ_{max}^2 is the maximal standard deviation $\frac{n-1}{n^2}$ for n alternatives. The standard deviation is proportional to the expected gain of an agent, i.e., agents with higher standard deviation can expect a higher average gain. For example, an agent with low standard deviation which has equally low utilities for all alternatives of $\frac{1}{n}$ can at best expect to get this low utility, no matter what alternative is chosen. In contrast, an agent which has just one alternative with maximal utility (high standard deviation) will have better average gain because the probability of chosing this alternative is greater equal $\frac{1}{n}$.

For $w = \frac{1}{2}$ the selection strategy is equivalent to the maximal sum selection, whereas for $w > \frac{1}{2}$ it drastically increases the influence of utilities u_i. But other than with maximal sum selection, an agent cannot completely determine the outcome for a selection, unless it has weight 1 or it announces an alternative with utility 1. To avoid this we restrict all announced utilities to the interval $[\frac{\epsilon}{n}, 1 - \frac{\epsilon}{n}]$, with, e.g., $\epsilon = 0.1$.

For uniformly distributed utilities, we have analysed the robustness of this protocol (with exponent $s = 2$) in [FT99]: greedy lies can still successfully manipulate one decision because the better alternatives are chosen more likely. But they reduce the weight for future decisions to a degree which more than compensates the short term advantage. Cautious lies, on the other hand, make the selection of the preferred alternatives less likely. This loss cannot be compensated in future decisions by the increased weight. Neither pure nor mixed lying strategies have been found to successfully increase an agents gain.

For utility distributions with stronger preferences and higher conflict rates, our experiments revealed that the protocol with $s = 2$ can be successfully manipulated with cautious lies. By decreasing s, this effect can be compensated.

For choosing the right s, an arbiter needs some knowledge about the typical preference structure of the targeted market. Additionally, the scheme requires rather stable business relationships in order to use weights as a compensation against potential lies.

Especially in markets with a high volume of similar transactions among a relatively fixed set of traders, it accomplishes almost maximal net benefit and it is robust against manipulations.

The disadvantage of the deterministic protocol is that it only guards against uninformed lies but allows for informed lies, i.e., an agent who knows the interests of its opponent can always lie its utilities just to the point that the selection of the best alternative is guaranteed.

For successful informed lies, even partial information about the opponent's interests suffices. Distributions with a high conflict rate introduce such partial information: when an agent has a high utility for a particular alternative where he usually has a low utility, it likely does not have a conflict with its opponent. Thus, it can safely lie down its utility with little risk of not getting its best alternative and with substantial increase of future influence.

3.5 Probabilistic Selection

To overcome the problem of public information for situations with high conflict rates, we introduce a probabilistic selection scheme. If an agent can not completely foresee which alternative the arbiter takes, even if it has complete knowledge about the involved utilities and weights, it can also not rely on the effect of an informed lie with certainty. As has been shown in [FT99], this uncertainty suffices to avoid informed beneficial lies.

We accomplish nondeterminism with the following selection and weight adjustment scheme. With utilities $u_{i,t}$, $v_{i,t}$, and weights w_t, $1 - w_t$ as defined above, the arbiter selects alternative $a_{i,t}$ with probability $p_{i,t} = w_t u_{i,t} + (1 - w_t)v_{i,t}$ and adjusts weights to w_{t+1} on the basis of the expected gain $Gain()$ of each agent, i.e., $w_{t+1} = w_t - Gain(u_{0,t}, \ldots, u_{n-1,t}, w_t) + Gain(v_{0,t}, \ldots, v_{n-1,t}, 1 - w_t)$.

The larger the weighted sum of utilities for an action is, the more likely it will be selected. Furthermore, like with the weighted deterministic selection, an agent who can gain more than the other agent in one step will have less influence on the selection in the future. The average gain of an agent correlates with the standard deviation of the reported utilities: $Gain(u_0, \ldots u_{n-1}, w) = \sum_{i=0}^{n-1} p(a_i)u_i$. It takes the minimal value for $u_0 = \ldots = u_{n-1} = \frac{1}{n}$, and the maximal value for one $u_j = 1$ and all other $u_i = 0$. It is particularily suited for arbitration in highly conflicting situations because they tend to have exactly one alternative with a utility close to 1

In general, the agents will accumulate less overall benefit than with the deterministic protocols, because this protocol also selects suboptimal alternatives with a certain probability. However, better alternatives are selected more likely. Thus the agents will still get significantly better benefit than with a completely random selection, which would just gain $\frac{1}{n}$ per step[FT99].

With these characteristics, the probabilistic selection scheme has its strength in environments where the traders are well-aware of the opponent's preferences. Especially for asymmetric public information, it guarantees the less-informed agent fair outcomes.

3.6 Performance of Arbitration Protocols

To analyse our approach, we have experimented with the following utility distributions. Given n alternatives, we choose $n - 1$ random values x_i independently from a uniform

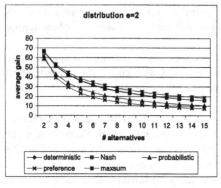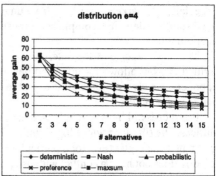

Fig. 1. Gain for honest agents for conflicting distributions without matchmaking

distribution between 0 and 1. We sort the x_i in ascending order and assign $x_0 = 0$ and $x_n = 1$. Then each u_i is defined by $x_{i+1} - x_i$ for $i = 0 \ldots n - 1$. This construction guarantees that the sum of utilities is 1. Furthermore, it avoids any bias, i.e., each alternative has equal chances to be the best. To model the behaviour of markets where agents with conflicting interests meet, we bias the distribution as follows. Each x_i is taken by some power $e \geq 1$. Thereby, alternatives with a small index get more frequently small utilities than alternatives with a large index. By assigning the utilities of one agent in ascending order, and the utilities of the other agent in descending order, we achieve a higher conflict rate with increasing e.

Figure 1 shows the average gain for honest agents with the number of alternatives n ranging from 2 to 15 for the different protocols. Due to our normalization, the relative gain decreases with n.

For a distribution biased with a factor 2 the maximal sum arbitration performs best, with Nash's arbitration and our deterministic protocol as close follow-ups. For $n > 2$, the very imprecise preference selection scheme performs worse than the probabilistic selection scheme. For the more extreme distribution biased with factor 4, again the maximal sum is the winner. The deterministic protocol performs slightly worse but clearly outperforms Nash's arbitration. For $n > 5$, even the probabilistic protocol is better than Nash. Again, the preference selection scheme performs clearly worst. Interestingly, with larger sets of alternatives, the overall performance of more biased distributions is slightly better although the conflict rate increases. This is due to the fact that with these distributions the conflict rate increases less than the average utility of the best alternative.

4 Matchmaking

4.1 Extended Setting

A natural extension to pairwise arbitration is the introduction of matchmaking as additional service of an arbiter. Instead of randomly formed pairs that visit the arbiter, a matchmaker can preferably pair agents with less conflicting interests and thereby achieve a better net benefit.

Like in the setting with only two agents, matchmaking should be robust against lies, i.e., no agent should benefit from falsifying its announced utilities.

For the investigation of matchmaking, we consider the following extended setting. We assume two equally sized sets of bargaining agents, one consisting only of suppliers, the other of buyers. Buyers and suppliers want to carry out repetitive trades among a predetermined negotiation set, and have opposing utilities which are distributed according to the biased distributions introduced in Section 3.6.

With these extensions, for example, the matchmaker can flexibly pair chip manufacturers and resellers with common interests among the alternatives in the negotiation set described in Section 3.1.

4.2 Protocol Adaptation to Matchmaking

The matchmaker proceeds as follows. First, it tries to find the best set of matching pairs. Because the number of different possible matching sets grows exponentially with the number of agents m, we use a heuristic approach: the matchmaker constructs a table which contains for all possible buyer/supplier pairs the expected outcome of matching them according to a particular arbitration scheme. From this table it chooses the best match for a randomly determined agent. The matched agents are discarded from the table, and the process continues until all agents are matched. This heuristic approach requires only an effort of $O(m^2)$ without decreasing the overall gain significantly and without favouring one particular (group of) agents. After the match is completed, it performs an arbitration for all matched pairs.

For weight-oriented arbitration schemes, agents that match will have weights that do not add up to 1. Thus, we have to normalize them by multiplying them with an appropriate factor. For example, assume one agent enters with weight 0.3, meaning that it had good gain in the previous exchanges, and the other agent with weight 0.9, meaning that it had significantly less than average gain recently. The weights are normalized with a factor $n_w = \frac{1}{0.3+0.9}$ resulting in weight pairs $w_{1,t} = 0.25, w_{2,t} = 0.75$. After the arbitration is performed, the new weights $w_{1,t+1}, w_{2,t+1}$ are denormalized by multiplying them with $\frac{1}{n_w}$. This allows weights to exceed the upper border of 1 but it disallows weights to become smaller than 0. Furthermore, the sum of weights of all agents remains constant.

Another necessary extension arises from the more frequent need to arbitrate decisions with different overall value, i.e., in one case $1 goods are exchanged, another might be about $100 goods etc. To arbitrate sequences of decisions with differing values $q_i > 0$, the presented weight adjustment schemes can be adapted as follows: given the weight adjustment $w_{t+1} = w_t - w_t d_1 + (1 - w_t)d_2$, where d_1, and d_2 are protocol-dependent factors determined from the normalized utilities of the agents, we need to calculate w_{t+q_i} rather than w_{t+1} for a decision of value q_i. This can be achieved by solving the recursive equation given above, which results in the following closed expression: $w_{t+q_i} = \frac{d_2+(1+d_1+d_2)^{q_i}(d_2(w_t-1)+d_1 w_t)}{d_1+d_2}$. Effectively, this repeats the weight adjustment q_i times.

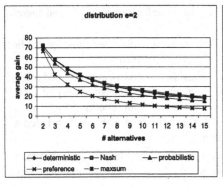 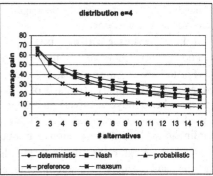

Fig. 2. Gain for 12 honest agents for conflicting distributions with matchmaking

4.3 Performance of Matchmaking

Figure 2 shows the average gain for 12 honest agents and matchmaking. Like in pairwise arbitration, the maximal sum, Nash's arbitration, and the deterministic protocol perform almost equally well for distributions biased with factor 2. However, the overall performance compared to pairwise arbitration increases by about 15% for larger n because the matchmaker favourably pairs agents with a reasonable compromise. Also the overall performance of the probabilistic protocol increases, whereas the preference selection remains almost at the level of pairwise arbitration. Similar observations hold for distributions with larger bias factor. But for larger bias factors, and thereby higher conflict rates, matchmaking has less room for optimization.

4.4 Simulation of Lies

For matchmaking with the deterministic arbitration scheme, we have investigated populations of agents that pursue different manipulation strategies. In order to assess how robust the protocols are against manipulations we compare the results with the maximal sum selection. Table 1 shows two major columns which consist a set of buyers (left) and suppliers (right). For the reported results we have used a fixed negotiation set of size $n = 4$. Additionally, we have assumed that all transactions have the same overall value.

We have simulated various manipulation strategies. A greedy agent lies its best alternative to 1, others to 0. A semi-greedy agent sgr increases its best alternative by a fixed constant if it exceeds the threshold value of $\frac{1}{n} + \sigma_{max}^2$. The cautiously greedy strategy cgt is similar except that is lies the best alternative to 1 when it exceeds the threshold. Agents that lie fully cautiously fct report for all alternatives $\frac{1}{n}$ except for the best which is slightly increased, vice versa for the worst. The semi-cautious lie sct groups all utilities around $\frac{1}{n}$ but preserves the preference structure of the alternatives. The standard deviation lie stv is an informed lie that knows the average standard deviation of an honest agent in the given population. It lies the best alternative as high as possible, and lowers the others accordingly without exceeding the given standard deviation.

For unbiased distributions with factor 1, honest agents perform best with the deterministic protocol. Only the *stv* strategy which is an informed lie performs slightly better. The greedy lies *cgt* and *sgr* which are successfully applied in the maximal sum scheme are avoided. Cautious lies like *sct*, which give less gain in the maximal sum scheme, become increasingly successful with stronger biased distributions in the deterministic case since a high weight is achieved. This can be avoided by decreasing the influence of weights on decisions which can be achieved by decreasing the factor s appropriately. The fact that honest agents in the buyer group perform better than honest agents on the supplier group can be explained by the chosen populations and the effect of their strategies, e.g., for stronger distributions, some manipulation strategies degenerate into pure altruism, benefiting all agents of the opposing population. This is reversed for the maximal sum selection.

In general, our experiments have shown that careful greedy lies can be worthwhile in matchmaking scenarios since they increase the chance of a better match. Although honest agents can be slightly outperformed in some situations by one specific lying strategy, there has been found no strategy that beats honest agents in general. Thus, the honest strategy has turned out to be most robust with varied environments. We have

protocol	dist	s	hon	sgr	hon	fct	sct	hon	hon	hon	hon	cgt	stv	hon
determ	1	2.0	48.4	48.3	48.3	41.4	45.2	48.3	48.4	48.3	48.4	39.9	49.8	48.4
determ	2	2.0	51.7	49.2	51.7	34.5	46.6	51.8	50.2	50.1	50.1	24.1	46.3	50.2
determ	4	1.7	56.4	34.8	56.5	23.4	54.5	56.3	48.9	49.1	49.2	8.4	33.4	49.1
determ	8	0.9	60.5	26.1	60.0	08.0	57.3	60.4	54.6	52.6	53.8	4.6	32.7	53.2
maxsum	1		48.3	54.8	48.4	21.8	27.3	48.5	49.9	50.3	50.3	58.1	48.6	50.5
maxsum	2		48.1	55.0	47.7	21.6	26.6	47.8	50.9	50.5	50.2	58.2	48.5	50.3
maxsum	4		47.0	61.6	48.2	8.6	9.5	47.7	52.8	51.9	52.7	69.6	39.0	52.5
maxsum	8		48.8	68.1	48.5	2.3	2.3	49.2	56.4	57.0	56.0	80.8	26.6	56.9

Table 1. Gain after $10,000$ steps for $n = 4$ alternatives with matchmaking

also experimented with mixed strategies, larger negotiation sets and the other arbitration protocols. These experiments revealed similar results, which we cannot present in detail due to space limitations.

5 Conclusion

We have introduced several protocols for arbitration among agents with conflicting interests. Compared to other models for business to business commerce, the protocols offer more flexibility and higher overall gain than trades along completely predetermined lines, such as fixed price selling, and they can be made robust against manipulations from which more flexible trading models, such as bilateral negotiations suffer. In addition, by virtue of arbitration, the agents do not need to make their interests known to each other. Furthermore, we have shown that the arbitration can be effectively combined with matchmaking, which further improves the overall gain by favourably pairing agents with little interest conflicts.

Future work will be in particular devoted to using more flexible and scalable negotiation sets. This comprises several extensions. Firstly, we will investigate ways to dynamically determine the actual negotiation sets, and analyse the potential of manipulations for such an approach. A side-issue of this is to arbitrate decisions in the case of only partially overlapping negotiation sets. Secondly, we will consider negotiation sets with continuous alternatives, which are convenient to represent whole ranges of options, such as price or delivery time. Finally, we will analyse means to combine our approach to avoid manipulations with complementary mechanisms, which either constrain the negotiation set and the allowed utilities within reasonable bounds, or at least detect fraud attempts.

References

[BGK95] E. Brickell, P. Gemmell, and D. Kravitz. Trustee-based extensions of anonymous cash and the making of anonymous change. In *Proceedings of the Sixth ACM-SIAM Symposium on Discrete Algorithms*, pages 457–466, 1995.

[FT99] P. Fankhauser and T. Tesch. Agents, a broker, and lies. In *Proceedings of Ninth International Workshop on Research Issues on Data Engineering: Information Technology of Virtual Enterprises*, pages 56–63, Sydney, Australia, 1999.

[GM98a] R. H. Guttman and P. Maes. Agent-mediated integrative negotiation for retail electronic commerce. In *Proc. of the Workshop on Agent Mediated Electronic Trading*, Minneapolis, Minnesota, May 1998.

[GM98b] R. H. Guttman and P. Maes. Cooperative vs. competitive multi-agent negotiations in retail electronic commerce. In *Proc. of the second Int. Conference on Cooperative Information Agents*, Paris, France, July 1998.

[GMM98] R. H. Guttman, A. Moukas, and P. Maes. Agent-mediated electronic commerce: A survey. *Knowledge Engineering Review*, June 1998.

[LR89] R. D. Luce and H. Raiffa. *Games and Decisions*. Dover Publications, Inc, Mineola, New York, 1989. Reprint. Originally published: New York, John Wiley and Sons, 1957.

[Nas50] J. F. Nash. The bargaining problem. *Econometrica*, 18:155–162, 1950.

[Rai82] H. Raiffa. *The Art and Science of Negotiation*. Harvard University Press, Cambridge, Mass., 1982.

[RZ94] J. S. Rosenschein and G. Zlotkin. *Rules of Encounter: Designing Conventions for Automated Negotiation Among Computer*. The MIT Press, Cambridge, MA, 1994.

[San95] T. W. Sandholm. Limitations of the Vickrey auction in computational multiagent systems. In Victor Lesser, editor, *Proc. of the first Int. Conference on Multi-Agent Systems*. The MIT Press, Cambridge, MA, 1995.

[SL95a] T. W. Sandholm and V. R. Lesser. Coalition formation among bounded rational agents. In *Proc. of the 14th Int. Joint Conference on Artificial Intelligence*, pages 662–669, Montreal, Canada, 1995.

[SL95b] T. W. Sandholm and V. R. Lesser. Issues in automated negotiation and electronic commerce: Extending the contract net framework. In *Proc. of the Int. Conference on Multi-Agent Systems*, pages 328–335, San Francisco, USA, June 1995.

[Tyg98] J. D. Tygar. Atomicity versus anonymity: Distributed transactions for electronic commerce. In *Proc. of the 24th Int. Conference on Very Large Databases*, pages 1–10, New York City, USA, 1998.

[Vic61] W. Vickrey. Counter specification, auctions, and competitive sealed tenders. *The Journal of Finance*, pages 9–37, 1961.

[ZR89] G. Zlotkin and J. S. Rosenschein. Negotiation and task sharing among autonomous agents in cooperative domains. In *Proc. of the 11th Int. Joint Conference on Artificial Intelligence*, pages 912–917, Detroit, Michigan, USA, August 1989.

Enabling Integrative Negotiations
by
Adpative Software Agents

Wolfgang Benn, Otmar Görlitz, Ralf Neubert[1]

Chemnitz University of Technology

Department of Computer Science

09107 Chemnitz, Germany

Abstract: One of the most important and complex aspects in Electronic Commerce is the automated negotiation between software agents. Most shopping assistance systems concentrate on price comparison agents or provide only the means to negotiating the price of articles. In our paper we present the model of an intelligent and adaptive software agent to support integrative negotiations of multiple interdependent properties of products. The agent is able to consider an arbitrary number of different properties whose values may be interdependent. Additionally, a ranking of the importance of the properties is maintained. Normalization of property values is an integral part of our model. The user does not need to transform desired values to abstract scales. Furthermore, normalization allows properties of different types to be the subject of one negotiation. Our agent can selectively act as a buyer or a seller of a product. The intelligent and adaptive behaviour throughout the negotiation is secured by a set of strategies, which determine the agent's proposals and its reactions to its counterpart. The realization of these negotiation strategies is based on ideas adopted from the field of neural networks and vibrations theory.

1 Introduction

With the emergence of online stores in the Internet and the vast possibilities that Electronic Commerce offers for trading in virtual market places or just looking for a bargain in the countless shopping sites, a new tool was required to support customers and retailers in electronic business. Shopping agents are software agents, specifically developed to represent users and their objectives in online shopping. Early shopping

---

[1] {Wolfgang.Benn, Otmar.Goerlitz, Ralf.Neubert}@informatik.tu-chemnitz.de

agents behaved like information agents. They only were able to collect price and availability information for a certain good [2]. Improved systems can also make recommendations based on the opinions of other individuals or agents [5]. Other approaches introduced more sophisticated agents, which could autonomously negotiate about the price in order to find the best possible deal for their clients [4]. Interestingly, there are simulation results reported, showing that well-informed shopping agents concentrating on price comparisons solely can lead to disastrous price-wars and subsequently decrease the business diversity and customer satisfaction [10].

Negotiation about the price is sufficient only if there are no other properties to consider when buying or selling commodities. But a customer might also have a strong interest in short delivery times or extended terms of guarantee. Moreover, the customer could be willing to make a tradeoff between the price and additional terms. Searching for an agreement on multiple goals and considering tradeoffs between the goals is called integrative negotiation [14]. We will also refer to it as negotiation about multiple interdependent attributes of a product or item. Probably, if the value of a product is not only measured by its price but additional factors and attributes, the price-war scenario can be avoided. To support automated integrative negotiations we have created a new model of a software agent. The agent is able to negotiate about an arbitrary number of attributes and can make tradeoffs between these attributes according to its client's preferences. In our model, the agent has no knowledge about the semantics of an attribute. The only information it needs is a range of preferred values and some measurement for the interdependencies between the attributes. Therefore the agent is able to negotiate about any product. Furthermore, in the negotiation itself it does not matter whether the agent should buy or sell something. So the agent is able to play either the role of the seller or the role of the customer [3].

The remainder of this paper is organized as follows: After a short overview of related work we introduce our basic concept of measuring interdependencies between attributes in the third section. Then we describe the principle behaviour of the agent and the procedure it follows to generate proposals in a negotiation. In the fifth section we introduce negotiation strategies the agent can follow and give a sketch of the agent's architecture. In the sixth section we give a game theoretic description of the agent's behaviour. We conclude our presentation with an example of a negotiation following our principles and a summary of the negotiation model.

2 Related Work

The application of software agent technology in Electronic Commerce is topic of various research projects. In [7] Guttman, Moukas, Maes gave a detailed survey. Guttman and Maes also proposed a model for agent-mediated integrative negotiations [6]. Chavez et al. introduced a project called Kasbah, the creation of a virtual agent marketplace [4]. Their agents also used simple negotiation strategies to find the best possible deal on the marketplace. Logical Decisions provides a software tool for defining multiple subgoals to facilitate integrative negotiations [15].

The negotiations of software agents in Electronic Commerce regarding coalition forming were discussed in [18]. An in-depth description of the agent concept and negotiations for coalition forming can be found in [11].

Keeney and Raiffa [9] gave a detailed analysis of multiple objective decisions, while Lewicki, Saundes and Minton [14] discussed the principles of negotiations. Rosenschein and Zlotkin [17] described strategies and negotiation protocols for BDI-agents to agree on cooperative work.

The game theoretic concepts we refer to in section six, are mostly results of Nash's and Harsanyis work. A detailed description can be found e.g. in [13] or [1].

3 Attribute Interdependencies

In integrative negotiations a tradeoff between multiple attributes of a product has to be found. Moreover, a negotiation agent should seek for the best possible tradeoff. Ideally, the agent should get the user's preferred values for all attributes. If this is not possible, it should demand a compensation for this loss in the value of another attribute. However, the compensation is not restricted to one attribute. The agent may demand better conditions for several attributes if it agrees to a lower value in a particular attribute. Consequently, we can define a square matrix whose dimension is the number of attributes to negotiate. Each cell $[i,j]$ contains the compensation in attribute j for the loss in attribute i's value. Therefore the diagonal entries in this matrix are zero.

Now the problem arises, how to compare the loss for one attribute with the gain for another. How should the agent calculate a price discount it has to demand for a longer delivery time? The problem aggravates if not all attributes have simple numerical values such as a price or an amount. The agent might need to demand a certain brand or special guarantee terms if it had to agree to a higher price than expected. We solve the problem of comparability between values of different attributes by translating every proposed and offered attribute value into a value that represents the client's satisfaction, which we call "satisfaction value". The satisfaction value can vary between 0 and 100 percent. 100 percent satisfaction means, the attribute has the value the agent's client intended or better, e.g. the delivery time for a product is two days or less. In order to calculate the lower boundary of the satisfaction interval, i.e. the attribute values that give 0 percent satisfaction, the user has to provide the range of acceptable values. For numerical or steady values, this would have the form *minimal value ... optimal value ... maximal value* where *minimal* or *maximal value* can be omitted if not applicable. For discrete types with no intrinsic order the user has to declare his preferred values and their ranking. By means of the satisfaction values all attributes are comparable, no matter which type they have or what the range of acceptable values is.

The entries in the compensation matrix also refer to satisfaction values. Each cell contains a fraction of the lost satisfaction value, which should in turn be gained in this attribute. For example, a value of 0.8 in cell $[i,j]$ means, 80 percent of the lost satisfaction in i should be gained in j. If attribute i's value is only satisfied at a rate of 50 percent, then the actual satisfaction of attribute j should be raised by 40 percent.

Please note that the satisfaction value cannot exceed 1.0 and cannot be lower than 0.0 .

Actually, all internal calculations for the agent are based on satisfaction values. Therefore we have implemented a "normalizer module" at the interface of the agent. The normalizer takes an offer with real values for the attributes as input and generates according satisfaction values. The agent calculates a counteroffer, described in satisfaction values, and the normalizer generates the corresponding attribute values as output. This is done for the different attribute types respectively. Currently four attribute types are supported, although the normalizer's architecture is suitable for the addition of further types. The supported attribute types are:

Steady type: this comprises numerical values. For instance, a price may vary between a minimum value of 75.00 and a maximum value of 140.00. Almost any intermediate value may be proposed.

Discrete type: discrete values have no intrinsic order, the user has to provide a list of acceptable values as well as their preferred order. For instance, preferred colours in the order *green, blue, red, yellow* with *green* most and *yellow* least preferred. Other colours have a satisfaction value of 0.0 . By default this will give the proposed colour *green* a satisfaction value of 100 percent, *blue* 70 percent, *red* 40 percent and *yellow* 10 percent.

Logical type: this comprises only the values *True* and *False*. The attribute might have a value or not. The preferred value yields 100 percent satisfaction, the opposite value 0 percent. For instance, renting a car may include taking out an additional insurance. If a customer wishes the insurance the proposal would yield 100 percent satisfaction. If the customer does not wish it the proposal would yield 0 percent satisfaction for him.

Bundle type: bundles are sets of several attributes with logical values. Bundles describe a group of properties or additions with no intrinsic order. An example would be additional car equipment like second front airbag, side airbags, second rear mirror, anti-lock braking system, leather seats. The user has to provide *True* or *False* values for every item in the set as well as a ranking for the items. In case of the car equipment a customer might have the following preferences: second front airbag: desired, rank 1; side airbags: desired, rank 2; second rear mirror: not desired, rank 4; anti lock braking system: desired, rank 3; leather seats: not desired, rank 4. Two or more attributes in the bundle may be assigned to a certain rank. The number of fulfilled attribute values and their rankings are used to compute the satisfaction value of a proposal.

In case one side wishes to negotiate an attribute the other side has no preferred value for, the normalizer allows a *don't care* value for every attribute type. The agent gets 100 percent satisfaction for any proposed value if it has a *don't care* value for this attribute.

Obviously, two agents have to agree about the attributes to negotiate before starting to make proposals. We intentionally do not tackle the problem of agreeing on a set of negotiable attributes in this paper. Matchmaking prior to the actual negotiation is a very complex task. There are research projects like TSIMMIS [20] and MOMIS [16], the Garlic prototype [19] and the InfoSleuth project [8] concerned with the intelligent integration of information, which is the conceptual base of the matchmaking process. Nevertheless, some major problems still persist. Our agent model can be combined with an external matchmaking procedure suitable for the actual problem scope. There are also many occasions, where the agent can be sent directly into online stores. In this case the user knows all negotiable attributes and no explicit matchmaking process is neccessary.

Unfortunately, to achieve the described frame for setting up complex attribute interdependencies and rankings, a user has to provide many parameters in advance of the negotiation. The question arises: Is the user able and willing to specify such an amount of inter-attribute relations? Moreover, can he always give exact numerical values? It has to be expected that often users do not have clear imagination about attribute interdependencies or they are unable to express them in numeric values. For the applicability of our negotiation approach, it seems imperative to provide an extensive interface to guide the user through the initialization of the negotiation parameters. Our mechanism of generating negotiation proposals has the advantage to create reasonable offers even without any compensation values. Only the specification of an attribute's worth (or ranking), described in the next section, is required.

4   Generation of Proposals

In addition to the compensation values the user has to provide a certain value for every attribute which determines the overall worth of this attribute. This worth is used as a kind of negotiation strength. The agent is more likely to make compromises for attributes with low worth and it will demand a high satisfaction value for attributes with a high worth.

The agent generates negotiation proposals considering the current satisfaction value, the negotiation strength and the compensations for every attribute. Furthermore, it takes into account whether the other side made compromises, i.e. if the counterpart has reduced its demands during the negotiation and therefore its later offers gave the agent a higher satisfaction value than earlier offers. With these data the agent calculates a compromise between its optimal values and the other side's latest offer. This compromise is returned as counteroffer. The negotiation goes on until an agreement on the value for every attribute is found or one of the agents loses patience and withdraws, i.e. it does not return a counteroffer, but informs the other side that it wishes to stop the negotiation instead.

The parallel generation of proposals for a number of attributes with respect to compensations is derived from Hopfield's model of a recurrent artificial neural network. We have implemented a very similar architecture in the proposal generation module of our agent. In this architecture the pendants of the neurons contain current satisfaction values of the attributes. The backward connections in this recurrent network contain the compensation values. A compromise value for every attribute is computed from the difference between offered values and the last proposal of the agent. This compromise is superimposed with the compensation values. Thus the network oscillates until a stable compromise is found. This stable compromise is given to the normalizer in order to form a counter offer.

The original Hopfield network is defined for unit values out of {-1,1} only. Furthermore, it does not converge for all possible combinations of values of the backward connections. These restrictions are not acceptable for our network model. However, the network will converge if all backward connections w are restricted to $0.0 \leq w < 1.0$. The network performs a damped oscillation and converges to a stable compromise. The proof is based on the calculation of amplitude values via an infinite series, which approaches a limit. The computation of the amplitude values results in a continued multiplication of the predecessor in the series with the compensation matrix. Because all entries in the matrix are bounded between 0 and 1 the amplitude values will eventually converge to a limit. Due to complexity and length, the proof is clearly beyond the scope of this paper.

The agent uses following algorithm to generate a negotiation offer:

A negotiation offer is a vector of satisfaction values for all attributes. Let $VV_i(t)$ the current proposal of the agent i and $vv_{ix}(t)$ the proposed value for attribute x.

If the agent has to propose the initial offer in the negotiation, it generates a vector with the value 1 for all attributes; i.e. it demands the optimal values for all attributes.

$$vv_{ix}(0)=1 \quad \forall x$$

Else, if it has to generate counteroffer, it calculates a compromise value $kv_{ix}(t)$ for every attribute x. This compromise value determines the maximum concession for the attribute in negotiation period t.

$$kv_{ix}(t)=kv_{ix}(t\text{-}2)\text{-}\Delta gv_{jx}(t_l)*(1\text{-}hv_{ix})$$

where $kv_{ix}(t\text{-}2)$ is the compromise value of the agent's last proposal, $\Delta gv_{jx}(t_l)$ denotes the concessions the other side j made for attribute x in the last l negotiation periods and hv_{ix} is i's worth of attribute x. The compromise value is therefore controlled by the personal attribute worth and the concessions the other side made.

The compromise value kv is then superimposed with the compensation values according to the compensation matrix.

$$vv_{ix}(tg=0) = kv_{ix}(t)$$

$$vv_{ix}(tg)=kv_{ix}(t)+\sum_y(1\text{-}vv_{iy}(tg\text{-}1))*w_{yx} \qquad tg=1..m$$

$$until \ \left| vv_{ix}(tg)\text{-}vv_{ix}(tg\text{-}1)\right| < \varepsilon \quad \forall x$$

A local counter tg is used to distinguish the network cycles until the oscillation is damped enough.

5 Negotiation Strategies

In its default behaviour, described in the previous section, the agent follows the user's preferences and the given parameters for the negotiation. This ensures that the automated negotiation follows the intentions of the user. But the agent might not be able to find an agreement with its counterpart if it had a high negotiation strength or demanded much compensation for compromises.

Often this is what the user exactly wishes: if no satisfying agreement can be found the deal is not accepted. But there are also cases, in which the user has a strong interest in finding an agreement and making the deal, even if this deal has a low satisfaction value. Then the agreement itself has a higher priority than the actual attribute values.

If the agent shall be able to pursue such higher level goals, it also requires a wider range of strategic decisions. An agreement might not be possible with the users preferred negotiation strength and compensations, that is why the agent has to change these negotiation parameters on its own. On the other hand, it should still try to find the most satisfying agreement. To enable the agent for strategic decisions we use ideas from the BDI-agent model [12,17]. Belief-Desire-Intention agents have perceptions and assumptions about their current state and the behaviour of other agents in their world. They have certain desires – the goals to achieve on the user's behalf. Lastly, they have intentions on how to change the state of their world in order to reach a state closer to the achievement of their goals.

The desires, the goals for the negotiation are given by the users preferred attribute values. The beliefs in the current state of the agent's world consist mainly of the difference between its latest offer and the optimal attribute values as well as the offers and the observed behaviour of the counterpart. To store the counterpart's reactions on the agent's offers, i.e. the counterpart's behaviour, we implemented an associative memory module for our agent. This memory is also used to make predictions for the counterpart's reactions on hypothetical offers. The core of our agent is a strategy module. This module contains the overall strategic goal, e.g. *Stay with the user's preferences* or *Find an agreement*. The module has also a function to calculate a value for the current state of the negotiation with respect to the strategic goal. From the current state's value and values of earlier states strategic decisions for changing the negotiation parameters (the negotiation strength and the compensations) are derived. These strategic decisions and a tactics module to actually carry them out, complete the intentions part of the agent. The full architecture of our negotiation agent is sketched in figure 2.

We have implemented a negotiation strategy *Find an agreement* in addition to the default strategy *Stay with the user's preferences*. The strategy *Find an agreement* allows the agent to change its negotiation parameters in order to increase the probability of an agreement with the other side. The agent permanently assesses the current negotiation situation. If a stagnation is discovered it calculates a strategic concession such that the other side should be encouraged to concede too. These calculations are based on the observed and memorized reactions of the other side, stored in the associative memory module.

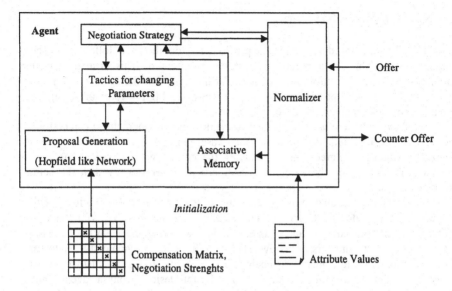

Figure 2: Architecture of the agent.

6   Game Theoretic Approach

In terms of the Game Theory, the negotiation protocol, which unfolds, can be described as noncooperative negotiation game with incomplete information. The information is incomplete in the sense that utility functions and patience is private information. Also, the overall negotiation strategy an agent follows is only known to itself. The negotiation resembles the Harsanyi-Zeuthen model, however, not the weaker player has to generate the next proposal. The proposals are generated mutually. The player who received the latest offer has to make a counteroffer.

In any game situation the player i has four strategies available:

(1) repeat its last offer,
(2) accept the proposal of the other player,
(3) make a concession and propose it as counteroffer,
(4) withdraw from the negotiation.

Actually, for every attribute a strategy $s_{i1} - s_{i3}$ is chosen independently during the generation of the proposal (they are interdependent in the compromise values however). To simplify these considerations, only the entire vector is viewed here, assuming an overall strategy according to strategy played in the majority of the attributes.

Playing strategy s_{i4} ends the game inevitably and both players receive their conflict utility c_i, c_j. We assume that playing strategy s_{i2} also ends the game. Both players receive a certain utility a_i, a_j for finding an agreement and the utility of the offer they agreed on: $u_i(VV_k(t))$, $u_j(VV_k(t))$ respectively; k determining the player who made this proposal. Playing strategy s_{i1} or s_{i3} prolongs the negotiation. Please note, it is quite possible to raise one's demands, i.e. demand more than in a previous offer. But this is not considered a rational behaviour and is only allowed for computational reasons. Thus, playing strategy s_{i3} always decreases the maximum utility for player i in the negotiation, while it simultaneously increases the minimum utility for player j (if an agreement is found). Playing strategy s_{i1} maintains the opportunity of a higher maximum utility for player i, but also does not increase the minimum utility for player j.

In its default behaviour, described in section four, an agent plays strategy s_{i3} if the other player did choose s_{j3}. The agent will concede only if it's minimum utility was increased in the previous negotiation step. The agent will play strategy s_{i1} if the other player did not decrease his demands. This behaviour should ensure that if an agreement is found, it provides the highest utility for the agent. Due to the zero-sum nature of the negotiation, an agreement is pareto optimal. Neither player can receive a higher utility without decreasing the other player's utility. An agreement is in equilibrium. An agent will only play strategy s_{i2} if the concession is equal to the concession of s_{i3}. Playing strategy s_{i1} against a default-behaviour agent would cause it's reaction s_{j1} and therefore only increase the probability that one agent plays strategy s_{k4}, which leads to the conflict utility. Equally, neither agent has an incentive to deviate from an agreement. However, an agreement is not necessarily optimal. Against a weak player it would be optimal always to repeat the initial offer with the optimum values for all attributes. A risk neutral player i could derive the maximum utility of $a_i + u(VV_i(0))$ with this strategy.

Agents following the overall strategy *Find an agreement* are more risk averse than default-behaviour agents are. Their strategic decisions let them play strategy s_{i3} (concede) even if the counterpart played s_{j1} (did not concede). This way, a stagnating negotiation (both sides play s_{k1}) should revive before one of the players withdraws. Because their agreement utility is higher than the actual utility of the proposal they agree on $(a_i > u_i(VV_k(t_n)))$, it is rational for them to decrease the maximum utility without previous increment of the minimum utility.

7 Negotiation Example

We will finish the description of our agent with an example of a negotiation. We instantiate two agents of our prototype. One agent, Mr. Shopkeeper, will play the part of a seller, while the other agent, Agent Jack, is a customer. We assume Agent Jack wants to rent a car. He agreed with Mr. Shopkeeper to negotiate the following attributes:

> **Price:** a steady type attribute; Agent Jack wants to pay 75.0, not more than 140.0; Mr. Shopkeeper wants to receive 120.0, at least 70.0 .
> **Duration:** a discrete type attribute; Agent Jack wants to rent the car for 4 days or 7 days or 2 days with decreasing satisfaction values; Mr. Shopkeeper wants to lend the cars for 1, 2, 4, 7, 14 days with decreasing satisfaction values.
> **Cylinder capacity:** a discrete type attribute; Agent Jack wants a car with 1800 ccm or 2000 ccm or 1500 ccm capacity with decreasing satisfaction

values; Mr. Shopkeeper wants to lend cars with capacities of 1500 ccm, 1200 ccm, 1800 ccm, 2000 ccm with decreasing satisfaction values.

Additional insurance: a logic type attribute; Agent Jack is self-confident and wishes none; Mr. Shopkeeper prefers to sell one.

The tables 1 and 2 show the negotiation values and the compensation matrices for the two agents. Of course, the other side knows neither the preferred values, nor the negotiation parameters for the agents.

Neg. Strength	Attribute	Compensations			
		Price	Duration	Capacity	Insurance
0.5	Price	-	0.6	0.6	0.8
0.8	Duration	0.5	-	0.0	0.0
0.6	Capacity	0.5	0.0	-	0.0
0.8	Insurance	0.7	0.0	0.0	-

Table 1: Negotiation parameters for the buyer.

Neg. Strength	Attribute	Compensations			
		Price	Duration	Capacity	Insurance
0.6	Price	-	0.5	0.7	0.8
0.7	Duration	0.3	-	0.6	0.8
0.4	Capacity	0.7	0.0	-	0.0
0.7	Insurance	0.6	0.8	0.0	-

Table 2: Negotiation parameters for the seller.

The attribute and negotiation values in this example are chosen arbitrarily. The buyer's negotiation parameters express his strong emphasis on the duration and his aversion to additional insurance. Price and capacity values are secondary objectives – he simply has to rent a car. However, all values will moderately influence the price he is willing to pay and the price influences the demands for the other attributes. The seller assesses all attributes nearly equally, except the capacity, which has a lower priority. There are some interdependencies in the seller's negotiation strategy: price and duration influence all other attributes, most notably the insurance. The capacity influences the price of course. The fact if he can sell an insurance or not will also influence the demanded price. Duration and insurance have a significant dependence and therefore a strong mutual influence.

If both agents negotiate in their default behaviour, they cannot find an agreement. Mr. Shopkeeper makes the initial offer:

Price 120, Duration 1 day, Capacity 1500 ccm, Insurance YES.

Agent Jack responds with:

Price 110.4, Duration 4 days, Capacity 2000 ccm, Insurance NO.

Although the values would permit a solution for both agents, it would give them too low satisfaction values. So the agents rather prefer not to agree. Finally, one agent loses patience. The agents have an internal counter for the negotiation steps and may decide when to give up. The last offers before timeout were:

Mr. Shopkeeper: *Price 110.4, Duration 4 days, Capacity 1800 ccm, Insurance YES.*
Agent Jack: *Price 110.4, Duration 4 days, Capacity 1800 ccm, Insurance NO.*

If Mr. Shopkeeper does not want to lose any business, he will negotiate with the strategy *Find an agreement.* So the final agreement is more important to him than the actual attribute values. In this case both agents can find an agreement. The initial offers are the same. Finally, Mr. Shopkeeper offers:

Price 110.4, Duration 4 days, Capacity 1800 ccm, Insurance NO,
to which Agent Jack agrees.

If Agent Jack also has a strong interest in renting a car and also follows the *Find an agreement* strategy, both can find an agreement again. The initial offers are the same. After some negotiation steps Agent Jack offers:

Price 110.4, Duration 4 days, Capacity 1800 ccm, Insurance YES
and Mr. Shopkeeper agrees.

8 Conclusion

In this paper we have presented a new model for automated integrative negotiation about multiple interdependent attributes. On the base of this model we have implemented negotiation agents and demonstrated their behaviour. The agents are able to autonomously generate negotiation proposals with respect to compromises and compensations for them. During the negotiation the agents can react to the behaviour of their counterpart and follow a higher-level negotiation strategy.

We showed that the normalization of attribute values serves as a semantic uncoupling. It becomes possible to negotiate about any product or subject without changing the intrinsic negotiation mechanisms. An important improvement for this system would be the addition of a matchmaking module. In the matchmaking process the negotiation partners agree about negotiable attributes of a product and their semantics. This is a substantial prerequisite for every negotiation. In our paper we assumed this as given knowledge.

We demonstrated that parallel generation of attribute values in a proposal with respect to a matrix of compensation values is a feasible method to reproduce interdependencies and preferences in complex attribute relations. In negotiations people always consider interdependencies, make compromises and demand compensations. Our approach improves the formalization of rational and intelligent negotiation. However, the formalization requires exact specification of negotiation parameters. Obviously, these parameters exist in negotiations between human beings, but most of them are only implicitly known and followed. To specify them in exact numbers is often very difficult. Nevertheless, the application of our negotiation approach in a shopping system with personal assistance agents would be advantageous. It provides the user with a more powerful tool to express his interests and gives him much better control over the negotiation activities of his personal assistance agent.

Further improvements of our model will comprise the inclusion of additional strategies and tests for the success of the agents in negotiations with agents based on different models. For purposes of convenient use, we are going to implement an improved user interface and extended features for result evaluation.

References

[1] R. Aumann, S. Hart (Ed.), Handbook of Game Theory with Economic Applications, North-Holland 1992.

[2] Bargain Finder, URL: http://bf.cstar.ac.com/bf .

[3] W. Benn, O. Görlitz, R. Neubert: An adaptive Software Agent for automated Integrative Negotiations, to appear in: Proc. of the 9th Annual European Conference and Exhibition on Multimedia, Micro Systems and Electronic Commerce EMMSEC-99, Stockholm, 1999.

[4] A. Chavez, D. Dreilinger, R. Guttman, P. Maes, A Real-Life Experiment in Creating an Agent Marketplace, Proc. of the 2nd Int'l. Conf. on the Practical Application of Intelligent Agents and Multi-Agent Technology (PAAM'97) 1997.

[5] Firefly Network, URL: http://www.firefly.com .

[6] R. Guttman, P. Maes, Agent-mediated Integrative Negotiation for Retail Electronic Commerce, Proc. of the Workshop on Agent Mediated Electronic Trading (AMET'98) 1998.

[7] R. Guttman, A. Moukas, P. Maes, Agent-mediated Electronic Commerce: A Survey, Knowledge Engineering Review 1998.

[8] InfoSleuth, URL: http://www.mcc.com/projects/infosleuth/ .

[9] R. Keeney, H. Raiffa, Decisions with Multiple Objectives: Preferences and Value Trade-offs, John Wiley and Sons 1976.

[10] J. Kephart, J. Hanson, J. Sairamesh: Price-War Dynamics in a Free-Market Economy of Software Agents, presented at the Artificial Life VI Conference, University of California at Los Angeles, California, June 29, 1998.

[11] M. Klusch, Cooperative Information Agents on the Internet (in German), Verlag Dr. Kovač 1997.

[12] K. Konolige, A deduction model of belief, Pitman Publishers/ Morgan Kaufmann 1986.

[13] H. Kuhn (Ed.), Classics in Game Theory, Princeton University Press, Princeton NJ 1997.

[14] R. Lewicki, D. Saunders, J. Minton, Essentials of Negotiation, Irwin 1997.

[15] Logical Decisions, URL: http://www.logicaldecisions.com .

[16] MOMIS, Mediator envirOnment for Multiple Information Sources, URL: http://sparc20.dsi.unimo.it/momis/index.html .

[17] J. Rosenschein, G. Zlotkin, Rules of Encounter. Designing Conventions for Automated Negotiation among Computers, MIT Press 1994.

[18] T. Sandholm, Agents in Electronic Commerce: Component Technologies for Automated Negotiation and Coalition Formation, in M. Klusch, G. Weiß (Eds.): Cooperative Information Agents II, Lecture Notes in Artificial Intelligence 1435, Springer Verlag 1998.

[19] The Garlic Project, URL: http://www.almaden.ibm.com/cs/garlic/ .

[20] TSIMMIS, The Stanford-IBM Manager of Multiple Information Sources, URL: http://www-db.stanford.edu/tsimmis/ .

An Adaptive Conversational Interface for Destination Advice

Pat Langley,[1] Cynthia Thompson,[2]
Renée Elio,[3] and Afsaneh Haddadi[4]

[1] DaimlerChrysler Research & Technology Center
1510 Page Mill Road, Palo Alto, CA 94304 USA
[2] Center for the Study of Language and Information
Stanford University, Stanford CA 94305 USA
[3] Department of Computing Science, Assiniboia Hall
University of Alberta, Edmonton, Alberta T6G 2H1
[4] DaimlerChrysler Research and Technology
Alt-Moabit 96a, 10559 Berlin, Germany

Abstract. In this paper, we describe the Adaptive Place Advisor, a conversational interface designed to help users decide on a destination. We view the selection of destinations as an interactive process of constraint satisfaction, with the advisory system proposing attributes and the human responding. We further characterize this task in terms of heuristic search, which leads us to consider the system's representation of problem states, the operators it uses to generate those states, and the heuristics it invokes to select these operators. In addition, we report a graphical interface that supports this process for the specific task of recommending restaurants, as well as two methods for constructing user models from interaction traces. We contrast our approach to recommendation systems with the more common scheme of showing users a ranked list of items, but we also discuss related work on conversational systems. In closing, we present our plans to evaluate the Adaptive Place Advisor experimentally and to extend its functionality.

1 Introduction

As society becomes more complex, humans are confronted with ever more alternatives in their activities. Today, we have more news to hear, more books to read, more songs to appreciate, and more places to eat than ever before. In addition, access to the World Wide Web has led to substantial growth in the number of information sources. Each new option gives people a greater variety of choices, but the sheer number of alternatives often makes an intelligent choice impossible without some computational assistance.

In response to this need, there have been increased efforts to design and implement intelligent aides for filtering web sites (e.g., Pazzani, Muramatsu, & Billsus, 1996), news stories (e.g., Lang, 1995), and other information sources. A related line of research and development has led to *recommendation systems*, which are not limited to filtering information but can be used for any task that requires choice among a large set of predefined items. Most research in this area has built on the literature in document retrieval, which assumes a specific approach to choice and a particular type of interaction.

However, when developing any intelligent system, especially one that will interact with humans, it seems important to make one's design decisions carefully. In this paper, we describe a *conversational* approach to recommendation systems that diverges from those based on information retrieval. The next section characterizes the traditional framework and its drawbacks, then outlines an alternative that appears to hold some advantages. After this, we present the Adaptive Place Advisor, a prototype system that incorporates this approach to recommendation. The conversational framework also supports user models at a finer grain than the usual item level, and we consider two ways of learning such models from interaction traces. Finally, we discuss related work on conversational interfaces and suggest some directions for future research.

2 Two Approaches to Recommendation Systems

As we have noted, one can view many decision-support tasks in terms of making *recommendations*. A recent workshop on this topic indicates the variety of real-world problems that one can formulate as recommendation tasks, including the selection of videos (Nguyen & Haddawy, 1998), television programs (Das & ter Horst, 1998), and books (Mooney, Bennett, & Roy, 1998). In generic terms, we can characterize the task as:

> Given a large set of items and a description of the user's needs, present
> to the user a small set of the items that are suited to these needs.

This statement covers all of the examples mentioned above, along with many others. However, note that our task statement is intentionally abstract, in that it does not specify certain details, such as how the user communicates his needs, the manner in which results are presented, or even the number of recommended items. Any specific approach to developing recommendation systems must take a position on these design issues.

We can illustrate this point by describing the most widely used framework for recommendation systems, which we will call the *ranked list* approach. In this scheme, the user specifies his needs with one or more keywords and the system presents an (often) long list of results, ordered by their predicted relevance to the user. This technique has a long history in information retrieval, where it was originally designed to help find documents or reports during library research. However, the basic method is quite general, and it underlies most search engines for the World Wide Web, which millions now use regularly for many quite different selection tasks.

Yet despite its current popularity, the ranked list scheme is not the only approach to making recommendations. We need only look to conversations between humans for a very different model of this process. Consider a situation in which one person, who we will call the *enquirer*, asks another person, who we will call the *advisor*, for assistance in deciding on a restaurant at which to have dinner:

Enquirer: Where do you think I should eat tonight?

Advisor: Well, what type of cuisine would you like?

Enquirer: What types are there?

Advisor: Some examples are Chinese, Indian, and Mediterranean.

Enquirer: Oh, maybe Indian.

Advisor: What quality rating would you like?

Enquirer: I don't care, as long as it's cheap.

Advisor: How do you want to pay?

Enquirer: No, I think I'd like Chinese instead.

Advisor: Okay, we'll switch to Chinese food.
What city do you prefer?

Enquirer: How about Berkeley?

Advisor: I know three cheap Chinese restaurants in Berkeley.
One is the Long Life Vegi House on 2129 University Avenue.
Does that sound alright?

Enquirer: Sure, that sounds fine.

Clearly, one could develop recommendation systems that attempt to mimic this type of human interaction, rather than relying on keyword searches and ranked lists. We will refer to such systems as *conversational* interfaces.

The interaction supported by conversational systems seems quite different from that found in the ranked list approach. The most important distinction is that the enquirer never hears about a complete item until only one, or at most a few, choices remain. Rather than being overwhelmed with items that compete for his attention, he interacts with the advisor to narrow down the choices in an iterative, manageable fashion. This interaction takes the form of a sequence of questions, most designed to eliminate some items from consideration. Answering these questions plays a similar role to giving keywords with the ranked list scheme, but the aim is remove alternatives rather than to simply order them. The conversational process can also help the enquirer better understand his own desires, since thinking about possible questions and answers may clarify goals in ways a ranked list does not.

Clearly, such dialogues seem better for recommendations that must be delivered by sound rather than visually. This makes the conversational approach well suited not only for advice between humans, but also for computer interfaces that must rely on speech, such as ones used while the enquirer is driving. However, they also seem ideal, independent of modality, for tasks like restaurant and movie selection, in which the user needs to converge on at most a few items. On the other hand, ranked list methods seem more appropriate for tasks like the selection of web pages or news stories, in which the user may well want to examine many options. In the next section, we describe the Adaptive Place Advisor, a computational assistant that takes this conversational approach to recommendation.

3 The Adaptive Place Advisor

We are interested in developing a conversational interface that has broad applicability to recommendation tasks, but our initial work has focused on a particular class of problems – *destination selection* – that seems especially relevant to drivers. Our prototype system, the Adaptive Place Advisor, aims to help the user select a physical location that is relevant to his goals. Again, the basic approach involves carrying out a conversation with the user to identify a place that matches his needs at the time.

We view this conversational process in terms of heuristic search, similar to constraint satisfaction in that it requires the successive addition of constraints on solutions, but also analogous to game playing in that the user and system take turns. Formulating the problem within a search framework means we must represent not only items, as in ranked lists, but also states of the conversation, as well as operators for advancing the conversation and heuristics for deciding which operator to apply on each step. This treatment also has some important implications for the modeling of user preferences. In this section, we discuss each of these issues in turn.

Our approach to destination advice draws heavily on an earlier analysis of the task by Elio and Haddadi (1998, 1999), which itself borrows ideas from linguistic research on speech acts (e.g., Searle, 1969). One difference between our formulations is that the previous work distinguishes between search through a task space and a dialogue space, whereas we aggregate these into search through a combined space. Another distinction is that user intentions plays a central role in their framework, whereas our less sophisticated approach sidesteps intentions by specifying system actions that are appropriate to different types of user responses. Nevertheless, both analyses view decision making as a process of successively refining constraints, which separates them from the ranked-list scheme.

3.1 Representation of Items and States

Many recommendation systems, since they focus on retrieving documents or Web pages, represent each item as a 'bag of words', that is, in terms of the words in the text that describes each item. In contrast, the Adaptive Place Advisor assumes a more constrained representation, similar to that found in a relational database. The system stores each item as a conjunction of attribute-value pairs, each specifying information likely to interest the user. For restaurants, these characteristics include attributes like their location, the cuisine served, the hours of operation, the method of payment, the price range, the availability of parking, requirements for reservations, and the name.

However, representing an item like a restaurant does not equate to describing the state of a conversation about such items. To encode conversational states, we must allow *partial* descriptions of items, which the Place Advisor specifies as a subset of attribute-value pairs. For example, after receiving answers to a few questions, the system may have determined that the user would prefer to eat someplace in Palo Alto that serves Thai cuisine and that does not require reservations. Earlier in the dialogue, this specification will tend to be less constrained, whereas later states will tend to include more attribute values. We can view each such partial description as a database query that has an associated, but implicit, representation consisting of all restaurants that match the query.

But this tells only half the story, since the Place Advisor must also represent its knowledge about a conversation's history. This includes information about attributes that remain unasked, that the system has asked but the user has indicated are undesired, and that the user has indicated are important enough to be fixed. The system must also keep track of attributes and values it has mentioned in response to a user query, as well as complete items the user has rejected as unacceptable. Most important, it must represent the dialogue operator(s) indicated by the user's most recent utterance, since these determine the system's appropriate response.

3.2 Dialogue Operators

Our view of conversational recommendation as search also requires us to specify the operators that take steps through the search space. Following Elio and Haddadi (1998, 1999), we group conversational actions if they achieve the same effect, so that two superficially different utterances constitute examples of the same operator if they take the dialogue in the same direction. Table 1 summarizes the operators assumed by the Adaptive Place Advisor, which differ somewhat from those in the earlier analysis.

Let us first consider the operators available to the system for advancing the conversation. The most obvious, ASK-CONSTRAIN, involves asking a question to constrain items, by proposing some attribute that does not yet have a value. In our example, we saw four examples of this operator, with the advisor asking questions about the cuisine, quality of the food, payment options, and the location (city). Asking such questions is the most central activity of conversational interfaces, at least for recommendation tasks, since it determines the ways in which the system constrains items presented to the user.

Another operator, SUGGEST-VALUES, answers a user's query about possible values for an attribute. In our example, this occurred in response to the enquirer's query about cuisine. Note that, in this case, the advisor lists only a few options rather than all possible choices, and if we want our interface to seem natural, its answers should have a similar character. In some cases, the advisor may decide to suggest values for an attribute without an explicit request, especially if the user's response is predictable. A similar operator, SUGGEST-ATTRIBUTES, responds to a user query about the possible characteristics of destinations.

Once the conversation has reduced the alternatives to a manageable number, the advisor must invoke RECOMMEND-ITEM, an operator that proposes a complete item to the user. In the restaurant domain, this involves giving the restaurant name, address, and similar information, as we saw at the end of our sample dialogue. In some cases, the process of introducing a constraint can produce a situation in which no candidates are satisfactory. When this occurs, the advisor applies the operator ASK-RELAX, which proposes dropping an attribute

Table 1. Dialogue operators supported in the Adaptive Place Advisor, with system operators in boldface and user operators in italics.

Ask-Constrain. Asks the user a question designed to constrain available candidates.

Ask-Relax. Proposes to the user that a constraint be removed to expand candidates.

Suggest-Attributes. Suggests to the user a small set of unused attributes.

Suggest-Values. Suggests to the user a small set of values for a given attribute.

Recommend-Item. Recommends to the user an item that satisfies the constraints.

Answer-Constrain. Answers a system question by giving a value for the attribute.

Reject-Constrain. Refuses to answer a system question by rejecting the attribute.

Accept-Relax. Accepts a system suggestion to relax a constrained attribute.

Reject-Relax. Rejects a system suggestion to relax a constrained attribute.

Replace-Attribute. Replaces a system question with a different attribute.

Accept-Item. Accepts proposed destination and ends the conversation.

Reject-Item. Rejects proposed destination and requests another recommended item.

Query-Attributes. Asks system for information about possible attributes.

Query-Values. Asks system for information about possible values of an attribute.

---

to expand the candidate set. A less drastic response, which we have not implemented, would replace an attribute's value with another having a similar effect.

Now let us turn to the operators that the system assumes are available to the human user. The most central action the user can take, ANSWER-CONSTRAIN, involves answering a question so as to specify the value of some attribute. Our example included two instances of this operator, in response to questions about cuisine and city. Each such answer further constrains the items the system considers for presentation to the user, and thus advances the dialogue toward its goal of identifying a few recommended restaurants.

But the Place Advisor does not assume the user will always answer its questions. If the person decides that the proposed attribute is inappropriate or less relevant than some other factor, he can reject the attribute or even replace it with another, using the operators REJECT-CONSTRAIN or REPLACE-ATTRIBUTE. We saw the second type of response in our example when the enquirer did not specify a restaurant quality, but instead replied 'I don't care, as long as it's cheap'. Note that, effectively, this utterance not only replaces one question with another, but also answers the second question. Replacements can also apply to attributes and values agreed upon earlier in the conversation, as happened when the user changed his mind about cuisine and decided on Indian food.

In addition, the user can explicitly accept or reject other proposals that the system makes, say for relaxing a certain attribute (ACCEPT-RELAX or REJECT-RELAX) or for a complete item once the system recommends it (ACCEPT-ITEM or REJECT-ITEM). We saw no examples of such rejections in our earlier scenario, but they take the same form as rejecting questions for contraction. Finally, the user can query about the available attributes (QUERY-ATTRIBUTES) or, if the system has asked a question, about possible values of that attribute (QUERY-VALUES), as we saw for cuisine in our example.

3.3 Operator Selection and Search Control

Any search process requires some control structure to constrain and direct it. In the Adaptive Place Advisor, selection of the dialogue operators themselves is largely bounded by the communication protocols that govern human dialogue. Of course, one side of the conversation is determined by the user, so here we are concerned with how the system selects its own actions.

Table 2 presents English paraphrases of the rules that specify the Adaptive Place Advisor's selection of questions and recommendations. These control rules are sensitive to the database query that the system constructs during its interaction with the user. Thus, the initial rule (Q1) initializes the query and welcomes the user. The second (Q2) selects an attribute to constrain the query when more than four candidates remain, then asks the user about this attribute. If the query has become so constrained that no items remain, the third rule (Q3) proposes to the user an attribute to relax. Finally, if the query returns only a few candidates, the last rule (Q4) selects one of these items and recommends it to the user.

Table 3 presents another set of control rules that are responsible for dealing more directly with user responses. Many of the conditions here refer to user-applied operators, which we assume another part of the Place Advisor infers from the user's behavior. For example, rule R1 handles situations in which the user answers a question with some value, thus constraining the database query, whereas rule R2 detects when the user has rejected an attribute and notes this fact for future reference.

Rules R3 and R4, respectively, handle the analogous cases in which the user accepts and rejects system proposals to relax a particular constraint. Similarly, rules R5 and R6 deal with acceptance and rejection of system recommendations about particular items. The seventh rule, R7, covers situations in which the user rejects a question the system has asked or decides to replace a question previously answered. The following two rules, R8 and R9, respond to user queries about available attributes and values, keeping track of what they tell the user to avoid repetition. The final condition-action rule, RW, is a default that, if the user has not yet replied, waits for a response.

As we noted above, the current implementation does not make use of an explicit representation of user intentions, as Elio and Haddadi assumed in their analysis. Nor does the Adaptive Place Advisor directly support subdialogues about side topics, such as for clarification of an attribute's values, as does their design. Rather, for both purposes, the system relies on information about the

Table 2. Control rules in the Adaptive Place Advisor that present questions to user.

```
Q1. If there is no database Query,
    Then let Query be an unconstrained query,
        Let Unasked be all known attributes.
        Let Asked be the empty set.
        Let Undesired be the empty set.
        Let Fixed be the empty set.
        Let Rejected be the empty set.
        Welcome the user.
Q2. If Size(Query) > 4,
    Then let Attribute be Select-Constrain(Query, Unasked, Undesired).
        Remove Attribute from Unasked.
        Add Attribute to Asked.
        Ask-Constrain(Attribute).
Q3. If Size(Query) = 0,
    Then let Attribute be Select-Relax(Query, Asked, Fixed).
        Ask-Relax(Attribute).
Q4. If 0 < Size(Query) < 4,
    Then let Recommended be Select-Candidate(Query, Rejected).
        Recommend-Item(Recommended).
```

---

history of the conversation and the dialogue operators that the user has invoked. We believe these will be sufficient to support natural conversations about destinations, but ultimately this remains an empirical question.

The rules described in Tables 2 and 3 establish some general guidelines about the flow of conversation, but some important choices still remain. One decision, denoted by the call to Select-Constrain in Rule Q2, involves determining the specific question the system should ask to constrain the query. To this end, the Adaptive Place Advisor selects the attribute that provides the most information and thus minimizes the uncertainty within the items C that satisfy the constraints already established. In mathematical terms, it selects the attribute a_i that minimizes, for the random variable c of possible items, the entropy measure

$$H(c|a_i) = \sum_{v_j \in a_i} \sum_{c_k \in C} -\log(p(c_k|a_i = v_j)) \cdot p(c_k, a_i = v_j) ,$$

where c_k is a particular item in the set C that the user may find acceptable and v_j is a possible value for attribute a_i. We can further compute

$$p(c_k|a_i = v_j) = \frac{p(c_k)}{\sum_{c_j \in C'} p(c_j)} ,$$

where C' is the set of items which satisfy the revised constraints that include

Table 3. Control rules in the Adaptive Place Advisor that handle user responses.

```
R1. If Response is Answer-Constrain(Attribute, Value),
    Then add Attribute Value as a constraint on Query.

R2. If Response is Reject-Constrain(Attribute),
    Then add Attribute to Undesired.
        Remove Attribute from Asked.

R3. If Response is Accept-Relax(Attribute),
    Then remove Attribute as a constraint on Query.
        Remove Attribute from Asked.

R4. If Response is Reject-Relax(Attribute),
    Then add Attribute to Fixed.

R5. If Response is Accept-Item(Recommended),
    Then halt the conversation.

R6. If Response is Reject-Item(Recommended),
    Then add Recommended to Rejected.

R7. If Response is Replace-Attribute(Attribute, New-Attribute),
    Then add Attribute to Undesired.
        Remove Attribute from Asked.
        Add New-Attribute to Asked.
        Remove New-Attribute from Unasked.
        Let Attribute be New-Attribute.

R8. If Response is Query-Attribute( ),
    Then let Attributes be
            Select-Attributes(Unasked, Asked, Suggested-Attributes).
        Add Attributes to Suggested-Attributes.
        Suggest-Attributes(Attributes).

R9. If Response is Query-Value(Attribute),
    Then let Values be Select-Values(Attribute, Suggested-Values).
        Add Values to Suggested-Values.
        Suggest-Values(Values).

RW. If there is no Response,
    Then wait for some response.
```

$a_i = v_j$. In addition, $p(c_k, a_i = v_j)$ is simply $p(c_k)$ if item c_k meets the revised constraints and zero otherwise.

As a first approximation, we assume that all items have equal probability, which means that $p(c_k) = |C|^{-1}$. The resulting measure behaves sensibly in simple situations. For instance, given a Boolean attribute that divides the remaining items into two groups of equal size and another that divides them into two unequal groups, the metric prefers the attribute that gives the even split.

Using this measure, the Adaptive Place Advisor computes the information to be gained by asking each possible question, then selects the one with the lowest entropy, breaking ties at random. This evaluation metric is similar to one often used in constructing decision trees from training data, except that it does not use class labels and it recalculates the expression during each conversation, rather than creating a permanent tree structure. This makes the question-selection strategy more akin to 'lazy' approaches to decision-tree induction, which construct only a single path through an implicit tree. In our domain, this path corresponds to a search trajectory through the space of conversational actions.

The system must make similar choices when suggesting attributes or values in response to a user query, and when recommending complete items that satisfy the specified constraints. On each conversational step, the Adaptive Place Advisor make predictions about which attribute to present and, given an attribute, about which value to suggest. In responding to a user query, the system simply presents the three most probable options not yet included in the query and not yet seen by the user. At the item level, the system combines its probabilities about attribute values to rank the candidate destinations and presents the most likely one the user has not yet seen.

The Adaptive Place Advisor must also select an attribute when it decides to relax its constraints because no candidate items remain. In this situation, the system selects the attribute that has not yet been rejected for relaxation by the user and that, when removed from the current database query, gives the smallest set of candidates. One could imagine more sophisticated evaluation metrics and even strategies for replacing one value with another, rather than removing the attribute entirely, but the current version takes the most straightforward approach to this issue.

3.4 A Graphical Interface for Conversational Advice

Our long-term plans for the Adaptive Place Advisor call for an interface that supports spoken conversations, drawing on techniques from natural-language processing and speech recognition. The system could then support interactions in a broad range of settings, including situations in which the user is driving an automobile. However, such interfaces are difficult to implement and not always robust, so our initial version instead relies on a graphical interface that we have designed to parallel the conversations we envision with the future system. Figure 1 shows the display, which includes boxes on the left for destination attributes, boxes on the right for their values, menu buttons for information about each, and a box at the bottom for the final candidates.

There exist direct analogues between interactions that occur with this interface and the dialogue operators we considered above. For example, the Adaptive Place Advisor asks a question by showing a new attribute in the left column, and the user answers a question by typing his preferred value in the corresponding box on the right. The person can also query the system about the attribute's

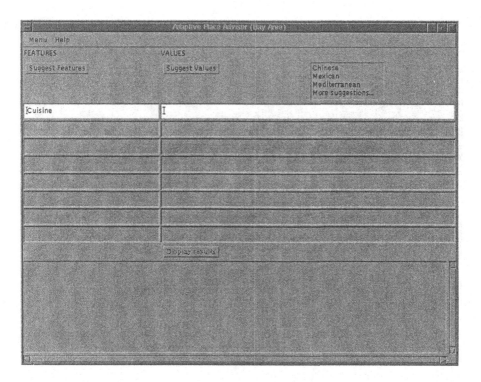

Fig. 1. Graphical display for the Adaptive Place Advisor, showing a state after the user has asked for information about the attribute 'cuisine' and received answers from the system.

values by clicking the menu on the top right, but Figure 1 shows that this menu presents only three values at a time, to reflect the limited bandwidth of spoken conversations. The user can request more values, but this requires an explicit request, which corresponds to a separate dialogue operator.

If the user wants to reject a question rather than answering it, he simply highlights and deletes the one proposed by the system, in which case it suggests another attribute. He can also replace one attribute with another by typing over the highlighted proposal. On a related note, the user can request information about alternative attributes by clicking the menu button on the top left, though again this presents only three options at a time, to reflect the nature of spoken dialogues. Similar actions are possible for values, which the user can reject by deletion or replace by typing over them. When the system decides it should relax an attribute, it highlights the proposed retraction, which the user can accept by typing 'return' or reject by taking any other keyboard action.

Figure 2 shows the graphical display after the conversation has reduced the candidate set to only three restaurants. In this case, the system displays detailed information about one candidate in the lower box, and the user can either accept

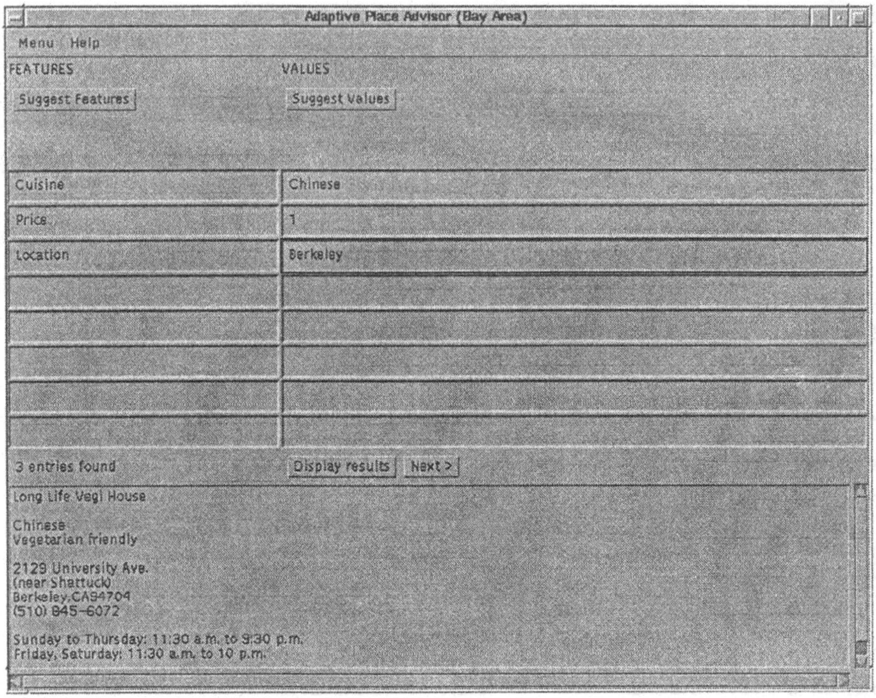

Fig. 2. Graphical display for the Adaptive Place Advisor, showing a state after the system has asked three questions and received answers from the user.

this recommendation or ask to see another alternative by clicking the 'Next' button. We could have designed the system to display all remaining candidates, but again we have constrained presentation to imitate the style of communication that occurs during human interactions.

3.5 Modeling User Preferences

We refer to the Adaptive Place Advisor as 'adaptive' because its design includes a module that constructs user models from interaction traces. However, our goal for user modeling differs from the one commonly assumed in recommendation systems, which emphasizes improving accuracy or related measures like precision and recall. We assume that the conversational nature of the Place Advisor will already give acceptable recommendations at the level of items like restaurants, so the system will not construct a user model at this level.

On the other hand, the dialogue process, if not well guided, can be tedious and time consuming, so we need user modeling to produce more *efficient* conversations. Just as interactions with a friend who knows your concerns can be more directed than one with a stranger, so dialogues with the Adaptive Place Advisor should become more directed over time, giving a form of speedup learning. This suggests modeling user preferences at a finer-grained level than in typical adaptive interfaces, focusing on the questions a user prefers to answer and the responses he tends to give, rather than at the level of entire items.

We are exploring two approaches to user modeling at the conversational level. The first represents the learned user model in direct probabilistic terms. For this, we need some way to predict the distribution of questions (attributes), as well as the distribution of answers (values), given other attribute-value pairs. One straightforward response is to use the naive Bayesian classifier (Langley, Iba, & Thompson, 1992), which we can train to predict the accepted attribute given other attribute values, as well as the value of some attribute given the same conditions. This method estimates and stores the conditional probability of each attribute value given the predicted entity, along with the probability of each entity. Naive Bayes fares well on many domains, despite its assumption of attribute independence, because it must estimate very few parameters, and it also deals cleanly with missing attributes for questions not yet answered. For example, suppose the system wants to predict the distribution of values for 'city' from the values of other attributes. If only 'cuisine' and 'price' are known, then naive Bayes simply ignores other attributes and uses these in predicting the city.

However, we need some way to combine statistics about the user's behavior with the system's generic mode of operation. Recall that the Place Advisor's default technique assumes a uniform distribution over items that, combined with the database, produces a probability distribution for each attribute conditioned on the attribute values already specified during the dialogue. Rather than using these as the final probabilities, we can use them as prior probabilities in the user model. Naive Bayes typically assumes uniform priors over classes and attribute values, but reliance on database queries seems a clean way to generate more informed priors that are relevant to the domain at hand. If the user's preferences disagree with these priors, his responses will alter the distributions in the user model, but to the extent that they do agree, the system will behave according to his wishes all the sooner.

Another approach is suggested by the Adaptive Place Advisor's similarity to case-based reasoning systems for help desks and related applications, which (as we discuss shortly) also engage in conversations of a sort. The basic idea is to store cases in a manner that represents details of a user's past dialogues, in terms of the questions he has accepted and the answers he has given, along with their order. The system would compare its description of the current dialogue state against stored traces to find cases that match closely, then use the selected case to decide on the next question. For instance, suppose the user and system have agreed on Chinese cuisine and medium price; if, during a previous interaction, the user accepted a question about the city under similar conditions, the system would ask about the city this time as well. We can apply the same basic scheme to predict the user's answers, which (if predictable enough) the system could offer as alternatives without an explicit user request.

A well-known characteristic of case-based methods is their sensitivity to the distance metric used for case selection. Here it seems natural to use the entropy measure described earlier to calculate the weights on attributes, since we intended it precisely to determine their relevance. But this raises another design issue, since we must decide when the system should rely on a retrieved case to select attributes or values and when it should use the entropy measure directly. One scheme would invoke a retrieved case only when its distance to the current situation fell below a given threshold and fall back on the entropy measure otherwise. This two-part response is less elegant than the probabilistic method discussed above, but a case-based approach offers many attractions, so we intend to explore this method as well.

4 Related Work on Conversational Interfaces

Although the ranked-list framework remains the most common approach to computer-assisted recommendation, we are not the first researchers to realize the potential of conversational interfaces. Rich (1979) describes one of the earliest systems, which carried out a textual conversation with a user, asking directed questions to infer their reading tastes for the purpose of book recommendation.

More recently, Allen et al. (1995) report on their ambitious TRAINS system, an intelligent assistant for planning tasks that converses with users in spoken natural language. Like the Place Advisor, the program interacts with the user to progressively construct a solution, though the knowledge structures are partial plans rather than constraints, and search involves operators for plan modification rather than database contraction and expansion. Each conversational step addresses issues about when, where, and how to complete a plan while ensuring no conflicts occur, rather than selecting a single item, as in our work. TRAINS lacks any mechanism for user modeling, but the overall system is considerably more mature and has been evaluated extensively.

Smith and Hipp (1994) describe another related project, this one concerning a conversational interface for circuit diagnosis. Their system aims to construct not a plan or a set of constraints, but rather a proof tree. The central dialogue operator, which requests knowledge from the user that would aid the proof process, is invoked when the program detects a 'missing axiom' that it needs for its reasoning. This heuristic plays the same role in their system as does the Place Advisor's heuristic for selecting attributes to constrain destination selection. The interface does some limited user modeling, but only infers user knowledge during the course of one conversation, not over the long term, as in our approach.

Perhaps the most closely related effort comes from Rich and Sidner (1998). Their COLLAGEN system supports conversations about complex tasks like scheduling a sequence of airline trips, relying on a graphical interface for interactions between the user and an advisory system. Their approach also builds upon theories of discourse to support an interactive decision-making process. One difference from the Adaptive Place Advisor is that COLLAGEN includes a more sophisticated model of dialogue that makes provision for interruptions, as well incorporating a more general representation of the resulting plan. However, their system's initiative seems to focus on suggesting tasks that the user should next address, making it less directive than the approach we have taken.

Dowding et al. (1993) and Seneff et al. (1998) have also developed conversational interfaces that give advice about air travel. Like the Place Advisor, their systems ask the user questions in order to reduce candidates, treating the choice of selecting airline flights as the interactive construction of database queries. Natural language and speech play a central role in both decision aids, making them more mature than our work on destination advice. However, neither system includes a component for user modeling to make conversations more efficient, despite the clear differences among individuals in this domain.

Linden, Hanks, and Lesh (1997) present another interactive travel assistant that carries out conversations through a graphical interface. Their system also asks questions in an effort to narrow down the available candidates, using similar dialogue operators to those we described earlier, and they share our aim of satisfying the user with as few interactions as possible. Their response to this challenge relies on a 'candidate/critique' approach to problem solving, in which the system presents candidate solutions to the user, who then critiques the solutions. From these responses, the system infers a user model stated as weights on attributes of travel choices, such as price and travel time. Unlike the Adaptive Place Advisor, it does not carry these profiles over to future conversations, but one can envision a version that stores longer-term models.

Aha, Breslow, and Maney's (1998) work on 'conversational case-based reasoning' also has connections to our research. Their effort focuses on troubleshooting printers and similar tasks, and their approach relies on interactions with the user to retrieve cases from memory that will recommend actions to correct some problem. The system supports simple textual interactions, using part-of-speech tags and keyword matching, but it relies primarily on a graphical interface for presenting and answering questions. The dialogue operators and basic flow of control have much in common with the Adaptive Place Advisor, in that answering questions increasingly constrains available answers. However, one significant difference is that they let the user select which of several system-generated questions to answer next, and which of several presented cases (items) is closest to his needs. Their system also supports inference of some fields based on the values of others, which reduces the number of questions it must ask the user.

We have focused here on conversational interfaces, but research on user modeling has been more widespread in traditional recommendation systems. Pazzani, Muramatsu, and Billsus (1996) report a content-based approach that recommends web pages, whereas Shardanand and Maes (1995) describe a collaborative method that suggests movies. Other systems that induce user models focus on filtering news stories (Lang, 1995) and electronic mail (Segal & Kephart, 1999). Nor has this idea been limited to recommendation tasks, with other adaptive user interfaces addressing generative problems like note taking (Schlimmer & Hermens, 1993), route advising (Rogers, Fiechter, & Langley, 1999), and interactive scheduling (Gervasio, Iba, & Langley, in press). Langley (1999) gives a more thorough review of research on the topic of adaptive interfaces.

5 Concluding Remarks

In this paper, we described the initial version of the Adaptive Place Advisor, an intelligent assistant designed to help people select a destination, specifically a restaurant. Unlike most recommendation systems, which accept keywords and produce a ranked list, this one carries out a conversation with the user to progressively narrow his options. And unlike other adaptive interfaces, it constructs user models at the level of dialogue actions rather than the level of complete items. We viewed the dialogue process in terms of problem-space search, describing the various states, operators, and heuristics involved. We also described two approaches to user modeling, one relying on case retrieval and the other on probabilistic summaries, that should lead to more efficient conversations as the system gains experience with the user.

Although we have a detailed design and a partial implementation of the Adaptive Place Advisor, clearly more work lies ahead. First, we should carry out pilot studies with the current graphical version to get experience with users' responses. This may reveal design flaws in the system, such as the need for additional dialogue operators. If these studies are encouraging, we should then run more systematic experiments to evaluate our two approaches to user modeling. Our main hypothesis here is that conversation time will decrease as the system gains experience with a user, and that this reduction will occur more rapidly than when user modeling is not included. But we are also interested in the details of this improvement, including the learning rate and the asymptotic accuracy, so we will collect learning curves that plot performance against the number of conversations.

On another front, we must still replace the graphical interface with one that incorporates natural language and speech. The generation module should be straightforward, since we can rely on canned phrases to ask questions and propose answers. The understanding process will be more challenging, but our design should encourage constrained dialogues, often with one-word answers, that can be handled by existing software packages. Moreover, the presence of a user model should aid speech recognition by providing probability distributions over the user's answers.

In the longer term, we intend to expand the framework to take into account other factors, such as the user's willingness to explore new cuisines or cities and his desire for variety. We might represent the former with a single factor indicating the probability, based on past responses, that the user will accept an attribute value the system has not suggested before. We could represent the user's bias about variety as the average time between selections of a given attribute value, though we might also associate a variety parameter with items themselves. For example, some users may be willing to eat Chinese food once a week and others only once a month, and for some people variety among restaurants may be more important than variety in cuisine or location.

We also hope to extend our conversational approach to other types of destinations, such as hotels and theaters, and to link the system to other driving assistants like the Adaptive Route Advisor (Rogers, Fiechter, & Langley, 1999), which recommends routes to a specified destination. Our goal for such additions is to provide new functionality that will make the Adaptive Place Advisor more attractive to users, but also to test the generality of our framework for adaptive recommendation. In turn, these should bring us closer to truly flexible computational aides that carry out natural dialogues with humans.

Acknowledgements

We thank Lei Wang for implementing the basic version of the Adaptive Place Advisor described in this paper, Sean Stromsten for the information-theoretic analysis of attribute selection, and Stanley Peters for enlightening discussions about the design of conversational interfaces.

References

Aha, D., Breslow, L., & Maney, T. (1998). Supporting conversational case-based reasoning in an integrated reasoning framework. *Proceedings of the AAAI Workshop on Case-based Reasoning Integrations* (pp. 7–11). Madison, WI: AAAI Press.

Allen, J., Schubert, L., Ferguson, G., Heeman, P., Hwang, C., Kato, T., Light, M., Martin, N., Miller, B., Poesio, M., & Traum, D. (1995). The TRAINS project: A case study in building a conversational planning agent. *Journal of Experimental and Theoretical Artificial Intelligence*, 7, 7–48.

Das, D., & ter Horst, H. (1998) Recommender systems for TV. *Proceedings of the AAAI Workshop on Recommender Systems* (pp. 35–36). Madison, WI: AAAI Press.

Dowding, J., Gawron, J., Appelt, D., Bear, J., Cherny, L., Moore, R., & Moran,D. (1993). GEMINI: A natural language system for spoken-language understanding. *Proceedings of the 31st Annual Meeting of the Association for Computational Linguistics* (pp. 54–61). Columbus, OH.

Elio, R., & Haddadi, A. (1998). *Dialog management for an adaptive database assistant* (Technical Report 98-3). Daimler-Benz Research & Technology Center, Palo Alto, CA.

Elio, R., & Haddadi, A. (1999). On abstract task models and conversation policies. *Proceedings of the Agents '99 Workshop on Specifying and Implementing Conversation Policies*. Seattle, WA.

Gervasio, M. T., Iba, W., & Langley, P. (in press). Learning user evaluation functions for adaptive scheduling assistance. *Proceedings of the Sixteenth International Conference on Machine Learning*. Bled, Slovenia: Morgan Kaufmann.

Lang, K. (1995). NEWSWEEDER: Learning to filter news. *Proceedings of the Twelfth International Conference on Machine Learning* (pp. 331–339). Lake Tahoe, CA: Morgan Kaufmann.

Langley, P. (in press). User modeling in adaptive interfaces. *Proceedings of the Seventh International Conference on User Modeling*. Banff, Alberta: Springer.

Langley, P., Iba, W., & Thompson, K. (1992). An analysis of Bayesian classifiers. *Proceedings of the Tenth National Conference on Artificial Intelligence* (pp. 223–228). San Jose, CA: AAAI Press.

Linden, G., Hanks, S., & Lesh, N. (1997). Interactive assessment of user preference models: The automated travel assistant. *Proceedings of the Sixth International Conference on User Modeling* (pp. 67–78). Chia Laguna, Sardinia: Springer.

Mooney, R. J., Bennett, P. N., & Roy, L. (1998). Book recommending using text categorization with extracted information. *Proceedings of the AAAI Workshop on Recommender Systems* (pp. 70–74). Madison, WI: AAAI Press.

Nguyen, H., & Haddawy, P. (1998). The decision-theoretic video advisor. *Proceedings of the AAAI Workshop on Recommender Systems* (pp. 77–80). Madison, WI: AAAI Press.

Pazzani, M., Muramatsu, J., & Billsus, D. (1996). SYSKILL & WEBERT: Identifying interesting web sites. *Proceedings of the Thirteenth National Conference on Artificial Intelligence* (pp. 54–61). Portland, OR: AAAI Press.

Rich, C., & Sidner, C. (1998). COLLAGEN: A collaboration manager for software interface agents. *User Modeling and User-Adapted Interaction, 8*, 315–350.

Rich, E. (1979). User modeling via stereotypes. *Cognitive Science, 3*, 329–354.

Rogers, S., Fiechter, C., & Langley, P. (1999). An adaptive interactive agent for route advice. *Proceedings of the Third International Conference on Autonomous Agents* (pp. 198–205). Seattle, WA: ACM Press.

Schlimmer, J. C., & Hermens, L. A. (1993). Software agents: Completing patterns and constructing user interfaces. *Journal of Artificial Intelligence Research, 1*, 61–89.

Searle, J. (1969). *Speech acts.* New York: Cambridge University Press.

Segal, R. B., & Kephart, J. O. (1999). MailCat: An intelligent assistant for organizing e-mail. *Proceedings of the Third International Conference on Autonomous Agents* (pp. 276–282). Seattle, WA: ACM Press.

Seneff, S., Hurley, E., Lau, R., Pao, C., Schmid, P., & Zue, V. (1998). GALAXY-II: A reference architecture for conversational system development. *Proceedings of the Fifth International Conference on Spoken Language Processing* (pp. 931–934). Sydney: ASSTA.

Shardanand, U., & Maes, P. (1995). Social information filtering: Algorithms for automating 'word of mouth'. *Proceedings of the Conference on Human Factors in Computing Systems* (pp. 210–217). Denver, CO: ACM Press.

Smith, R., & Hipp, D. (1994). *Spoken natural language dialog systems: A practical approach.* New York: Oxford University Press.

Anticipation Delegation,and Demonstrations: Why Talking to Agents Is Hard

MICHAEL LEWIS

School of Information Sciences

University of Pittsburgh

ml@sis.pitt.edu

Abstract. Interacting with a computer requires adopting a metaphor to guide our actions and expectations. When we choose to build and use agents we are committing to interact with a domain indirectly. Whether this is a good choice or not will depend on the ease and accuracy with which we can instruct our agents. Current approaches range from specialized agents programmed to perform specific tasks, to learning programs which get on-the-job training looking over a user's shoulder. In the expert case very little communication is needed because the agent already knows what it is going to do. In the novice case the raison d'etre of agent learning is to relieve the user of the tedium of instructing it. The vast middle ground of tasks of moderate complexity too infrequent for targeted implementations or empirical learning goes largely untouched. Three current projects at our laboratory address aspects of this problem. The first, a series of experiments in which subjects are aided by fallible agents examines the role of trust in providing a context for communication. The second project compares the effectiveness of communication to adapt an agent plan with human planning which is critiqued by an equally informed agent. The third project uses a variety of learning and interaction techniques to help a user communicate the information needed to access and extract information on a subsequent autonomous visit.

1. Introduction

Interacting with a computer requires adopting some metaphor to guide our actions and expectations. Most human-computer interfaces can be classified according to two dominant metaphors: *agent* or *environment.* Interactions based on an agent metaphor treat the computer as an intermediary which responds to user requests. In the environment metaphor a model of the task domain is presented for the user to interact with directly.

The power of the environment approach which provides advertisement and unique identification and selectability of available objects and actions is reflected in the ascendance of graphical user interfaces (GUI's). The value of the agent metaphor to interaction only becomes apparent when objects are not present or fully visualizable and actions are repetitive, delayed, or poorly specified. The distinctions between agent and environment based HCI are very similar to those between manual and automated action in the physical world. It is much simpler for us to drive a car or set a table than to instruct a robot to do so, yet we would rather adjust a thermostat or program a milling machine than repeatedly performing these actions by hand. While the computer offers the ultimate in flexible automation, instructing it do what we wish may be arbitrarily hard for humans as demonstrated by the difficulty experienced in using traditional programming and scripting languages. The growing popularity of "agent-based" interaction reflects the emergence of an increasingly powerful and complex computing environment bringing with it desires to perform flexible tasks involving multiple or unknown objects by users who do not wish or may not have the ability to program.

The greatest impediment to assisting human users lies in communicating their intent and making results intelligible to them. .

By this we mean that today in almost all cases the limiting factor in HCI is not computing cycles or connectivity to information sources or characteristics of peripherals (the machine side) but in the user's ability and/or willingness to communicate these desires and sift, organize, and represent the machine's response to satisfy them (the human side). So, for example, although I have a Perl interpreter for which I could in principle write a script which would visit a list of web sites, extract particular information from each, perform comparisons, and return the result to my Inbox, I will almost certainly not do so. The effort of prescribing how to navigate, how to parse HTML at each of the sites, and how to analyze and return the results is infinitely more difficult than pushing buttons and following links on my browser myself. It would probably remain more difficult even if I had to repeat the search ten or fifteen times. Even when the time to search repeatedly equaled the time to program, I would still prefer the manual search because of the lower cognitive effort. As this example suggests, scripting languages may fit our definition as maximally powerful instructable "agents", yet they fail miserably in satisfying Negreponte's [6] desire for an implacable butler or mine for a no hassle autonomous web searcher. The problem is a human variant of Turing equivalency. Scripting languages or for that matter assembly code may meet the letter of a definition of agents but the spirit clearly lies in the ease with which our desires can be communicated.

1.1 A Cybernetic Model

Don Norman (1986) characterizes human-computer interaction as the problem of bridging twin gulfs of execution and evaluation. The execution side of the cycle involves translating a goal into a sequence of actions for achieving that goal. The evaluation side involves using feedback from the domain to compare the result of the action to the goal. The model is cybernetic rather than logical in that attention to parts of the environment and processing of these inputs are determined by prior actions and subsequent actions are in turn functions of previous feedback. A crucial feature of this model is that tampering with either side of the loop can lead to detrimental or unanticipated results. If the execution side is automated the human may fail to observe effects of actions and be unable to correct errors or modulate ongoing behavior. If the evaluation side is automated the human may be unable to track the effect of actions and adjust to their results. Norman proposes seven stages of action in this model to link the user's goals to the world The stages of execution are: forming an intention to act, translating this intention into a planned sequence of actions and executing that sequence. The stages of evaluation are perceiving the state of the world, interpreting this perception in light of prior action and evaluating that change with respect to initial goal. The gulfs refer to the interface/metaphor which separates the user's goals from the application domain in which they must be realized.

While some agent-based systems may require no more human interaction than a conventional GUI, they should support the same cycle of action, feedback, and interpretation. This will in general be more difficult because the greater flexibility and autonomy which made a task suitable for an agent also make monitoring and evaluating more difficult for the human. Except in cases where task performance is completely correct and deterministic (as in the case of a command to open a file or delete a document) uncertainties may need to be addressed even in the simplest interactions.

Just as our networked computing infrastructure has given rise to multi-agent systems and cooperative computing paradigms, it has become a medium for human coordination and cooperation. The role of agents in this environment for facilitating human-human interactions is a second crucial research issue.

1.2 Desiderata for Human Agent Interaction

Graphical user interfaces have succeeded by providing advertisement, unique identification and selectability of available objects and actions to their users. To be a viable alternative, intelligent agents must also convey these types of information. More precisely they must:

1) Advertise their availability
   users must be made aware of the agent's existence and how to access it

2) Advertise their service domains
   users must be made aware of the types of services an agent can perform, or arrange to have performed (multi-agent systems)

3) Advertise their capabilities
   users must be made aware of the precise nature of services actually available

4) Advertise their "instruction language"
   users must be made aware of how to specify parameters and objects to "customize" the services they request

5) Advertise opportunities for monitoring
   users must be made aware of how they may monitor task performance

Over the past three years we have conducted a series of experiments aimed at identifying strategies for improving human-agent performance in the presence of errors, aiding in human-human cooperation, choosing between human/machine initiative, and hybrid forms of instruction combining programming by demonstration, learning, and command. In conducting these experiments we have attempted to: identify issues likely to be important for proposed uses of agents such as aggregation, interpretation, and presentation of information and test them at simplified tasks which allow us full experimental control..

2. The Tandem Simulation

Two of our experiments used a low fidelity simulation (TANDEM) of a target identification task, jointly developed at the Naval Air Warfare Center-Training Systems Division and the University of Central Florida and modified for these experiments. The TANDEM simulation was developed under the TADMUS (tactical decision making under stress) program of the US Office of Naval Research and simulates cognitive characteristics of tasks performed in the command information center (CIC) of an Aegis missile cruiser.

The cognitive aspects of the Aegis command and control tasks which are captured include time stress, memory loading, data aggregation for decision making and the need to rely on and cooperate with other team members (team mode) to successfully perform the task. The more highly skilled tasks of the individual team members involving extracting and interpreting information from radar, sonar, and intelligence displays is not modeled in the simulation. Instead of interpreting displayed signals to acquire diagnostic information about targets, TANDEM

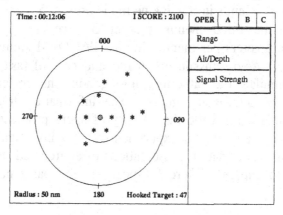

Figure 1. The TANDEM Display

participants access this information manually from menus. In accessing new information, old information is cleared from the display creating the memory load of simultaneously maintaining up to 5 parameter values and their interpretation.

In the TANDEM task subjects must identify and take action on a large number of targets (high workload) and are awarded points for correctly identifying the targets (type, intent, and threat). and taking the correct action (clear or shoot). A maximum of 100 points is awarded per target for correct identification and correct action. Users "hook" a target on their screen by left-clicking on the target or selecting "hook" from a menu and specifying a target's unique contact number. Only after a target is hooked can they access information relative to that target. In team configuration TANDEM consists of three networked pc's each providing access through menus to five parameters relative to a "hooked" target. Their tasks involve identifying the type of contact (submarine, surface, or aircraft), its classification (military or civilian), and its intent (peaceful or hostile). Each of these decisions is made at a different control station and depends on five distinct parameter values, only three of which are available at that station. Subjects therefore must communicate among themselves to assure that they have all hooked the same target and subsequently exchange parameter values to classify the target. It the team finds a target to be hostile it is shot, otherwise it is cleared and the team moves on to another target.

In standalone mode all of the information is made available on a single pc with the station specific parameters accessed using three distinct menus. Menus in standalone mode present 5 parameters each. In team mode the three menus present 3 (overlapping among team members) parameters per menu. Just as TANDEM simulates cognitive aspects of the Aegis missile command and control task, it provides a context to simulate the gathering, aggregation, and presentation of C2I information by intelligent agents. The information found on menus remains ground truth while the validity of agent processed information can be manipulated by the experimenter. To investigate impacts on human-human coordination presentations of aggregated information can be tailored to support different aspects of the participants' cognitive tasks.

2.1 Trust, Error, and Uncertainty

Many of the complex of issues involving mutual human-machine modeling, awareness, and coordination are captured by the anthropomorphic term trust. If we examine the considerations that enter into our decision to delegate a task to a subordinate, instruct the subordinate in how to perform the task, monitor that performance, or authorize some class of tasks without follow-up, our trust in the subordinate will almost certainly play an explanatory role. Closer consideration will show our use of the term to be multidimensional. The trust we have that our secretary will remember to pick up the mail, is distinct from our trust that she will compose a postable business letter, which in turn is distinct from our trust in the lawyer who assures us that the letter is not actionable. A merger of several taxonomies proposed by Lee and Moray (1992) distinguishes:.

1) trust which is based on observed consistency of behavior (*persistence* or *predictability*)I trust my watch to keep relatively accurate time
2) trust which is based on a belief in competence or well formedness (*competence* or *dependability*).I trust the recipe for hollandaise
3) trust which is based on faith in purpose or obligation (*fiduciary responsibility* or *faith*)I trust my physician to monitor my health

As bases for human modeling of machine agents this taxonomy suggests that agents can be made predictable by: 1) consistently pairing simple observable actions with inputs, or 2) making the causes and rules governing an agent's behavior transparent or 3) making the purpose, capability, and reliability of the agent available to the user. Muir [5] refers to the process of acquiring predictive models of these sorts as *trust calibration*. The idea being that performance will be better for human-machine systems in which trust is accurately calibrated because the human's model will allow more accurate predictions. The greater predictability of consistent or competent agents should also make boundary conditions and "brittleness" more apparent and remediable. Agents trusted on faith, by contrast, would require a very high degree of reliability across their range and more communication to maintain accurate coordination.

Where information sources are unreliable or information processing algorithms are uncertain, brittle, or error prone, usefulness of their services will depend on how readily they can be incorporated into their user's model of the situation. The first TANDEM experiment manipulates error, error source, and transparency of presentation to address the questions of task allocation (under what conditions should automated information processing be curtailed or eliminated) and information presentation (can choice of presentation context affect the usability of processed information). We hypothesize that effective human/agent performance requires a precise calibration of trust so that the decision maker can accurately interpret an agent's communications and anticipate its limitations. This calibration will depend both on experience and supporting evidence.

2.2 Standalone TANDEM Experiment

We classify information presentations into three types which roughly parallel the level of trust they rely upon for interpretation:(1) aggregated, (2) integrated, and (3) synthesized. The reported experiment pairs error-making and error-free data presentations with differing degrees of inspectability to observe the effects on decision quality, reliance on agent provided information and reported confidence. .

Displays

Each agent provided one of three possible levels of information.

To manipulate the subjects' trust of the agents' presentations, errors were introduced. In the control condition, both menus and agent presented errorless values. Errors were of three types: data errors (display levels 1,2,&3), classification errors (display levels 2&3), or decision errors (display level 3). Data errors occurred when the agent displayed different data than the ground truth shown on the corresponding menus. This type of error was explained to subjects as "problems with the agent's sensors". Classification errors occurred when the agent placed data in the wrong column of the display table (level 2, placing an altitude reading of 1000 feet in submarine column for example) or used a wrong classification to determine assignment type and certainty factor (level 3). Decision errors occurred when the oracle assigned an incorrect "type" to a target independent of target data. Classification and Decision errors were explained to the subjects as "software problems". Errors of the different types were equated by matching corresponding rates to the multinomial reference distribution followed by data errors (5 independent parameters with 1/3 probability of error {.132, .33, .33, .164, .04, .004} for 0-5 errors). Only one source of error was presented during a TANDEM session. Buttons presses to access agent information, menu selections, target hooks, classifications, and final actions and times were collected along with simulation states for each subject. Agent displays tested showed:

1) aggregated information (list) -- a list of parameters and values

2) integrated information (table) -- a table showing categorized values

3) synthesized information (oracle) -- target type assignment with certainty factor.

Method

Sixty targets were distributed in several concentric rings on the screen. The circle closest to the center is referred to as the "circle of fear" and the amount of time a target spent in this circle before being identified was measured as penalty time. The number of targets identified while in this penalty circle, targets identified outside of the penalty circle, and targets hooked but not resolved were all measured. Ratings of "trust" of simulated information agents using scales developed and validated by Muir [5] were also gathered from each subject. These ratings, on a scale of 1(low) to 5 (high) focused on issues of dependability, predictability, accuracy, reliability and an overall "assessment of trust in the agent. Seventy-eight paid subjects recruited from the University of Pittsburgh community participated in the experiment. Data from eight subjects were excluded from this analysis due to equipment failure, incomplete data, or failure to follow instructions. Subjects received standard instructions and a sheet of tables showing the correspondence between parameter values and identification decisions. Subjects were assisted through a five minute training session operating the simulation and then completed two 15 minute experimental trials, concluding the session by completing a "trust in automation" [5] survey.

Results

Performance was analyzed using a repeated measures analysis of variance with session as the within subject factor and types of error and level of agent as between group factors. Effects of session were significant ($p < .05$) for each of the dependent measures reported. Where differences were found between groups, data was pooled across the two sessions and Post hoc analyses conducted using Tukey's HSD to identify reliable differences among the conditions.

Performance measures reported in preliminary form in Lenox et al. [3] fell into three groups which can be categorized as targets engaged, targets engaged within penalty circle, and agent use/correct identification. The number of targets shot or cleared, number of targets engaged, and score were affected by the type of presentation, the type of error and the interaction between presentation and error type. Errorless presentations led to processing more targets and the table presentation led to processing more targets (p < .04).

The number of non-penalty targets engaged, number of penalty targets engaged, and time targets remained in the penalty circle were affected by the presence of errors and particularly decision errors (p < .04). Subjects' willingness to activate an agent depended on the type of agent and the presence/absence of errors. Subjects activated the agents more often in the no error condition and activated the oracle more often than the other agents (p <.05). Subjects' ratings on 10 of the 11 scales on Muir's trust in automation questionnaire were lower for agents committing errors (p < .05)

Ratings of trust in automation using scales developed by Muir [2] were collected at the conclusion of the experiment. Subjects' ratings on 10 of the 11 scales were lower (p < .05) for agents committing errors and were not affected by the level of agent.

The level 2 (table) agent provided the best support for the target identification task. Although subjects consulted the level 3 (probability assignment) agent more than either of the other two agents, their scores were lower than subjects using level 2 agents and errors in the probability assignment led to longer penalty times. Regardless of their source, errors affected subjects' performance, reliance on agents and ratings of trust in a similar manner. Contrary to our expectations, presentation did not appear to affect the subjects' ratings of trust or penalty times.

These results demonstrate the dangers of using agents to collect, aggregate, and process information without providing their user the ability to monitor and evaluate their product. The participants rated their trust of the level-3 oracle as highly as the others and accessed it more often yet performed more poorly than the others. Equally clear was the failure of processed information to provide added value when errors occurred. Subjects using the level-2 (Table) agent with classification errors, for example, had available on their agent display exactly the same information as those using the level-1 (List) agent without errors yet performed less well.

2.3 Supporting Individuals vs. Teams

We have developed a framework for examining the different ways that machine agents can be deployed in support of team performance. One option is to support the individual team members in completion of their own tasks. Another option is to allocate to the machine agent its own subtask as if we were introducing another member into the team. In this case all the issues associated with communication and coordination among team members become relevant [1], [8], [9].

The third option is to support the team as a whole by facilitating communication, allocation of tasks, coordination among the human agents, and attention focus. A basic tenet of this approach is that teamwork skills exist independent of individual competencies. The performance of teams, especially in tightly coupled tasks, is believed to be highly dependent on these interpersonal skills.

The second TANDEM study examines different ways of deploying machine agents to support multi-person teams: 1) supporting the individual (within a team context) by keeping track of the information

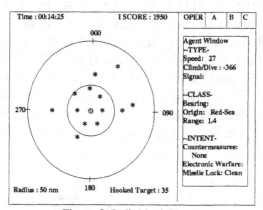

Figure 2: Individual Agent

he has collected and in sense, helping the individual with his task and with passing information to team mates (Individual Clipboard); 2) supporting communication among team members by automatically passing information to the relevant person which should reduce communication errors and facilitate individual classification (Team Clipboard); and 3) supporting task prioritization and coordination by providing a shared checklist (Team Checklist). We hypothesized that the Individual Agent should aid the individual task and aid communication among team members (Figure 2). This agent shows all data items available to an individual team member (in this case, ALPHA) and fills in the values for the data items as the subject selects them from them from the menu. The values under the TYPE

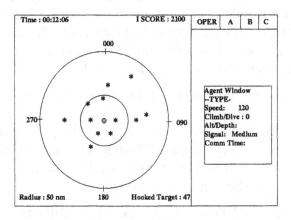

Figure 3 Team Clipboard

heading assist the individual with their task while the other team members may need the remaining values. The Team Clipboard Agent should also aid the individual task and aid team communication to a greater degree than the Individual Agent (Figure 3) should. This agent aggregates values from all members of the team to help the individual with his/her task. It automatically passes values as they are selected from the menu to the appropriate team member. Thus, when altitude/depth is selected from a menu, it is passed to an individual team member

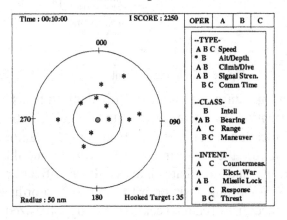

Figure 4: Team Checklist Agent

(ALPHA) who can use it to make the type identification. We hypothesized that this agent should reduce verbal communication among team members and reduce communication errors. The third agent, Team Checklist, should aid team coordination (Figure 4). This agent shows who has access to what data. For example, all three team members (ALPHA, BRAVO, CHARLIE) have access to speed, but only BRAVO has access to "Intelligence". The final condition is a control where we observed team performance without the aid of any machine agent. This is the standard TANDEM paradigm used by Jentsch, et al [9]. The goal of the study is to examine the impact of the aiding alternatives on: 1) communication patterns, 2) data gathering strategies, 3) reliance (i.e., use of) on the intelligent agents, and 4) performance.

Method

Teams of three subjects were recruited for this study. Each team was assigned to one of four conditions: 1) control, 2) individual agent, 3) team clipboard agent, or 4) team checklist agent. TANDEM was used with three-person teams, each member with a different identification task to perform (air/surface/submarine, military/civilian, and peaceful/hostile). One person was assigned to ALPHA, one to BRAVO and one to CHARLIE. ALPHA, BRAVO and CHARLIE had different items on their menus and different tasks during the trials. ALPHA identified the type of target (air, surface or submarine); BRAVO determined whether the target was civilian or military; CHARLIE determined whether the target was peaceful or hostile. In addition, CHARLIE acted as the leader by indicating the type, classification and intent of each target to the system and taking the final action (shoot or clear).

There were five pieces of information for each identification task, three of which must agree in order to make a positive identification. These pieces of information were distributed among the three team members. Each team member saw different data items on the menus and had three data items required for his/her identification task and several other items that the other team members might need to complete their tasks. Thus, the subjects needed to communicate with one another to perform their tasks for roughly two-thirds of the targets. All five pieces of information might agree for a particular target, however, in many cases, the ambiguity of the data was manipulated such that only three pieces agreed.

The targets were divided into three groups: 1) easy—all three pertinent items on the individual's menu agree; 2) medium—only two items on the menu agree, a team member must ask one or both teammates for data; and 3) hard—two items on the menu agree, but do not provide the correct solution. For example, ALPHA's task was to identify the type of target. If the target was easy, all three items on ALPHA's menu indicated the same type (e.g., air). If the target was of medium difficulty, one or two values would indicate air and the other indicate submarine. If the target was hard, both of ALPHA's menu items indicate air, but the remaining three items from ALPHA's menu and the other team members indicate surface. Thus, the target is a surface vessel. Subjects had no way of knowing the difficulty level of the targets.

Each team participated in a 90-minute sessions which began with a 15-minute training session in which the TANDEM software and team goals were explained. The team was told to identify as many targets as possible, as accurately as possible during the 15-minute trial. After the training session, the team participated in three 15-minute trials. At the conclusion, subjects were asked to complete a brief questionnaire.

Several forms of data were collected during the trials: 1) performance data from Tandem logs including the type and number of targets hooked and classified, the percentage of targets correctly identified, and the number of times the agents were activated; 2) communication data encoded from observers or audio tapes including the number of requests for data (e.g., does anyone have initial range?), the number of responses (e.g., range is 5.6 nm), the number of target identifications (e.g., it's civilian), and the number of confirmations (e.g., target is sub, civilian); 3) observer data including ratings on team communication, situation assessment, leadership ad supporting behaviors; and 4) questionnaires completed by the subjects before they leave.

Results

The performance data reported in this paper are based on five teams per condition. Time per target varies for both the target difficulty and across conditions. For example, teams took approximately 450 seconds per target to process hard targets in the control condition, 350 seconds in the individual agent condition, 250 seconds in the team clipboard condition, and 150 seconds in the team checklist condition.

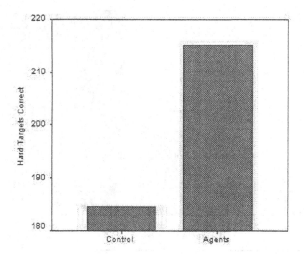

Figure 5:

Using a repeated measures design with four conditions there were significant order effects across the three trials for the proportion of correct targets (p<.009), the time per target (p<.0001), and the total targets hooked by a team (p<.0001). Effects were also found across the target difficulties (easy, medium, and hard) for the proportion of correct targets (p<.0001) and the time per target (p<.0001). In pairwise comparisons for time per target, the control condition differed from the team clipboard agent (p<.03) and the control condition differed from the team checklist agent (p<.02).

Grouping all agent conditions (individual agent, team clipboard agent and team checklist agent) into one condition, showed that agent aiding was superior to the no aiding condition (control) over the three trials on the proportion of correct targets (p<.0001), time per target (p<.0001) and total targets hooked (p<.0001).

Subjects learned across the trials, hooking more targets, spending less time on any particular target and getting more targets correct. As Figure 6 shows, aiding teamwork directly (team clipboard/checklist) proved more effective than supporting team members at their individual tasks despite the reductions in memory load and ready accessibility to

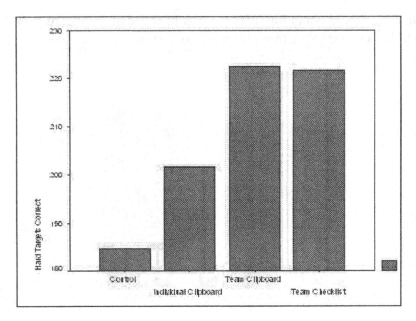

Figure 6:

parameters for sharing provided by the individual clipboard. The potential for coordinating human-human interactions through agent systems seems a particularly promising approach because of the high payoff and the reusable and largely domain independent character of the agents' tasks.

3. MokSAF Experiment

Human decision-makers, particularly military commanders, face time pressures and an environment where changes may occur in the task, division of labor, and allocation of resources. Information such as terrain characteristics, location and capabilities of enemy forces, direct objectives and doctrinal constraints are part of the commander's "infosphere." This information is routinely gathered and organized through geographical and other information systems. Information within the infosphere has the opportunity for data fusion, situation visualization, and "what-if" simulations. Software agents have access to all information in the infosphere and can plan, criticize, and predict the consequences of actions using the information at a greater accuracy and finer granularity than the human commanders can

These agents cannot consider information outside the infosphere unless it is explicitly translated in a compatible form.. This extra-infosphere data consists of intangible or multiple objectives involving morale, the political impact of actions (or inaction), intangible constraints, and the symbolic importance of different actions or objectives. Military commanders, like other decision-makers, have vast experiential information that is not easily quantifiable. Commanders must deal with idiosyncratic and situation-specific factors such as non-quantified information, complex or vaguely specified mission objectives and dynamically changing situations (e.g., incomplete/changing/new information, obstacles, and enemy actions). When participating in a planning task, commanders must translate these intangible constraints into physical ones to interact with planning agents. The issue then becomes how should software agents interact with their human team members to incorporate these intangible constraints into the physical environment effectively.

3.2 The Planning Environment: MokSAF

A computer-based simulation called MokSAF was developed for these experiments and two agent interfaces are currently undergoing evaluation. MokSAF is a simplified version of a virtual battlefield simulation called ModSAF (modular semi-automated forces). MokSAF allows two or more commanders to interact with one another to plan routes in a particular terrain. Each commander is tasked with planning a route from a starting point to a rendezvous point by a certain time. The individual commanders must then evaluate their plans from a team perspective and iteratively modify these plans until an acceptable team solution is developed.

Figure 7 shows the MokSAF Environment, including the terrain map and the toolbar. The terrain consists of soil (plain areas), roads (solid lines), freeways (thicker lines), buildings (black dots), rivers and forests. The rendezvous point is a red circle and the start point is a yellow circle on the terrain map. As participants create routes with the help of the Path Planner Agent or the Critique Agent, the routes are shown in bright green. The second route shown is from another MokSAF commander who has agreed to share a route.

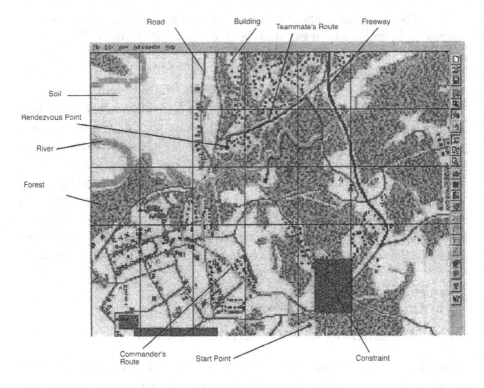

Figure 7 MokSAF

The partially transparent rectangles are social constraints that the user has drawn on the terrain map to indicate to the agents which areas should be avoided. Once these constraints have been drawn on the map, the Path Planner Agent will not draw a route through these coordinates and the Critique Agent will inform the user that a constrained area has been violated.

3.3 MokSAF Agents

Two different software agents which interact with the human team members in the planning task have been developed for MokSAF. The first agent, the Path Planner Agent, guides the human team members through the route-planning task and performs much of the task itself. This agent acts much like a "black box." The agent creates the route using its knowledge of the physical terrain and an artificial intelligence planning algorithm that seeks to find the shortest path. The agent is aware of physical constraints only. Commanders must translate the intangible constraints into physical ones by drawing constrained areas on the maps.

The second agent, the Critique Agent, analyzes the routes drawn by the human team members and helps them to refine their plans. In this mode, the human and agent work jointly to solve the problem (e.g., plan a route to a rendezvous point). The workload should be distributed such that each component matched to its strengths. Thus, the commander, who has a privileged understanding of the intangible constraints and utilities associated with the mission, can direct the route around these constraints as desired. However, the commander may not be as knowledgeable about the terrain and so the agent can indicate where the path is sub-optimal due to violations of physical constraints.

The commander draws the desired route and requests that the Critic Agent review the route for physical violations or to indicate ways in which the path could be improved. The commander can iteratively improve the plans until a satisfactory solution is reached.

Method

In the current MokSAF pilot experiments, a deliberative, iterative and flexible planning task is examined. There are three commanders (Alpha, Bravo and Charlie), each with a different starting point but the same rendezvous point. Each commander selects units for his/her platoon from a list of available units. This list currently contains M60A3 tanks, M109A2 artillery units, M1 Abrams tanks, AAV-7 amphibious assault vehicles, HMMWVs (i.e., hummers), ambulances, combat engineer units, fuel trucks and dismounted infantry. This list can be easily modified to add or delete unit types. With the help of one of the software agents, each commander plans a route from a starting point to the rendezvous point for the specified platoon.

Once a commander is satisfied with the individual plan, he/she can share it with the other commanders and resolve any conflicts. Conflicts can arise due to several issues including shared routes and/or resources and the inability of a commander to reach the rendezvous point at the specified time. The commanders must coordinate about the number and types of vehicles they are planning to take to the rendezvous point. The mission supplied to the commanders provides them with a final total of vehicles required at the rendezvous point. In addition, the commanders are told that they should not plan a route that takes them on the same path as any other commander and that they should coordinate their routes to avoid shared paths.

MokSAF 1.0 was used for this pilot study. It consists of the standard terrain map and markings, a toolbar as seen in Figure 5, a communication window where commanders can send and receive messages and share plans, and a constraint tree. The two different agent interfaces described above were evaluated. Fifteen teams consisting of three-persons were recruited (10 teams in the Planner Agent condition and five in the Critic Agent condition) from the University of Pittsburgh and Carnegie Mellon University communities. Participants were recruited as intact teams, consisting of friends or acquaintances. Each team member had a different starting point, but all had the same rendezvous point. Teammates needed to communicate with one another to complete their tasks successfully.

Each team participated in a 90-minute session that began with a 30-minute training session in which the MokSAF environment and team mission were explained. The team was told to find the optimal path between the start and rendezvous points, to avoid certain areas or go by other areas, to meet the mission objectives for numbers and types of units in their platoon, and to avoid crossing paths with the other commanders. After the training session, the team participated in two 15-minute trials. Each trial used the same terrain, but different start and rendezvous points and different platoon requirements. At the conclusion, participants were asked to complete a brief questionnaire.

Results

We examined time to share a route for the three commanders and found that the Planner Agent interface had an advantage over the Critic Agent interface ($p < .005$ for Alpha, $p < .063$ for Bravo and $p < .006$ for Charlie). Groups using the Planner Agent spent less time creating their individual plans before sharing them with their teammates.

We also examined the individual path lengths for each commander at two points in each trial when routes were first shared with the team and at the end of the 15-minute trial. The ending path lengths for Alpha (p <.001), Charlie (p < .001) and combined

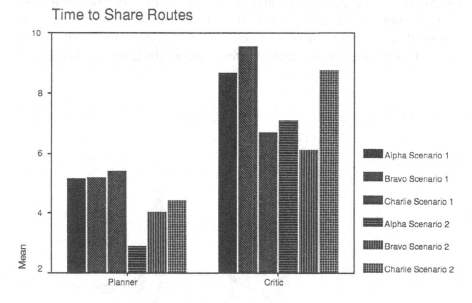

Figure 8

were better using the Planner Agent Interface than with the Critic.

It is expected that path lengths between the first time a route was shared and at the end of a trial would vary due to issues related to conflict resolutions among the teammates. There was a significant difference in the change in path lengths from these two points in time (p < .018). Figure 6 shows that participants using the Critic Agent interface made more changes in their paths. This change could be due to the state in which the route was in when first shared; that is, the routes drawn by the participants may have required additional refinement during the trial. Another possible reason for the change in the paths could be due to interactions with teammates.

Participants were asked to create optimal routes given certain confounding factors (e.g., avoiding constraints, going to designated areas, and avoiding traveling on the same paths as other commanders). They were also asked to plan as a group numbers and types of units at the rendezvous point. We found that there was no difference in this selection of units in either agent interface condition.

In its current form, the Path Planner has been shown to provide a better interface for both individual route planning and team-based re-planning. While the individual plans for Critic users in the Alpha and Bravo roles were not significantly different from Planner users in quality, it took them substantially more time to construct their routes. The eventual coordinated routes were uniformly better for each of the individual positions in the planner group and for the team as a whole.

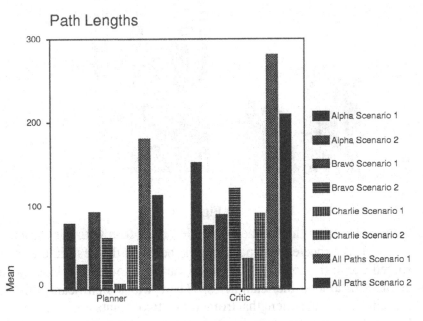

Figure 9

Despite this clear superiority, participants in the Planner group frequently expressed frustration with the indirection required to arrange constraints in the ways needed to steer the planner's behavior and often remarked that they wished they could "just draw the route by hand".

In the Critic condition complaints focused more closely on the minutiae of interaction. In its current form, the user "draws" a route in MokSAF by specifying a sequence of points at the resolution of the terrain database. To do this, she clicks to specify an initial or intermediate point in the path and then clicks again at a second point. A sequence of points is then drawn in a straight line between these locations. A route is built up incrementally by piecing together a long sequence of such segments. Although MokSAF provides tools for deleting unwanted points and line segment "rubberbanding" for moving control points, the process of manually constructing a long route is both tedious and error prone. While the Planner automatically avoids local obstacles such as trees and closely follows curves in roads due to their less costly terrain weights, a user constructing a manual route is constantly fighting unseen obstacles which void her path or line segments which stray a point or two off a road into high penalty terrain. The anticipated advantages of heuristic planning and cooperation among human users were largely lost due to the necessity of focusing on local rather than global features of routes.

The experience we have gained in developing and evaluating the critic interface will be used to redesign and test a new hybrid version of the task in which automated path planning will be performed within an approximate path drawn by the human user. Of the lessons learned in this initial test of our agent-based alternatives, the difficulty of creating good interfaces for communicating human intent stands out. The Planner interface which minimizes this communication was very successful in its initial implementation. The Critic interface, by contrast, will require substantial revision before it approaches the planner in articulatory directness and fluency. We hope that subsequent refinements to the Critic may allow a more thorough comparison of the effects of agent and human initiative on team planning and re-planning tasks.

4. InfoWrapper

One of the most commonly cited tasks to be solved by agent technologies is seeking out and extracting information from the World Wide Web. The problem is actually much more difficult than it seems and despite many efforts agents do not yet intelligently seek out new sites and extract information from them although many systems will return URLs likely to contain desired information. While parsing HTML is fairly straight forward, specifying the information to be extracted from a content/user oriented view is much more complex. A promising approach to this problem is to treat it as one of human-agent cooperation. Web pages have been designed and formatted to promote human discriminations and judgements so while the tagging conventions of HTML may be commonly violated their appearance is tightly controlled and "intelligible" to humans. If we can devise the means for the human to communicate her discriminations and semantic judgements to the agent it should be possible for the joint system to develop site specific information extractors fairly efficiently. What is needed is some form of "programming by example" with provisions for indicating and discriminating among procedural instructions (accessing successive pages for instance), informational templates (the boundaries and constituents of classified ads or example) and string constants/variables for matching. From the user's perspective, one would like to access a page through a browser, select (highlight) an instance of the items to be searched, and associate the selection's constituents with a schema for testing and extracting matching instances. The design challenge is to build an interface which make this kind of direct manipulation specification as transparent as circling a classified ad and underlining an object's name and price.

Unlike the controlled experiments with TANDEM and MokSAF, our efforts in developing the InfoWrapper follow an iterative prototyping plan where through development and testing we explore a range of potential interaction schemes for bridging the gulf between what the user sees and what the agent parses. The InfoWrapper has by far the most complex task of conveying human intent of the systems we have studied. Like TANDEM, it must operate in an open environment where errors are likely and mechanisms for monitoring and evaluation must be designed in. Like MokSAF, there are many possible ways to allocate tasks and control with good choices likely to emerge only after repeated testing. We believe that the future of human agent systems will lie in such multi-method interactions which can combine demonstration, direct manipulation, machine learning, and command language in effective enough ways to bridge Norman's gulfs and allow communication of complex intents and perceptions.

Acknowledgements

This research has been sponsored by ONR grant N-00014-96-1-1222.

References

1. P. M. Jones and C. M. Mitchell. Human-computer cooperative problem solving: Theory, design, and evaluation of an intelligent associate system. *IEEE Transactions on Systems, Man, and Cybernetics*. SMC-25(7), pages 1039-1053, 1995.

2. J. Lee and N. Moray. Trust, Control Strategies, and Allocation of Function in Human-Machine Systems. *Ergonomics* 35(10), pages 1243-1270, 1992.

3. T. Lenox, L. Roberts, and M. Lewis. Human-Agent Interaction in a Target Identification Task. In *1997 IEEE International Conference on Systems, Man, and Cybernetics*, pages 2702-2706, Orlando, FL: IEEE, 1997.

4. J.T. Malin, D.L. Schreckenghost, D.D. Woods, S.S. Potter, L. Johannesen, M. Holloway, and K. D. Forbus. *Making Intelligent Systems Team Players: Case Studies & Design Issues. Human-Computer Interaction Design* (NASA Technical Memorandum 104738). Houston, TX: NASA Johnson Space Center, 1991.

5. B. Muir. Trust in Automation: Part I. Theoretical Issues in the Study of Trust and Human Intervention in a Process Control Simulation. *Ergonomics*, 39(3), pages 429-460, 1994.

6. N. Negroponte. *Being Digital*. New York, NY: Alfred Knopf,1996.

7. D. Norman. *Cognitive Engineering. In User Centered System Design: New Perspectives on Human-Computer Interaction*, eds. D. Norman and S. Draper, pages 31-61, Hillsdale, NJ: Lawrence Erlbaum, 1986.

8. E. M. Roth, J. T. Malin, J. T and D. L. Schreckenghost. Paradigms for Intelligent Interface Design. In M. Helander, T. K. Landauer, and P. Prabhu (Eds) *Handbook of Human-Computer Interaction*, Second Edition, pages 1177 -1201, 1997.

9. K. Smith-Jentsch, J. H. Johnston, S. C. Payne (in press). Measuring team-related expertise in complex environments. To appear in J. A. Cannon-Bowers and E. Salas (eds.), *Decision Making Under Stress: Implications for Individual and Team Training*. Wash., DC: American Psychological Association.

A Cooperative Comprehension Assistant for Intranet-Based Information Environments

Ludger van Elst and Franz Schmalhofer

German Research Center for Artificial Intelligence (DFKI),
University Bldg. 57, Erwin-Schroedinger-Str., D-67663 Kaiserslautern
{elst, schmalho}@dfki.uni-kl.de

Abstract. A cooperative comprehension-assistant is described which represents text documents at three different levels of abstraction (surface, propositional and situational levels of representation). At the *surface level* texts are represented as bags of words without any linguistic structure. For the *propositional level* a definite but evolutionary growing set of predicates and concepts is used for selectively representing the most interesting parts of each text. By a latent semantic analysis the *situational level* is calculated as the third level, which is a parsimonious representation of the complete contents of a document with respect to some previously established frame of reference (metric vector space). Together the three levels provide more flexibility as well as precision for assisting human comprehension, document storage, retrieval and distribution. Furthermore, it is shown how this comprehension assistant is applied for knowledge dissemination in a particular kind of intranet-based information environment (oligo-agent system). The individual and social components of knowledge sharing within such an environment are described by knowledge construction and knowledge integration processes. To take the problem of long-term maintenance into account, the comprehension assistant and the oligo-agent system is embedded in a life-cycle model of cooperative knowledge evolution, consisting of a seeding phase, the system's evolutionary growth and periodical reseedings.

1 Introduction

The successes of the internet as well as intranets have been tremendous. There are now about 320 million pages in the World Wide Web. On any given day a powerful search engine cannot even identify all these pages. Only a relatively small portion (6 million) of these pages can be identified within a day. With intranets there is the similar problem, that it is often quite difficult to find the most relevant knowledge for a particular task at hand. The large amount of electronically available information in combination with the continuously occurring changes of the stored information make the task of finding the best document available quite difficult.

Anyone who has frequently used the search engines on the internet has had the experience that the retrieved information did not satisfy his particular needs although the desired information was indeed available in the net: The retrieved information is often redundant and some portion of it may be quite irrelevant with respect to the particular query. In order to alleviate this problem we have developed a cooperative comprehension assistant for a particular type of multi-agent information system which was termed oligo-agent system [15]. In this paper we describe the comprehension assistant which uses multiple levels of representations as has been suggested by theories of human cognition. Thereafter it will be shown how this comprehension assistant can be utilized for the storage, distribution and retrieval of information in an intranet-based information environment. Finally, a summary will be presented.

2 A Cooperative Comprehension Assistant

2.1 Knowledge Construction and Integration for Document Comprehension

It is well known that one of the core tasks for systems of multiple agents (cf. [1]) is to establish a shared context to allow for collaborative problem solving [9]. This is especially true for human-centered approaches to knowledge management where the information landscapes consist of human *and* artificial agents. Here, a mutual understanding of the structure and contents of the organizational memory is central to enable the different actors to take over their specific responsibilities and achieve an overall performance that is sufficient for the respective needs of the multiple participants [11]. We therefore employ a comprehension assistant within the social coordination region [15]. This assistant was developed according to the principles of a cognitive theory of text comprehension, namely the CI-theory [10], and yields knowledge representations of texts that are therefore relatively similar to the knowledge representations that humans form when they read a text. Hence they are well suited for establishing mutual understanding.

To take the problem of long-term maintenance into consideration, this approach is embedded in a life-cycle model of cooperative knowledge evolution, consisting of a *seeding phase*, the systems *evolutionary growth* and periodical *reseeding* [8].

As it is shown in Figure 1, two types of processes are employed to establish a shared context among the information providers and the information consumers by the comprehension assistant. Whereas the various *knowledge construction processes* are quite general and therefore well suited for all the different participants (perhaps leading to redundant or inconsistent portions of information in some participants' views or with respect to specific purposes), the *knowledge integration processes* yield a more coherent view and are therefore more closely tied to an individual user. The construction processes are based on various specific assumptions for the representation of the documents. This frame of reference is negotiated between the participants in the seeding phase and should stay quite constant during the evolutionary growth where more and more users and documents participate in the system while other documents may be deleted and some users may no longer participate. After a while, the chosen frame of reference,

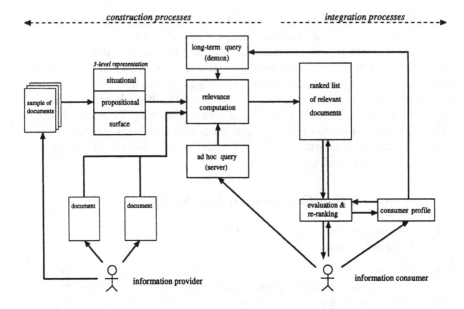

Fig. 1. Knowledge construction and knowledge integration processes for three-level representations as a means for accomplishing mutual understandings among information providers and information consumers

i.e. the "blueprint" of the organizational memory, may no longer be appropriate and the new representational assumptions must be negotiated (reseeding). Next we will describe the three-level representations of text documents with their respective construction processes in more detail.

2.2 Three-Level Representations

The most important task of the comprehension assistant is to represent text documents on a) a surface, b) a propositional and c) a situational level. While the surface level is quite word-oriented, the two other levels utilize more abstract representation spaces (discrete spaces for the propositional level and continuous spaces for the situational level).

surface level: On this level, documents are seen as "bags of words". Hereby we enforce an abstraction from the linguistic structure of the text as well as from concrete semantics of the words. Technically speaking, the representation space is a highly dimensional vector space where the dimensions are all the words that occur in all documents. Documents and queries are vectors in this space and the relevance of a document with respect to a specific query is approximated by the similarity of the two vectors (e.g. the cosine). Most search engines that are in use nowadays are based on this vector space model (e.g. [13]) and the problems like low precision and recall values due to polysemy or synonymy are well known. However, the method works very fast and can easily be understood by novice users as it doesn't require a deeper theory. Furthermore, a good portion of practical problems can be solved with the assistance of this level, as the application of WWW search engines shows. The only arrangements that have to be made in the seeding phase is the specification of parameters like stop word lists, the concrete weighting schema and similarity function. Much past research has be done in this area [5].

propositional level: This level of representation abstracts from the specific words to diminish some of the problems of the surface level. On this level, documents are represented in a discrete representation space that is based on a fixed vocabulary which has to be negotiated in the seeding phase. On the basis of a pre-defined list of propositions which may consist of concept terms and/or predicate argument terms, each sentence will be searched for these specific propositions. Technically speaking, this amounts to searching for specific terms or combinations of terms in a sentence. Thereby synonyms will be matched to the same concept or proposition. Such propositions are called CL-Propositions which stands for "controlled language propositions". These CL-Propositions have the following basic properties:

- CL-Propositions are predicates that contain no variables.
- Predicates must be elements of a controlled language, i.e. elements of an emerging ontology.
- The terms of the controlled language as well as strings can be used as arguments.
- CL-Propositions can be related to various segments of a document, e.g. sentences or paragraphs. Here, the choice of the controlled language is pivotal.

Basically, CL-propositions are normal forms of selected sentences. By the application of some prototypes of CL-propositions and a thesaurus that maps the words of the documents to the controlled language selected sentences may be represented in this controlled language. The number of prototypical CL-propositions may be at first small, but with the use of the system it may incrementally grow to larger numbers (for a more detailed description see [7]).

situational level: The situational level of a document will be generated as a vector in a latent semantic representation space [12]. Alternative situation models of a text may thereby be constructed by using alternative semantic spaces. For example, a text which describes a computer science department of an American university may be represented in the space of academic department descriptions of all academic disciplines in the whole world or in the more detailed representation space of computer science departments in North America. The selection of a representation space thus determines the scope and the frame of reference [4] for the interpretation of a text.

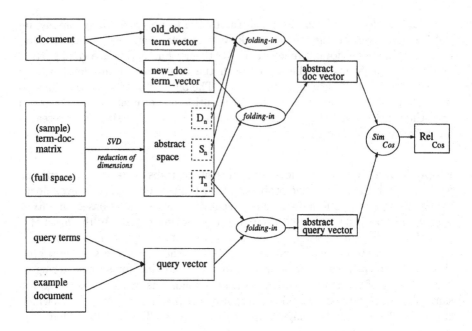

Fig. 2. Technical specification of the construction processes at the situation level

Figure 2 summarizes the technical description of the situation level. Of central importance for the situational level is the abstract space which is shown in the center of the figure. This abstract space is obtained from the standard term-document matrix [13] by a singular value decomposition [6] which results in a reduced but still high dimensional semantic space that is represented by three matrices (D, S, T). These matrices contain the row and the column entities (matrices T and D) of the original term-document matrix as well as scaling values (diagonal matrix S) in such a way that by multiplying D, S and T the original matrix is approximated. Here, an abstraction is achieved by the reduction of dimensions. As is shown at the top region of Figure 2, old as well as new documents can subsequently by represented by abstract document vectors (*folding in*). As is shown in the bottom region of Figure 2, any user query (in the form of some sequence of search terms of the length i, $1 \leq i \leq$ m, or in the form of some example document) may also be folded into the abstract representation space and thereby yield an abstract query vector. For any given query, the most relevant documents (on the basis of the abstract semantic space) may now be determined by some similarity measure (e.g. Sim_{Cos}, the angle between the abstract document vectors and the abstract query vector) which is defined in the abstract space. The three levels thus allow a user to search for documents in a way that is adjusted to his prior domain knowledge.

We will now explain the usefulness of the three levels of representations by an example: Suppose, there is an intranet with a web-page for each computer science course that has been offered by any instructor worldwide. Furthermore, there are requests by a large number of international students for acquiring some specific computer science training. As the terminology is quite varied across different countries, a broker that uses only the surface forms of the course descriptions and the student request will not necessarily find the best match. For example, in some contexts, computer science, informatics, and electrical engineering may indeed be treated as synonyms. (When a university does not have a computer science department, a true computer science course may be offered by the department of electrical engineering).

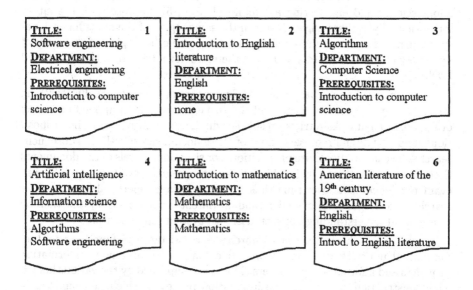

Fig. 3. Six hypothetical web-pages about academic classes

As a minute example, imagine that there are n=6 courses offered, where each course is described by a web page, as is shown in Figure 3. Furthermore, there are high school graduates who are interested in studying artificial intelligence and do not yet have much knowledge about this field. When using a search engine with the search key "artificial intelligence" they would find only page 4. When using the search key "computer science", they would find page 3. With such a surface oriented search, the users are literally getting what they are requesting.

With the three-level representation and the described comprehension assistant, on the other hand, these users may find what they really wanted, even when they are not knowledgeable enough to explicitly request it. In the information environment of the oligo-agent system for course brokering, the propositional level would encompass concepts like "engineering", "humanities" and "natural sciences". At the propositional level, "electrical engineering", "computer science" and "information science" would therefore all be mapped onto "engineering". In the latent semantic space of the situational level, all web-pages about science courses would be represented by vectors in the same vicinity of the metric vector space. Web pages about humanity courses would similarly build a cluster, however, at a quite different location of the latent semantic space.

With the comprehension assistant, the high school graduates would again start out by using "artificial intelligence" as search key. With the retrieved page 4, there would also follow the propositional unit "engineering", which would subsequently retrieve the pages 1 and 3, but not page 5 (nor pages 2 and 6), because mathematics is not mapped onto "engineering" at the propositional level. However, when the search is extended to the situational level, all pages about science and engineering are found (1, 3, 4, 5), because with the latent semantic analysis these pages cluster in the same region of the multidimensional space, just like all humanity courses cluster in some other region of the space of university courses. Courses 2 and 6 are therefore not retrieved at the situational level.

In summary, if a user has little or no knowledge of what he is really searching for, he may use some key terms and the surface level is then applied as in any other search engine. As retrieval result he will, however, also obtain the propositional and situational representations of those documents as well. In subsequent searches he can now use those propositional or situational levels of the documents that most closely correspond to his interests as a search key. The search for relevant text documents over time thus advances from a superficial level (surface search) to a deeper level of understanding (latent semantic space) and thereby to a mutual understanding between user and system representations.

Figure 1 also shows how the comprehension assistant can function as a tool for mutual understanding and cooperative comprehension among information providers and information consumers. This is accomplished by the various knowledge construction and knowledge integration processes which are depicted in Figure 1.

The different roles of the participating agents can lead to quite conflictive goals. For example can the structure of an information archive that is "optimal" for the librarian be very different from the structure that is "optimal" for the distributors. Therefore, the various frames of reference (or representational assumptions) that build the basis of the comprehension assistant must be negotiated between the agents. An initial coordination of the individual and the global concerns of the different users is already achieved at the definition time of all potential communications within the intranet. This coordination is accomplished by a more or less representative sample of documents from which a three-level representation and the associated relevance scores are established. Information-identification is initiated by long-term queries as well as ad hoc queries. The most relevant information (i.e. the right documents) become explicitly specified (information identification time). Integration processes [7] form consumer-centered views (e.g. individual re-ranking) and allow an information consumer to converse about his individual relevance rankings of the various selected documents on the basis of the three-level representation (cf. [16]). Figure 4 shows the particular interface which is used for conversing about the individual relevance of documents. Through the various sliders and buttons, the parameters of the integration processes (e.g. the weighting of different topics or the desired level of abstraction) can easily be manipulated and the effects can be seen immediately.

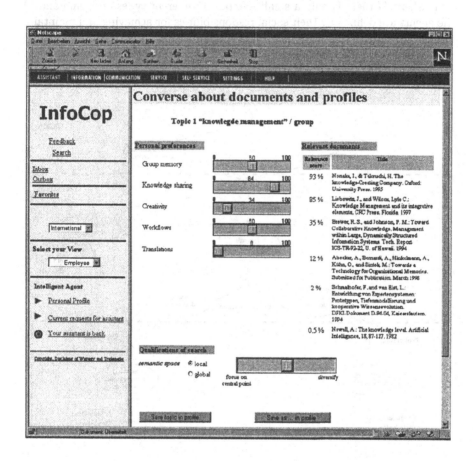

Fig. 4. A dynamic query interface for conversing about the personal relevance of documents

It should be noted that the comprehension assistant does in no way replace the human comprehender. Quite to the contrary, the comprehension assistant and its human users are cooperating with one another and thereby enhance but also somehow change the human comprehension process. This is comparable to the changes which are occurring in text composition when an author switches from a manual typewriter to a word-processor with spelling and grammar checkers. As is well known, certain qualities of the task execution are modified by using the new technology [2].

3 Embedding in a Multi-agent System

Figure 5 shows how the described comprehension assistant is embedded in an oligo-agent system. An oligo-agent system is a special kind of multi-agent system, where 1) there is only a small number of different types of agents and 2) the agents are defined by their social responsibilities for achieving and maintaining certain qualities of the whole agent-system and the particular information environment in which they operate (cf. [15]).

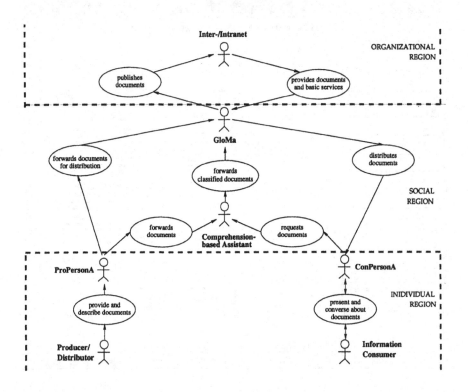

Fig. 5. The structure of the oligo-agent system for distribution and comprehension assistance within the organizational memory

We will now explain how the comprehension assistant is utilized for the various distribution- and comprehension-based tasks which have to be performed within an intranet. At first we have to explain some additional specifications. Repositories of potential information consumer groups and document groups as well as templates of distribution and interests-lists are held in a relational database system (RDBS). Based on these repositories, specific distribution and interests-lists are constructed (or chosen) and refined. These tasks also specify information as to when the information should be delivered. A demon acts upon this information. Whenever a *specific distribution* or *interests list* reaches its *distribution time* this demon computes the delivery information which basically consists of a table of (user, document info)-pairs. This table is processed by a standard delivery mechanism (e.g. e-mail), sending the document notifications to the user's inbox. The delivered information is filtered by the consumer agent (ConPersonA) and thus categorized individually. Each category has *presentation time* information which is used by a ConPersonA-demon to initiate presentation via the special user interface that is shown in Figure 4 and allows for individualized ranking and selection of documents.

How the *document providers* and *information consumers* of the intranet can employ the distribution and comprehension assistant to improve their consensual understanding of documents in the organizational memory is shown in the form of a use-case diagram (see Figure 5). A document provider (who may be either an author or a distributor) can publish a document in the organizational memory in one of two ways. He may have his own ideas as to where in the intranet (i.e. the virtual library) the document should be stored and to whom it should be distributed. In this case he would directly forward the documents and/or distribution list to GloMa, the global manager that has access to and maintains a representation of the organizational memory. Alternatively, he can call on the comprehension assistant, that will then make suggestions as to where the document is to be stored and who should be informed about its publication. In either case, GloMa will eventually store the newly published information in the organizational memory and distribute the information via the personal agents to the potential information consumers.

In addition to this *push-oriented approach* to knowledge management, the integrated assistant also provides a sophisticated *information pull* solution that is based on content and meta-content descriptions of the documents as well as user interests. With the personal agent and the described dynamic queries interface (see Figure 4), a user can specify his interests to the comprehension assistant, that will in turn communicate to GloMa which will then provide the specific documents.

4 Summary

The described cooperative comprehension-assistant that is to be applied for knowledge dissemination in an organization (i. e. the right documents to the right people at the right time) can be more generally characterized through the following design specifications and accomplishments:

1. Based on theories and models of human text comprehension [10], [14], a fully automated comprehension assistant with *three levels of representations* is used to achieve mutually shared representations between the oligo-agent system and their users. With increasingly more people applying this system, the mutual understanding may be shared among increasingly more people and increasingly more documents.

2. *Individual* and *global concerns* are coordinated in an oligo-agent system with shared responsibilities. While the individual agents are client-based, the global agent runs on an application server.
3. GloMa uses an RDBS to keep and maintain repositories that are used for the definition of user profiles (information consumers), document groups and distribution and interests-lists. Thereby it is possible to use the available information, consisting of document attributes, document contents and organizational structures as a whole. Concerning the *distribution and interest identification tasks*, GloMa maintains a continually updated representation of the *information environment* at the *relevant level of abstraction*.
4. *Decoupling* of *definition time*, *information-identification time* and *presentation time* allows distribution to be determined either by the *individual* or as a *common responsibility* of administrator, author, distributors and information consumers. These responsibilities may concern *one-shot distributions* as well as *periodical repetitions* of some general distribution specification.

From an application point of view, the functions that are provided by the comprehension assistant and its embedding in the oligo-agent system can be compared to the Fishwrap system [3]. The information consumer gets a personalized view of the information environment. This view consists of individual aspects that are based upon a semantic document analysis as well as upon organizational aspects (distribution lists), in which a distributor determines the portion of information that is delivered to the consumer. However, unlike an individualized newspaper, the proposed system has a very sophisticated representation about the ripeness and expiration time for relevant information. This allows for a different "date of publication" for each "line" of the newspaper. The combination of these elements leads to a flexible tool for handling different aspects of information distribution and information utilization which are the core problems of document and knowledge exploitation in the knowledge society.

References

1. Ambite, J. L., and Knoblock, C. A.: Agents for Information Gathering, *IEEE Expert*, *September/October*, 1997.
2. Boy, G. A.: Cognitive Function Analysis. *NATO-ONR Workshop Presentation*, *Washington D.C.*, 1997.
3. Chesnais, P. R., Mucklo, M. J, and Sheena, J. A.: The Fishwrap Personalized News System. *http://fishwrap-docs.www.media.mit.edu/docs/dev/CNGlue/cnglue.html*, 1997.
4. Clancey, W. J.: *Situated Cognition: On human knowledge and computer representations*. New York: Cambridge University Press, 1997.
5. DARPA (Ed.): *Proceedings of the 6th Message Understanding Conference (MUC-6), Columbia, Maryland, November 6-8, 1995*. Morgan Kaufmann, San Francisco, 1996.
6. Deerwester, S., Dumais, S., Furnas, G., Landauer, T., and Harshmann, R.: Indexing by Latent Semantic Analysis. *Journal of the American Society for Information Science*, 41(6), 391–407, 1990.

7. van Elst, L.: Ein kooperativer Informationsassistent zum gemeinsamen Verstehen von Textdokumenten (*An information assistant for the cooperative comprehension of text documents*). Master Thesis, Department of Computer Science, University of Kaiserslautern, 1998.

8. Fischer, G., McCall, R., Ostwald, J., Reeves, B., and Shipman, F.: Seeding, Evolutionary Growth and Reseeding: Supporting the Incremental Development of Design Environments. In *Proceedings of ACM CHI94 Conference on Human Factors in Computing Systems, 2, p. 220*, 1994.

9. Fischer, G., and Redmiles, D.: Enhancing Indirect Long-Term Collaboration with Intelligent Agents. NSF-Grant IRI-9311839, Boulder.

10. Kintsch, W.: *Comprehension: A Paradigm for Cognition.* Cambridge University Press, 1998.

11. Krauss, R. M., and Fussell, S. R.: Mutual knowledge and communicative effectiveness. In J. Galegher, R. Kraut, C. Egido (Eds): *Intellectual Teamwork: Social and technological foundations of cooperative work, pp. 111-146.* Hillsdale, New Jersey: Lawrence Erlbaum Associates, 1990.

12. Landauer, T.K., Foltz, P.W., and Laham, D.: Introduction to Latent Semantic Analysis. *Discourse Processes*, 1998.

13. Salton, G.: *The Smart Retrieval System Experiments in Automatic Document Processing.* Prentice Hall, 1971.

14. Schmalhofer, F.: *Constructive Knowledge Acquisition: A Computational Model and Experimental Evaluation.* Mahwah, N.J.: Lawrence Erlbaum Associates, 1998.

15. Schmalhofer, F., and van Elst, L.: An oligo-agent system with shared responsibilities for knowledge management. In D. Fensel, and R. Studer: *Proceedings of EKAW '99*, Springer-Verlag, 1999.

16. Williamson,C., and Shneiderman, B.: The Dynamic HomeFinder: Evaluation dynamic queries in a real-estate information exploration system. *Proceedings of the ACM SIGIR'92 Conference, Copenhagen, Denmark, (June 1992), pp. 338-346*, 1992.

Author Index

Springer
and the
environment

At Springer we firmly believe that an
international science publisher has a
special obligation to the environment,
and our corporate policies consistently
reflect this conviction.

We also expect our business partners –
paper mills, printers, packaging
manufacturers, etc. – to commit
themselves to using materials and
production processes that do not harm
the environment. The paper in this
book is made from low- or no-chlorine
pulp and is acid free, in conformance
with international standards for paper
permanency.

Springer

Lecture Notes in Artificial Intelligence (LNAI)

Lecture Notes in Computer Science